The Politics of Prisoner Abuse

The United States and Enemy Prisoners after 9/11

DAVID P. FORSYTHE

When states are threatened by war and terrorism, can we really expect them to abide by human rights and humanitarian law? David P. Forsythe's bold analysis of US policies towards terror suspects after 9/11 addresses this issue directly. Covering moral, political, and legal aspects, he examines the abuse of enemy detainees at the hands of the US. At the center of the debate is the Bush Administration, which Forsythe argues displayed disdain for international law, in contrast to the general public's support for humanitarian affairs. Forsythe explores the similarities and differences between Presidents Obama and Bush on the question of prisoner treatment in an age of terrorism and asks how the Administration should proceed. The book traces the Pentagon's and CIA's records in mistreating prisoners, providing an account which will be of interest to all those who value human rights and humanitarian law.

DAVID P. FORSYTHE is currently Professor Emeritus of Political Science at the University of Nebraska–Lincoln. He has been a visiting professor at universities in Geneva and Utrecht, and in 2008 he held the Fulbright Distinguished Research Chair of Human Rights and International Studies at the Danish Institute of International Studies, Copenhagen. He has also been on staff for the United Nations University in Tokyo, and has been a consultant to both the UN Office of the High Commissioner for Refugees and the International Red Cross and Red Crescent Movement.

The Politics of Prisoner Abuse

The United States and Enemy Prisoners after 9/11

DAVID P. FORSYTHE

CAMBRIDGE UNIVERSITY PRESS
Cambridge, New York, Melbourne, Madrid, Cape Town,
Singapore, São Paulo, Delhi, Tokyo, Mexico City

Cambridge University Press
The Edinburgh Building, Cambridge CB2 8RU, UK

Published in the United States of America by Cambridge University Press, New York

www.cambridge.org
Information on this title: www.cambridge.org/9780521181105

First published 2011

Printed in the United Kingdom at the University Press, Cambridge

A catalog record for this publication is available from the British Library

Library of Congress Cataloging in Publication data
Forsythe, David P., 1941–
The politics of prisoner abuse : the United States and enemy prisoners after 9/11 / David P. Forsythe.
p. cm.
ISBN 978-1-107-00466-5
1. Torture – United States. 2. Political prisoners – Abuse of – United States. 3. Prisoners of war – Abuse of – United States. 4. September 11 Terrorist Attacks, 2001. 5. War on Terrorism, 2001–2009. I. Title.
HV8599.U6F67 2011
355.1′296 – dc22

2011010558

ISBN 978-1-107-00466-5 Hardback
ISBN 978-0-521-18110-5 Paperback

The measure of a country is how it acts in peril.

(David M. Brahms, Brig. Gen., US Marines (ret.), quoted in Richard Bernstein, "Guantánamo Lawyers Showed Their Moral Fiber," *New York Times*, October 6, 2010, www.nytimes.com/2010/10/07/us/07iht-letter.html)

Contents

Preface

This is a book about US policies toward enemy prisoners after the Al-Qaeda terrorist attacks on New York and Washington of September 11, 2001. It analyzes the central moral, political, and legal factors in the US policy making process that led the George W. Bush Administration to abuse prisoners on a widespread basis. It also covers the early years of the Barack Obama Administration.

This study is based primarily on information already in the public domain. Its creativity and originality lies in the synthesis presented and the conclusions drawn. It does not purport, for the most part, to have uncovered new evidence from primary sources. That the United States abused prisoners after 9/11 is not in doubt. Questions remain about the scope of the abuse, the thinking of various officials in the making and implementation of policy, how often the abuse rose to the level of torture or inhuman treatment, and how often it led to increased US security. The undeniable fact is that high US officials knowingly authorized the severe abuse of various prisoners in various places, often as part of enforced disappearances or secret detention, in the face of legal prohibitions. How this came about merits full discussion. So does the question of what to do after the fact.

This book is intended for those seriously interested in this subject, including scholars, advanced university students, and others in the attentive public seeking to affect future policy on detention and interrogation matters. My intent is to pull together all the key factors in one source.

Unfortunately some of the existing studies on the topic are legalistic and arcane or otherwise obfuscatory. Some studies are helpful but fail to connect all the dots and are not fully clear and systematic. Many academic experts, especially those who teach advanced students, often fail to write in a clear and straightforward manner. This work tries to present fact and interpretation clearly, with a minimum of esoteric cant from academe, but also with a minimum of journalistic excursions into personalized trivia. In particular, legal mumbo jumbo is translated into clear English. Despite the quest for a readable presentation, great care has been taken regarding accuracy. The manuscript has been read by a number of colleagues in various disciplines and professions. Finally, we know a lot more now compared to when some of the previous studies were compiled. It has actually been an advantage to lag behind some early studies.

This book is also intended to be "one stop shopping," that is, comprehensive. In the extensive reference notes one can find further information on the topic. What we know on this subject thus far has come out in piecemeal fashion – a social science article here, a legal article there; a newspaper report here, a magazine article there; an internet blog or web site here, a television program there. Some of the early sources are decidedly dated. This book attempts to pull the major threads together into a coherent whole, be readable, and be as up-to-date as possible.

In my career of university teaching stretching over four decades, I never ceased to be reminded of how little my students know about more recent political history. The students I taught circa 2010 knew almost nothing about the Cold War, including seminal events such as the Suez Crisis or the various Soviet invasions of Eastern Europe. For those same students in 2010, the Al-Qaeda attacks of nine years earlier were a fuzzy event, most of my class members being about eleven years old at the time. To the extent that this book is assigned in university classes in political science and international relations, it should provide a useful overview of events, processes, and major issues to be considered.

I use the term "enemy prisoners" with care. It is a general term that may at times include other notions such as terror suspects, prisoners of war, unlawful combatants, civilian detainees, and so forth. Other authors have used various legal and political terms. It is important not to prejudge various individuals by assigning legal labels like "prisoner of war" or "unlawful enemy combatant" at the start. The focus here is on the detention and interrogation of those thought to represent violent danger to the security of the United States after 9/11. In Iraq after the US invasion of 2003 they might be armed insurgents, perhaps at certain times legally covered by international humanitarian law (IHL, the laws of war or of armed conflict). But beyond Iraq they might also be individuals picked up in Gambia or Pakistan and then shipped off to Guantánamo, whose link to the laws of war is not a matter of broad agreement. They might in fact be civilians who did not take part in hostilities, or perhaps really fighters of some sort. They might even be, on occasion, US citizens and not aliens (foreigners). So the safest, most general, and most non-legal term to use at the start is "enemy prisoner." It is the term used to advantage in the memoirs by Richard B. Myers, the retired Chairman of the Joint Chiefs of Staff (JCS). The Bush Administration, mainly through the CIA and the Department of Defense (DOD), viewed these prisoners as probable enemies of US security. That is the core focus. Of course if an enemy prisoner properly qualifies as a prisoner of war (POW) or falls into another legal category, that should be acknowledged because that affects personal rights and protections.

I also use terms like "torture" and "inhuman treatment" with some prudence. As with the legal categories for prisoners, one should take care with different categories of abuse. "Abuse" is a non-legal term that perhaps has four legal levels: (1) torture; (2) severe mistreatment that is cruel, inhuman, or degrading (CID, inhuman or cruel for short); (3) humiliating treatment; and (4) lesser abuse. Precision requires that we not rush to legal judgment about the extent or levels of abuse. After all, the national and international case law on the meaning and manifestations of the different categories is not so extensive. It is also not crystal clear. The European Court of Human Rights (ECHR) has itself reached different judgments at different times on what constitutes torture. That European Court and the European Commission on Human Rights (now defunct) sometimes disagreed on how to characterize prisoner abuse, as in Northern Ireland, looking at the same facts. New research suggests that even the distinction between torture and CID is misleading, in that supposedly lesser forms of abuse may produce more lasting distress in some persons than supposedly greater forms of abuse.

Above all, the book tries to highlight the importance of what has happened. The US government, which often articulates the notion of American exceptionalism and claims to represent an especially good nation, and which has throughout its history claimed a role in world affairs of leading others toward more freedom under the rule of law, has detained thousands without legal charge, often in secret, then severely abused a certain percentage of them. There is no doubt but that much of what the United States has done is prohibited by international and national law. To some legal experts, US leaders are criminals who should be prosecuted, if not under US law then under international human rights or humanitarian law. In the view of these experts, US leaders have committed grave breaches of the 1949 Geneva Conventions or war crimes under IHL, which can lead to universal jurisdiction – that is, the right of any government to try the individuals regardless of nationality or place of the crime. Likewise, many of these same experts are sure that US leaders have authorized torture, also prohibited by the 1984 UN Convention against Torture (Torture Convention for short), to which the notion of universal jurisdiction likewise applies. In legal fact, the Torture Convention prohibits not just torture but also inhuman treatment (without, it might be noted, defining the latter).

One can also acknowledge that the term "terrorism" is subject to much disagreement. It is not defined in international law, and the International Criminal Court (ICC) does not include terrorism in its subject matter jurisdiction. For many, terrorism consists of violent attacks on civilian or military targets by those posing as civilians, in maneuvers falling short of guerrilla or irregular warfare, in an effort to spread terror broadly, for political purposes. This being primarily a political rather than legal study (although legal factors need to be covered), it is not necessary to dwell on why international law remains vague on the definition of terrorism. It is sufficient to note that the law bypasses this ambiguity by prohibiting a variety of acts – e.g. attacks on civilians, mistreatment of prisoners, interference with civilian aircraft, the taking of hostages, etc.

We need to be clear about how US abuse of prisoners on a broad scale came to be. Was it, or some of it, justified in an age of terrorism in the context of weapons of mass destruction (WMD)? Has the United States done great damage to international efforts to promote human rights and human dignity under law, or is this concern greatly misguided? Did the Bush Administration gravely endanger the rule of law, constitutional government, and democratic checks and balances at home, or was Vice President Cheney correct that President Bush was just restoring presidential power to its proper place after unwise restraints imposed by particularly the Congress from the 1970s on? Was the Bush Administration really acting so differently from other liberal democracies like the United Kingdom or Israel that had faced terrorism in the past? Campaign rhetoric aside, did the Administration of Barack Obama essentially continue the policies of the preceding Administration on many key points? What should the United States do in the aftermath of various strained legal interpretations and widespread abuse? These and other questions are hugely important for the future of the United States and the world, and we all need clear thinking about them.

My conclusion comprises a bleak paradox. When governments, democratic or otherwise, perceive an existential threat, they will almost certainly go to the "dark side" of prisoner abuse. Yet that apparent fact does not absolve persons of progressive (read liberal) persuasion from the responsibility to struggle against that tendency. If one believes in the objectives of universal human rights, the rule of law, and limited rather than total war, one has the obligation to contest the views of Dick Cheney and John Yoo and other advocates of going to the dark side. The key is a political and subjective factor: not to engage in threat exaggeration, which normally also involves a self-critical appraisal of one's own virtue. After 9/11 the George W. Bush war council had such an elevated view of American greatness, and such a dark view of the threat of terrorism (albeit also manipulated to pursue long-standing agendas), that abuse of prisoners followed on a large and serious scale. This did great damage to international human rights and humanitarian law, as well as great damage to American democracy and its constitutional principles. Trying to ensure that these policies of abuse are not replicated is no easy matter.

I would like to thank George Aldrich, Gabor Rona, and William Aceves for helping me make my legal points as clearly as possible. Peter Maslowski gave me the perspective of a military historian. Some friends in the British Red Cross helped me refine some of my points about the role of the United Kingdom, past and present. My colleague Patrice McMahon read the entire manuscript with a keen eye. Lindsey Forsythe, Annette Kovar, Ryan Hendrickson, and Barb Flanagan read parts of the manuscript for clarity and organization. Jay Osiovitch helped locate many legal documents. Jalele Defa and Ryan Lowry were helpful student assistants. Others played important roles but wish to remain unnamed. Two referees for Cambridge University Press were central to final revisions. Once again John Haslam at that Press was a wonderful editor. Naturally any remaining errors of fact and interpretation are mine.

David P. Forsythe
Lincoln, NE
December 2010

Abbreviations and acronyms

ABA	American Bar Association
ACLU	American Civil Liberties Union
AI	Amnesty International
AP	Associated Press
AUMF	Authorization to Use Military Force
BSCT	Behavioral Science Consultation Team (DOD)
CID	cruel, inhuman, or degrading (treatment)
CIL	customary international law
CJSOTF	Combined Joint Special Operations Task Force
CoE	Council of Europe
CSRT	Combatant Status Review Tribunals
CTC	Counter-terrorism Center (US Executive Branch)
DOD	Department of Defense
DOJ	Department of Justice
DTA	Detainee Treatment Act
ECHR	European Court of Human Rights
ETA	Euskadi Ta Askatasuna (Basque militant group)
EU	European Union
FBI	Federal Bureau of Intelligence
FDR	Franklin D. Roosevelt
FISA	Foreign Intelligence Surveillance Court
FOB	Forward Operating Base
GC	Geneva Convention
GID	General Intelligence Department (Jordan)
GTMO	Guantánamo Bay Detention Facility
GWOT	Global War on Terror
HRF	Human Rights First
HRW	Human Rights Watch
HVD	high-value detainee

IAC	International Armed Conflict
ICC	International Criminal Court (World Court)
ICCPR	International Covenant on Civil and Political Rights
ICJ	International Commission of Jurists
ICJ	International Court of Justice
ICRC	International Committee of the Red Cross
ICTR	International Criminal Tribunal for Rwanda
ICTY	International Criminal Tribunal for the Former Yugoslavia
IG	Inspector General (CIA)
IHL	international humanitarian law
IRA	Irish Republican Army
JAG	Judge Advocate General
JCS	Joint Chiefs of Staff
JPRA	Joint Program for the Recovery of Assets (DOD)
JTF	Joint Task Force
KGB	Soviet Intelligence Agency
MC	Member of Congress
MCA	Military Commissions Act
MI	Military Intelligence
MP	Military Police
NATO	North Atlantic Treaty Organization
NGO	non-governmental organization
NIAC	Non-International (Internal) Armed Conflict
NIE	National Intelligence Estimate
NSA	National Security Adviser
NSC	National Security Council
NVA	North Vietnam People's Army
OEF	Operation Enduring Freedom
OLC	Office of Legal Counsel (DOJ)
OPR	Office of Professional Responsibility (DOJ)
POW	prisoner of war
RUDs	reservations, understandings, and declarations
SERE	Survival, Evasion, Resistance, Escape (US military training program)
SF	Special Forces
SIB	Science Intelligence Board
SOP	Standard Operating Procedure

TJ	transitional justice
TRC	Truth and Reconciliation Commission
UN	United Nations
VC	Viet Cong
WCA	War Crimes Act
WMD	weapons of mass destruction

1 Torture and political morality in historical perspective

The interrogation of someone like a terrorist suspect can be a real ethical dilemma. The available options may all be bad in some way.

(David Perry, Professor of Ethics, US Army War College, quoted in the *Christian Science Monitor*, May 26, 2004)

September 11, 2001 confronted the George W. Bush Administration with tough choices – to put it mildly. Any democratic government would have faced tough choices responding to similar events, given the Al-Qaeda attacks on New York and Washington that killed just under 3,000 persons, mostly civilians. (The 1941 Japanese attack on Pearl Harbor, preventive self-defense in the Japanese view, their version of the Bush Doctrine, had killed a little more than half that number, mostly military personnel.) When it came to treatment of what were called terror suspects or more generally enemy or security prisoners, which is the focus of this study, many liberal democratic governments had faced tough choices in the past: the British in dealing with violence by the Provisional Irish Republican Army (IRA) concerning Northern Ireland, the West German government in dealing with attacks on civilians by the Red Army Faction and other violent groups, Italy confronting the Red Army Brigades, Spain wrestling with ETA (Euskadi Ta Askatasuna, the nationalist/separatist organization) about Basque issues, India in dealing with Islamic militants incensed over New Delhi's control over much of Kashmir from 1947, Israel in dealing with Palestinian and other attacks since 1948 and especially after 1967, etc. The dilemmas were in fact old, even if some in the Bush Administration thought that everything had changed after 9/11.[1]

[1] For comparative analyses see further Alison Brysk and Gershon Shafir, eds., *National Insecurity and Human Rights: Democracies Debate Counterterrorism* (Berkeley: University of California Press, 2007). I have a chapter in this book

This chapter outlines the three basic options open to the US government with regard to prisoner treatment in the context of terroristic total war – meaning unrestricted covert attacks by those posing as civilians, including on civilians. (There is no definition of terrorism in international law, owing to political disagreement as well as the difficulty of capturing complex phenomena in legal terminology.) The chapter then notes a drift in US policy from a relatively good record on treatment of enemy prisoners during the Second World War, especially in Europe, to a two-track policy thereafter: support for relevant human rights and humanitarian law norms in public, but a shift toward abuse – including torture – in secret, by both the CIA and the Pentagon. A kind analysis would say that what Bush did was to bring honesty to the subject, namely to bring US abuse of security suspects into the realm of public policy, whereas in the past it had been hidden in secrecy. A less kind analysis would say that what Bush did was to undermine the long quest to oppose torture and inhuman treatment, and thus open the flood gates to more abuse in the future, both at home and abroad.

This introduction sets the stage for what follows, namely analysis of the widespread abuse of enemy prisoners during the Bush Administration, much of it intended, as the secret maneuvers sought to bypass the public prohibitions. At the end of this introduction I indicate the specific arguments to follow in the various chapters. Throughout my analysis, one central question is whether a cost-benefit analysis supports the wisdom of harsh interrogation – was the actionable intelligence gained from abuse truly necessary and worth the long list of negatives inherent in the illegal process? Another persistent concern is, "what next," especially since secret abuse never stays secret forever.

Political morality: two-and-a-half views

In terms of general moral principles relevant to prisoner treatment, the choices were fairly clear – as they had been for others in times past.

regarding the United States. Also Robert Art and Louise Richardson, *Democratic Counter Terrorism: Lessons Learned* (Washington, DC: United States Institute of Peace, 2007). On the history of democracies and torture, see Darius Rejali, *Torture and Democracy* (Princeton: Princeton University Press, 2006).

Human rights as trumps

On the one hand there was the absolutist opposition to, and legal prohibition against, torture and other major mistreatment of suspected enemies. In any ranking of human rights, the right to life and to what experts called the overlapping rights of personal integrity (no summary execution, no forced disappearances [secret detention], no torture, no mistreatment amounting to cruel, inhuman, or degrading treatment [CID]), all loomed large. This moral view commanded much respect, which is precisely why it is codified in much law. At the core of classical liberal thinking is respect for the individual, his autonomy, her capacity for reason and choice.

From the time of Henry Dunant and the first Geneva Convention for War Victims in 1864, it had been widely accepted, at least in theory, that when a combatant was out of the fight due to injury, the wounded soldier was entitled to humane treatment as an individual. He ceased being an active political agent and reverted to being a person meriting humane attention. This liberal logic was expanded to prisoners of war in the 1907 Hague regulations at the turn of the century, and then in the practice of the First World War – a practice further codified in the 1929 Geneva Convention on the subject. All of this was reaffirmed in the 1949 Geneva Conventions for war victims. Combatants when out of the fight were not to be abused, and civilians were never to be the objects of attack. (The episodic history of sparing war victims who are not active combatants is much longer than from just 1864 and thereafter.)[2]

Especially the 1949 Geneva Conventions for the Protection of Victims of Armed Conflict prohibit all of the above violations of personal integrity rights, covering both combatants and civilians, in both international and internal war. Geneva Convention III, together with Additional Protocol I (API) from 1977, prohibits abuse of all sorts of detained combatants when *hors de combat* (out of the fight) in international war. Geneva Convention IV, especially in the light of the same API, provides similar coverage for all civilians in international armed conflict or occupation resulting from that armed conflict. All four Conventions from 1949 contain Common Article 3 that

[2] For one source among many see Adam Roberts and Richard Guelff, eds., *Documents on the Laws of War* (Oxford and New York: Oxford University Press, 3rd edn., 2000).

prohibits abuse of all prisoners in internal armed conflict (internal war, or civil war). In such situations, one of the fighting parties is a non-state actor – e.g. the rebel side in a civil war. The United States ratified the 1949 Geneva Conventions in 1955 and adopted legislation translating them into national law, including via the 1996 War Crimes Act (WCA), later amended. Geneva standards on treatment of prisoners are written into various versions of the US Army and Marine field manuals. Reference to the Geneva Conventions is printed on US military identification cards.

The 1984 UN Convention against Torture prohibits torture in all places at all times, whether in peace or war, with no exceptions for situations of "national emergency." Prohibition of CID can be read as absolute or not, but if so read this has to be from inference, context, and legislative history, the body of the treaty primarily referring to torture.[3] The United States ratified in 1994, but restricted the definition of torture, made the treaty itself inapplicable in federal courts, and in other ways minimized legal change and effects.[4] The 1966 International Covenant on Civil and Political Rights (ICCPR) contained the same prohibitions in more general terms, which Washington ratified in 1992, although again the United States undermined its enforcement at home. Other international documents (often called instruments because the category included more than treaties) reinforced humane standards for prisoner treatment.[5]

Until 2001 the United States had officially and generally supported almost all of the international legal developments designed to regulate the treatment of prisoners so as to protect human dignity.[6] As will be shown, the United States might have violated these same standards from time to time, especially in the shadowy game of covert action that all states practiced regardless of their overt statements and policies. Still, in its official and overt policies, Washington had endorsed the view that prisoners, even those that fought against the United States, were entitled to humane detention and interrogation. As was true of all other states,

[3] John T. Parry believes that CID is not absolutely prohibited. *Understanding Torture: Law, Violence, and Political Identity* (Ann Arbor: University of Michigan Press, 2010), p. 5.

[4] See further *ibid.*

[5] E.g. UN Standard Minimum Rules for the Treatment of Detainees.

[6] The United States has never ratified Protocols I and II additional to the 1949 Geneva Conventions. More on this in chapter 2.

implementation did not always match legal requirements, but still, formal acceptance held out the promise of progressive achievement in implementation over time.

This absolutist moral–legal position does not prohibit expedient (self-interested) concerns. By adopting an absolute ban on torture and stigmatizing lesser mistreatment, the detaining authority might capture the high moral ground in the effort to win the hearts and minds of the civilian base of the enemy. Humane detention and interrogation might reduce the number of those who could otherwise become enemy terrorists or other combatants, or perhaps continue fighting rather than surrender. An absolute ban might contribute to one's self-interest under notions of reciprocity. And a commitment to humane policies might solidify morale, cohesion, and self-respect on the home front. Perhaps most importantly, many security officials believe that the route of humane interrogation is the right route for obtaining accurate intelligence.

In the last analysis, the absolutist position allows for pursuit of national security by all *humane* means possible, but it cannot guarantee that it has tried *every* means at its disposal.[7] This posture leaves a government open to challenge by its hard line critics if a major terrorist attack succeeds in penetrating defensive efforts. A sizable proportion of American society, for example, elevates the defense of the country, by torture if necessary, over considerations of adhering to human rights and humanitarian norms intended to protect the human dignity of all.[8] For many, their version of nationalism trumps the cosmopolitanism entailed in serious attention to human rights and humanitarian law. Even brutal or cruel defense of national objectives trumps the project to protect the fundamental rights of all. As the International Committee of the Red Cross (ICRC) understands because of its widespread prison visits in times of war or other national emergency, it is not very popular to seek humanitarian protection for those viewed as the enemy.[9]

[7] See further Yuval Ginbar, *Why Not Torture Terrorists? Moral, Practical, and Legal Aspects of the "Ticking Bomb" Justification for Torture* (Oxford and New York: Oxford University Press, 2008).

[8] According to one poll in June 2009, 40 percent of Americans sampled opposed a flat ban on torture in all situations, Program on International Public Attitudes, University of Maryland, June 25, 2009.

[9] David P. Forsythe, *The Humanitarians: The International Committee of the Red Cross* (Cambridge: Cambridge University Press, 2005).

David Rodin has made a trenchant defense of the absolute ban on torture and inhuman treatment of terror suspects.[10] He says that a number of US public policies entail increased deaths for Americans but this is widely accepted: lenient hand gun laws contribute to more than 25,000 murders each year; elevated highway speed limits contribute to about 43,000 traffic fatalities annually; and so on. Deaths from terrorism, which might have been prevented by torture, fall into this same line of thinking. If a terrorist blew up an airplane with hundreds on board, and if that terrorist might have been blocked by torture of his colleagues leading to actionable intelligence, that is no different from the other public policies he cited which led directly to deaths for Americans. An absolute commitment to humane interrogation, he says, entails a possible price that is the price we pay for upholding our best values. Terrorism, he continues, cannot defeat us; only we can defeat us, by abandoning our democratic and human rights values.

However, it is difficult for an elected US official to make this argument – namely, that American civilians might die if we uphold our values against torture or other cruelties. At least some political opponents can be counted on to attack this view, as we note in the next section.

National security as trumps

By comparison to the absolutist position in defense of fundamental rights of personal integrity, there was utilitarian thinking about the greatest good for the greatest number. In this view, the torture or other cruel abuse of certain prisoners could be justified if the moral good derived from abuse was judged to be greater than the limited bad derived from otherwise unacceptable treatment of certain individuals. According to this reasoning, the defense of a liberal democratic nation-state could well entail the torture or other major abuse of terrorists opposed to liberal democracy. This is the lesser evil approach. The core value is a quest for actionable intelligence in the short run to protect the "good society," even though this may entail "bad" for certain detainees

[10] Remarks by David Rodin, "Torture, Rights, and Values: Why the Prohibition of Torture is Absolute," Carnegie Council for Ethics, June 26, 2008, www.cceia.org/resources/transcripts/0051.html.

who attack, or might attack, that good society.[11] It has long been argued in the realist political tradition well represented by Henry Kissinger, even in the Christian realist tradition represented by Reinhold Niebuhr, that the courageous national political leader or diplomat may have to take action normally considered evil in order to secure a larger legitimate good. Torture, normally an evil between individuals inside a secure democratic state, might be justifiable in an insecure world where the existence of a democratic state might come into question.

In the case of 9/11, so this second argument goes, Al-Qaeda sought to impose an ancient theocracy inimical to freedom in general, and especially gender equality, as seen in Taliban rule in Afghanistan first from Kandahar and later from Kabul. Al-Qaeda was said to be effectively intertwined with those extreme ruling Taliban. Some chose the label of Islamofascism to refer to this rule. Al-Qaeda and its shadowy allies observed no limits, attacking civilians, beheading prisoners, and otherwise pursuing a strategy of total war, limited only by the means at their disposal. Better to engage in the coercive interrogation of Al-Qaeda and Taliban suspects – and those similar to them – than run the risk of the demise of free societies, even if the latter manifested some defects here and there.

After all, so it is argued, democratic polities and the constitutions, statutes, and treaties they adopt do not constitute a suicide pact in which the law is to be upheld regardless of the danger to democracy itself.[12] For John Yoo, as we will see the author of some "torture memos" in the Bush Administration, the US Constitution allows the President to order torture if necessary to provide for the common defense, whatever treaties and statutes might say.[13] In a different but equally disturbing view, when democracies face an existential threat, they will do what is necessary to defend their way of life.[14] In this view, threats to fundamental

[11] See especially Michael Ignatieff, *The Lesser Evil: Political Ethics in an Age of Terror* (Princeton: Princeton University Press, 2004).

[12] Richard A. Posner, *Not a Suicide Pact: The Constitution in a Time of National Emergency* (New York: Oxford University Press, 2006).

[13] John Yoo, *War by Other Means: An Insider's Account of the War on Terrorism* (New York: Grove/Atlantic, 2006); and *Crisis and Command: A History of Executive Power from George Washington to George W. Bush* (New York: Simon & Schuster, 2005).

[14] Paul Kahn, *Sacred Violence: Torture, Terror, and Sovereignty* (Ann Arbor: University of Michigan Press, 2008).

sovereignty are not subject to the rule of law. In this argument, some see killing and torture in defense of the nation as a sacred commitment, not subject to secular legal restraint, just as Islamic militants see violent attacks on Americans as a sacred cause. One does not have to buy into the religious angle to understand the seriousness of this view. As the secular former Secretary of State Dean Acheson said apropos of the 1962 Cuban missile crisis, when state sovereignty is at stake, one should not expect law to constrain policy.[15] In these views, classical liberals, particularly the legalistic elements among them, should adjust to a dangerous world and adopt utilitarian thinking in times of national emergency.

If one accepts particularly the Posner–Yoo view, troubling questions follow. Suppose the President overstates the threat from enemies, or misuses a situation of threat to pursue other agendas? When and if these situations manifest themselves, if the President has unlimited authority as Commander in Chief, what institution has the authority to right the ship of state? And, since these views look to the President as the man on horseback to save the nation, what is the difference between democratic exceptionalism under an all-powerful president and a fascist glorification of the great man theory?[16] If George W. Bush could legally order torture, why not Pinochet, the Chilean dictator, or Franco, the Spanish dictator? They, too, thought they were saving a good Christian society from dastardly enemies, including godless Bolsheviks and Leninists, whether foreign or domestic.

Winston Churchill supposedly said, apropos of the Second World War, that truth is so important it has to be protected by a thicket of lies. In similar paradoxical reasoning, some contemporary thinkers argue that liberal democracy, human rights, and the rule of law are so important that they have to be defended with secret detention and abusive interrogation in the face of ruthless enemies. This is, if you will, the reasoned argument for torture.

(Much utilitarian thinking assumes that number matter, that it is morally justifiable to torture a few to protect the many. But once one

[15] Quoted in Abram Chayes, *The Cuban Missile Crisis: International Crises and the Role of Law* (New York and London: Oxford University Press, 1974), p. 1.

[16] Just as there has been a resurgence in the debate over torture, so there has been renewed interest in the legal theories of Carl Schmitt who defended Hitler and the German Third Reich given the chaos and insecurity of Weimar Germany in the inter-war years.

starts down this road, why not torture the many to protect the few? Why not torture many terror suspects to ensure that even a few innocent civilians are spared injury or death? This latter view might be termed consequentialist rather than utilitarian. Here, political morality depends on appreciation of outcomes and does not stop at categorical imperatives. Such a theoretical discussion about types of moral argument, and the exact dividing line between utilitarian and consequentialist arguments, is not the central point here.)

Splitting the difference

A third school of thought tries to split the difference, more or less, between the moral absolutists and the utilitarian relativists by arguing for limited exceptions to the absolute prohibition on prisoner abuse. Hence Alan Dershowitz of Harvard Law School argued for "torture warrants," under which Executive interrogators would have to get court permission to depart from the absolute prohibitions found in law in order to deal with the "ticking time bomb scenario." In this logic, the necessity of national security could override normal legal protections for the prisoner who was very likely to have knowledge of future and significant attacks on a just society. But the checks would need to come from outside the Executive branch, from an independent judiciary or other independent body, to ensure against a version of "force drift," namely the anticipated tendency to turn the limited exception into the general rule.[17] Some advocates of "the lesser evil" approach agreed on the need for strict limits to abuse.[18]

In Israel from 1999 the Supreme Court imposed an absolute ban on torture but allowed for the possibility of the "necessity defense" – namely, that some exceptions might be allowed *ex post facto* if the security services could reasonably show that torture was necessary for Israel's national security.[19] This is similar to Dershowitz's torture

[17] Alan Dershowitz, *Why Terrorism Works: Understanding the Threat, Responding to the Challenge* (New Haven: Yale University Press, 2003), where he argues that terrorism is never justified but torture sometimes is.

[18] Ignatieff, *The Lesser Evil.*

[19] For an overview, among several sources, see Gershon Shafir, "Torturing Democracies: The Curious Debate on the 'Israeli Model,'" in Brysk and Shafir, *National Insecurity.*

warrants, in that the general and absolute ban on torture (and mistreatment) remains, but there is a formal effort to allow for the supposedly rare and very limited exception. The Israeli experience will get more attention in Chapter 7.

In the United States after the Al-Qaida attacks, the 9/11 Commission recommended the creation of a new civil liberties panel to oversee the detention process.[20] The Bush Administration was opposed and Congress never took up the issue. Similar concern about civil liberties and the collection of information in the United States led to a moribund body, the Privacy and Civil Liberties Oversight Board.[21] The US Civil Rights Commission took no interest in enemy prisoners after 9/11, even when American citizens were declared "unlawful enemy combatants" and deprived of their constitutional rights.

A central problem in this third approach remains: how to ensure that strict limitations do indeed occur concerning exceptional abuse? Even apart from the delicate question of torture for national security, it is well known that those charged with supervision and oversight tend over time to get co-opted, whether one speaks of those overseeing off-shore oil and gas drilling in 2010, or those who were supposed to regulate the railroads in the past. The Israeli example of trying to implement the necessity defense in law, to mitigate punishment under an absolute ban on torture, is highly problematic in this regard, meriting fuller discussion in Chapter 7. For now it suffices to say that the Israeli security services and others have been reluctant to cooperate with judicial doctrine, in that the country cannot show a series of follow-on cases demonstrating the application of the doctrine of necessary exception.

In sum thus far, these competing views of political morality, of how to do as much good as possible for the liberal democratic nation and as little bad to individuals, in the context of violent power struggles, manifest an interesting history in US policy debates. For reasons of time and space I limit myself to the era since 1941. One could go back to the US revolutionary war and study George Washington's refusal to countenance the abuse of captured British soldiers. One could also examine the importance of Abraham Lincoln's statement that military

[20] *9/11 Commission Report* (New York: Barnes & Noble, 2006), p. 395.

[21] Richard B. Schmitt, *Los Angeles Times*, "Civil Liberties Board Dormant, Despite Relevant Issues," reprinted in *Lincoln Journal Star*, February 26, 2006, p. A-4.

necessity does not permit of cruelty, and then his adoption of the Lieber Code, intended to protect primarily Confederate prisoners in the American civil war.[22]

Political morality applied: the Second World War

During the Second World War for the most part the Roosevelt and Truman Administrations, and the military, accepted the absolutist position contained in the then-existing laws of war (also called international humanitarian law [IHL], also called the law of armed conflict). In general the United States treated German (and other Axis) prisoners of war (POWs), and even many of their Japanese counterparts, correctly in the light of the 1929 Geneva Convention on Prisoners of War. That is not to say that incidents of abuse did not occur concerning German POWs – and such abuses were more prevalent against the Japanese. But US general policy, especially regarding European enemy combatants, was to engage in humane interrogation and detention even for those undertaking aggression and carrying out deadly attacks on US military personnel. (The killing of active enemy combatants is legal in armed conflict.) With regard to Germany and the United States, both bound by the 1929 Convention, no doubt notions of reciprocity pushed Washington in this direction.[23]

In 2009 President Barack Obama asserted that his policies on detention and interrogation followed the British record in the Second World War – in that Prime Minister Winston Churchill had refused to go down

[22] For a brief reference to both George Washington and Abraham Lincoln, see James P. Pfiffner, *Torture as Public Policy: Restoring US Credibility on the World Stage* (Boulder and London: Paradigm Publishers, 2010), Chapter 1.

[23] For a readable overview of POWs in the Second World War see Niall Ferguson, *The War of the World: Twentieth-Century Conflict and the Descent of the West* (London: Penguin, 2006), part IV. A short, scholarly treatment is Joan Beaumont, "Protecting Prisoners of War, 1929–95," in Bob Moore and Kent Fedorowich, eds., *Prisoners of War and their Captors in World War II* (Oxford and London: Berg, 1996), pp. 277–299. She notes that both the United Kingdom and the United States tried to avoid some of their legal obligations under the 1929 Geneva Convention by redefining some German POWs late in the war as "surrendered enemy personnel" or "disarmed enemy forces." As we will see after 9/11, unilateral legalistic definitions continued to be used to evade the intent of the laws of war. See also ICRC, *Report on Activities During the Second World War: Volume II, Central Agency for Prisoners of War* (Geneva: ICRC, 1948).

the road of torture.[24] As usual, the historical record is more complicated than simple. It seems the British record was relatively good with regard to rank-and-file Axis POWs. But it has been asserted, with some evidence, that the British tortured some high-value German POWs in "the London Cage," hiding them from visits by the ICRC (whose visits were customary but not mandated in the 1929 Geneva Convention).[25] As for German spies, not subject to POW protections, it seems the British authorized secret and harsh interrogation, using sleep deprivation and other techniques we will come to examine in this study. One sub-unit of this "Camp 020" in Germany seems to have spun out of control, with German detained spies looking similar to Jewish victims of the German concentration camps.[26]

Philip Zelikow, the Executive Director of the 9/11 Commission, has correctly asserted that the United States had somewhat similar policies for high-value detainees (HVDs) in the Second World War.[27] The US military ran a secret facility, Fort Hunt or Camp 1142, in Virginia in which presumed German HVDs were isolated and interrogated, some under pressure.[28] While the coercive measures employed seem mild by comparison to subsequent actions by various governments in situations like the Korean and Vietnam Wars, nevertheless the facility was hidden from the ICRC. The 1929 Geneva Convention was bypassed. Sleep

[24] For a brief reference and discussion see "Did Obama Misquote Churchill?," FactCheck.org, May 5, 2009, www.factcheck.org.2009/05/did-obama-misquote-churchill/.

[25] For a short treatment see Ian Cobain, "The Secrets of the London Cage," *The Guardian*, November 12, 2005, www.guardian.co.uk.uk/2005/nov/12/secondworldwar.world, who used, among other sources, ICRC archives. For a less reliable account by the commander of this facility, see A. P. Scotland, *The London Cage* (London: Evans, 1957). See also Parry, *Understanding Torture*, p. 107.

[26] Oliver Hoare, *Camp 020: M15 and the Nazi Spies* (London: UK Public Records Office, 2001); and Ian Cobain, "The Interrogation Camp that Turned Prisoners into Living Skeletons," *The Guardian*, December 17, 2005, www.guardian.co.uk.uk/2005/dec/17/secondworldwar/topstories3.

[27] Philip Zelikow, "A Dubious C.I.A. Shortcut," *New York Times*, April 24, 2009, www.ntimes.com/2009/04/24/opinion/24zelikow.html.

[28] For a short introduction, see the three-part series on National Public Radio, the first of which was on August 18, 2008. "Breaking the Silence of a Secret POW Camp," www.npr.org/templantes/story/story.php?storyId=93635950. See also Petula Dvorak, "A Covert Chapter Opens For Fort Hunt Veterans," *Washington Post*, August 20, 2006, www.washingtonpost.com/wp-dyn/content/article/2006/08/19/AR2006081900856.

deprivation, threats, and other measures were sometimes employed on the prisoners who were "disappeared" for several weeks to several months. Only later were the prisoners transferred to regular POW camps and the ICRC informed. According to oral histories by American personnel who worked there, most interrogations were conducted humanely.

Moreover, as Peter Maguire has shown, from time to time the United States did authorize harsh treatment for other POWs.[29] For example, when US military authorities identified some German POWs as having participated in the shooting of US POWs in the Malmédy massacre during the Battle of the Bulge, they were taken to Schwabish Hall in occupied Germany, isolated, and dealt with harshly. At least one fatality by suicide was recorded. This is in addition to the more frequent unauthorized abuse, even killing, immediately after capture. So the US record regarding prisoner protection during the Second World War was not perfect, as it never is for any state in war, but there was not a wholesale rejection of the notion of a humanitarian quarantine for detained enemy fighters.

Perhaps surprisingly with regard to Japanese POWs, the US search for actionable intelligence was often by humane interrogation in which a premium was placed on building trust between the American interrogator and the Japanese detainee, even if this situation did not obtain all the time.[30] The first, humane course was pursued despite Japan's often brutal treatment of US POWs and thus in the absence of full reciprocity. Perhaps this was at least partially because late in the war the US homeland and its democracy were not perceived as being directly at stake, even if global power and control were. (The arbitrary relocation and detention of Japanese-Americans from the West Coast, a policy widely supported within the Franklin D. Roosevelt [FDR] Administration and indeed the country, suggested considerable fear

[29] Peter Maguire, *Law and War: An American Story* (New York: Columbia University Press, 2001).

[30] Stephen Budiansky, "Truth Extraction," *The Atlantic*, June 2005, www.theatlantic.com/doc/print/200506/budiansky, reporting on the record of Sherwood F. Moran, Maj., US Marines, a record apparently well known in military intelligence circles. See also Elaine Woo, *Los Angeles Times*, May 4, 2006, in the obituary about the similar record of Otis Cary, a Navy interrogator, www.boston.com/news/globe/obituaries/articles/2006/05/04/otis_cary_his_sly_interr.

about homeland security at least early in the war, however misguided. It is relevant for later discussions that the US Supreme Court approved this arbitrary detention of Japanese-Americans.) Military honor, self-respect, and quest for accurate information all pushed in this same policy direction of US humane treatment of Japanese POWs, even though there was considerable abuse and even killing of prisoners especially soon after capture. For the United States even in the Pacific theatre of war, the considered search for actionable intelligence, as compared to the release of frustrated passions immediately after capture, was often by humane means.

The conclusion certainly from the Japanese case was that the United States could often get the information it was seeking, mostly about military details, from humane interrogation. Of course the United States knew who the Japanese enemy was, and mostly where it was, and in general what its strategic objectives were. Its interrogation of Japanese military prisoners was more tactical than strategic. Still, there must have been considerable temptation to engage in abuse of prisoners to discover the where and when of the next military attack. American lives were at stake, if not homeland security. Moreover, the dividing line between strategic and tactical information is not always crystal clear.

From a post-9/11 perspective it is remarkable that the United States dealt with most German and many Japanese prisoners according to the humane quarantine prescribed by IHL, even though global hegemony was at stake in the contest between the Allied Powers and fascism/militarism. American lives were at stake around the world in 1941–1945, and yet the United States as a matter of broad policy and general practice, especially in Europe, did not resort to forced disappearances, torture, and inhuman treatment – even though some unauthorized abuse and death of prisoners always occur in warfare, and some authorized abuse was directed at a few HVDs.

Political morality changes: the Cold War

In the Cold War, things were different. Stimulated especially by Chinese and North Korean coercive manipulation of US POWs, Washington began to look seriously at what came to be called "no touch torture," also called "clean torture" or "torture lite" – the breaking down of a prisoner's will to resist his captors through largely psychological pressures like sleep deprivation and solitary confinement – combined with some non-fatal and non-scarring physical pressures like being locked into "stress positions" and manipulation of heat and cold. For American prisoners in Chinese and North Korean captivity during the Korean War there was no humanitarian quarantine, but rather a continuation of the brutal political struggle after the combat had ended. During some phases of Chinese detention, almost 40 percent of American POWs died.[31] The Chinese manifested a relatively high rate of success in getting US POWs to confess to germ warfare and other war crimes, confessions apparently willingly given but false.[32] The CIA thus funded research, led by a Canadian to supposedly escape direct US accountability, centered on the breaking down and reprogramming of the human psyche. This started primarily as an attempt to understand and protect against what had happened to US POWs in the Korean War.[33]

However, it seems the British had used some of these same techniques against German HVDs – with London perhaps influenced by reports of harsh interrogation techniques coming out of the Soviet Union.[34] The historical record is not crystal clear, but American officials might have been looking not only at Chinese communist policies in Korea, but also at earlier Russian communist policies, the latter perhaps having an effect on British anti-fascist policies.

The US research, centered on psychological pressures albeit entailing some physical torment, was then applied to a few Soviet intelligence agent (KGB) captives and others, along with injection of drugs like LSD, as the CIA program morphed into coercive intelligence gathering.[35] The CIA asserted that it was certain that it could break prisoners,[36] and this

31 Beaumont, "Protecting Prisoners of War," p. 285.

32 Rejali, *Torture and Democracy*.

33 The essential reference is Alfred W. McCoy, *A Question of Torture: CIA Interrogation, from the Cold War to the War on Terror* (New York: Owl Books, for Henry Holt, 2006). See also Parry, *Understanding Torture*.

34 See p. 12 above for references to British interrogation in the Second World War. It is possible that Soviet abuse of prisoners affected both the British in the Second World War and the Chinese in the Korean War. As Rejali, *Torture and Democracy*, shows, information about torture travels horizontally through informal means rather than simply vertically by command.

35 See Mark Bowden, "The Dark Art of Interrogation," *The Atlantic*, October 2003, at www.theatlantic.com/doc/print/200310/bowden, and the literature cited there.

36 Kubark manual (1963), and Human Resource Exploitation Training Manual (1983), available on the internet. A reliable source is the National Security Archive at George Washington University, www.gwu.edu/~nsarchiv/.

conclusion eventually affected US military training known as SERE (Survival, Evasion, Resistance, Escape), as US military personnel were trained in how to survive, evade, resist, and escape from expected pressures if captured by the communists. SERE was not designed to elicit information, but to oppose its coercive and illegal extraction. But it was eventually reverse engineered for US intelligence purposes.[37]

So both the CIA and the DOD, the latter through such instruments as the School of the Americas, now known as The Western Hemispheric Institute for Security Cooperation, at Fort Benning, GA, got into the business of teaching and supervising coercive interrogation, especially regarding Latin America.[38] CIA research on and use of torture seeped into military affairs as well. As Benjamin Wittes of the centrist Brookings Institution has written, "American forces trained Latin American governments in the use of tactics forbidden to themselves . . ."[39] Even if the Pentagon were to turn out not to be *the* hub for the spread of Hemispheric torture, word spread about interrogation techniques, as the various security services and military establishments exchanged views and experiences.[40] The United States

[37] On the reverse engineering of SERE for intelligence purposes see M. Gregg Bloche and Jonathan Marks, "Doing unto Others as they did unto Us," *International Herald Tribune*, November 14, 2005, www.iht.com/bin/print_ipub.php?file=/articles/2005/11/14/opinion/edbloche.php.

[38] The DOD, including when Dick Cheney was Secretary of Defense and David Addington was one of his assistants, was found to be allowing the teaching of abusive interrogation to Hemispheric military officials via what was then the School of the Americas from 1984. Also, there were ample human rights violations by graduates of that school. The DOD claimed that such instruction was not authorized, but tellingly there were no punishments for those directly involved. For one treatment see Kathryn Sikkink, *Mixed Signals: US Human Rights Policy and Latin America* (Ithaca and London: Cornell University Press, A Century Foundation Book, 2004), pp. 202–207. For more critical coverage see Greg Grandin, *Empire's Workshop: Latin America, The United States, and the Rise of the New Imperialism* (New York: Owl Books, for Henry Holt, 2006, 2007), pp. 107 and *passim*; and Jane Mayer, *The Dark Side: The Inside Story of How the War on Terror Turned Into a War on American Ideals* (New York: Doubleday, 2008). See also Jennifer K. Harbury, *Truth, Torture, and the American Way: The History and Consequences of US Involvement in Torture* (Boston: Beacon, 2005) about the torture death of her husband in Guatemala by persons on the CIA payroll. Also Parry, *Understanding Torture*.

[39] Benjamin Wittes, *Law and the Long War: The Future of Justice in the Age of Terror* (New York: Penguin Press, 2008), p. 30.

[40] Rejali, *Torture and Democracy*, believes in decentralized information sharing in Latin America, not DOD master tutelage. On the role of France in spreading torture in Latin America, based on its experiences in Algeria and Indochina, see

knew that Chinese and North Korean abuse had produced false confessions by American military personnel about US use of germ warfare and other subjects, but Washington developed its own science of abuse for intelligence gathering.

Bush policy toward enemy prisoners after 9/11 has been said by some to constitute the "Latin Americanization" of world affairs.[41] What the United States encouraged and supervised, and presumably benefited from, in places like Guatemala during the Cold War, greatly influenced the treatment of terror suspects and other enemy prisoners after 9/11. In other words, what the United States taught and advised primarily in Latin America during the Cold War, the Bush Administration came itself to practice widely after 9/11. The CIA claim that it was inexperienced in coercive interrogation after 9/11 needs to be seen in the context of its own research on, and links to, precisely this subject, especially via the Phoenix Program in Vietnam as covered below. In 2001 the CIA might not have been recently experienced in the practice of directly managing detention centers, and in 2002 it might not have had on board a stable of experienced interrogators, but it certainly manifested a great deal of presumed knowledge about torture and mistreatment. It researched, taught, and supervised torture and lesser forms of abuse, even as it tried to mostly leave the direct application to others. The DOD was eventually implicated in this process, especially via the SERE program. As is evident, CIA, DOD, and FBI personnel are not hermetically sealed off from one another. They often interact and share knowledge and experiences, even as they failed to properly coordinate to prevent 9/11.[42]

Thus after Korea, the United States via both the CIA and DOD got into the business of prisoner abuse in a serious, if often quiet and indirect, way. At the same time, the overt policy of Washington was to support the 1949 Geneva Conventions and, more reluctantly, the human rights documents protecting prisoners that emerged from negotiations at the United Nations. I say "more reluctantly" because several circles of opinion in the United States on the right or conservative side

Marie-Monique Robin, "Counterinsurgency and Torture," in Kenneth Roth *et al.*, eds., *Torture: Does It Make Us Safer? Is It Ever OK? A Human Rights Perspective* (New York: The New Press, for Human Rights Watch, 2005), pp. 44–54.

[41] Grandin, *Empire's Workshop*.

[42] On the failure of CIA and FBI cooperation before 9/11, see the *9/11 Commission Report*.

have never liked the United Nations and the documents emerging from it, viewing those developments as unwise infringements on a virtuous nation. Even when the United States got around to ratifying several of these UN human rights instruments, the Senate, in giving its consent to ratification, imposed reservations that gutted the documents of legal effectiveness in US courts. The overall US relationship to internationally recognized human rights, mostly negotiated through the United Nations, is more ambivalent than fully supportive.[43]

Somewhat ironically in the light of the policies of the George W. Bush Administration, it can be recalled that it was the United States that led the movement to revise IHL after the Second World War, wanting to strengthen POW protection and being proud of its record in this regard ever since the adoption of the Lieber Code in its civil war.[44] (The Lieber Code that was designed to protect Confederate prisoners, among other objectives, in civil war was adopted at more or less the same time as the first Geneva Convention in 1864 for the protection of wounded soldiers in international war. So there were humanitarian developments regarding the laws of war on both sides of the Atlantic at this time.)

US policy in the Vietnam War showed an effort to have it both ways. From 1966 the US military, working with the non-governmental ICRC, the official guardian of IHL, declared parts of IHL applicable to the armed conflict. (In the Vietnam War, just like the "global war on terrorism," there was question about what legal framework applied. Was it an international war between two independent states – North and South Vietnam? Or was it an internal war within one Vietnam between two Vietnamese factions, with outside intervention by mainly the United States?) The central point for present purposes remains: in quest of better protection of US military personnel captured by enemy forces, and thus primarily in search of reciprocity, the United States was relatively generous in its official approach to captured enemy fighters – although the realities on the ground remain debated.

According to a key military directive in 1967, the United States afforded POW status to a variety of irregular or guerrilla fighters, not

43 See further, David P. Forsythe, "The U.S., the U.N., and Human Rights," in Margaret Karns and Karen Mingst, eds., *The United States and Multilateral Institutions* (New York: Unwin Hyman, 1990, 1992), pp. 261–288.

44 Beaumont, "Protecting Prisoners of War," p. 280.

just North Vietnamese regulars.[45] The situation was complex, because there were many different types of irregulars on the North Vietnamese side, with some Vietnam People's Army (NVA) regulars embedded with some Viet Cong (VC) units. According to another authoritative source, US policy was to *treat* not just NVA regulars but also aligned VC fighters as POWs, whatever their official legal *status*, as long as they were not spies, saboteurs, and terrorists.[46] According to yet other sources, US policy was to treat all detained enemy fighters as entitled to at least the minimum protections provided by Common Article 3 of the 1949 Geneva Conventions.[47] So it remains unclear what exactly was the controlling legal norm, or whether there was one, for the US military regarding especially detained VC. The political fact remains that the US intention was to take a generous approach to the question of whether enemies, including irregular fighters, merited humane treatment when captured. The driving concern in the field was pragmatic: self-interested reciprocity.

[45] Military Directive Number 381–46, December 26, 1967, Annex A, reprinted in the *American Journal of International Law*, 62, 3 (July 1968), pp. 766–767. This classification of various enemy units or actors was so complex as to present obvious difficulties for implementation in the field. The evolution and contents of this directive were confirmed by: ICRC Archives: 202/69, Saigon, 28 May 1966, memo from ICRC delegate to ICRC Headquarters detailing interactions with US military officials. Annex II of this memo provides emerging US definitions regarding prisoners. Annex III provides a copy of USMAC–Vietnam, Directive Number 190–3, May 24, 1966, regarding categories of prisoners. When at this general juncture the DOD sought to clarify and refine its treatment of captured prisoners, it sought the expertise of the ICRC "off the record." The ICRC was invited to "seminars" at which the various issues were discussed.

[46] Hans-Peter Gasser, "An Appeal for Ratification by the United States," in "Agora: The US Decision Not to Ratify Protocol I to the Geneva Conventions on the Protection of War Victims," *American Journal of International Law*, 81, 4 (October 1987), pp. 912–925. Gasser was an ICRC lawyer with good access to US diplomatic personnel.

[47] James Gebhardt, *The Road to Abu Ghraib: US Army Detainee Doctrine and Experience*, Global War on Terrorism Occasional Paper 6 (Fort Leavenworth: Combat Studies Institute Press, n.d.). Also David P. Forsythe, "Legal Management of Internal War: The 1977 Protocol on Non-International Armed Conflict," *American Journal of International Law* 72, 2 (April 1977), pp. 272–295 drawing on contacts with US military officials. My view now of this subject is that: (1) the official designation of enemy prisoners as POWs was too complicated to be workable in the field; (2) over time reference to Common Article 3 replaced the reference to POWs *de facto*; and (3) much brutality persisted in field interrogations given primarily the irregular nature of the war and lack of much reciprocity by the other side.

The United States made some effort, no doubt incomplete, to impose its legal views on the South Vietnamese military through such measures as a joint interrogation center in Saigon. Some of the military directives pertaining to relations with South Vietnamese authorities referred to Geneva Convention Common Article 3.[48] This somewhat still fuzzy record is highly relevant to the post-9/11 situation, as particularly the various VC fighters were out of uniform and represented a non-state party (from the US point of view).

This is not to say that US military interrogation in the Vietnam War was a perfect model of attention to legal and humanitarian rules, even if superior to the record compiled by both Saigon and Hanoi. There is much documented abuse of enemy prisoners by the US military in the Vietnam War.[49] But it is accurate to say that parts of the US military establishment in Southeast Asia paid relatively serious attention to IHL even in the case of captured VC. Many US military interrogators did observe the restrictions imposed particularly by Common Article 3 of both Geneva Conventions III and IV, if not the other relevant articles of those treaties – principally no torture or other inhuman or degrading treatment of enemy fighters. Thus, there was a broad attempt by the US military to protect enemy fighters in detention, even if captured out of uniform.

And with regard to terrorists – namely, those who did not display arms openly and fight under recognizable command – while they were not given the status of fighters, as civilians in a war zone officially they were not to be tortured – even if many were turned over to the not-so-tender mercies of the Saigon authorities. They could be interrogated, of course, and then prosecuted, and if convicted then executed.

At the same time, the United States adopted the covert Phoenix Program that resulted in considerable torture and murder.[50] This was run primarily by the CIA but with some military personnel seconded to

48 Author emails with Maj. James Gebhardt, 2009.

49 See Rejali, *Torture and Democracy*; and Beaumont, "Protecting Prisoners of War."

50 Douglas Valentine, *The Phoenix Program* (New York: Morrow, 1990); McCoy, *A Question of Torture*, pp. 61–74 and *passim*; William E. Colby and James McCargar, *Lost Victory: A First Hand Account of America's Sixteen-year Involvement in Vietnam* (Chicago: Contemporary Books, 1989); and M. Moyar, *Phoenix and the Birds of Prey: The CIA's Secret Campaign to Destroy the Viet Cong* (Annapolis: Naval Institute Press, 1997). Also Parry, *Understanding Torture*.

the Agency. This "pump and dump" operation, with brutal interrogation on a sizable scale, with many innocents caught up in the process in a quest for actionable intelligence, often followed by such measures as throwing the victim out of a helicopter, was not dissimilar from what democratic France had engaged in during the Algerian war – namely, the torture and summary execution of "terror suspects." Indeed, it seems that the Phoenix Program was greatly influenced by brutal French policies in Algeria in 1954–1962 and in Indochina in 1947–1954.[51] And just as French torture and summary execution did not lead to victory in Algeria and Indochina, and maybe not even to victory in the battle for Algiers, so US covert terror and summary execution did not lead to victory in Vietnam.[52] (It is of passing interest that while the CIA was asserting the ability to break prisoners by no touch torture, as per assertions in the Kubark manual, in Vietnam it resorted to brutal forms of traditional torture, followed by murder, in quest of actionable intelligence. Practice would seem to undercut the general claims about the effectiveness of torture lite.)

Be all that as it may, officially in public Washington supported IHL and military honor, while in the shadows it sometimes acted little differently from colonial France. The British, too, used coercive interrogation and killings in the Northern Ireland troubles, just as they had used violent interrogation in places such as Aden and Kenya.[53] After 9/11 there were a number of American statements about the US government's long-standing, consistent, and unblemished support for the

[51] Robin in Roth *et al.*, *Torture.*

[52] For a summary of the French experience see David P. Forsythe, "United States Policy toward Enemy Detainees in the 'War on Terrorism,'" *Human Rights Quarterly*, 28, 2 (May 2006), pp. 465–491. See Rejali, *Torture and Democracy*, for the argument that the useful role of French torture in the battle of Algiers has been much overstated. After 9/11, the Pentagon showed the 1966 movie "The Battle of Algiers." See further Raphaelle Branche, "Torture of Terrorists? Use of Torture in a 'War against Terrorism': Justifications, Methods and Effects: The Case of France in Algeria, 1954–1962," *International Review of the Red Cross*, no. 867 (September 2007), pp. 543–560.

[53] For an overview see Colm Campbell, "Northern Ireland: Violent Conflict and the Resilience of International Law," in Brysk and Shafir, *National Insecurity*, p. 71 and *passim*. See Rejali, *Torture and Democracy*, for British colonial and racist torture in Kenya. There was also British torture in Aden. On this general subject see further Maguire, *Law and War*. Also Parry, *Understanding Torture*. Note that in 2010 the British government acknowledged the unjustified killing of peaceful protesters in Belfast in 1972.

Geneva Conventions.[54] None of these accounts referred to the Phoenix Program (which had some military involvement) in Vietnam or US complicity (including by the military) in torture in political violence in places like Guatemala, Honduras, and El Salvador, *inter alia*.

Conclusion

It is helpful at this point to step back for a moment from our central focus on prisoner treatment and look at the US record on international law more generally. While the United States was formally accepting the principles of state sovereignty and domestic jurisdiction, it was overthrowing governments, some of them genuinely elected, in Iran, Guatemala, Chile, Congo/Zaire, Brazil, and so on.[55] The US policy of unilateral forceful regime change did not start with Iraq in 2003. US foreign policy, like the foreign policies of many if not most others, has long manifested much hypocrisy and many double standards.[56] Or, more charitably, the United States like most other states endorses norms in international law more as aspirational statements than as rules they are truly ready to abide by in daily affairs.

If true about international law in general, this US hypocrisy also remains true regarding the legal standards designed to protect enemy prisoners during the Cold War. There was public endorsement of enemy prisoner protections while there was also an active covert program entailing enemy prisoner abuse. Many especially in the military, however, clung to traditional military honor and respect for the laws of war, and thus strongly supported humane detention and interrogation of captured fighters from the other side.[57]

In the last analysis, why the United States had a relatively better record of protecting prisoners during the Second World War (especially

[54] See, for example, P. Z. Kelley and Robert F. Turner, "War Crimes and the White House," *Washington Post*, July 26, 2007, www.washingtonpost.com/wp-dyn/content/article/2007/07/25/AR2007072501881.html.

[55] For a popular, readable account see Stephen Kinzer, *Overthrow: The United States and Regime Change from Hawaii to Iraq* (New York: Henry Holt, 2007).

[56] Stephen Krasner, *Sovereignty: Organized Hypocrisy* (Princeton: Princeton University Press, 1999).

[57] For a very good analysis of the importance of notions of military honor for the functioning of IHL in the Balkan Wars of the 1990s, see Michael Ignatius, *Warrior's Honor: Ethnic War and the Modern Conscience* (New York: Holt, 1998).

regarding Europeans) compared to the Cold War is not easy to answer. Was European and Asian communism after 1945 really a greater threat to the United States than European fascism and Asian militarism before then? Was there a difference in the need for actionable intelligence in the era of WMD? Was it that the brutalities by the Asian communists, perhaps borrowing some techniques from the Soviets, pulled Washington down to their level? Was it that most liberal democracies increasingly turned nasty when they felt their security, even their colonial possessions, threatened? Was it that a subconscious racism informed American treatment of many (a) Japanese and (b) Vietnamese, and (c) non-Westerners after 9/11, in the same way that France harshly treated Algerians and the British the Kenyans – with perhaps the British translating their foreign experiences into prisoner policy in Northern Ireland?[58]

Whatever the answers, the United States had opened the door to generalized torture and abuse before 9/11. The Bush Administration eventually wound up bringing US abusive interrogation out of the shadows and into public debate, although Bush, Cheney *et al.* hardly intended to do that.

Most probably the Bush principal officials saw themselves as adopting our third version of political morality: the half-way house of limited cruelty toward dangerous and unprincipled terrorists, stopping short of torture. But it often did not play out that way, and it provoked a

[58] For examples of racist statements by US military officers regarding the Japanese in the Second World War see Ferguson, *The War of the World*. For double standards in the US approach to the laws of war based on attitudes toward opponents see Maguire, *Law and War*, Introduction. On the importance of decline in reciprocity in asymmetrical warfare see Mark Osiel, *The End of Reciprocity: Terror, Torture, and the Law of War* (Cambridge: Cambridge University Press, 2009). Relatedly Stephanie Carvin, in *The US and the Politics of the Laws of War* (New York: Columbia University Press, 2010), believes that "culture" explains much about the US history of application of the laws of war, by which she means formal fighting versus irregular insurgency. Thus captured British or Confederates were treated relatively humanely, or at least the official intention was to do so, while captured Native American fighters were often treated very badly. She argues that the Spanish in the Philippines were treated better than the Filipino insurgents. She also argues that Mexicans were relatively well treated by the United States. Other works, however, have noted a strong strain of racism in US foreign policy. See, e.g., Michael L. Hunt, *Ideology and US Foreign Policy* (New Haven: Yale University Press, 1987).

national public debate on a subject long taboo in polite company – the ethics of torture.

The book

Chapter 2 reviews the basic views of the Bush Administration on foreign policy, including the question of treatment of enemy detainees. Basic assumptions and general orientations very much affected specific policies toward prisoners. I argue that one should not spend vast amounts of time debating who was a realist and who was a neo-conservative. Bush, Cheney, Rumsfeld, and Rice and most of their immediate associates agreed on a radical, expansive, and unilateralist hard line response to 9/11. Spearheaded by Cheney, they were contemptuous of various legal restraints on what they wanted to do – especially the restraints found in international law. It was their views at the top that led to CIA forced disappearances, torture, and inhuman treatment. It was their views that led to widespread military abuse, sometimes including torture, at places like the Bagram Air Force Base in Afghanistan and the Guantánamo Naval Base on the island of Cuba. And it was this permissive context that contributed directly to the appalling situation at Abu Ghraib prison in Iraq. While some lower-level persons exceeded instructions, the push for widespread abusive interrogation was instigated, authorized, and (badly) managed from the very top.

Chapter 3 shows how the general views of the top Bush officials were implemented. The key first step was to arrange for civilian lawyers, politically appointed, to provide the legal memos that attempted to gut the 1949 Geneva Conventions and the 1984 UN Convention against Torture, among other legal standards. This was combined with the effort to screen out or disregard the other military and civilian lawyers who could be anticipated to object. Central to developments were the memos written by John Yoo in the Justice Department's Office of Legal Counsel (OLC), the office that pronounces on legal matters for the Executive Branch. Cheney's legal counsel, David Addington, drove the process, Yoo wrote many of the key memos, and Rumsfeld's general legal counsel, William Haynes, facilitated key decisions, as did White House lawyers like Alberto Gonzales. Attorney General Ashcroft and some others duly signed off on most of the memos. Once the standard legal norms applicable to enemy prisoners were deconstructed, for the military no precise rules about interrogation were clearly and consistently put into place. For the CIA, the precise rules in fact permitted torture and inhuman treatment, and were supervised by high officials.

Chapter 4 shows how the military situation played out in Afghanistan, Guantánamo, and Iraq. There is no doubt but that the new detention and interrogation rules for the Taliban and Al-Qaeda, and others associated with them, were intended to facilitate abuse at places like Bagram and Guantánamo. While high Bush officials might have intended the military to abuse without crossing the lines into torture, the process often did not work out that way. Contributing to the evolution of affairs was the high-level demand for actionable intelligence, whatever the theoretical limits imposed by various memos emanating eventually from Rumsfeld's office. Moreover, there was a clear decision by Rumsfeld's office to transfer some hard line personnel and abusive lessons out of Bagram and Guantánamo to Iraq, although the Administration had agreed that particularly the 1949 Geneva Conventions fully applied to its invasion and occupation of that country. As a bipartisan US Senate report was to state, the military guidelines were permissive and confused.

Chapter 5 focuses on the CIA program of kidnapping, secret transfer to foreign countries known for abusive interrogation, and management of its own secret prisons. An ICRC report from 2007, fully leaked in 2009, left no reasonable doubt that the CIA had engaged in torture or inhuman treatment of a certain number of disappeared persons. There was also no doubt that this program had been authorized and supervised by high Bush officials, especially after President Obama released various internal legal memos from the Bush era. Numerous other reports from journalists and human rights organizations, plus published claims by released prisoners, presented circumstantial evidence attesting to CIA complicity in abusive interrogation by states such as Egypt, Syria, Uzbekistan, and others. This situation gave pointed rise to the troubling question of how should the United States respond to the fact that high authorities had authorized major abuse. If Washington supported various forms of transitional justice (TJ) abroad, from criminal court trials to truth commissions, what about at home in the wake of torture and CID treatment especially by the CIA?

Chapter 6 focuses on due process questions, and particularly on the debate about the fate of enemy prisoners during and after interrogation. Here one confronts the question about what constitutes due process for prisoners suspected of hostile intent or action and seized in various parts of the world, including sometimes in theatres of armed conflict like Afghanistan and Iraq. The options range from open-ended administrative detention, to trial in US federal courts, to trial in US military courts, to proceedings in special tribunals such as Military Commissions or new security courts. Much attention was focused on the validity of the US information that led to seizure, on whether there was a reliable review of initial government claims, and on whether the detainee had been subjected to torture or some other form of inhuman treatment. On this matter, which included complex norms on rules of evidence and defendant's rights, eventually the courts as well as Congress were much involved in the conversation about what should be done. Particularly after torture or lesser forms of inhumane treatment, there was no apparent satisfactory policy that would meet consensus standards of due process.

Chapter 7 provides a review along with summary conclusions about the politics of abuse. It notes that in the United States after Bush II, there were advocates for all three views of political morality noted in Chapter 1: no torture or inhumane treatment, endorsement of torture or inhumane treatment, and trying to split the difference. There was also a spirited debate about TJ – namely whether to prosecute for past actions, authorize a truth commission, or just "move forward." The central point is to note the US difficulty in coming to terms with the past, as in France, because the abuse of enemy prisoners was authorized at highest levels to try to protect the country. Given the strength of different forms of nationalism, this kind of retrospective and evaluation is usually difficult, as particularly some French intellectuals had already noted. Given nationalism and the nation-state system of world affairs, the cosmopolitan project to implement freedom from torture and inhumane treatment of enemy prisoners is usually a difficult and uphill battle in times of insecurity, as democratic leaders feel strong pressures to do whatever is necessary to defend the country, and its arguably innocent civilians, from attack.[59] Ultimately the chapter argues for a total and

[59] In the view of those who support violent attacks on civilians, the latter are not seen as politically innocent. They may be non-combatants, but through election of certain leaders, lack of opposition to certain policies, and payment of taxes to support those policies they are seen as politically engaged and responsible. In certain circles of opinion, their active or passive acceptance of perceived injustices makes them permissible targets in irregular total war.

absolute ban on torture and cruel treatment, but advocates an improvement on the Israeli model of allowing for "the necessity defense" in order to mitigate punishment for well-considered exceptions. But the key to this model is the integrity of political leaders and especially judges in taking the model seriously.

2 *Political morality and the Bush Administration*

Because of [Bush's] decisions, America has squandered much of its global leadership role . . . This may take a generation to fix, or it may never be fully fixed, in which case the second Bush presidency will mark the beginning of a long-term decline in American status. This didn't have to happen. We need to make some sense of how it did.

(Jacob Weisberg, *The Bush Tragedy*, New York: Random House, 2008, p. xix)

The greatest dangers to liberty lurk in insidious encroachments by men of zeal, well meaning, but without understanding.

(Louis Brandeis, quoted in Joseph Margulies, *Guantánamo and the Abuse of Presidential Power*, New York: Simon & Schuster, 2006, p. 85)

Chapter 1 reviewed the three main positions on the question of treatment of enemy detainees: no major abuse; major abuse as the lesser evil; and selective but controlled abuse. It also showed that progressively into contemporary times the United States had continued to oppose prisoner abuse in public, but had often adopted and propagated the abusive methods of its adversaries in secret. The chapter also noted that liberal democracies like Britain, France, and Israel, among others, had pursued their version of national security in quite harsh ways at times.

The central point of Chapter 2 is that the mix of persons and principles in the George W. Bush Administration produced a foreign policy in general that was aptly characterized by two analysts as unilateralist and revolutionary.[1] This was so especially in its first term. Part of this

[1] Ivo H. Daalder and James M. Lindsay, *America Unbound: The Bush Revolution in Foreign Policy* (Washington, DC: Brookings, 2006).

general orientation was a deep skepticism about, or actual disdain for, international law and organization.[2] Bush's policy on enemy prisoners, reflecting these primary traits, aspired to limited abuse of enemy prisoners in defense of the virtuous United States and in violation of much international and domestic law, but it wound up with extensive abuse including torture.

Intersecting this foreign policy orientation was a domestic consideration of major importance – namely, as pushed primarily by Vice President Cheney, that the presidency had been unduly limited by Congress and the Courts since the 1970s. Hence, in this view, Bush needed to reassert the virtually unlimited authority of the President in times of national emergency. This domestic focus on constitutional checks and balances, and especially on presidential "war powers," was to lead to the remarkable argument that if the President needed to abuse enemy prisoners, even to torture them, the President had the plenary or residual authority to do so. No congressional statutes, court orders, or treaty provisions could properly limit his decisions. Hence some views about domestic law and politics were as revolutionary as about foreign policy and international law.

These general views provided the context within which specific decisions were taken about law and policy pertaining to enemy prisoners. We should have a proper view of the forest before dwelling on the nature of particular trees. Or, general views about law and politics, both at home and abroad, impacted particular decisions about detention and interrogation of enemy prisoners.

Foreign policy orientations

Analysts often employ the labels of "realist" or "liberal" to denote the general political orientation of various foreign policy officials. (With regard to the second position, one *used to* speak of "liberal." Such was the cultural power of right-wing discourse, especially after Ronald Reagan, that the world "liberal" became widely associated with idealistic or impractical opinions or some other negative connotation like big government spending, and so the label "progressive" came into use to

[2] Francis Fukuyama argues that this trait of skepticism about international law was consistent with the fundamental principles of neo-conservatism in his *America at the Crossroads: Democracy, Power, and the Neoconservative Legacy* (New Haven: Yale, 2006).

avoid the term "liberal."[3] Even earlier, at least for realists, liberalism was often associated with idealism, again implying an unrealistic or impractical orientation.)

To these two presumably classic orientations of realism and liberalism, for present purposes one might add two other views. The label "neo-con" or "neo-conservative" came into broad use from roughly the 1970s. There was never agreement on what it referred to, either for policies or persons. This did not prevent its widespread use among both journalists and academic analysts. Moreover, many political scientists became enamored with the philosophy of constructivism. This translated into political arguments asserting that beneath the surface for realists, liberals, and neo-cons there were more fundamental if subjective ideas about personal and group identity and roles. To make a long complicated story short on this point, some positions in the torture debate were driven by notions of military or national honor. These arguments most fundamentally hinged primarily on conceptions of proper identity and role.

These general orientations will be developed further below. To be sure there were other labels or theoretical (general) policy positions noted from time to time – like Marxist, neo-Marxist, or revisionist. Some observers of foreign policy officials use the two categories of "crusaders" and "pragmatists" (neo-cons would be crusaders and realists would be pragmatists).[4] Others describe Bush principal officials as "democratic imperialists" and "assertive nationalists."[5] Some scholars talk about Jacksonian nationalists, with perhaps Patrick Buchanan in mind.[6] One can find studies of foreign policy making that use multiple and complex categories.[7] There are, in addition, analysts who view leaders through the lens of various psychological theories. The fundamental point remains that we need some systematic overview of the general orientations of high US policy makers after 9/11 in order to get the big picture of what transpired.

[3] Note the creation in Washington of the think tank called the Center for American Progress, which was liberal.

[4] John G. Stoessinger, *Crusaders and Pragmatists: Movers of American Foreign Policy* (New York: W. W. Norton, 1985).

[5] Daalder and Lindsay, *America Unbound*.

[6] Walter Russell Mead, "The Jacksonian Tradition and American Foreign Policy," *The National Interest*, 58 (1999), pp. 5–29.

[7] Jon Western, *Selling Intervention and War: The Presidency, the Media, and the American Public* (Baltimore: Johns Hopkins, 2005).

Realism

In the United States from the start of the Cold War in 1947, if not from Pearl Harbor in 1941, the dominant perspective for the study of international relations in academic circles has been realism. This can be based either on the view that evil leaders will always confront the nation (Hitler, Stalin, Mao, Ho Chi Minh, Osama bin Laden), or that a global system of competing states will always produce security dilemmas requiring tough responses. Hence we find classical realism as developed by Hans Morgenthau or structural realism as developed by Kenneth Waltz. As is often the case in academe, numerous variations sprouted, such as offensive and defensive realism.

Leaders like Richard Nixon and Henry Kissinger can be accurately if generally described as realists. Their priority values were the management of national power for the benefit of US national security as they defined it; they emphasized primarily state power even if its exercise violated international law or harmed particular individuals; they did not hesitate about supporting brutal authoritarians like Augusto Pinochet in Chile or the Shah in Iran as long as that relationship was seen as in the US national interest as they defined it; they were certainly wary of moral crusades; they did not hesitate to lie and misrepresent in behalf of the national interest as they saw it; they were deeply pessimistic about how much one could improve the human condition. As structural realists, their core view was that a dangerous world required security policies that should not be judged by the traditional canons of domestic, individual morality.

When, for example, Kissinger came around to concern for human rights and national self-determination in Southern Rhodesia, which was widely recognized as independent Zimbabwe in 1980, it was mainly because he was worried about the Soviet Union using those issues to spread its power in southern Africa. Kissinger could give ringing public endorsements about democracy and human rights in South America, then tell his authoritarian and brutal allies that it was just for US domestic consumption – to placate his liberal critics. It was Nixon and Kissinger who developed better relations with Mao's China (and Mao was one of the great mass murderers of the twentieth century), so as to cause additional difficulties for the Soviet Union, the main US protagonist. This is classic realist maneuvering, in the tradition of Metternich (Kissinger's role model) and Machiavelli, without regard to traditional ideas of individual morality in a domestic context.

Even if realism can be defined and its variations noted, it remains more a philosophical orientation than a rigorous social science theory that leads to precise understanding about foreign policy.[8] It probably makes some sense to say that George Herbert Walker Bush (Bush I) was mostly a realist, and that George W. Bush (Bush II) campaigned as a realist but as President represented some other set of values and decisions.

Neo-cons

Some analysts are fond of the label "neo-conservatism." This label supposedly suggests the priority values of hard (coercive) national power joined with some assertive version of expansive morality in a Manichean struggle between good and evil. (Realists like Nixon and Kissinger were content to manage power relations so as to try to avoid disaster, which is minimalist morality. Kissinger argued that détente with the USSR, which reduced the dangers of nuclear war, was a moral policy.) In a common cliché, neo-conservatives are supposedly former liberals interested in expansive morality but who got mugged by (international) reality.

According to Stefan Halper and Jonathan Clarke, neo-conservatives unite around the themes of: (1) seeing the world in moralistic terms of good versus evil; (2) displaying an eager willingness to use hard power in this central moral struggle; (3) articulating a primary focus after the Cold War on the Middle East and Islam; (4) believing in the essential goodness of the United States, along with a general disregard for the opinions of others; (5) hence displaying a general disregard for much international law and organization, and alliances.[9] Jacob Heilbrunn notes considerable diversity in the neo-con camp but emphasizes their need for an evil enemy in a Manichean struggle, with a concern for Israel at the center of their policies whether in the era of communism or terrorism. To him, neo-cons are disputatious, firm believers in the

[8] On realism as a philosophical orientation rather than a precise theory, see Jack Donnelly, *Realism and International Relations* (Cambridge: Cambridge University Press, 2005). Also Samuel Barkin, "Realism, Prediction, and Foreign Policy," *Foreign Policy Analysis*, 5, 3 (July 2009), pp. 233–247.

[9] Stefan Halper and Jonathan Clarke, *America Alone: The Neo-Conservatives and the Global Order* (Cambridge: Cambridge University Press, 2004). See also Tom J. Farar, *Confronting Global Terrorism and American Neo-Conservatism: The Framework of a Liberal Grand Strategy* (New York: Oxford University Press, 2008), although his conception of neo-conservatism is not crystal clear.

benefits of hard power, and above all sure of the accuracy of their views.[10] Francis Fukuyama agrees that neo-conservatives display great variety in their views but argues for four principles: concern for democracy, human rights, and state internal politics; skepticism about international institutions; belief that American power can be a force for good; and skepticism about social engineering by governments.[11] He downplays any inherent connection to Israel. James Mann believes that Bush's war cabinet was comprised of Vulcans whose formative belief was that the United States in Vietnam was engaged in a noble cause for freedom which could have been won had Washington worried less about international opinion and been more willing to exercise its full hard power.[12] Central to all of these views is unilateralism and certitude. Among those labeled neo-conservatives one does not find much (any?) reference to the dangers of that mindset called the arrogance of power.[13]

If neo-cons are ultra-nationalists with a belief that the United States is the central force for good in the world and should not hesitate to use hard (coercive) power, there were certainly some neo-cons in the Administration of Bush II. Pentagon officials Paul Wolfowitz and Douglas Feith are usually cited in this regard, and probably the President himself. There were other neo-cons advising the Administration such as Richard Perle. Whether Vice President Cheney and Secretary of Defense Donald Rumsfeld are properly classified as neo-cons we will address later in this chapter. The point to be made here is that Bush II was not a prudential realist in the tradition of his father. As we will see, he did not carefully calculate power relations with a view to

10 Jacob Heilbrunn, *They Knew They Were Right: The Rise of the Neo-Cons* (New York: Anchor, 2009). He suggests that neo-cons cannot make up their collective mind as to whether they are militant Wilsonians or not, trying to spread democracy and other virtues by force or not. See especially p. 15.

11 Fukuyama, *America at the Crossroads*.

12 James Mann, *Rise of the Vulcans: The History of Bush's War Cabinet* (New York: Viking, 2004).

13 According to J. W. Fulbright, one of the leading critics of US policy in Vietnam, a great part of the problem for Washington stemmed from an arrogance of power, a belief that the United States could solve distant and complex problems through assertion of unilateral hard power. Its wisdom and power were so great the government could afford to block out competing views. Fulbright, *The Arrogance of Power* (New York: Random House, 1966). See also Peter Beinart, *The Icarus Syndrome: A History of American Hubris* (New York: Harper: 2010) for a more recent and broader treatment of the same theme.

simply protecting the power and independence of the United States. He was, rather, optimistic about the ability to transform the Middle East in a more democratic direction through such measures as the invasion of Iraq. When the Kissinger protégé and perceived realist Brent Scowcroft (who was national security advisor under Bush I and a mentor for Condoleezza Rice) said that he hardly recognized (the policies of) Dick Cheney any more, he certainly implied that his realist circles were uncomfortable with the basic directions of much US foreign policy under Bush II.[14]

Liberalism

I will assume for present purposes that a foreign policy liberal would show a strong commitment to: the fate of all individuals and thus human rights, the advancement of multilateralism and hence international law and organization, diplomatic solutions to problems rather than wars of choice, and optimism about the prospect of making progress in world affairs.[15] A conventional if erroneous reading of Woodrow Wilson was that he was a foreign policy liberal who stood above all else for democracy promotion as a means to enhanced security, through institutionalized measures such as international law and the League of Nations.[16] Hence one finds many references to "Wilsonian liberalism" among analysts of international relations.

Was Franklin D. Roosevelt (FDR) a liberal in the supposed Wilsonian tradition? FDR (with Churchill) did indeed issue the Atlantic Charter in 1941 justifying the Second World War in terms of liberal principles; he was an architect of the United Nations; he was opposed to colonialism; and he saw (inconsistently to be sure) human rights as an important subject at home and abroad.[17] He also authorized the unjustified and arbitrary internment of Japanese-American citizens during the Second

[14] See Jeffrey Goldberg, "Breaking Ranks," *The New Yorker*, October 31, 2005, www.newyorker.com/archive/2005/10/32/051031fa_fact2.

[15] For one comparison of liberalism and realism in foreign policy see Stephen W. Hook, *US Foreign Policy: The Paradox of World Power* (Washington, DC: CQ Press, 2nd edn., 2008), p. 68.

[16] See further Fukuyama, *America at the Crossroads*.

[17] It seems that the US and other governments make appeals to human rights and other liberal principles during times of stress in order to rally support, as per the Atlantic Charter in 1941, then try to back away from the ringing statements thereafter, whereupon human rights groups and others try to hold the governments to their original statements. See Roger Normand and Sarah Zaidi,

World War, for which the United States eventually apologized and paid reparations. He authorized military commissions that were in reality kangaroo courts leading to a quick death penalty for Nazi saboteurs.[18] He looked fairly favorably on "Uncle Joe" Stalin despite his brutalities and aggressions. Actually not just FDR, but Woodrow Wilson himself, was not a consistent Wilsonian liberal in international relations.[19]

Given the state system of international relations and the fact that the central problem of guaranteeing state security and prosperity has never been solved, and given the persistent bellicose nationalism that bubbles up from domestic sources, it is difficult to find consistent liberalism in contemporary US foreign policy. The fate of Jimmy Carter is instructive in this regard, as he started out in 1977 emphasizing human rights and the need to move away from an "inordinate" fear of communism. After the Soviet invasion of Afghanistan in 1979, he wound up pushing for greater military spending and aligned with many authoritarian regimes, such as Communist but independent Poland, in the name of containing the Soviet Union.

Suffice it to say that there were few if any liberals in the Bush II Administration. As we will show, those dissenting from the drift of much but not all prisoner policy, like Secretary of State Colin Powell, were motivated by a combination of prudent realism and conceptions of American and military honor. There were certainly some moderates in the Bush Administration, but more as prudential realists than liberals.

Constructivism

Constructivist theorists stress that much reality is constructed via perceptions that depend greatly on notions of identity and self-image. Constructivism in this sense, if you will, is a pre-theory that can feed

Human Rights at the UN; The Political History of Universal Justice (Bloomington: Indiana University Press, 2008).

18 Pierce O'Donnell, *In Time of War: Hitler's Terrorist Attack on America* (New York: New Press, 2005).

19 Wilson blocked a Japanese proposal at Versailles to introduce the norm of racial equality into the League of Nations Charter, he refused to commit the United States to the protection of endangered Armenians in the Ottoman Empire and successor state of Turkey, and he authorized unilateral force in Central America not required for US self-defense. At home, in a different notion of liberalism, he insisted on full racial segregation in the federal work force. On the complexity of Wilson, see Lloyd Ambrosius, *Wilsonianism: Woodrow Wilson and his Legacy in American Foreign Relations* (New York: Palgrave Macmillan, 2002).

into the other theories of foreign policy. It is an approach quite relevant to the present study because of notions of military honor and a version of American exceptionalism. For example, while some military officials might be realists in the sense of Nixon and Kissinger, doing whatever was necessary to protect the US national interest as they defined it, other military personnel might be greatly affected by notions of military honor. These latter, as professional military, might object to torture and/or mistreatment of the enemy prisoner because that is not what being professional military personnel is about. For Michael Ignatieff, there were many atrocities in the Balkan Wars of the 1990s because the fighters displayed little sense of warrior's honor.[20]

Michael Walzer in his major study of morality and war notes the role of military honor:

> Among professional soldiers, the war convention [the laws, rules, practices, etc. that govern fighting] often finds advocates of a special kind. Though chivalry is dead and fighting unfree [because of the draft, at the time he wrote] professional soldiers remain sensitive (or some of them do) to those limits and restraints that distinguish their life's work from mere butchery. No doubt, they know with General Sherman that war is butchery, but they are likely to believe that it is also, simultaneously, something else. That is why army and navy officers [there is no reason to exclude the air force; marines were technically part of the navy] defending a long tradition, will often protest commands of their civilian superiors that would require them to violate the rules of war and turn them into mere instruments for killing.[21]

Whether in the military or not, some might say, as John McCain did say at one point, that torture is not something that Americans do. Reportedly the lead lawyer in Bush's National Security Council staff, John Bellinger, III, said the same thing, which is supposedly why he got excluded from much policy making by Vice President Cheney and his allies.[22]

Fundamentally, the early McCain and the Bellinger positions are constructivist arguments based on notions of identity. These can feed

[20] Michael Ignatieff, *The Warrior's Honor: Ethnic War and the Modern Conscience in the Balkans* (New York: Metropolitan/Holt, 1998).

[21] Michael Walzer, *Just and Unjust Wars: A Moral Argument with Historical Illustrations* (New York: Basic Books, 1977), p. 45.

[22] Jane Mayer, *The Dark Side: The Inside Story of How the War on Terror Turned Into a War on American Ideals* (New York: Doubleday, 2008), p. 68. At one point Bellinger confronted John Yoo, the key lawyer on torture issues in the DOJ, about being excluded from meetings.

into a liberal policy position on the one issue of prisoner treatment, namely an absolute ban on torture and other cruelty, but the argument hinges mostly on a conception of national and/or professional identity, with some attention to self-interest in the form of reciprocity. But constructivism can feed into other views as well. For Dick Cheney, if we assume he was motivated primarily by intense American patriotism, his view of his identity led to rigid and unending endorsement of major abuse (even after he left office). Cheney arguably identified strongly with a United States that was such a pillar of virtue in the world, in the face of horrible enemies, that significant abuse of enemy prisoners was justified.

General overview

Where does this review of foreign policy labels leave us when it comes to the foreign policies of Bush II, in general and with regard to enemy prisoners? First, it remains more art than science to characterize with certainty the prevalent and persistent general orientation of most foreign policy decision makers. This is why there is such a plethora of terms floating around as various observers, some quite serious and careful, search for an accurate way to summarize foreign policy orientations. Nixon and Kissinger would seem exceptional in their systematic commitment to one approach – realism. Most policy makers leave a mixed record that is difficult to summarize easily. They tend to change over time, with Reagan and Bush II arguably becoming more centrist – maybe even more liberal – in their second terms. Reagan, for example, came to see Gorbachev as a reliable negotiating partner, wanted to move toward nuclear disarmament, and foresaw an enhanced security role for the United Nations.

Second, despite the caveat above, it is reasonably clear that the early foreign policy of Bush was the result of both a certain neo-con push combined with offensive if not aggressive realism. Cheney and Rumsfeld were basically assertive and quite brutal realists, with the religiously inclined President susceptible to the siren song of doing God's work through militant American exceptionalism. With the likes of Paul Wolfowitz, Douglas Feith, and Richard Perle pushing for such measures as a war of choice in Iraq and abuse of enemy prisoners, it was no wonder that Bush foreign policy could be fairly and accurately characterized as revolutionary and unilateralist. As will be shown, those prudent realists, some with a sense of military honor, like Colin Powell with misgivings about the direction of Bush foreign policy, were first cut out and then forced out, for the most part (Condoleezza Rice being the major if partial exception).

Third, given the above, we should not be surprised that traditional understandings of law and morality did not fare very well in the Bush Administration, especially in the first term. The basic climate inside the Bush Administration after 9/11 was one of dire threat, hence the need for new thinking. The core reputation and power of the United States had been challenged. The Al-Qaeda attacks were the perfect pretext for Cheney to push for unlimited presidential power, for Rumsfeld to push for a transformed military, for Wolfowitz and Feith to push for the removal of Saddam Hussein who had been such a thorn in the side of Israel in particular. Traditional understandings of the restraints imposed by law, restraints linked to reciprocal self-interests and military honor, had little role in Bush's new thinking.

Just as it was years before we had a fulsome view of other Administrations, so it will be some years before we have a relatively complete view of the Administration of Bush II. In the meantime, it is worth making interpretations as best we can, for considerable information is already in the public domain. One of the fundamental points expounded here is that the policy views at the top drove events on down the line. What happened at the Bagram Air Force Base in Afghanistan, at Guantánamo on Cuba, at Abu Ghraib prison in Iraq, and at the CIA secret prisons, did not happen willy nilly in a policy vacuum. There were a few bad apples at the bottom of the barrel, as always, but prisoner abuse happened mostly because of command responsibility, both civilian and military. Taking the key policy decisions were Bush officials who wanted a free hand to engage in coercive interrogation, in pursuit of a maximum but narrow and short-term conception of national security. Some key players also thought the imperial presidency, even the imperial presidency on steroids, a desirable situation. They were quite dismissive of legal rules and some traditional American ideals to the contrary.

The President and Vice President

Benjamin Wittes of the Brookings Institution has suggested that most Presidents, faced with the horrors and uncertainties of 9/11, would have been tempted to do what Bush II did in authorizing abuse of prisoners: "What president, sworn to protect America from threats foreign and domestic, is really going to forgo the information that the highest-value detainees may have stored in their brains? Presidents do not err on the side of restraint in those situations on which they believe the country's ultimate fate depends."[23] The political theorist Michael Walzer said much the same thing: "political leaders can hardly help but choose the utilitarian side of the dilemma [by emphasizing the nation they are sworn to defend rather than the rights of enemy prisoners]. That is what they are there for. They must opt for collective survival and override those rights that have suddenly loomed as obstacles to survival."[24] At the heart of John Yoo's understanding of the US Constitution is the argument that all war-time Presidents have expanded presidential power without much attention to legal restraints, whether Lincoln, Wilson, FDR, or Truman.[25] John McCloy, an advisor to FDR and later a hawkish cold warrior, was not the only one to opine, then and now, that when it comes to perceived national security, legal documents, including the US Constitution, are but scraps of paper.[26] Dean Acheson, Secretary of State for President Truman, and widely considered a tough and perhaps arrogant realist, said at the time of the Cuban missile crisis that law doesn't play much of a role when the security of the state is seen as endangered.[27] Therefore some academics theorize that executive departure from legality under extreme conditions is to be

[23] Benjamin Wittes, *Law and the Long War: The Future of Justice in the Age of Terror* (Washington, DC: Brookings, 2008), p. 121.

[24] Walzer, *Just and Unjust Wars*, p. 326.

[25] John Yoo, *The Powers of War and Peace: The Constitution and Foreign Affairs After 9/11* (Chicago: University of Chicago Press, 2005).

[26] John J. McCloy, at the time of the forced relocation of Japanese, including US citizens of Japanese descent, as quoted by Jean Edward Smith in *FDR* (New York: Random House, 2007), p. 551. In reality, those relocated posed no threat to US security.

[27] "The power, position and prestige of the United States had been challenged by another state; and law simply does not deal with such questions of ultimate power – power that comes close to the sources of sovereignty." Quoted in Abram Chayes, *The Cuban Missile Crisis: International Crises and the Role of Law* (New York and London: Oxford University Press, 1974), p. 1. In reality, Soviet missiles in Cuba did not really change the strategic military balance between the United States and the USSR, which is why Secretary of Defense McNamara at the time said the missiles presented a political problem – the appearance of a Soviet success in foreign policy. McNamara aside, there was an overblown threat assessment at that time also.

expected, but insist that the process be transparent and that there be some type of evaluation to pass judgment on the "necessity argument."[28]

The Bush team did not make a transparent necessity argument as such, much less invite review during or after the fact. What the Bush principals and lawyers did was twist the law to try to give the appearance of legality, at least to their satisfaction and that of their supporters, in a secret process that avoided competing views and authoritative review for as long as possible. They did not say that they had the right to exceed the law. They said, as we shall see in Chapter 3, that existing law either did not apply to situations like detention at Guantánamo, or permitted the abusive policies they adopted. Some, like John Yoo, also made the argument that the Commander in Chief during war-time was virtually omnipotent, which comes close to the necessity argument. That argument itself comes close to a Fascist view of law and leadership, since the necessity argument sees executive power as above mundane law. (We lack a consensus definition of fascism.) Yoo's democratic Commander in Chief is very close to the caudillo on horseback (Pinochet? Franco?) who rises above law to save the organic nation from itself. There will be more on this in Chapter 3. It is with reason that the scholar John T. Parry sees rational liberalism on a continuum with romantic fascism.[29] It is with reason that another scholar, Paul W. Kahn, sees militant Islamists and those advocating an unlimited American response in religious terms, both acting in terms of sacred violence.[30]

Whether or not we can reasonably expect law to restrain in a national emergency, which is what international law requires, a major feature of Bush's decisions after 9/11 was a lack of systematic review of policy options – and a lack of careful consideration of long-term problems that might be encountered in the path contemplated. There was a rush to judgment in a chaotic policy making process after the dust had settled from the Twin Towers and part of the Pentagon, as will be shown

[28] For an excellent overview of this arguments, with pros and cons, see Victor V. Ramraj, ed., *Emergencies and the Limits of Legality* (New York and Cambridge: Cambridge University Press, 2008).

[29] John T. Parry, *Understanding Torture: Law, Violence, and Political Identity* (Ann Arbor: University of Michigan Press, 2010).

[30] Paul W. Kahn, *Sacred Violence: Terror, Torture, and Sovereignty* (Ann Arbor: University of Michigan Press, 2008).

below. Bush II trusted his personal instincts and was not enamored of careful policy planning and review.[31] Moreover, with hindsight it is fair to say that the threats from Al-Qaeda, and especially from Iraq, were maximized, as Cheney, Rumsfeld, and Wolfowitz, among others, seized upon 9/11 to implement long-held preferences and policy objectives. Among the principals only Powell sometimes hesitated, and he was marginalized. Given 9/11 and fears of more attacks, the humane values codified in much law were thrown away in the quest for enhanced national security.[32]

By conservative Republican standards Bush was often seen a pragmatic, centrist governor in Texas who reached out to Democrats for agreement on many policy questions and who in the 2000 presidential campaign ran as a realist.[33] He was supposedly skeptical of do-goodism causes like foreign nation-building and other so-called "social work" by Great Powers,[34] and in the 2000 campaign he put out the line that if the United States was humble and careful about uses of power the country would be widely respected.[35] He was clearly more unilateralist than multilateralist, but then that is a characteristic shared by many Republicans. In one of the 2004 presidential campaign debates, he said he would never ask for a "permission slip" from the United Nations in order to take needed action.[36] This line played well in American society, even if it did not fit well with some political realities in a globalized world where even a Superpower could benefit from allies and collective approval.

31 See Ron Suskind, *The Way of the World: A Story of Truth and Hope in an Age of Extremism* (New York: Harper, 2008), p. 5 and *passim*.

32 See especially Mayer, *The Dark Side*.

33 Lou Cannon and Carl M. Cannon, *Reagan's Disciple: George W. Bush's Troubled Quest for a Presidential Legacy* (New York: Public Affairs, 2008). The clearest statement about Bush's official position on foreign policy prior to election was by Rice, "Promoting the National Interest," *Foreign Affairs*, 79, 1 (January–February 2002), pp. 45–62. The argument was supposed to be realist, but there was evidence of much naïveté, such as the position that since every other state wanted what the United States wanted, US exercise of power was benign.

34 This line was developed in print by Michel Mandelbaum, "Foreign Policy as Social Work," *Foreign Affairs*, 75, 1 (January–February 1996), pp. 16–32.

35 See the discussion on the Jim Lehrer NewsHour on PBS, the transcript of which can be found at www.pbs.org/bb/politics/jul–dec00/for-policy_10–12.html.

36 See Chris Suellentrip, "The Post-Debate Debate," *Slate*, October 2, 2004, www.slate.com/ID/2107682.

Being largely unread in world history and inexperienced in foreign policy, Bush was never a thoughtful and prudent realist; his realist image was built on little more than campaign phrases. He had no real ideology or philosophy or theoretical world view at the start of his presidency. (Nor did President Carter, despite his image as a liberal.) After 9/11 Bush was highly influenced by a group of policy advisors who had long seen the United States as the engine for goodness in the world (the neo-cons) and who believed in the broad exercise of US military power without much restraint (the neo-cons and the offensive realists/assertive nationalists). The former tended to talk in moralistic terms and mostly had great affection for Israel. The latter eschewed traditional moralistic approaches and stressed strictly US interests, chief among which was a very expansive notion of US security. What counted among these advisors was not theoretical labels but a common belief in (1) the enormous danger faced by the United States after 9/11; (2) the need for radical, preventative, "forward leaning" action; and (3) a conviction that they were correct in their views and had little need for other opinions and rules that constrained their initial impulses and decisions. Particularly Vice President Cheney and a few others down the line also believed in the need for enhanced presidential authority as a domestic, constitutional matter.

As a late-comer to religion in the form of a vague deist Christianity (even if "born again," his religion lacked theological specifics), Bush believed the United States was divinely blessed and a moral force for good in the world. Cabinet meetings started with prayer. The President's day started with religious devotionals. Some Pentagon reports to him quoted biblical passages. There was a Manichean, good versus evil thinking that was clearly manifest in his pronouncements after 9/11.[37] Bush's religion gave him a certain certitude that could morph into rigidity and lack of reflection.[38]

Bush's thinking reflected a moralistic and crusading American exceptionalism. This exceptionalism led to exemptionalism, in that the United

[37] See further Jacob Weisberg, *The Bush Tragedy* (New York: Random House, 2008). Also Shirley Anne Warshaw, *The Co-Presidency of Bush and Cheney* (Stanford: Stanford University Press, 2009), especially the chapter entitled "God and George W. Bush: The Faith Based Presidency."

[38] Richard Brookheiser, "Close Up: The Mind of George W. Bush," *Atlantic Monthly*, April 2003, www.atlanticmonthly.com/doc/200304/brookheiser. See also Suskind, *The Way of the World*.

States was seen as too virtuous to be bound like ordinary nations under international law.[39] In the US National Security Strategy Statement of 2002, international law was mentioned along with weak and corrupt nations as an undesirable drag on Washington. Clearly after 9/11 Bush was incensed that Al-Qaeda had dared to attack the democratic and virtuous United States, and he was personally engaged in the response in visceral terms. His response combined religiosity with a type of Texan machismo. He later issued a macho challenge to the insurgents in Iraq to "bring it on," who responded with increasingly deadly attacks for some years. Bush personified what Walter Hixon has termed the core of a culturally determined foreign policy: "a manly, racially superior, and providentially destined 'beacon of liberty,' a country which possesses a special right to exert power in the world."[40] This was but a variation of the long-held view that central to the US place in the world was a sense of American greatness, its providentially ordained Manifest Destiny.[41]

Bush's response to 9/11 morphed into a rhetorical global crusade and war against all terrorism everywhere, a dubious concept since terrorism in its various forms and causes has been around for a long time, and will be for a long time. (According to the Human Security Report, in 2008 there were about 11,800 terrorist attacks in the world.) Moreover, terrorism is a method of political action, and one does not make war on a method. In reality, Bush showed little interest in eradicating terrorism in places like Sri Lanka, where it had been used for a long time by the Tamil Tigers, was unconnected to Middle East terrorism, and was apparently in the British or Indian sphere of influence. But Cheney and Rumsfeld pushed the notion of a global war on terrorism that went far beyond Osama bin Laden and Al-Qaeda, and far beyond

[39] See further John G. Ruggie, "Doctrinal Unilateralism and its Limits: America and Global Governance in the New Century," in David P. Forsythe, Patrice C. McMahon, and Andrew Wedeman, eds., *American Foreign Policy in a Globalized World* (New York: Routledge, 2006), pp. 31–50.

[40] Walter Hixon, *The Myth of American Diplomacy: National Identity and US Foreign Policy* (New Haven: Yale University Press, 2008), p. 1. See especially chapter 10 on post-9/11 developments. I find Hixon's thesis overstated, in that he argues the cultural influences on US foreign policy are so strong that individual decision makers count for little (p. 240), but in general he is right to stress a manly (read militaristic) national identity that is both powerful and insecure at the same time.

[41] Michael H. Hunt, *Ideology and US Foreign Policy* (New Haven: Yale University Press, 1987).

Afghanistan, in order to implement their long-standing agendas. By framing the issues as a crusade for freedom, they appealed to Bush's moralistic but unsophisticated leanings. Cheney in particular knew "how to push Bush's buttons," at least in the first term.[42]

According to Bush, either one was for or against the United States. There was no complex, in-between position. One is reminded of similar comments by the moralist John Foster Dulles during the Cold War when he was Secretary of State for most of the Eisenhower Administration, who railed against supposed Third World neutralism. Bush's second inaugural address outlined such a rhetorical crusade for freedom around the world that he made Jimmy Carter and his talk about human rights look like a crafty and prudent realist.[43]

Much of Bush's swagger played very well in American politics immediately after 9/11, since the country was in a highly nationalistic and truculent mood after the attacks, but its appeal waned as time passed – as indicated in the President's declining popularity in his second term. By 2008 some 80 percent of respondents to various public opinion polls thought the nation was on the wrong track in general,[44] and more than half came to believe the invasion of Iraq had been a mistake (compared with more than two-thirds who supported the invasion when it commenced). By 2008 the President's overall popularity hovered around 20 percent and slightly below, very low by historical standards, and even lower than President Nixon in 1974 at the time of his resignation after the Watergate scandal. (Yet Bush had been re-elected in 2004.) By early 2009 those Americans willing to identify as Republicans had declined to 22 percent. Figures changed by the 2010 congressional elections, as many voters swung back into the Republican column two years into Barack Obama's term.

Driving some of Bush's moralistic and macho response may have been a competition to out-do his father, Bush I, supposedly a prudent realist. The elder Bush had left Saddam in power after the first Persian Gulf War of 1991, had thus refused to take the fight to Baghdad, and had, moreover, lost a bid for a second term in large part by not being

[42] See especially Barton Gellman, *Angler: The Cheney Vice Presidency* (London: Penguin Press, 2008).

[43] www.msnbc.msn.com/id/6848112/.

[44] David Leonhardt and Marjorie Connelly, "81% in Poll Say Nation is Headed on Wrong Track," *New York Times*, April 4, 2008, www.nytimes.com/2008/04/04/us/04poll.html.

crusading enough for the American religious right wing. The workings of an Oedipus complex are as intriguing as they are incapable of absolute proof. For now one can plausibly believe that George W. Bush loved and respected his father, and at the same time was in competition with him for who would have the greater legacy as President. This latter factor could have encouraged Bush II first to revolutionary change and then to rigidity when his various radical policies became controversial.[45]

For Bush II, his Texan machismo, belief in American moral greatness as divinely inspired, lack of knowledge and experience in foreign affairs, confidence in his personal instincts, and competition with his father's legacy all drove him toward radical, not cautious, positions. Above all, he was counseled in these directions by Cheney and Rumsfeld, who eclipsed Rice and Powell in the first Bush II Administration. It is likely that he wanted to show his greatness by bold actions, particularly in the face of doubts about his abilities by northeast elitist liberals whether at Yale or the *New York Times*. As Weisberg has suggested, Bush's over-confidence masked considerable insecurities.[46] When things went wrong, he showed a lack of reflection and flexibility.[47] Ronald Reagan had shifted away from misguided policies in Lebanon in the early 1980s (he removed US ground troops), had changed course in both the Philippines (he instituted more distance from Marcos) and Chile (more distance from Pinochet), and had, in a somewhat muddled way, accepted responsibility for equally misguided policies in the Iran-Contra Affair (trading weapons to Iran for the release of American hostages in Lebanon, with the proceeds of arms sales going to support the Contras in Central American in violation of US statutory law). Bush seemed mostly incapable of adjusting course when the train went off the tracks.

As we will see, Bush fought to the end of his administration for CIA secret prisons unsupervised by the ICRC, and for the option of CIA

[45] See further Weisberg, *The Bush Tragedy*. On friction between father and son about the conduct of US foreign policy, see James Risen, *State of War: The Secret History of the CIA and the Bush Administration* (New York: Free Press, 2006), p. 1.

[46] Weisberg, *The Bush Tragedy*, p. 172. Daalder and Lindsay, *America Unbound*, miss this point, seeing Bush simply as confident.

[47] According to the Cannons, *Reagan's Disciple*, this was Bush's major failing compared to Reagan.

abusive interrogation of supposedly HVDs. He was willing to talk about closing Guantánamo, but then transferred certain CIA prisoners there which made its closing more difficult. He accepted a rewriting of the US army field manual regarding interrogation, but this was only after the US Supreme Court had forced his hand in the 2006 *Hamdan* judgment holding that parts of the laws of war applied to the proclaimed Global War on Terror (GWOT). He could not bring himself to remove his first Secretary of Defense, Donald Rumsfeld, who directly oversaw various major débâcles such as the Abu Ghraib prison scandal, until after the Republican defeats in the 2006 congressional elections. He continued to consult with Rumsfeld after the latter left office. Bush did belatedly increase troop levels in Iraq, those low levels being one of the principal defects of his earlier decisions (as advised by Rumsfeld), and the "surge" contributed to increased relative security there as of 2010 – along with other shifts in policy. But this was a tactical shift in support of the constant strategic objective of continuing to stabilize Iraq after the invasion.

There is a competing view. Jack Goldsmith, a Bush official, has argued that on prisoner affairs Bush, pushed by Rice, began to change course around 2003 and moved away from the more extreme positions adopted immediately after 9/11 under the dominant influence of Cheney.[48] While there seems some truth to Goldsmith's interpretation as laid out in *The New Republic*, it is overstated. As noted above, Bush persisted in the attempt to keep a free hand on prisoner matters especially via the CIA until first the Congress (2005, Detainee Treatment Act or DTA) and then the US Supreme Court (2006, *Hamdan* judgment) forced some change in Bush's prisoner policy. Bush did not rein in Cheney in battles on Capitol Hill, as the Vice President fought John McCain and other Members of Congress (MCs) during 2005 regarding prisoner legislation. Bush fought any judicial review of his prisoner policies in each and every court case. Bush never did respond affirmatively to ICRC efforts to get information about "ghost detainees" (hidden prisoners); there was no moderate shift on such questions. Bush never insisted, even after the Abu Ghraib scandal became public in 2004, on a proper review of prisoner policy in military installations. He let Rumsfeld stall and cover up, as we shall see in Chapter 4. He advanced the careers of, or otherwise rewarded, those who authorized

[48] "The Cheney Fallacy," *The New Republic*, May 18, 2009.

or administered prisoner abuse – Jay Bybee, William Haynes, Alberto Gonzales, Geoffrey Miller, etc. This is hardly the mark of a President who has seriously rethought previous policies.

Bush was clearly pushed in his radical orientations by Cheney. If Cheney were to turn out to be the most powerful Vice President in American history, it is because Bush allowed that to happen. If the Bush Administration in its first term had no real national security review process on many questions, normally handled by the National Security Advisor (NSA) and staff, but rather security policy making by the President closeted with the Vice President, it is because Bush preferred it that way. It was also the case that Condoleezza Rice was personally too close to Bush, too supportive of what he wanted, to give him the objective vetting of policies that he needed.[49] If Cheney and his chief aides, David Addington and Scooter Libby, were inordinately successful in controlling much policy by controlling the paper flow and attendance at meetings, and thus by controlling which Executive Branch officials were in or out of the game of decision making, whether on energy policy, or environmental policy, or prisoner policy, it was because Bush allowed that to happen. If NSA Rice and Secretary of State Colin Powell were both often marginalized during Bush's first term, it is because the President allowed the Vice President (and his ally, Donald Rumsfeld, the Secretary of Defense) to win the internal battles.

If Addington, for Cheney, turned out to be a main architect of much prisoner policy, it is partly because Bush surrounded himself with weaker legal figures like the lawyers Alberto Gonzales and Harriet Miers, who were no match for the bright and assertive Addington. Bush's inattention to details, acknowledged in passing by a supporter like Douglas Feith, gave Cheney and Rumsfeld and their aides much room to maneuver.[50] The fact was that the early process for making

[49] See especially Elisabeth Bumiller, *Condoleezza Rice: An American Life, A Biography* (New York: Random House, 2007). See also Weisberg, *The Bush Tragedy*: "where Bush went, Rice would follow" (p. 149). And see Risen, *State of War*, p. 64. Ivo H. Daalder and I. M. Destler, *In the Shadow of the Oval Office: Profiles of the National Security Advisers and the Presidents They Served – From JFK to George W. Bush* (New York: Simon & Schuster, 2009) consider Rice the weakest of all national security advisors since 1947. Colin Powell, as interviewed by Karen De Young, also found Rice unwisely deferential to whatever Bush wanted.

[50] Feith says that Bush was not much interested in tactics, but preferred the big ideas of strategy. *War and Decision: Inside the Pentagon at the Dawn of the War on*

foreign and security policy in the Bush II presidency was unsystematic, to put it kindly, as indicated by the analysis of, *inter alia*, Richard Haass, an establishment figure who was in the Bush II State Department.[51] From Bush's inexperience and inattention arose the "co-presidency" of Bush–Cheney, with Cheney in the driver's seat regarding, *inter alia*, national security and detainee policy – at least early on.[52]

According to Ron Suskind in a persuasive interpretation, Cheney believed that if there was a 1 percent chance that another government might possibly make serious trouble for the United States in the future, the Bush team should engage in regime change.[53] International legal prohibitions on such actions made no difference. The law requires a clear and present danger for the exercise of self-defense, not just a future and possible danger.[54] But this 1 percent doctrine was not limited to Cheney. It was shared by Secretary of Defense Rumsfeld and his principal advisors like Douglas Feith, Paul Wolfowitz, and Stephen Cambone.[55] Distressingly, the uniformed military also bought into this view. The Joint Chiefs of Staff (JCS) Chair after Hugh Shelton, Richard B. Myers, accepted this view. NSA Rice was of similar opinion. Whether with regard to the invasion of Iraq or the treatment of enemy prisoners, most of the top of the Bush Administration believed in the need for radical action and a disregard for existing rules. They believed

Terrorism (New York: Harper, 2008), p. 62. For confirmation see Gellman, *Angler*, p. 7.

51 Richard N. Haass, *War of Necessity, War of Choice: A Memoir of Two Iraq Wars* (New York: Simon & Schuster, 2009). On Bush's chaotic policy making process see also Michael R. Gordon and Bernard E. Trainor, *Cobra II: The Inside Story of the Invasion and Occupation of Iraq* (New York: Pantheon, 2006).

52 Warshaw, *The Co-Presidency*.

53 Ron Suskind, *The One Per Cent Doctrine: Deep Inside America's Pursuit of its Enemies Since 9/11*(New York: Simon & Schuster, 2006).

54 For one authoritative view, one highly important for both legal and political reasons, see the Israeli scholar Yoram Dinstein, no dove, *Aggression and Self-Defense* (Cambridge: Cambridge University Press,4th edn., 2005).

55 Feith in his memoirs makes clear that they all used 9/11 to rush into a broad preventive war that was not particularly oriented toward Afghanistan, the Taliban, and Al-Qaeda. They used 9/11 to do what they had long wanted to do, which was to topple Saddam Hussein and remake the world according to their pre-set desires. See *War and Decision*, pp. 4, 9, 13, 15, 49, 84, 87, and *passim*. One reason they focused on Iraq early on was that there were obvious military targets there, which was not the case in lesser developed Afghanistan! Their goal was to eliminate anyone, anywhere in the world, that might do the United States harm in the future. This is neither conservatism nor realism.

they would create their own realities.[56] 9/11 affected their judgments about traditional American values like human rights and the rule of law, with damaging results. Their concern to prevent similar attacks on the homeland overwhelmed any other consideration. There was no balance between a tough response to 9/11 and respect for the rule of law and presumed traditional American values. There was also little awareness that overreaching on national security could actually increase insecurity – by fomenting more anti-Americanism and hampering cooperation with friends. This is probably what Al-Qaeda wanted: to provoke the United States into overreaction and thus to make its position in the world more controversial.[57] Since the Bush principals knew they were right, they felt little need to explain their controversial and specific views to the country and abroad; they were content to take decisions secretly.

Feith is correct that Secretary of State Colin Powell neither fully bought into the Cheney–Rumsfeld view nor fully opposed it. Powell did not agree with the prevailing threat assessment about Al-Qaeda and Iraq, and he was opposed to abuse of prisoners by the military.[58] But he participated in meetings at which abusive interrogation methods for the CIA were discussed, which apparently drew more protest from Attorney General Ashcroft than from Powell, so far we know now. And Ashcroft seemed to be objecting more to the high-level discussion in the White House than to use of the brutalities.[59] Powell's disagreements with the rest of the principals of the Bush Administration took the form of stalling and playing for time, hoping that something would happen to slow down the revolutionary trends. But apparently he never considered resigning, as Secretary of State Cyrus Vance had resigned in opposition to Carter's military raid on Iran in 1980 to try to free American hostages. William Jennings Bryan had also resigned as Secretary of State to protest President Wilson's handling of relations with Germany before the United States entered the First World War. Powell's model was Secretary of State George Marshall under Truman, another military man, who strongly objected to Truman's recognition of Israel but stayed loyal to his Commander in Chief.[60]

[56] See Suskind, *The One Percent Doctrine*.
[57] See Suskind, *The Way of the World*.
[58] Karen De Young, *Soldier: The Life of Colin Powell* (New York: Vintage, for Random House, 2006, 2007).
[59] See Mayer, *The Dark Side*, p. 143. Also Gellman, *Angler*, p. 178.
[60] De Young, *Soldier*.

According to Charlie Savage, Cheney believed presidential power had been seriously eroded since the 1970s.[61] It followed that Bush should cut out Congress from most policy making roles, especially given the threats to national security, and should operate as unilaterally within the United States as in international relations. It is quite clear, as will be shown in Chapter 3, that Cheney and his principal lawyer David Addington, "Cheney's Cheney," and other lawyers particularly in the DOJ, did not believe that US constitutional or statutory law really restrained the President in times of threats to national security. They were all particularly dismissive of treaty limitations and customary international law. They were ultra-nationalists who believed in the virtue and wisdom of the United States, not in the values found in international law. In sum, Cheney, who in foreign affairs was supposedly an offensive realist, and thus single-mindedly devoted to American power, far from seeing the imperial presidency as a threat to US constitutional government, wanted an even stronger presidency that would circumvent Congress – and the Courts – more often. In this he was enabled by a number of politically appointed lawyers, who told the Vice President what he wanted to hear, and who then passed that "advice" to the President, who accepted it. Bush wound up making revolutionary claims to presidential power, and about "signing statements" and a "unified theory of executive power"– explained on pp. 90–91.

It was in this context, as we shall see in some detail in Chapter 3, that John Yoo in the DOJ, in the key Office of Legal Counsel, could advance the idea that the President could legally order the torture of prisoners in violation of international and national law if in the President's view US national security so required. It was in this context that Bush was advised to issue many "signing statements" arguing that under the "unified theory of executive power," the President has the residual, plenary authority to violate treaties and statutes in the name of national security. (If this were true for Bush as US President, why not true for Saddam Hussein or Slobodan Milošević?) And it was in this context that Cheney publically endorsed the waterboarding of certain enemy

[61] Charlie Savage, *Takeover: The Return of the Imperial Presidency and the Subversion of American Democracy* (New York and Boston: Little, Brown, 2007). It is more likely that the imperial presidency never went away after either 1941 or 1950, but had gone through relative ups and downs. See also Frederick A. O. Schwarz, Jr. and Aziz Z. Huq, *Unchecked and Unbalanced: Presidential Power in a Time of Terror* (New York: The New Press, 2007).

prisoners, although he used euphemisms for the process (it was a "no brainer" to be supportive of a "dunk in the water"). Earlier Cheney had said to the press that in responding to 9/11, the United States would need to act "on the dark side" and "with every means at its disposal."[62]

The more flexible Reagan, who (unlike Cheney) came around to seeing Gorbachev as a reliable partner for peace and progressive change, had been urged to change a variety of policies by a variety of persons ranging from Secretary of State George Shultz to Nevada Senator Paul Laxalt, *inter alia*. Bush II, on the other hand, was not known to have encouraged open policy debates or a serious review of past decisions.[63] More than one observer found him to be secretive, content early on to lean on Cheney, comfortable with the likes of legal advisors in the White House like Alberto Gonzales and Harriet Miers (and Rice) who were loyal and did not much challenge. If those who dissent are marginalized and/or undercut, like Powell and General Shinsheki (the latter had recommended more troops for Iraq than especially Wolfowitz was prepared to discuss, and wound up with a career detour), this naturally has a dampening effect on efforts to give the President a wide range of honest opinion.

Relevant is the decision making that led to the invasion of Iraq, for it too showed a rush to judgment and lack of long-term perspective. Immediately after 9/11 both Rumsfeld and Wolfowitz raised the issue of seizing the moment to effectuate regime change in Iraq, regardless of the lack of evidence of Saddam's complicity in the Al-Qaeda attacks. (In fact, Cheney, Rumsfeld, and Wolfowitz had been focused on Iraq from the first days of the Bush II Administration even before 9/11.) Bush ordered contingency planning for the invasion by November 2001. Only belatedly was a National Intelligence Estimate (NIE) produced to justify the invasion, which came after Bush had already decided to invade based on his intuitive judgment as supported by virtually all of his top appointees.[64] Apparently both French and British intelligence

[62] For an overview see especially Mayer, *The Dark Side*.

[63] This is mainly why the conservative Cannons, champions of Reagan, are highly critical of Bush.

[64] On the lack of an NSC review regarding the invasion of Iraq, and other NSC weaknesses in Bush's first term, see Haass, *War of Necessity*; Risen, *State of War*; Daalder and Destler, *In the Shadow of the Oval Office*; and Gordon and Trainor, *Cobra II*. Also James Bamford, *A Pretext For War: 9/11, Iraq, and the Abuse of America's Intelligence Agencies* (New York: Anchor, 2005).

reports, based on contacts with high Iraqi officials, informed the Bush White House that Saddam had no WMD, but Bush dismissed them and proceeded with the 2003 invasion.[65]

Daniel Benjamin of the Center for International and Strategic Studies has accurately analyzed the consequences, even had the follow-on occupation been competently managed, which it was not. "The invasion played into the radical Islamists' view of the United States – namely, a country out to steal Islamic lands and oil wealth, destroy Islam, prop up Israel, and support Arab secular autocrats. Not surprisingly, the invasion was thus a magnet for Islamic fighters to concentrate on the occupying forces, given that they were more accessible than the distant US homeland. Foreign fighters spearheaded the violent resistance to the Coalition Forces in Iraq, creating prolonged violence and increased numbers of prisoners – and more abuse of those detainees. None of this was contemplated, or even apparently recognized after the fact, by the Bush Administration."[66] In reality, long-range planning and prudent calculation was not the hallmark of the Bush–Cheney team. One sees it in the invasion of Iraq, but the same qualities were at play in detainee affairs.

The Secretary of Defense and the head of the CIA

Halper and Clarke consider Rumsfeld, like Cheney, to be an offensive or aggressive realist, but sharing a number of values with the neo-cons.[67] Weisberg says that Rumsfeld flew with the neo-con flock but was not one of them.[68] A biography also asserts Rumsfeld was not a neo-con.[69] This is hair-splitting *par excellence*. Now it may be true that self-styled realists focus on power and someone's view of national interest, whereas the so-called neo-cons want to infuse power and interest considerations with a Manichean morality. Most neo-cons, more than realists, display profound affection for Israel. Some realists find the US attachment to Israel to be a distraction from the real national interest,[70] whereas most neo-cons, many of whom are Jewish, are very

[65] Suskind, *The Way of the World*.

[66] Daniel Benjamin, "Notes on the Future of Terrorism," www.ifi.org/files/politique_etrangere/Benjamin.

[67] Halper and Clarke, *America Alone*. [68] Weisberg, *The Bush Tragedy*.

[69] Bradley Graham, *By His Own Rules: The Ambitions, Successes, and Ultimate Failure of Donald Rumsfeld* (New York: Public Affairs, 2009).

[70] Famously, John Mearsheimer and Steven Walt, in *The Israeli Lobby and US Foreign Policy* (New York: Farrar, Straus, Giroux, 2007).

strong supporters of Israel – not just of Israel but of right-wing governments there.[71] Be that as it may, both realists and neo-cons mostly denigrate international law, international organizations like the United Nations and even sometimes the North Atlantic Treaty Organization (NATO), and especially human rights treaties. Trying to differentiate realists from neo-cons can turn into an academic exercise that obscures their common beliefs in an unrestrained United States that is engaged in global war with a dangerous Islamofascism. To be fair, as Feith notes, a number of supposedly liberal Democrats bought into Bush's radical paradigm about invading Iraq, traumatized as they were by 9/11, sympathetic as they were to Israel – and misled as they were by a number of Bush–Cheney statements. One sees this in Democratic votes to invade Iraq even absent a clear and present danger from Saddam, and in their lack of opposition to abusive interrogation when briefed about it (although debate continues as to the specifics of CIA briefings to MCs).

Focusing on elusive theoretical differences can also obscure a hallmark of the Bush Administration, including Rumsfeld as Secretary of Defense. That characteristic is arrogance combined with ignorance.[72] Neither Bush, nor Cheney (and Addington), nor Rumsfeld were open to much dissent. Rumsfeld in particular was reminiscent of Robert McNamara when Defense Secretary under Presidents Kennedy and Johnson. Both Secretaries wanted to make major changes in Pentagon culture and policies, and both were intolerant of other points of view. Cheney and Rumsfeld in particular simply cut out of the policy making process those who had a different view. This was a major reason for the débâcle of Iraq under occupation and during transition. Neither Rumsfeld nor Jerry Bremer, in direct charge of the US occupation, turned out to understand much about Iraqi society but both thought

[71] Feith in his memoirs downplays his well-known sentiment for, and connections with, the Israeli right. Compare especially Heilbrunn, *They Knew They Were Right*. Also Mayer, *The Dark Side*. Michael Isikoff and David Corn, in *Hubris: The Inside Story of Spin, Scandal, and the Selling of the Iraq War* (New York: Crown, 2006), p. 77, note that Richard Perle and Douglas Feith, *inter alia*, did consulting for some right-wing, expansive Israeli circles in the 1990s. They recommended regime change in Iraq at that time.

[72] See further especially Andrew J. Bacevich, *The Limits of Power: The End of American Exceptionalism* (New York: Holt, 2008). Also Stanley Hoffmann, "The High and the Mighty: Bush's National Security Strategy and the New American Hubris," *American Prospect*, 13, 24 (January 13, 2003), p. 24.

they did, and proceeded to issue various disastrous edicts. Most Iraqi experts, the State Department, the Army War College which had extensive studies on military occupation, and many relevant others were simply cut out of the policy process. The Coalition Provisional Authority in Iraq was often staffed with the Republican Party faithful rather than with Iraqi or development experts. Experts on democracy promotion like Larry Diamond of the generally conservative Hoover Institution at Stanford were asked to serve as consultants and then ignored.[73] The war in Afghanistan was also mismanaged over time, despite the early successes.[74]

On the arrogance and incompetence of the Bush Administration, with Rumsfeld at the center, see the damning critique by the centrist Leslie Gelb in the establishment journal, *Foreign Affairs*.[75] In 2008 a federal government review of waste and incompetence in Iraq circulated, once again detailing the expensive missteps of the DOD and its subcontractors during the occupation and insurgency.[76] A biography of Rumsfeld confirms his arrogant, abrasive, and domineering personality (but without explaining how he got that way).[77]

Two key advisors to Rumsfeld were Paul Wolfowitz and Douglas Feith. They were widely seen as convinced neo-cons, or democratic imperialists if one prefers, long in favor of regime change in Iraq even before 9/11, long critical of the way IHL had developed, long sympathetic to conservative Israeli circles, for whom they had worked as consultants during the Clinton years, long champions of an expansive United States when in the Reagan Administration. Feith in particular had some impact on prisoner policies, as noted in Chapter 3. Under the façade of great attachment to the Geneva Conventions, as we shall see,

[73] Larry Diamond, *Squandered Victory* (New York: Time Books, 2005).

[74] For a short overview see David Rohde and David E. Sanger, "How the 'Good War' in Afghanistan Went Bad," *New York Times*, August 12, 2007, www.nytimes.com/2007/08/12/world/asia/12afghan.html.

[75] Leslie H. Gelb, "Necessity, Choice, and Common Sense," *Foreign Affairs*, 88, 3 (May–June 2009), esp. p. 65. For a highly academic study making the same point about poor decision making and bad management, see David Mitchell and Tansa George Massoud, "Anatomy of Failure: Bush's Decision Making Process and the Iraq War," *Foreign Policy Analysis*, 5, 3 (July 2009), pp. 265–286.

[76] James Glanz and T. Christian Miller, "Official History Spotlights Iraq Rebuilding Blunders," *New York Times*, December 14, 2008, www.nytimes.com/2008/12/14/world/middleeast/14reconstruct.html.

[77] Graham, *By His Own Rules*.

he worked to undercut their application to prisoners held in Afghanistan and Guantánamo. He brushed aside issues of command responsibility for what happened at Abu Ghraib, including the role of his boss, Rumsfeld.[78]

A third key advisor to Rumsfeld on prisoner affairs was William Haynes, the Pentagon's top civilian lawyer. As we shall see, he worked closely with Addington to often exclude critical military lawyers from key decisions about prisoner treatment, anticipating their interest in military honor and the Geneva Conventions. He was a central part of the Bush Administration efforts to keep many key decisions from being vetted in the normal review process, and to keep most uniformed lawyers in the Office of the Judge Advocate General (JAG) and State Department lawyers from playing influential roles on prisoner affairs. Haynes, Wolfowitz, and Feith (and Cambone) could not have done what they did had Rumsfeld been truly interested in international human rights and humanitarian law – just as Addington could not have been so influential without the backing of Cheney. Some say Rumsfeld was uninterested in prisoner affairs early on,[79] but he took key decisions that resulted in much abuse, and he was deeply implicated in torture at Guantánamo, as well as the Abu Ghraib prison scandal and its attempted cover up after the fact, as will be shown later.

Interestingly, no one much debates whether George Tenet, head of the CIA from 1997 to 2006, was a realist or a neo-con. Perhaps that is because of the assumption the head of the CIA was supposed to be a pragmatic technician and not a policy maker (although that was an entirely incorrect assumption about William Casey when he headed the CIA under Reagan). The general debate here is more about politics and psychology than about general orientation to foreign affairs. The central question is whether Tenet could speak truth to power, or whether he so much liked to be liked, and wanted to be part of the inner circle of the Bush Administration, that he allowed Bush, Cheney,

[78] See Feith's memoirs. Compare the discussion of Abu Ghraib in Chapter 4.

[79] Richard B. Myers, with Malcolm McConnell, *Eyes on the Horizon: Serving on the Front Lines of National Security* (New York: Threshold, for Simon & Schuster, 2009). Myers was head of the JCS from 2002 to 2005. Despite his endorsement of abusive interrogation by the military, or maybe because of it, President Bush awarded him the Distinguished Service Medal. For Myers as a compliant follower, see Bacevich, *The Limits of Power*.

and Rumsfeld to cherry pick from intelligence reports, saying things in public that discounted the questions and caveats found in the raw intelligence memos.

We know that the CIA caved in on whether Bush should say in his 2003 State of the Union speech that Saddam was seeking uranium for nuclear weapons in Niger, which was a highly questionable statement, but which the CIA allowed to be mentioned as attributed to foreign intelligence. (Rice and the National Security Council [NSC] also have responsibility here.) We know that Tenet sat behind Colin Power when he made his famous, or infamous, speech at the United Nations in 2003 attributing all sorts of aggressive intentions, and dangerous weapons including mobile biological labs, to Saddam. Many of Powell's statements turned out to be false, but there was Tenet, lending the CIA's authority to Powell's misstatements.

The central debate about Tenet is actually over whether he was just incompetent in not obtaining accurate intelligence and in feeding erroneous reports on up the line, or whether he knowingly allowed those reports to be politicized.[80] Cheney visited CIA headquarters numerous times, no doubt pushing the Agency to give the reports he wanted. Neither alternative is very encouraging regarding Tenet's legacy – incompetence or politicization. After Tenet resigned to spend more time with his family in 2006 (!), Bush awarded him the Medal of Freedom Award, the highest governmental honor for civilians. (Tenet received the award along with Tommy Franks and Jerry Bremer. It is hard to think of any three persons at the second tier of the US government who did more damage to US foreign and security policy than these three, since Franks, when in charge of the invasion of Iraq, had no specific plans for the follow-on occupation of Iraq, and Bremer mismanaged the plans that later were put into place.)

There is no doubt but that Tenet was in favor of abusive interrogation, arguing that it provided actionable intelligence.[81] We do not know if he willingly endorsed that policy at the outset, or whether he had to be pushed into it. We know that some CIA agents were hesitant to get into the business of abusive interrogation, fearing the

[80] For a critical view of Tenet and the CIA see Bamford, *A Pretext for War*. Bamford is an expert on the intelligence community.

[81] George Tenet, *At the Center of the Storm: My Years at the CIA* (New York: HarperCollins, 2007).

legal consequences. To these agents in 2002, it looked illegal. We do not know if Tenet initially questioned the wisdom of the CIA's secret prisons, or what position he took, if any, on the matter of what would be done with prisoners after they had been waterboarded or otherwise tortured. We do not know what calculation he might have made about whether abusive interrogation, on balance, did or did not contribute to US security when the negatives were factored into the equation, because he showed no awareness of those negatives in his public comments.

Michael Hayden took over for Tenet at the CIA. He testified to Congress that the CIA had waterboarded three prisoners during 2002 and 2003. As will be shown, there are other ways to torture prisoners than by waterboarding. Neither Hayden nor Ashcroft's replacement as Attorney General, after Gonzales, Michael Mukasey, were clear in their public statements about what constituted torture, whether they approved or disapproved of the practice, and whether those who commissioned torture should be or would be prosecuted.

Conclusion

Bush, Cheney, and Tenet have all stated publicly that "enhanced interrogation techniques" have produced valuable actionable intelligence that has saved lives. In their view they adopted a modified "lesser evil approach," with effective controls to keep prisoner abuse within reasonable limits.

Just as US leaders do not call torture by its name, so as to avoid unpleasant realities, so many persons talk about a war of choice rather than a war of aggression. We dull our senses by such circumlocutions. Also, sometimes those who seek to manipulate language to mask reality wind up manipulating themselves: they come to believe in their own distortions. This process is well captured by the analysis of Adam Hochschild, who noted how the use of phrases like "enhanced interrogation techniques" and "aggressive interrogation" sought to cover up the reality of torture and other proscribed action.[82] US high officials, seeking to avoid the reality of what they had authorized and supervised, might have come to believe their own propaganda – in this case that severely abusing supposed "HVDs" was somehow not illegal

[82] "What's in a Word? Torture," *New York Times*, June 21, 2004, Op-Ed, p. 11.

torture.[83] According to a CIA spokesperson, "The agency's terrorist detention program has used lawful means of interrogation, reviewed and approved by the Department of Justice and briefed to the Congress."[84] According to President Bush at the very end of his presidency, "I firmly reject the word 'torture.' Everything this administration does had a legal basis to it; otherwise, we would not have done it."[85] In reality, various officials, ranging from the Vice President's Office down to CIA agents "in the field," had worried about the legal implications and personal responsibility of their actions.[86]

If we assume for now that abusive interrogation and especially waterboarding did produce actionable intelligence of some value on some occasions, with effective controls for any misinformation that came out of the process, one still needs to ask whether there were more negatives than positives. Did that abusive process, which included torture (waterboarding is a mock execution through near asphyxiation, which clearly is psychological torture) make the United States more hated and despised around the world?[87] Did it produce more commitment by

[83] According to one well-informed and privileged study, Lyndon Johnson lost touch with reality about Vietnam in the latter stages of his presidency; his optimistic statements, driven by intense desires and fear of failure and rejection, ran counter to developments in that Asian country. See Doris Kearns Goodwin, *Lyndon Johnson and the American Dream* (New York: St. Martin's Press, 1976, 1991). On Presidents believing what they need to believe, see Bacevich, *The Limits of Power*, p. 42.

[84] Jane Perlez, Raymond Bonner, and Salman Masood, "An Ex-Detainee of the US Describes a 6-Year Ordeal," *New York Times*, January 6, 2009, www.nytimes.com/2009/01/06/world/asia/06iqbal.html.

[85] Patrick O'Connor, "Bush Defends Interrogation Record," pertaining to a TV program on Fox News, as reported via Yahoo.News, January 11, 2009, http://news.yahoo.com/s/politico/20090111/pl_politico/17320.

[86] Scott Shane and David Johnston, "US Lawyers Agreed on Legality of Brutal Tactic," *New York Times*, June 7, 2009, www.nytimes.com/2009/06/07/us/politics/07lawyers.html. Also David Johnston and Scott Shane, "Interrogation Memos: Inquiry Suggests No Charges," *New York Times*, May 6, 2009, www.nytimes.com/2009/05/06/us/politics/06inquire.html. The CIA created a legal defense fund for the two consultants who helped devise and implement the Agency's abusive interrogations in the secret prisons, thus acknowledging legal controversies surrounding the policies adopted. Adam Goldman and Matt Apuzzo, AP, "CIA Gave Freelance Waterboarders $5 million Legal Shield," December 17, 2010.

[87] On waterboarding as torture, see especially Gary Solis (of the US Military Academy at West Point), *The Law of Armed Conflict: International*

persons to join terrorist organizations and try to damage the United States? Did it undermine other US policies like democracy promotion and advancing human rights and the rule of law? Did it undermine American confidence and consensus and self-esteem at home? Was it part of widespread abuse of prisoners that spun out of control and led to much unnecessary damage to innocent persons? Was it part of growing secrecy in the Executive Branch that is dangerous to constitutional government? Was it truly necessary to avoid major destruction when it was employed? Was Senator John Rockefeller IV (D, WV) correct when he said that abusive interrogation "has produced valuable intelligence, but the question is at what cost?"[88]

At what price should US national security be pursued, and what is the conception of that security? And, as Chapter 3 explores, what is the role of law and lawyers in the process?

Humanitarian Law in War (Cambridge: Cambridge University Press, 2010), p. 441 and *passim.*

88 Scott Shane, "On Torture, 2 Messages and a High Political Cost," *International Herald Tribune*, October 29, 2007, www.iht.com/bin/printfriendly.php?id=8107346.

3 *Bush lawyers: the politics of legal interpretation*

Before you can torture anyone, you must first torture the law.

(Richard Cohen, *Washington Post*, April 28, 2009)

Not since the Nazi era have so many lawyers been so clearly involved in international crimes concerning the treatment and interrogation of persons detained in war.

(Jordan J. Paust, Capt., US Army (ret.), *Columbia Journal of Transnational Law*, 2005)

The United States professes to be a nation committed to democracy and the rule of law, under which liberal or humane values are supposed to loom large. After all, the Nazis had laws, too, so rule of law *per se* is not the issue. For liberal democracies the point is to use law to formalize and lock-in a commitment to liberal values such as human rights and human dignity. The real test comes in hard cases where it is not easy and self-evident to apply a law of liberal values. Many of these hard cases arise when democratic governments think they face genuine national emergencies that threaten the life of the nation. Most of the principal officials in the Bush Administration thought that 9/11 presented such a hard case. Colin Powell did not (at least after he left office), believing that Osama bin Laden and Al-Qaeda did not present an existential threat to the United States, and believing that Washington should respond to terrorism like Spain and some of its other European partners – with better intelligence and policing, but not a "global war" and foreign invasion and abuse of enemy prisoners.[1]

As is now evident the President, under the early influence of particularly Cheney, wanted to have a free hand to deal with terrorism and

[1] Karen De Young, *Soldier: The Life of Colin Powell* (New York: Vintage, for Random House, 2006, 2007), pp. 518–519.

related prisoner questions. This meant, among other measures, producing unilateral and strained interpretations of relevant international law like the 1949 Geneva Conventions, customary IHL, and the 1984 UN Convention against Torture. And it meant trying to circumvent restraining influences from Congress and the Courts – restraints crucial to constitutional (limited) government. Officials associated with Cheney and Rumsfeld used 9/11 to implement desires that predated the Al-Qaeda attacks. Cheney and Secretary of Defense Donald Rumsfeld, along with key assistants like Paul Wolfowitz and Douglas Feith, all members of the imperialistic Project for a New American Century, had long wanted the chance to try to remake the world without much restraining effects from international law and foreign opinion.[2] The result of such motivations was a disturbing belief that they could not respond to twenty-first-century terrorism without behaving similar to their twentieth-century enemies, especially the Chinese communists in the Korean War, when it came to treatment of enemy prisoners.

Clear law and supporting regulations are especially important for large bureaucracies like the US military that function according to rules. Remove the legal framework and the derivative regulations, or confuse them, and bureaucracies can become dysfunctional. It was to prove important that the Bush Administration rejected traditional views of much law normally relevant to enemy prisoners in war, but many in the US military were not clear about what legal rules were controlling and when they applied. Moreover, if some abuse is said to be all right in a shifting and unclear process, others down the line evidently thought that more abuse is even better.

The result of this combination of persons and preferences was that the Bush Administration wound up with policies that at worst played fast and loose with the evident meaning of much international and domestic

[2] As noted in Chapter 2, the view that the United States alone should dominate the world, and remain dominant, has a discernible history culminating as of the late 1990s in the political campaign called the Project for a New American Century, stimulated by a feeling that the Clinton Administration was not tough enough. It is a view that is often linked to Israel, and the benefits to Israel that would flow from such a situation – including the removal of Saddam Hussein in Iraq. On the "neo-cons" and, for many of them, their Israel-centered anti-terrorism, replacing their Israel-centered anti-communism, see especially Jacob Heilbrunn, *They Knew They Were Right: The Rise of the Neo-Cons* (New York: Anchor, 2009).

law, and at best ignored the humane policy direction that the law suggested. Bush wound up endorsing widespread extraordinary rendition (kidnapping and transfer to foreign countries for abusive interrogation), forced disappearances (secret detention by the United States and others), torture and inhuman treatment of various detainees in various places, controversial procedures for the trial of those said to be "unlawful enemy combatants," and attempts to shield high American officials who had been involved in gross violations of human rights, or war crimes under humanitarian law, from prosecution and other forms of accountability. The Bush team, by so doing, sent the message to others like China and Pakistan, Syria and Uzbekistan, Egypt and Syria, *inter alia*, that it was alright to crack down, to repress, to torture. During 2010 a UN study by independent experts concluded that under the influence of the US "war on terror," secret detention has expanded in the world.[3]

The resulting situation raised the question of whether the United States during the Bush Administration was similar in certain respects to "national security states" as in Argentina and Chile and certain other South American countries in the 1970s and 1980s – countries in which law ceased to be a liberal and independent force and became nothing more than a unilaterally devised means to enhance unlimited and brutal Executive power in the quest for complete national security.[4] If President Bush could constitutionally order serious abuse to protect national security as he saw it, as John Yoo of the Bush DOJ opined, why not the dictator Pinochet in Chile? The latter saw himself as a Christian bulwark who was saving Chile in the face of godless Communist subversives. The whole point of the Nuremberg (and Tokyo) trials after the Second World War was to establish the supremacy of the humane values found in international law over national decisions to abuse, to torment. The Bush approach to the detention and interrogation of

[3] UN News Service, "UN Experts Point to Widespread Use of Secret Detention Linked to Counter-terrorism," January 26, 2010, www.un.org/apps/news/printnews.asp?nid=33586. UN Doc. A/HRC/13/42, 26 January 2010, advance edn., "Joint Study on Global Practices in Relation to Secret Detention in the Context of Counter-terrorism."

[4] See further Rebecca Evans, "South American Southern Cone: National Security State, 1970s and 1980s," in David P. Forsythe, ed., *Encyclopedia of Human Rights* (New York: Oxford University Press, 2009). The South American national security states used traditional physical torture and killed many opponents, whereas the Bush interrogation policies were intended to be different.

enemy prisoners, whether similar to past national security states or not, started with efforts to circumvent the traditional understanding of the international legal framework governing the treatment of prisoners in conflicts.

Early indications, Fall 2001 to Spring 2002

Much has been made of statements to the press by Cheney that after 9/11 the United States would have to operate on "the dark side" and use "any means" in responding to terrorism.[5] Slightly later Cofer Black, a counter-terrorism expert in the CIA said the "gloves were coming off."[6] This phrase was repeated in certain military messages pertaining to Iraq in 2003.[7] Immediately after the attacks of 9/11 there was great fear of other attacks, particularly fear of other sleeper cells within the United States. An anthrax scare followed the mass murder of 9/11 that saw airplanes turned into hi-tech battering rams. Cheney took the lead in advocating not only abuse of prisoners but also preventative strikes to remove governments like Saddam Hussein's in Iraq that might create problems in the future.[8] Later, as already noted, he openly endorsed waterboarding even if he used a euphemism – namely, that to subject terrorists to a "dunk in the water" was a "no brainer."[9] But it took some time and considerable effort for this view to prevail within the Bush Administration and also for it to be translated into specific policies.

In the meantime large bureaucracies such as the US military establishment acted as they have always acted. Certain military officials assumed that the laws of war, primarily as found in the 1949 Geneva Conventions, would be applicable in Afghanistan and at Guantánamo

5 See especially Jane Mayer, *The Dark Side: The Inside Story of How the War on Terror Turned Into a War on American Ideals* (New York: Doubleday, 2008).

6 Hearing, US House and Senate Intelligence Committees, 107th Congress (2002), p. 6.

7 "Senate Armed Services Committee Inquiry into the Treatment of Detainees in US Custody," available on the internet, p. xxiv.

8 See especially Ron Suskind, *The One Percent Doctrine: Deep Inside America's Pursuit of its Enemies Since 9/11* (New York: Simon & Schuster, 2006). If there was a 1 per cent chance Saddam might cause the United States trouble, he should be taken down.

9 Dan Eggen, "Cheney's Remarks Fuel Torture Debate," *Washington Post*, October 27, 2006, p. A 9, www.washingtonpost.com/wp-dyn/content/article/2006/10/26/AR2006102601521.

once it was evident there was an international armed conflict between the United States and Afghanistan from October 2001. Thus the ICRC, widely seen as the guardian of IHL and the humanitarian organization that does more prison visits around the world than anyone else, especially in war, was given permission by various officials in the DOD (explained in Chapter 4) to operate both in Afghanistan and at the Guantánamo detention facility.[10]

Given that the United States used regular military force openly (as well as various actions covertly) in Afghanistan from October 2001 to oust the Taliban government and to try to destroy Al-Qaeda, the two being intertwined, it was difficult for the Bush Administration to completely ignore the laws of war designed historically to regulate international armed conflict among states. Moreover, the UN Convention against Torture applies in peace and war, with no exceptions for any kind of national emergencies. Still further, the 1966 International Covenant on Civil and Political Rights (ICCPR) does not permit derogation from its ban on torture and mistreatment even in times of national emergency that "threaten the life of the nation." Since the United States had entered a reservation to this latter treaty at the time of ratification, indicating that no individual rights of action existed under this treaty for would-be plaintiffs in US courts, the Bush Administration consistently ignored this Covenant since it feared no restraining action under its terms from those courts.

Four decisions early on

Given the existence of particular international and national laws, after 9/11 the Bush Administration addressed a number of legal issues. For present purposes we highlight four of them. In retrospect, there is no doubt that the various legal interpretations, and the process in which they were developed, were part of a policy perspective intended to facilitate abusive interrogation. It was not as if the key policy makers asked about the meaning of the law. Rather, they sought only those interpretations that advanced their predetermined policy objectives.

10 See further the ICRC web site, ICRC.org, esp. Yves Sandoz, "The International Committee of the Red Cross: Guardian of International Humanitarian Law," written in 1998. Also David P. Forsythe, *The Humanitarians: The International Committee of the Red Cross* (Cambridge: Cambridge University Press, 2005).

Key lawyers, mainly in the DOJ's Office of Legal Counsel, responded over several years, from 2001 to at least 2005, by rationalizing "a predetermined and illegal result."[11]

Torture

First, since the United States was a party to the UN Convention against Torture, the key Bush legal papers said that torture only occurred when there was an intent to cause severe mental and physical pain (not when it occurred as a by-product of seeking information), when that pain left lasting damage, and when that pain was associated with damage that approached the level of organ failure.[12]

The first part of this legal position was perhaps consistent with the US War Crimes Act (WCA), as affected by US legislation to implement the UN Convention against Torture, even if the latter was not consistent with relevant treaty language. That is to say first of all that the US WCA, presumably intended to implement the 1949 Geneva Conventions and other relevant parts of the laws of war, as of 2001 clearly prohibited (a) torture, (b) cruel, inhuman, or degrading (CID) treatment, and (c) humiliating treatment.[13] Under this domestic legislation, torture was defined by cross-reference to the statute implementing the Torture Convention.

In that second domestic statute[14] it was said, either by poor drafting or by clever intent, that: "'torture' means an act committed by a person acting under the color of law specifically intended to inflict severe physical or mental pain or suffering (other than pain or suffering incidental to lawful sanctions) upon another person within his custody or physical control." So under this US law, to be guilty of torture, the dominant view during the Bush years was that one has to have the specific intent to cause severe pain. This is not what the Torture Convention states. There it is written that the infliction of severe pain for any reason whatsoever is prohibited, regardless of intent. The Bush lawyers seized on this discrepancy to argue that if a US official had

11 David Cole, "The Torture Memos: The Case Against the Lawyers," *New York Review of Books*, 56, 15 (October 8, 2009), www.nybooks.com/articles/23114?utm.

12 See Karen J. Greenberg and Joshua L. Dratel, eds., *The Torture Papers: The Road to Abu Ghraib* (Cambridge: Cambridge University Press, 2005) for a compilation of relevant documents.

13 US Code, Title 18, section 2441.

14 US Code, Title 18, section 2340.

the intent to extract actionable intelligence, but severe pain occurred as a by-product, the interrogator or superiors could not be held liable for torture. This is a good example of the legalistic arguments employed by Bush lawyers to get around the prohibition of torture in international law.

Particularly the last part of this first Bush Administration interpretation was so extreme, and so at variance with the plain sense meaning and legislative history of the Torture Convention, that it was withdrawn by later Bush officials in the DOJ. But as drafted by John Yoo in the Office of Legal Counsel, and approved by Jay Bybee, head of that office, it was exactly the interpretation that Cheney, Rumsfeld, and Tenet, and their lawyers, wanted. It sought to enable the abusive interrogation that had long been evolving through CIA and DOD channels, abuse that mostly avoided some measures like electric shocks and pulling out fingernails but still could cause severe mental and physical pain. These officials and their lawyers did not want a good-faith interpretation of the Torture Convention and derivative US law, because they carefully tried to freeze out of the policy making process those that could be expected to object to the emerging interpretation. They wanted a politicized interpretation – one that would free them to pursue the policy of abusing prisoners. The Administration was to say repeatedly that it did not torture, but this was only plausible if one accepted its greatly constricted definition of torture.

Related to torture was the notion of CID: behavior that was cruel, inhuman, or degrading. The Universal Declaration of Human Rights (UNDHR, a resolution adopted by the UN General Assembly in 1948), the ICCPR, and certain other international legal instruments prohibited both torture and CID equally.[15] The Torture Convention, however, while mentioning CID, dealt only with torture in the body of the document. This left room for US officials to argue that the ban on CID was not absolute, was subject to being balanced against the needs of national security, did not apply to US interrogators and jailers abroad, and only referred to the extreme measures just fractionally short of torture – behavior that in terms of US constitutional law would shock

[15] Nigel S. Rodley, "Torture: International Law," in David P. Forsythe, ed., *The Encyclopedia of Human Rights* (New York: Oxford University Press, 2009), vol. 5, pp. 65–74.

the conscience of a reasonable person.[16] If that were not sufficient, Bush lawyers argued that what the CIA was authorized to do, such as body slamming and waterboarding, *inter alia* and in combination, did not constitute even CID.[17]

"Geneva" and fighters

Secondly, the Bush Administration, having said that the President could suspend "Geneva" in Afghanistan (and thus was above the law) but would not, then said that the 1949 Geneva Conventions did indeed apply there from the Fall of 2001. But this statement was made meaningless as far as prisoners were concerned. In early 2002 President Bush said that the Taliban as an armed force would not be recognized as POWs when captured and would not be provided with the legal protections laid out in 1949 Geneva Convention III (the POW Convention). The Administration noted that Geneva Convention III required POWs to have fought under organized command, wearing identifiable insignia as combatants, carrying arms openly, and implementing the laws of war. The Administration's position hence emphasized the 1949 language negotiated after the Second World War, and ignored relevant practice since that time.

The issue here was whether unprivileged combatants, meaning those who took up arms but without qualifying for POW status, should be seen as having no protections under the Geneva Conventions, or protected by Geneva Convention IV for civilians rather than Geneva Convention III for traditional warriors. The Bush Administration adopted the former view (unlawful enemy combatants had no IHL protections), whereas eventually the Obama Administration followed the

[16] See further John T. Parry, *Understanding Torture: Law, Violence, and Political Identity* (Ann Arbor: University of Michigan Press, 2010). Also Peter Jan Honigsbert, *Our Nation Unhinged: The Human Consequences of the War on Terror* (Berkeley: University of California Press, 2009), p. 24. On states formally accepting the notion of universal human rights, but then making self-serving arguments about jurisdiction and other legal concepts to undermine the protection of human rights see Mark Gibney, *International Human Rights Law: Returning to Universal Principles* (New York: Rowman & Littlefield, 2008).

[17] See further Cole, "The Torture Memos." A good overview of Bush legal memos dealing with torture, CID, and humiliation can be found in Scott Shane and David Johnson, with James Risen, "Secret U.S. Endorsement of Severe Interrogations," *New York Times*, October 4, 2007, www.nytimes.com/2007/10/04/washington/04interrogate.html.

traditional understanding and adopted the second view (unprivileged combatants were civilians who had taken up arms and were thus covered by other parts of IHL rather than Geneva Convention III).

In this controversy the Bush position ignored some French and American experience in past wars, as noted in Chapter 1. It can be briefly recalled that in the Algerian and Vietnam Wars both states had officially given POW treatment, more or less, to organized fighters on the opposite side. That is, both Paris from 1961 and Washington from 1966 had considered Algerian nationalist fighters and VC fighters, when captured, to be entitled to the usual treatment accorded POWs – principally no torture or mistreatment, and in general a humane detention for the duration of the armed conflict. At least that was the general policy position of the two democratic states, whatever the record of implementation in the field. The origin of the US policy mandating humane detention for VC fighters in the Vietnam War centered on the quest for reciprocity and better treatment for captured Americans.[18]

Largely because of the need to regulate irregular, guerrilla, asymmetrical warfare as in Algeria from 1954, and elsewhere, 1977 Additional Protocol I (API) to the Geneva Conventions specified that for those captured in international armed conflict with open arms, or arms visible prior to attack, they were entitled to humanitarian protections as combatants when captured even if not wearing military uniforms.[19] As long as they were identifiable as fighters, and were not those posing as civilians and, for example, throwing a grenade into a market place, they should, when detained, be treated as other fighters *hors de combat* (out of the fight).[20] The US delegation to the 1974–1977 Geneva

[18] See the appropriate references in Chapter 1. We noted there some ambiguity in the historical record as to whether captured irregular enemy fighters were to be treated as POWs, or perhaps treated in conformity with the more general Geneva Convention Common Article 3.

[19] API, Art. 75. See further Adam Roberts, "Keeping the Unlawful Combatants Out of Legal Limbo," *Washington Post Outlook*, February 3, 2002.

[20] See especially Hans-Peter Gasser, "An Appeal for Ratification by the United States," in "Agora: The US Decision Not to Ratify Protocol I to the Geneva Conventions on the Protection of War Victims," *American Journal of International Law*, 81, 4 (October 1987), pp. 912–925. Gasser was an ICRC legal official. His clear exposition has been subsequently distorted by various American ultra-nationalists – not only repeatedly by Douglas Feith but also by Jack Goldsmith and John Yoo.

Diplomatic Conference on Humanitarian Law, led by a tough State Department lawyer, George Aldrich, supported this formulation – having helped to negotiate it. It codified US practice, or some US practice, in the Vietnam War. In the US delegation under Aldrich was the head of Army JAG (Judge Advocate General Corps, the military lawyers), George Prugh, and the head of Air Force JAG, Walter Reed. Also in the US delegation was Professor Richard Baxter of Harvard University, an eminent academic authority on the laws of war and at one time editor-in-chief of the *American Journal of International Law*. They all supported API, in an effort to expand humanitarian protections and reciprocity.

By the time API came up for discussion about ratification in Washington, Ronald Reagan had replaced Jimmy Carter, and Douglas Feith was in charge of the Administration's review of the new Protocol. Feith was highly sympathetic to Israel and closely aligned with right-wing circles in that state, which strongly opposed API since it was seen by Israel as giving enhanced status to certain Palestinian militants and others engaged in violence against the Jewish state.[21] Feith distorted API, as he continued to do in his later memoirs, saying that it gave protection to terrorists. In precise fact, it did not. It distinguished fighters who carried arms openly prior to attack, or were taken with open arms during attack, from terrorists who posed as civilians while executing covert violence.[22] Admittedly, in "the real world" it can be difficult to always distinguish the guerrilla or irregular fighter from terrorists, especially since states, who negotiate and accept treaties, have never defined "terrorism" to the satisfaction of all. But that is the distinction API tried to make. Feith prevailed both with the US military and with the Reagan Administration, with President Reagan finally declaring that he could not support API given the lack of endorsement from the military. (There were other reasons for the US opposition to API that need not concern us here.) The United States has never ratified API – or APII for that matter, which expands humanitarian rules for internal war beyond Geneva Convention Common

[21] Mayer describes Feith as a "passionate Zionist"; Mayer, *The Dark Side*, p. 122.

[22] The key 1967 US military directive for the treatment of enemy prisoners in Vietnam, cited in Chapter 1, which fed into API, clearly and consistently distinguished irregular fighters, entitled to POW treatment if not also status, from spies, saboteurs, and terrorists.

Article 3. It is now widely accepted that certain parts of these legal instruments have passed into customary international law since 1977.[23]

Feith, having played the role of spearheading the opposition to API in the Reagan era, found himself as Under Secretary of Defense for Policy in the George W. Bush Administration, having been selected by Rumsfeld.[24] He sought to block any meaningful application of Geneva Convention III in Afghanistan, in effect arguing that no consideration should be given to past detention practice and API, even as non-binding guidelines to policy, and that to recognize the Taliban fighters as entitled to a humanitarian quarantine would be to protect terrorists, because some Al-Qaeda elements were intertwined with the Taliban forces. In his memoirs Feith takes the position that only by sticking to the letter of 1949 law can one reward regular fighters with POW protection, and thus try to entice irregular fighters into open combat with uniforms, etc.[25] But the problem with that view, as the United States discovered in Vietnam, was that irregular fighters will not in fact be so enticed, because it would put them at a military disadvantage. And in the meantime they are killing your own captured troops.

So in Vietnam the United States had taken the decision to seek reciprocity from the VC by officially treating them when captured as POWs, or at least as protected by Common Article 3 (as explained in Chapter 1) in the hopes of securing better treatment for American soldiers captured

[23] For the argument that the United States accepts much of API as customary international law, including the sections on combatant protections, see Michael J. Matheson, "The US Position on the Relation of Customary International Law to the 1977 Protocols Additional to the 1949 Geneva Conventions," *American University Journal of International Law and Politics* (1986), pp. 419–431. Matheson was in the Legal Office of the US Department of State. Also William Howard Taft, IV, "The Law of Armed Conflict: Some Salient Features," *Yale Journal of International Law*, 28, 2 (Summer, 2003), pp. 319–325. Taft was State Department Legal Advisor under Colin Powell. See also Jordan J. Paust, "Post 9/11 Overreaction," *Notre Dame Law Review*, 79, 4 (2004), pp. 1335–1364. See US Army, *TJAG Handbook* (2002), where it is stated that API, Art. 75 is either CIL or acceptable practice.

[24] See Douglas J. Feith, *War and Decision: Inside the Pentagon at the Dawn of the War on Terrorism* (New York: Harper, 2008).

[25] This view is supported by certain legal scholars such as Michael Reisman, "Holding the Center of the Law of Armed Conflict," *American Journal of International Law*, 100, 4 (October 2006), pp. 852–860. The fact remains that in Vietnam this view did not operate to protect US POWs, which is why the US military took a different approach.

by them. This practical consideration, expanding humanitarian protection to all captured fighters on the basis of self-interest, namely hoped-for reciprocity, was simply ignored by Feith and those who followed his lead. Among those were the JCS after 9/11, who in effect repudiated, at least until 2005–2006, what the military thought wise in Vietnam. One of the more disappointing aspects of events after 9/11 was the failure of the JCS to insist on humane interrogation and treatment of detained enemy fighters at Guantánamo and other military installations.[26]

Aldrich, who certainly knew something about the Vietnam War having been a legal advisor to Henry Kissinger during the prolonged Paris peace negotiations, and also knowledgeable about API, as head of the US negotiating team, argued that the Taliban fighters should have been recognized as entitled to a status similar to POWs since they were the *de facto* army of Afghanistan. Aldrich believed past practice and API should serve as guides to policy, not the precise wording of the 1949 Geneva Convention III.[27] In his view, civilians who take up arms were protected by Geneva Convention IV and its Common Article 3.

The ICRC, and the American Bar Association (ABA) for that matter, argued that if the Taliban were not seen as POWs when captured, then they had to be seen as protected persons under 1949 Geneva

[26] Richard Myers, Chairman of the JCS from 2002 until 2005, has written his memoirs. In his view he was a champion of "Geneva." In reality, he was not. See Myers, with Malcolm McConnell, *Eyes on the Horizon: Serving on the Front Lines of National Security* (New York: Threshold, for Simon & Schuster, 2009). He approved the supposedly limited abuse in military facilities, and in fact it was during his tenure as Chairman, in the Summer of 2002, that a JCS study called for tougher interrogation at Guantánamo. He tried to suppress the Abu Ghraib photos of abuse in early 2004. When in response to those photos Rumsfeld commissioned an inquiry by Gen.Taguba, leading to a report in March, Myers admitted in May he had not even read the report. *Newsweek*, May 24, 2005, www.msnbc.msn.com/id/4989422. He was widely known to defer to Rumsfeld and Haynes on detainee affairs. See Graham, *By His Own Rules: The Ambitions, Successes, and Ultimate Failure of Donald Rumsfeld* (New York: Public Affairs, 2009); and Tim Golden, "After Terror, A Secret Rewriting of Military Law," *New York Times*, October 24, 2004, www.nytimes.com/2004/10/24/international/world. Also De Young, *Soldier*, p. 416. Also Andrew J. Bacevich, *The Limits of Power: The End of American Exceptionalism* (New York: Henry Holt, 2008, 2009), p. 97.

[27] George Aldrich, "The Taliban, Al Qaeda and the Determination of Illegal Combatants," *American Journal of International Law*, 96, 4 (October 2002), pp. 891–898. Also Aldrich, book review, *American Journal of International Law*, 100, 2 (April 2006), pp. 495–499, esp. p. 497.

Convention IV, the convention for civilians in international armed conflict and resulting occupation. In the ICRC and ABA view, once there is international armed conflict all individuals captured by a fighting party are either lawful fighters covered by Geneva Convention III or civilians covered by Geneva Convention IV – if in the latter case they are of the nationality of the fighting party. Thus, for US personnel in civilian agencies fighting in Afghanistan (such as paramilitaries for the CIA), they would be protected persons under Geneva Convention IV when captured (unless considered as spies). For the ICRC, there are no other options. Civilians who take up arms may be fairly considered as unprivileged combatants, but they still retain the protections of Geneva Convention IV.[28] The Bush Administration's argument that the Taliban represented a mostly unrecognized government and a largely failed state makes no difference, because Geneva Convention III explicitly states (Article 4(3)) that non-recognition of a government cannot be a basis for denying POW status to members of its armed forces. Reference to "failed states" is political or academic or journalist jargon rather than part of legal discussion.[29]

Nevertheless, the Feith view prevailed in the Washington of Bush II, dovetailing as it did with the arguments of John Yoo and others, and the President declared that no Taliban fighters would be considered protected by what came to be called "Geneva," a synonym for IHL. According to Philippe Sands, a persistent critic of the Bush Administration, Feith was very proud of his role in sinking any practical application of Geneva in Afghanistan, even though those four Conventions were said to be formally applicable. According to Sands, Feith was very proud of his getting the US military, and especially General Myers, to endorse Geneva in the abstract while not understanding that its practical effects for prisoners were gutted. Thus the Bush Administration, with JCS support, saw both Taliban and Al-Qaeda personnel as "unlawful enemy combatants." In this view, they were protected by neither Geneva Convention III nor Geneva Convention IV.[30]

[28] ICRC web site, "ICRC Reactions to the Schlesinger Panel Report, August 9, 2004."

[29] In his memoirs Yoo asserts that John Ashcroft was the origin of arguments about failed states and Afghanistan. If true, this shows that the US Attorney General did not understand the Geneva Conventions.

[30] Philippe Sands, *Torture Team: Rumsfeld's Memo and the Betrayal of American Values* (New York: Palgrave, 2008). The Bush position has interesting ramifications. Israeli armed settlers would seem to have no protection under IHL

"Geneva" and terrorists

Thirdly, the Bush Administration declared that even though it was engaged in a Global War on Terror (GWOT), principally against Al-Qaeda but not limited to them, "Geneva" (meaning IHL) was "quaint" and did not apply. Al-Qaeda was a non-state party and thus not entitled to sign and ratify humanitarian treaties. It attacked civilians and thus did not observe the laws of war. And it was a global phenomenon, not limited to Afghanistan. Thus Al-Qaeda operatives when captured (and presumably those from other transnational terrorist networks) did not even benefit from Geneva Convention Common Article 3, the article common to all four of the 1949 Geneva Conventions and intended to regulate internal war involving non-state parties in addition to the government. Common Article 3, among other norms, prohibits torture, and inhuman and degrading treatment, for all detainees in non-international armed conflict. So the President invoked the broad prerogatives of Commander in Chief in war, while seeking to avoid the usual legal limits on that role, at least regarding the Taliban and Al-Qaeda.

It is reasonable to say that in the Fall and Winter of 2001 Afghanistan was characterized by an international armed conflict between the United States and Afghanistan, and also an internal war between the Taliban government and its armed and organized domestic opponents led by the Northern Alliance. Whether there is agreement with this view or not, civilians taking up arms in *international* war are widely seen as still falling under the provisions of Geneva Convention IV. This was the US view in Vietnam (and also, in fact, in Iraq from Spring 2003). They may be interrogated, prosecuted, convicted, and given the death penalty (depending on national law), but they are not to be tortured or treated cruelly when detained. If civilians directly participate in hostilities in an *internal* war, more or less the same norms pertain regarding detention and interrogation, although the wording of Common Article 3 is more general than in Geneva Conventions III and IV. (The ICRC has a legal right of visitation to all prisoners in international armed conflict, and may offer its services to the parties in internal armed conflict.) Of course, making this legal framework effective in the face of deadly

when and if captured by Palestinian or other Arab militants. They could be seen as "unlawful enemy combatants" from the Palestinian view, as armed civilians. In US military history, "unlawful combatants" were considered to be spies and saboteurs, not organized militias like the Taliban.

enemy attacks has never been easy. In addition, the UN Convention against Torture, as noted, applies in all situations, regardless of the presence of armed conflict or not, and clearly prohibits torture while mentioning CID treatment.

The Administration's public position was that while no part of IHL pertained to Al-Qaeda detainees, and also to Taliban fighters, they would be treated humanely, consistent with "the principles of Geneva," unless "military necessity" required otherwise.[31] So the Bush team borrowed the language of military necessity from the laws of war to say, in effect, that Taliban and Al-Qaeda detainees would be treated humanely unless US officials thought it necessary to treat them inhumanely. This was a rare public statement from Washington asserting that it was the policy of the United States to treat some persons inhumanely. It was a strange and troubling argument to say that IHL did not require humane treatment of all those detained, whatever their status as combatant or civilian.

As John Yoo, one of the key lawyers in these affairs, made clear in later explanations, the various legal interpretations reflected the desire to clear away the legal impediments to coercing prisoners.[32] According to more than one critical lawyer, such as retired JAG Jordan Paust, there was in the Bush Administration a criminal conspiracy to violate the law. While paying lip service to "the principles of Geneva" in a public relations campaign, Bush officials eliminated the precise rules governing detention and interrogation linked to Afghanistan and Al-Qaeda. Even the conservative Jack Goldsmith, no great friend of international law

[31] For the origins of this language, as driven by Cheney and Addington, who were worried about prosecution for war crimes, see especially Barton Gellman and Jo Becker, "Pushing the Envelope on Presidential Power," Washington Post Web Q and A, June 25, 2007, http://blog.washingtonpost.com/cheney/chapters/pushing_the_envelope_on-Presi/index.html.

[32] See especially Jordan J. Paust, *Beyond The Law: The Bush Administration's Unlawful Responses in the "War" on Terror* (Cambridge: Cambridge University Press, 2007), particularly p. 30. In his book *War by Other Means: An Insider's Account of the War on Terrorism* (New York: Atlantic Monthly Press, 2006), Yoo says first that he was just interpreting the law, but then he immediately contradicts himself by saying that a definite policy preference (for a free hand in dealing with prisoners) drove his legal interpretations. See pp. 29 and 35. According to Yoo, one did not ask what the law required, but whether invoking the Geneva Conventions would be a help or hindrance to the Bush Administration. This is a self-incriminating (if honest) narrative that supports the damning interpretation by Paust. Conspiracy to violate the law is a federal crime.

and for a brief time a key legal official on the Bush team, said that the Bush legal war council launched a blitzkrieg against laws they didn't like: "they blew through them in secret based on flimsy legal opinions that they guarded closely so no one could question the legal basis for the [coercive] operations."[33] Goldsmith may have repeated Feith's distortions of API, but during his short stay in Bush's DOJ he did try to alter some of the faulty assertions emanating from Yoo and other civilian political appointees.

"Geneva" and Guantánamo

Fourthly, after arguing that neither Taliban nor Al-Qaeda agents, when captured, fell under any part of "Geneva," the Administration designated Guantánamo (or GTMO, or Gitmo) as a holding and interrogation center for supposedly important detainees seized in Afghanistan or elsewhere. The Administration hoped that it would be a legal black hole, not subject to oversight by US courts since in the Administration's view it was technically under Cuban sovereignty. Other locales were initially considered as *the* major interrogation center in the GWOT, but GTMO was secure, distant from the media and other prying eyes, and hopefully beyond the reach of US courts. However, in a process explained in Chapter 4, the ICRC was given permission to be there from the first arrival of prisoners in January 2002, interviewing them about their conditions and treatment, and making their normally discreet reports to US officials.[34]

To the ICRC at Guantánamo, their actions were not much affected by US arguments that "Geneva" did not apply. The ICRC visited political or security detainees in situations short of war, and detainees in internal

33 Quoted in Mayer, *The Dark Side*, p. 70.

34 The ICRC believes discreet reports to detaining authorities maximizes access to prisoners and produces humanitarian improvements in conditions over time. It reserves the right to go public if: discreet efforts have been tried and found wanting, the inhumane issues constitute clear violations of international human rights and humanitarian standards about conditions, and the organization believes publicity will enhance prisoner conditions. The organization also reserves the right to go public if the detaining authority publishes selective parts of its reports. The present author has argued (*The Humanitarians*) that the ICRC is a very conservative organization, tradition-bound, affected by a commitment to discretion as found widely in Swiss culture, and willing to wait for a considerable period of time to see improvements for prisoners. It occasionally disengages from prison visits with a public statement, but believes it has a duty under "Geneva" to stay generally engaged in a situation of international armed conflict.

war, just as they visited POWs and legally protected civilian detainees in international war. The basic humanitarian point was the same across the various categories of prisoners. The central objective was to work for humane conditions devoid of torture, inhuman, or humiliating or degrading treatment. Interrogation was of course permitted, but not inhumane or degrading interrogation. So while the ICRC headquarters disagreed with US legal interpretations about IHL's applicability to Afghanistan and the GWOT, its delegates in the field went about quietly contesting the emerging US policy of harsh detention and abusive interrogation.

The policy making process early on

In taking the legal positions it did, the Bush Administration was greatly guided by Vice President Cheney and his aide David Addington, even though they had no official position in the military chain of command and were not supposed to be directly in charge of national security policy. But as events played out, Addington emerged as the chief legal thinker on the Bush team, reflecting Cheney's preferences. He worked closely with William Haynes, II, General Counsel at the Pentagon and the top civilian lawyer in the DOD. Haynes owed his position to Addington.[35] When the American John Walker Lindh was captured among the enemy forces in Afghanistan, it was Haynes who gave the green light for his abusive interrogation.[36] Alberto Gonzales, legal counsel to the President, was also involved in the inner legal circle, but more as a front man for Addington than in any other role. Gonzales was a key transmission point from the legal war council to Bush. He certainly was no intellectual match for the bright and assertive Addington. An assistant to Gonzales, Timothy Flanigan, was also part of the inner legal circle, or legal war council.

A key player in the legal war council was John Yoo, who wrote several key memos that emerged from the OLC in the DOJ. The early Yoo memos were signed by Jay Bybee, head of the OLC, and sometimes approved by John Ashcroft, Bush's first Attorney General. But it was Yoo who wrote much of them. It is the OLC that is charged with establishing the official US Executive position on legal matters, including those stemming from international law. It was the OLC that had the

[35] Mayer, *The Dark Side*, p. 63. [36] See *ibid.*, pp. 94, 97.

official last say on Executive legal concerns about the Geneva Conventions and the Torture Convention, not the Legal Office in the State Department or the OLC in the DOJ. The traditional view sometimes offered up was that the OLC was to be at least relatively independent, non-partisan, and non-political. In fact, as one holder of the office noted candidly, the head of the OLC was supposed to be an enabler for the President, helping him do what he wanted done, but not cross over the line into clear illegality.[37] Under Bush, the OLC became an advocate for Administration policy.[38]

Yoo, like Addington and Haynes, was a civilian political appointee. As events were to demonstrate, he gave key but one-sided opinions, in effect giving Addington and Cheney the legal opinions they wanted. As noted, some of the Yoo memos were eventually discredited and rescinded when made public, and/or when others took over his position. In his memoirs Yoo attributes this change to caving in to public opinion, but in fact the memos, like his memoirs, were clearly part of a political project. Some of the memos were "too much" even for the conservative Goldsmith, head of OLC in the Bush Administration for a short time. Yoo was eventually investigated by an agency of the DOJ for possible misconduct, and the resulting DOJ report of almost 300 pages, started during the Bush years, recommended that Yoo and Bybee be referred to their state bar associations for possible sanctions.[39] In the view of this extensive study, both failed to present candid, independent, and objective legal advice to their clients. Both were seen as yielding to political pressure. But this report was overruled by higher authorities in the DOJ of President Obama, on the grounds that the standard for ethics violation was not clear, especially in the context of extreme fear after 9/11.[40] The matter was then shelved by the Obama Administration and by the Congress. As critics pointed out, letting Yoo and Bybee escape sanction meant that panic in high places took precedence over accountability for

[37] Jack Goldsmith, *The Terror Presidency: Law and Judgment Inside the Bush Administration* (New York: W.W. Norton, 2007).

[38] Cole, "The Torture Memos."

[39] DOJ, Office of Professional Responsibility, "Report," July 29, 2009, http://graphics8.nytimes.com/packages/pdf/politics/20100220JUSTICE/20100220JUSTICE-OPRFinal Report.pdf.

[40] David Margolis, "Memorandum for the Attorney General," January 5, 2010, http://graphics8.nytimes/packages/pdf/politics/20100220JUSTICE/20100110JUSTICE-DAGMargolisMemo.pdf.

enabling torture and other abuse of prisoners, keeping the door open for a repeat performance in the future.[41]

In his memos on torture, Yoo never indicated that others might well view the approved interrogation techniques as illegal, opening up the prospect for US officials of prosecution in foreign and international courts, if not in the United States itself. Other memos within the Bush Administration offered cautionary tales and even referred to the contemplated interrogation techniques as "torture."[42] Yoo ignored all this. However, he was supported by most of the other top lawyers in the DOJ, even by those who believed abusive interrogation was unwise from a policy standpoint.[43] But Yoo never advised his clients, namely Bush, Cheney, Rumsfeld, and Tenet, *inter alia*, about the legal risks in the recommended course of abusive action. To some centrist lawyerly observers, he engaged in advising his clients how to violate the law, a transgression of professional ethics. In their view, he failed to speak legal truth to power.[44] But this critical view did not carry the day in Washington.

In the meantime, he remained a major architect, with Addington, of the project to dismantle any meaningful legal restraints on the Bush team from the Geneva Conventions and the Torture Convention. Once

[41] See, for example, David Luban, "David Margolis Is Wrong," *Slate*, February 22, 2010, www.slate.com/toolbar.aspx?action=print&id=2245531. Also Bruce Ackerman, "How to Keep Future John Yoos Under Control," *Washington Post*, February 23, 2010, p. A 19, www.washingtonpost.com/wp-dyn/content/article/2010/02/22/AR2010022203550.

[42] See further Peter Finn and Joby Warrick, "In 2002, Military Agency Warned Against 'Torture,'" *Washington Post*, April 25, 2009, www.washingtonpost.com/wp-dyn/content/article/2009/04/24/AR2009042403171_p.

[43] Scott Shane and David Johnston, "US Lawyers Agreed on Legality of Brutal Tactic," *New York Times*, June 7, 2009, www.nytimes.com/2009/06/07/us/politics/07lawyers.html. These lawyers, Republican political appointees, relied not on the Torture Convention but on the wording of the US implementing legislation passed in 1996, discussed above.

[44] Richard B. Bilder and Detlev F. Vagts, "Speaking Law to Power," *American Journal of International Law*, 98, 2 (2004), starting at p. 189. On the weakness, legally speaking, of the torture memos see esp. David Luban, "Liberalism, Torture, and the Ticking Bomb," in Karen Greenberg, ed., *The Torture Debate in America* (Cambridge: Cambridge University Press, 2006), pp. 35–83; Harold H. Bruff, *Bad Advice: Bush's Lawyers in the War on Terror* (Lawrence: University Press of Kansas, 2009). Also Robert K. Goldman, "Trivializing Torture: The Office of Legal Counsel's 2002 Opinion Letter and International Law Against Torture," *Human Rights Brief*, 12, 2 (Fall 2004), pp. 1–4.

the OLC speaks, others in the Executive Branch can say that they acted under authoritative guidance, making domestic prosecution for wrongful conduct very unlikely. In effect, the OLC can give a "get-out-of-jail" card to other officials.

A key maneuver in the battle of the legal memos was the ability of the legal war council to cut out of the process other officials that might have a different view. Hence both Secretary of State Colin Powell and State Department Legal Advisor William H. Taft, IV did not find out about the emerging Bush policy toward Geneva Convention III and the Taliban fighters until it was too late. By the time they objected, stressing the importance of self-interest and reciprocity in respecting the laws of war, Bush had already approved what Cheney wanted, Addington had arranged, Yoo and Haynes had facilitated, and Gonzales eventually explained, namely the dismantling of the legal barriers to abusive interrogation. Even though Bush took a decision on "Geneva" with important repercussions abroad without even consulting his Secretary of State, apparently Powell never considered resigning over the issue, since it arose early in Bush's first term, and Powell was the collegial military man who continued to support the unit even when his advice was disregarded.[45] Powell later participated in meetings where specific abusive techniques for the CIA were discussed.[46]

Being cut out of early policy decisions was also the fate for many of the uniformed military lawyers (members of the JAGs) at the Pentagon, who by tradition shared the views of Powell, who was of course a military man. Haynes kept them in the dark until it was mostly too late, involving only those other military lawyers early on who could be counted on to support the emerging policy of abuse. The same was also true in large part for National Security Council (NSC) lawyers under Rice. She herself appears to have been cut out of key meetings and decisions by Cheney in particular, despite being officially responsible for coordinating all aspects of national security policy.[47] She did discuss specific interrogation techniques, and she conveyed the authorization to

[45] De Young, *Soldier*, Epilogue. [46] Mayer, *The Dark Side*, p. 143.

[47] On the weakness of Rice as National Security Advisor see Elizabeth Bumiller, *Condoleezza Rice: An American Life, A Biography* (New York: Random House, 2007); and Ivo H. Daalder and I. M. Destler, *In the Shadow of the Oval Office: Profiles of the National Security Advisers and the Presidents They Served – from JFK to George W. Bush* (New York: Simon & Schuster, 2009), esp. Chapter 8. Stephen Hadley, Rice's number two, undercut her by secretly sending copies of

abuse CIA prisoners to that Agency.[48] After the fact, she claimed that since the techniques were based on the "Survival, Evasion, Resistance, Escape" (SERE) military training program, which had not left permanent damage to individuals, they should be seen as acceptable.[49] She also reportedly claimed that, Nixon-like during the Watergate affair, if President Bush authorized abuse, it had to be legal.[50]

Her principal legal advisor on the NSC, John B. Bellinger, III, was also cut out of many important meetings precisely because he was not sympathetic to the emerging policy of abusive interrogation. Yoo wrote that Bellinger, and legal advisor Taft at the State Department, had an "accommodating attitude" toward international law,[51] meaning – one supposes – that they took the law seriously. The 2009 DOJ ethics report on Yoo and Bybee documents that Bellinger, the NSC's top lawyer, was not informed of several key legal memos written by Yoo until they had already been issued. Cheney and Addington were not known to be fond of dissent on major issues, nor was Rumsfeld.[52] By all accounts Bush prized loyalty to him. He did not seem to value open debate and certainly not open dissent. He preferred one-on-one discussion, often with Cheney – at least in his first Administration.

Hence by the winter of 2001–2002, the rule of law pertaining to enemy prisoners linked to Afghanistan had largely been dismantled, as far as Bush policy was concerned, in a battle of memos and meetings inside the Executive Branch in Washington. Even within the Executive, legal experts who were seen as liable to dissent were often excluded. Congress was not involved. The United States has no national human

certain communications to the Office of the Vice President. Hadley had worked for Cheney earlier.

48 George Tenet, *At the Center of the Storm: My Years at the CIA* (New York: HarperCollins, 2007); Mayer; *The Dark Side*; and Jan Crawford Greenburg, Howard L. Rosenberg, and Ariane de Vogue, "Bush Aware of Advisers' Interrogation Talks," ABC News, April 11, 2008, http://abcnews.go.com/print?id=4635175.

49 Joby Warrick, "Top Officials Knew in 2002 of Harsh Interrogations," *Washington Post*, September 25, 2008, p. A 7, www.washingtonpost.com/wp-dyn/content/articles/2008/09/24/AR2008092403355.

50 Editorial, "The Torture Debate: The Missing Voices," *New York Times*, May 7, 2009, www.nytimes.com/2009/04/07/opinion/07thu1.html.

51 Yoo, *War by Other Means*, p. 32.

52 See the biography of Rumsfeld by Bradley Graham, *By His Own Rules*, p. 344 and *passim*, who portrays the Secretary of Defense as a difficult and petulant personality, someone who enjoyed debate on tactics but was not tolerant toward those who disagreed with his major objectives or who challenged his turf.

rights institute to turn to for independent and objective interpretation of human rights and humanitarian law. Some other democratic states have one but not the United States.[53] The last thing Cheney and Addington wanted was objective interpretation based on the plain meaning and negotiating history of human rights and humanitarian treaties, with follow-on national legislation such as the 1996 WCA. Customary international law never entered the picture. A long-term view of the law, its integrity, or its usefulness to the United States in the long run, did not figure at all. The overriding concern was immediate and political: to free US personnel for abusive interrogation. The rest was window dressing for public consumption, and to try to protect against any future criminal prosecution for war crimes or crimes against humanity.

While the civilian lawyers in the Office of the Vice President and the DOJ developed their strained interpretations, the Pentagon's top lawyer, William Haynes, also a civilian political appointee, was already contacting the military's Joint Program for the Recovery of Assets (JPRA), which is the agency that runs SERE. The point was to reverse engineer SERE, originally intended to counter illegal abuse by enemy authorities, in order to develop it for intelligence gathering for the United States. The trail of memos and advice was to lead from the DOD's JPRA, anxious to play a larger role in US policy making, to CIA interrogation of HVDs, as approved by the DOJ, and then back to the Pentagon in the form of interrogation at Guantánamo. The abusive techniques, authorized first for the CIA and Gitmo, were to migrate to both Afghanistan and Iraq – although abuse in Afghanistan was already under way. The Geneva Conventions and the Torture Convention were effectively bypassed, despite some lip service in Washington.[54]

Spring 2002 to December 2002

The general outline of the Bush policy on enemy prisoner affairs was developed in the Fall and Winter of 2001–2002 as per the analysis above. Its application became important during the course of 2002.

53 See Julie Mertus, *Human Rights Matters: Local Politics and National Human Rights Institutions* (Stanford: Stanford University Press, 2009).

54 For an official overview see the Levin report, or "Senate Armed Services Inquiry," compiled by that Senate committee and which commanded bipartisan support.

Focus on the CIA

By the Spring of 2002 (late March to early April), even though Guantánamo had been designated the primary holding and interrogation center for terror suspects and was by then operational, the CIA found itself in possession of several HVDs – or those presumed to have important knowledge of Al-Qaeda and/or other terrorist operations. After the decision was taken to hold in secret CIA prisons first of all Abd al-Rahim Al-Nashiri, presumably involved in the bombing of the *S. S. Cole* in Yemeni waters, and Abu Zubaydah, a supposed high-level Al-Qaeda operative, the question then arose as to which interrogation techniques should be employed, and about their legality. Strange as it may seem, this covert intelligence agency is rife with lawyers. Not so strangely, some of the CIA persons directly involved were concerned that some of the techniques being discussed seemed to them quite possibly in violation of the law.[55] Some objected, but the coercive program went forward. With prescience, various circles in the Agency insisted on clear authorization from the highest levels of the US government. CIA Director Tenet said the authorization came from above him, namely from "the administration," the DOJ, and the NSC.[56] "The administration" included President Bush, who in his memoirs published in 2010 acknowledged that he authorized the abusive interrogation implemented by the CIA. Logically, this admission opened the door wider to his prosecution in foreign or international courts, however unlikely that was politically.[57]

From early 2002 until August of that year there then followed a continuation of the battle of legal memos over what constituted torture and what might be permitted in the form of lesser forms of coercive interrogation by the CIA. CIA officials were in touch with SERE officials. Finally in August, Bybee as head of the OLC produced a list of approved interrogation techniques,[58] after much discussion by high Bush officials including Rice, Rumsfeld, Powell, and Ashcroft.

[55] See Mayer, *The Dark Side*, pp. 162–163. Also Shane and Johnston, "US Lawyers Agreed." Recall from Chapter 2, n. 86, that the CIA set up a legal defense fund to cover some of those who planned and applied the abusive interrogation methods, such was the controversial if not clearly illegal nature of those methods.

[56] Tenet, *At the Center of the Storm*, pp. 241–242.

[57] George W. Bush, *Decision Points* (New York: Crown, 2010).

[58] "Memorandum for John Rizzo, Acting General Counsel of the Central Intelligence Agency, August 1, 2002," posted on the web site of the ACLU.

President Bush was aware of these discussions.[59] Backed by this memo, which was released by the Obama Administration in the Spring of 2009, the CIA began – or perhaps continued – various forms of coercive interrogation, including waterboarding (mock execution by simulated drowning) of at least three prisoners. There is some evidence that the abuse started before the August memo, and that sometimes DOJ officials like Yoo gave verbal advice to the CIA before August 1. Other techniques included removal of clothing for prolonged periods, incarceration in a coffin-like box, prolonged solitary confinement, subjection to extremes of heat and cold, disorientation through manipulation of time and space, slamming prisoners into walls, and other measures, sometimes used in combination. When fourteen HVDs held by the CIA were transferred to Guantánamo in 2006 and interviewed separately by the ICRC, that organization concluded, and so advised the United States in a discreet process, that what had happened to some of these detainees clearly constituted torture or CID.[60]

The FBI had withdrawn from the CIA interrogation of Zubaydah in opposition to the nature of his treatment. It also refused to participate in the "enhanced interrogation techniques" implemented by the military at Guantánamo and other military facilities. A 2008 review of these matters by the Inspector General for the DOJ, covering the period 2001–2004, concluded that only in a few instances did FBI agents participate in the abuse of prisoners, Bureau policy being otherwise. The Bureau was slow, however, in notifying agents of their responsibilities in this regard, and it was not effective in contesting "CIA and Pentagon" abuse.[61]

[59] Editorial, "The Torture Sessions," *New York Times*, April 20, 2008, www.nytimes.com/2008/04/20/opinion/20sun1.html.

[60] The ICRC report, at first summarized to certain reporters by one or more dissidents in Washington, was eventually given – presumably by one of them – to the journalist Mark Danner. Danner quoted extensively from the report, whereas earlier press accounts had given only a second-hand summary. See Danner, "The Red Cross Report: What it Means," *New York Review of Books*, 56, 7 (April 30, 2009). The ICRC report was eventually posted on the web site of the *New York Review of Books*. It can also be found on the web site of the National Security Archives and other places.

[61] Statement of Glenn A. Fine, before the House Committee on Foreign Affairs, Subcommittee on International Organizations, June 4, 2008, www.justice.gov/org/testimony/t0806/final.pdf. He summarizes a report of some 400 pages: "A Review of the FBI's Involvement in and Observations of Detainee Interrogations in Guantánamo, Afghanistan, and Iraq," May 2008, on line at the National Security Archive.

Focus on the military

In the meantime, abusive interrogation migrated to Guantánamo as run by the Pentagon. From the beginning of the Bush Administration, there had reportedly been much tension and turf wars between the CIA and DOD, between Tenet and Rumsfeld.[62] As the CIA reportedly began to get useful intelligence out of its Black Sites, Rumsfeld became dissatisfied with the lack of intelligence gleaned from Gitmo. The DOD seemed to be falling behind the CIA in intelligence gathering.[63] The CIA also was disappointed at the lack of information obtained from Gitmo prisoners, sent its own representative to the US prison on the island of Cuba, and reported that many of the detainees there were either not connected to terrorism or not high enough in any chain of command to have important information.[64] This early evaluation was confirmed by later reports.

Nevertheless, SERE authorities briefed and trained not only CIA but also military intelligence personnel. Particularly after the Bybee legal memo of August 1, 2002, SERE interactions with military personnel responsible for Gitmo increased.[65] Pushed by Rumsfeld, the JCS approved the policy position of toughening the interrogation regime at Gitmo.[66]

Two further decisions are noteworthy. First was the dispatch of several officers, and eventually Maj. Gen. Geoffrey Miller (in November 2002), as new commanders at Guantánamo with instructions to intensify the harsh detention regime there.[67] This is covered in more detail in Chapter 4.

The second decision was an extraordinarily secret effort by Addington and Haynes to bring the military mostly on line with the

[62] According to Graham, *By His Own Rules*, Rumsfeld had a low opinion of CIA intelligence and did not want the CIA encroaching on DOD prerogatives. See also Mayer, *The Dark Side*. Rumsfeld and Tenet did cooperate, however, on a number of issues.

[63] Tenet strongly defended the usefulness of abusive interrogation. Mayer concludes that Rumsfeld authorized the abuse of al-Qahtani in part because he was losing some of the bureaucratic turf wars to Tenet and the CIA.

[64] Mayer, *The Dark Side*. [65] "Senate Armed Services Committee Inquiry."

[66] Jameel Jaffer and Amrit Singh, *The Administration of Torture: A Documentary Record from Washington to Abu Ghraib and Beyond* (New York: Columbia University Press, 2007), p. 5.

[67] See Karen Greenberg, *The Least Worst Place: Guantánamo's First 100 Days* (New York: Oxford University Press, 2009).

harsh interrogation policy already instituted by the CIA, but to make it look as if the tough policy arose from lower military levels. The politically appointed civilian lawyers still drove policy, but they sought to pin the onus on the uniformed military as far as Gitmo was concerned.

In September 2002 Addington, Haynes, Alberto Gonzales from the White House, and John Rizzo the CIA lawyer, plus others including lawyers from the OLC, made a secret trip to Guantánamo. This was soon after Bybee's "torture memo" of 1 August, and just after SERE training of military interrogators. At Gitmo a group of high Bush officials arranged for a request for tougher interrogation guidelines to be sent up the military chain of command by the Gitmo commanding officer at that time, General Michael Dunlavey, as counseled by his legal advisor, Diane Beaver.[68] A Senate report called the Beaver legal memo "profoundly in error and legally insufficient."[69] The techniques in the memo drew objections not only from the FBI but also from the Pentagon's Criminal Investigative Task Force.[70] Beaver later indicated in Senate testimony that she never expected the views of a Lt. Col., namely herself, to become the final word on the subject of Gitmo interrogation, and she apologized for any errors she may have made in her analysis. She suggested that others above her hid behind her report in order to avoid responsibility.[71] This remarkable Administration effort to shift responsibility from civilian political appointees to the uniformed military shows that Addington *et al.* knew very well the controversial nature of their enterprise. They sought to cover their tracks, as they pushed the military to emulate the harsh abuse being implemented by the CIA.

As this Beaver–Dunlavey request circulated through various levels of the extensive military hierarchy, several line officers, like Gen. James Hill, head of SouthCom, with jurisdiction over Gitmo, questioned the appropriateness and/or legality of parts of the drafts, but early on none were willing to flatly object to the content, perhaps fearing falling out of favor with higher echelons. Or, they wanted to protect themselves by making sure higher officials in Washington were the ones to explicitly establish the interrogation rules. No one in the operational military chain

[68] The Beaver memo can be viewed at www.defenselink.mil/news/Jun 2004/d20040622doc3.pdf. The memo is also reproduced in Greenberg and Dratel, *The Torture Papers*.

[69] "Senate Armed Services Committee Inquiry," p. xxvii.

[70] *Ibid.*

[71] Her statement to the Senate Armed Services Committee can be found at www.fas.org/irp.congress/2008_hrs/160708beaver.pdf.

of command for Gitmo wanted to jeopardize his or her career by taking a firm stand in favor of traditional military law and military honor.

The draft, however, produced considerable criticism from various Pentagon legal officials in Washington. Legal officials in all four services raised serious questions about the memo. In response, Capt. Jane Dalton, senior legal advisor to Richard Myers, JCS Chair, started the kind of comprehensive legal review of interrogation techniques that Beaver and Hill had hoped for. But Gen. Myers ordered Capt. Dalton to stop the legal review, as requested by Pentagon General Counsel Haynes.[72] The Senate Armed Services Committee in 2009 called this abortive legal review process in the Pentagon a grave error of judgment by both Haynes and Myers.[73] In December 2002, Rumsfeld then signed off on a series of interrogation techniques for the military, with the first category being the mildest, the second category more intense, and the third category the most severe and only to be employed after specific approval by the Secretary of Defense.[74] The concrete trigger for these events was the treatment of Mohammed al-Qahtani at Gitmo, a presumed intended hijacker in the 9/11 events (details of his interrogation are covered in Chapter 4).

Push back and confusion on the military side

It was at this point that former Admiral Alberto J. Mora (ret.), then a civilian advisor on legal affairs to the Navy, found out about the process of rule making. In a crucial showdown with Haynes, he did take a

[72] "Senate Armed Services Committee Inquiry." This Committee report had bipartisan support, being unanimously adopted with the endorsement of the likes of Senators John McCain, Joe Lieberman, and Lindsey Graham. As already noted, in his memoirs *Eyes on the Horizon*, Myers presents himself as a great defender of "Geneva," but he does not comment on the Walker study at all. In general, the statements in this memoir confirm the view of Myers by Sands, *Torture Team*, namely that when it came to "Geneva" and treatment of prisoners, the JCS Chair was not very astute about what happened. Myers' memoir also fails to deal candidly with command responsibility for what happened at Abu Ghraib.

[73] "Senate Armed Services Committee Inquiry."

[74] For a review of the process whereby Rumsfeld issued three categories of abusive interrogation, then pulled back two of them under pressure from Mora, then created the Walker group which issued still more approved techniques, see James P. Pfiffner, *Torture as Public Policy: Restoring U.S. Credibility on the World Stage* (Boulder and London: Paradigm, 2010), Chapter 2.

principled stand and threatened to object in a written memo, thus producing a paper trail about events.[75] At that point Haynes interceded with Rumsfeld, and the most severe interrogation techniques were rescinded. Thus began some of the confusion about what was and was not permitted to military interrogators. Rumsfeld's original list of harsh techniques had meanwhile been circulated to Afghanistan.[76]

As the Pentagon backed off from some of the more intense abuse of al-Qahtani at Gitmo, Rumsfeld ordered Haynes to convene a Working Group of selected military lawyers to review interrogation techniques. State Department lawyers were excluded. In the first half of 2003 this Working Group, advised by John Yoo, somehow managed to conclude that certain abusive interrogation techniques were legal, overriding the objections of a number of JAG lawyers.[77] The Yoo key memo was extreme, arguing that those in the Executive branch had unlimited powers to do whatever was necessary to protect the country.[78] This Working Group under the tactical leadership of Mary Walker thus continued the effort to authorize coercive interrogation by the military.[79] The Yoo–Haynes–Walker approach mirrored the Yoo–Bybee memo of August 1, 2002 in that both documents authorized a combination of abusive measures that would shock much of the country when publicized later, but contended implausibly that US policy fell short of torture or inhuman treatment. The Walker report gave some legal cover to Rumsfeld and others in the DOD, although many independent lawyers questioned the group's conclusions.[80] The Senate Armed

75 Mora compiled a detailed report on his efforts, which can be found at http://en.wikisource.org/wiki/Statement_of_Alberto_J_Mora_on_interrogation_abuse,_Jul.

76 Senate report, *op.cit.* 77 Jaffer and Singh, *The Administration of Torture*, p. 16

78 Dan Eggen and Josh White, "Memo: Laws Didn't Apply to Interrogators," *Washington Post*, April 2, 2008, p. A 1. Also David Johnston and Scott Shane, "Memo Sheds New Light on Torture Issue," *New York Times*, April 3, 2008, p. A 15. The ABA criticized Yoo's position as inconsistent with "time-honored" interpretations of law. See Greenberg and Dratel, *The Torture Papers*.

79 A centrist view was that Walker was very "political" and followed the lead of Yoo and others. See *The American Lawyer*, August 6, 2004, www.americanlawer.com. Earlier, Walker had sought to absolve various Air Force officers of sexual and religious misconduct at the Air Force Academy. See www.sourcewatch.org/index.php?title=Mary_Walker.

80 Possibly one version of the Walker report was given to inquiring members of Congress while another, more harsh version was given to General Miller at Gitmo. Mayer, *The Dark Side*, pp. 234–235. See also Jaffer and Singh, *The Administration of Torture*, p. 15.

Services Committee was highly critical of this report that enabled continued mistreatment in military facilities.[81] Once again the Pentagon leadership reaffirmed a policy of abuse toward prisoners, including for detainees at Gitmo. All of this occurred despite the clearly stated concerns by many JAG officials, military criminal investigation officials, and the FBI – not to mention also by independent lawyers and human rights groups.

Looking ahead

By the Summer of 2005 certain elements within the Administration tried to return to the more traditional military policy of humane interrogation and detention. This effort was led by Deputy Defense Secretary Gordon R. England and the Deputy Assistant Secretary of Defense for Detainee Affairs Matthew Waxman, along with Philip Zelikow and John Bellinger who were close to Secretary Rice at the State Department. But once again core reform efforts were opposed by Cheney and Rumsfeld and their assistants.[82] In the wake of the Abu Ghraib controversy, the DOD did set up an office of detainee affairs. Some saw this as leading to more systematic attention to those issues, while others thought it was a bureaucratic maneuver to control ICRC reports, reduce further leaks of embarrassing material, and minimize the impact of humanitarian concern. Clearly positive was a reduction in the number of "ghost prisoners" in military facilities, and in general the treatment of detainees held by the military became more humane over time.[83]

Still, it was in 2005 that Steven Bradbury in the OLC in the DOJ produced a secret memo arguing that not only had the CIA not engaged in torture, but its "enhanced interrogation techniques" did not constitute even CID conduct. One also needs to keep in mind that in Bush-sponsored congressional legislation during 2005 and 2006 (the

[81] "Senate Armed Services Committee Inquiry," p. xxviii.

[82] See the testimony by Philip Zelikow before the Senate Judiciary Committee on May 13, 2009 at http://judiciary.senate.gov/pdf/09-05=13ZelikowTestimony.pdg. See further Gellman and Becker, "Pushing the Envelope." See also Graham, *By His Own Rules*, pp. 540–544. Also Tim Golden, "Detainee Memo Created Divide in White House," *New York Times*, October 1, 2005, www.nytimes.com/2006/10/01/washingtton/01detain.html.

[83] See Graham, *By His Own Rules*, p. 544 and *passim*.

Detainee Treatment Act [DTA], and the Military Commissions Act [MCA]), the Republican-controlled Congress removed humiliating treatment as a war crime in US law, while prohibiting the prosecution of any US official who conducted interrogations but could show that his actions were believed to be legal. So even as the Bush team reduced the practice of mistreatment of presumed enemy prisoners in US places of detention, it continued to rely on DOJ lawyers to block any US prosecutions for past action. The implicit logic of the various memos and legislative maneuvers was to say that past US behavior toward enemy prisoners was only humiliating, not torture or CID, and humiliation of prisoners was no longer a war crime with individual responsibility.[84] Of course these maneuvers by the Bush team did not bind foreign or international courts.

Congressional deference until 2005

After 9/11 the Congress, unfortunately learning nothing from its Gulf of Tonkin resolution in 1964 that effectively gave Lyndon Johnson a much-regretted blank check for waging war in Vietnam, hastily passed a vague and open ended authorization to use force in the GWOT. The Administration claimed, and US courts eventually accepted, that under this resolution (which passed without committee hearings or protracted debate) the Executive alone could set much – but not all – detention and interrogation policy.

During Bush's first six years the Republicans controlled both houses of Congress. For most of the first four of those years the majority was not much interested in enemy prisoner affairs, sharing not just the President's political party but also his view that one needed to take exceptional measures to avoid further attacks on the United States.[85] It can be recalled that some two-thirds of Congress voted for the invasion of Iraq even though Saddam Hussein presented no clear and present danger to the United States. With regard to both treatment of enemy prisoners and preventive war, many Democrats supported the Administration, reflecting a national climate of fear if not paranoia.

84 A good review remains Shane and Johnston, "US Lawyers Agreed."
85 The congressional and national mood was well captured by Joseph Lelyveld, "Interrogating Ourselves," *New York Times Magazine*, June 12, 2005, starting at p. 36.

During this time, congressional oversight of Bush's foreign policies was moribund.[86]

It appears to be the case that a number of Democrats in Congress were briefed by the CIA in executive session on detention and interrogation matters. It does not seem to be the case that any objected to what they heard. The CIA claimed that it was very explicit to MCs in briefings about the treatment afforded HVDs held in secret locations abroad. Some Democrats, however, most prominently Speaker of the House Nancy Pelosi, challenged some of the CIA claims about candid briefings.

As the Administration's policies proved inconclusive in Afghanistan and encountered major difficulties in Iraq, and when photos of gross abuse of prisoners at Abu Ghraib prison in Iraq surfaced in the Spring of 2004 to compound various earlier reports of mistreatment, public and congressional opinion begin to shift. The President's popularity began to wane. When Democrats won control of both houses of Congress in the congressional elections of 2006, the shift became pronounced. Democratic control meant more hearings held and more critical reports issued regarding the Bush era. Congressional oversight resumed.

In fact, significant congressional developments had started before 2006. After the Abu Ghraib photos were circulated in early 2004 detailing shocking behavior by US personnel in Iraq, several Republican Senators took the lead in a push back against Bush detention and interrogation policies. This gave the Democrats political cover to join in the criticism of the Administration's record. Led by Senators John McCain, John Warner, and Lindsey Graham, all Republicans and all with strong links to the military, the Congress passed the DTA in Summer 2005. Despite the Administration's strenuous objections, led by a very determined Vice President Cheney, this legislation required the military, and also the CIA when operating in military facilities, to abide by the interrogation techniques listed in the US Army field manual, which prohibited most of the abusive methods in use from 2001–2002. The bills had been adopted by overwhelming majorities in each house, which thus took a presidential veto out of play. Bush signed the legislation. He did, however, append a "signing statement" indicating he might bypass the statute in certain unspecified situations, consistent

[86] Norman J. Ornstein and Thomas E. Mann, "When Congress Checks Out," *Foreign Affairs*, 85, 6 (November–December 2008), pp. 67–82.

with the so-called "unitary theory" of executive power already noted.[87] The bill was not entirely progressive, as it did not pertain to the CIA outside of military facilities, and it also provided legal immunity to any US actor who could show a reasonable belief that his or her action toward prisoners was legal at the time.[88]

With considerable reason it can be said that until the 2005 DTA the US abuse of enemy prisoners after 9/11 was not just a Bush policy but a national policy, since in reality both the President and the Congress, both Republicans and Democrats, supported it – or at least did not actively oppose it. Zelikow, the moderate Republican, made this point when testifying in 2009. Bush and most of the Republicans may have done so more willingly than most of the Democrats. The latter, particularly in the Fall of 2004 prior to elections, may have feared the electoral results of appearing to be soft on national security issues. Certainly the Republicans, led by their chief strategist Karl Rove, tried to paint them in those colors as he constructed a campaign based on fear of further attacks from ruthless enemies. This strategy worked in the sense of producing the re-election of Bush II, and in the sense of delaying a growing sense of congressional unease over prisoner policy.

It was also the case that the public either knew or could have known about abuse of prisoners from 2003. There were extensive and accurate reports by the media and non-governmental organizations (NGOs) from that time.[89] Yet there was no groundswell of public criticism until after the Abu Ghraib photos, which helps to explain the Democrats' reticence on the issue. To some observers, the entire nation was responsible for approving torture.[90]

It proved significant, however, that in a context of no further successful attacks on the homeland, those with a belief in American military honor such as McCain, Warner, and Graham could energize identity politics in a way that led to a rejection of the Bush policies of

[87] The White House, "President's Statement on Signing of H.R. 2863," December 30, 2005, www.whitehouse.gov/news/releases/2005/12/print/20051230-8.html.

[88] See the analysis in the *Harvard Journal of International Law* at www.law.harvard.edu/students/orgs/hrj/iss19/suleman.shtml.

[89] See for example the report of Human Rights First on deaths of enemy prisoners in US detention, "Command's Responsibility: Detainee Deaths in US Custody in Iraq and Afghanistan," January 6, 2005.

[90] Jacob Weisberg, "Our Tacit Approval of Torture," *Newsweek*, May 1, 2009, on-line, and in the printed magazine May 18, 2009, www.newsweek.com/id/105622.

abuse at least by the military. With appeals to "American values" and "military honor," supplemented by arguments about legal obligations and self-interest, moderate Republicans and Democrats proved uncomfortable, by overwhelming congressional majorities, with torture and CID treatment of enemy prisoners by the military.[91] In this changed political climate, moderates in the Administration could also move against not just torture but also inhuman treatment by the CIA.[92]

This course of events played out despite the fact that at certain times in response to certain questions, sizable segments of American public opinion, usually around 40 percent, indicated support for torture in the name of national security.[93] In one poll in 2009, 50 percent of the American public supported the use of abusive interrogation even though most respondents characterized the techniques as torture. 80 percent of Republicans approved, as compared to 25 percent of Democrats.[94] Perhaps more to the point, there were powerful players in Washington who were prepared to adopt "the lesser evil" approach which accepted the necessity of torture, whatever public opinion might prefer.

Conclusion

By 2002 both the CIA and the DOD had instituted an official process of abusive interrogation on the basis of approval by the highest civilian and military officials. CIA authorization and practice were in place

91 The record of the Congress on human rights and humanitarian affairs has been highly inconsistent over several decades. It was Congress that forced the Eisenhower Administration to back away from internationally recognized human rights circa 1953, and it was Congress that forced the Nixon Administration to pay more attention to at least some of those same international human rights circa 1973. It was Congress that institutionalized McCarthyism in the 1950s, and it was Congress that sought to rein in some of the CIA's brutal operations in the 1970s. See David P. Forsythe, *Human Rights and US Foreign Policy: Congress Reconsidered* (Gainesville: University Presses of Florida, 1988).

92 Zelikow testimony, before the Senate Judiciary Committee.

93 Paul Gronke *et al.*, "US Public Opinion on Torture, 2001–2009," *PS*, 43, 3 (July 2010), pp. 437–444. See further the blog associated with the *Washington Post* under the name of Chris Cellizza, May 7, 2009. http://voices.washingtonpost.com/thefix/white-house/polling-the-torture-debate.html?wprss.

94 PIPA (Program on International Public Opinion), University of Maryland, electronic news release, June 25, 2009. See also "Tolerating Abuse," *The Economist*, July 30, 2009, for similar data, at www.economist.com/daily/chartgallery,PrinterFriendly.cfm?story_id=14120009.

halfway through the year. The DOD attempt in Spring of 2003 to refine and limit the coercion in military facilities that had been started in 2001 and 2002 did not work in an operational sense. The Pentagon Working Group report (Walker report) might have given some legal cover to high military officials, but it did not greatly restrain action in the field. Oversight to keep the abuse truly limited often failed to manifest itself, whether at Gitmo, Abu Ghraib, or Bagram – as we shall see in Chapter 4. There was some limitation on paper, but particularly in military circles there was a high-level press for more "actionable intelligence" plus lack of oversight and supervision to ensure that coercive interrogation was controlled. Moreover, CIA abuse – sometimes constituting torture and sometimes CID – seemed to work, or at least was reported to work, thus creating incentives for a competitive Rumsfeld to go down a similar path on the military side.

Addington, representing Cheney, had succeeded in dismantling the conventional understanding of the meaning of the Geneva Conventions and the UN Convention against Torture. Aided principally by Yoo representing Ashcroft, and Haynes representing Rumsfeld, the Bush Administration proceeded down the road of torture and inhuman treatment. Many other Bush officials contributed to this process, even if some tried to apply the brakes.[95] In his memoirs, Tenet explicitly endorses "enhanced interrogation techniques" as necessary for national security and challenges those opposed to find a better way to protect the United States.[96] He and Cheney both argued that valuable intelligence was obtained from the CIA Black Sites, where torture clearly occurred as directed and supervised by high officials. When questioned about the interrogation of al-Qahtani at Gitmo, Rumsfeld replied that it was controlled and professional; he did not deny that it was abusive.[97]

[95] It seems that in Rumsfeld's office, Feith, Cambone, and Wolfowitz were all directly involved in the authorization and supervision of abuse. See Jaffer and Singh, *The Administration of Torture*, pp. 18, 24. It was already noted that many high lawyers in the DOJ supported the Yoo–Bybee "torture memo of 2002," which was reaffirmed in 2004 and 2005 after Yoo had left the Department. Shane and Johnston, "US Lawyers Agreed." These memos were conveyed to the CIA.

[96] Tenet, *At the Center of the Storm*.

[97] David Johnston and Thom Shanker, "Pentagon Approved Intense Interrogation Techniques for Sept. 11 Suspect at Guantánamo," *New York Times*, May 21, 2004, p. A 10. Also Agence France-Presse, "Pentagon Gives no Excuses for Suspect Treatment: Senators Aghast," Yahoo.News, June 13, 2005.

The President would say that the United States did not torture, but it did.[98] The President would say that the general policy of the United States was humane detention, but that was largely false, too, given the pervasive application of inhuman and humiliating treatment. A key reason for extraordinary rendition and forced disappearances was abuse. A key reason for secrecy in legal argument and policy making was to avoid any review of decisions that were obviously inconsistent with accepted legal understandings. When dissent arose it was mostly ignored, especially by Haynes, who was carefully watched by Addington, and Yoo who had extreme views on the subject. Addington was openly contemptuous of competing opinion, as seen by his congressional testimony.[99] Haynes struck a similar pose of obfuscation.[100] A key reason for the selection of Guantánamo was to avoid judicial oversight.

The implementation of policy unfolded in slightly different ways in military and CIA jurisdictions. It is to those facts that we now turn.

98 See Bush's press conference of March 16, 2005, for one of many examples.
99 Democracy Now, "Addington, Yoo Offer Little in House Torture Hearing," June 27, 2008, www.democracynow.org/2008/6/27addington_yoo_offer_little_in_house.
100 See the excellent analysis by Scott Horton, "Torture from the Top Down," *Harpers*, June 18, 2008, www.harpers.org/archive/2008/06/hbc-90003099.

4 *The military: Afghanistan, Guantánamo, Iraq*

The CIA has always operated to a significant degree outside the law. The military, by contrast, is at its core an institution committed to discipline and order, strictly governed by the laws of war. So the fact that illegal abusive tactics were officially authorized at the Pentagon's highest levels is in some sense more shocking than the CIA's crimes. We should expect more of the military.

(David Cole, "What to Do About the Torturers?," *New York Review of Books*, January 15, 2009)

As long as the United States – or any state, for that matter – has the power to detain at pleasure and in secret, abuse of detainees is inevitable.

(Michael Ignatieff, in Kenneth Roth *et al.*, eds., *Torture*, New York: The New Press, 2005, p. 23)

As the previous chapters have showed, when the United States used military force in Afghanistan in the Fall of 2001 and then opened the Guantánamo prison facility in January 2002, it deconstructed the international legal framework for the protection of prisoners in war, even as it declared a Global War on Terror (GWOT). The result was extensive abuse of prisoners, much of it intended by high policy makers. Iraq was supposed to be different, since the George W. Bush Administration declared the 1949 Geneva Conventions fully applicable to a situation of armed invasion and occupation, including those provisions pertaining to prisoners. But Iraq was *not* fundamentally different in 2003–2005. More or less the same extensive and chaotic abuse transpired as had been the case in Afghanistan. Moreover, there was a concerted attempt to transfer the early "lessons of Gitmo" to Iraq, despite the fact that at Gitmo the Bush team had asserted that "Geneva" did not apply whereas in Iraq it agreed "Geneva" did apply. The embarrassment of the prison scandal at Abu Ghraib prison in Iraq was the product, in part, of the more general US deconstruction of the rules for humane treatment of prisoners. Abu Ghraib was definitely not the simple result of a few "bad apples at the bottom of the barrel."

Regardless of what the CIA and "other government agencies" were doing in secret (see Chapter 5), the US military record in Afghanistan, Guantánamo, and Iraq left a deep stain on US military honor and US respect for the laws of war. The field record also left a dark stain on the more general American claim to the moral high ground in the global effort to expand liberal democracy – which is inherently linked to human rights and a liberal rule of law. Gitmo and Abu Ghraib and other less-publicized abuse impeded the US effort to win the hearts and minds of the Arab–Islamic world and isolate the jihadists. It is far from clear that the "actionable intelligence" gained offset these negatives. Rather, it is reasonably clear that on the military side the gains in strategic intelligence were minimal despite the abuse. The driving force behind events was the civilian leadership of the military, although many in the uniformed military aided and abetted the process, even while others in uniform fought determinedly against the policy of serious abuse.

Afghanistan

No doubt in war the overriding emphasis is on winning, with sometimes scant regard given in advance to the treatment of prisoners. Certainly in the early stages of the US military campaign in Afghanistan, which started in October 2001, prisoners fared badly. In addition to air power, the US operation featured small numbers of US special military forces and CIA operatives and relied on cooperation with an Afghan Northern Alliance militia not known for its devotion to the laws of war. As was true in much warfare, prisoners immediately upon capture were sometimes roughly interrogated and then executed, while the wounded were killed lest they return to the fight.[1] Some prisoners detained by the Northern Alliance, as assisted on the scene by CIA personnel, were held in medieval conditions; some suffocated or were otherwise killed in the

[1] Sean Naylor, *Not a Good Day to Die: The Untold Story of Operation Anaconda* (New York: Penguin, 2005). For example, a captured US soldier was interrogated and then executed, while US forces blew up a concentration of wounded enemy fighters who were out of the fight.

process. The Northern Alliance intentionally killed many Taliban prisoners. Its leader, Gen. Dostum, was on the CIA payroll and later became an advisor to the President of Afghanistan, so the US government resisted efforts to investigate the deaths.[2] Prisoner riots also led to the deaths of CIA and Northern Alliance personnel.[3] In the modern history of Afghanistan the killing of detained fighters and the massacre of civilians was a common occurrence, carried out by all the competing factions.[4] Suffocation of prisoners in transport containers was a common tactic, whether by the Taliban or its opponents.

At CentCom (the US DOD Central Command had operational responsibility for Afghanistan) there was an early inclination to treat prisoners as usual, meaning according to the laws of war.[5] Commander Tommy Franks started the process of establishing "Article 5 hearings" in Afghanistan to determine who was a POW and who was not.[6] One of the early reasons for transferring prisoners to Guantánamo was apparently humane, namely to get them out of the theatre of war and give them better conditions.[7] With the capture of the American John Walker Lindh, however, who was fighting with the Taliban, Secretary of Defense Rumsfeld and his general counsel William Haynes overruled CentCom's early orientation and ordered harsh interrogation. That was in the Fall of 2001. Lindh, despite being a US citizen, or maybe because of it, was treated very harshly – tied down while stripped naked in cold weather and denied medical attention for a time. In order to try to get a reduced sentence Lindh

[2] James Risen, "US Inaction Seen After Taliban P.O.W.'s Died," *New York Times*, July 11, 2009, www.nytimes.com/2009/07/11/world/asia/11afghan.html.

[3] Richard B. Myers, with Malcolm McConnell, *Eyes on the Horizon: Serving on the Front Lines of National Security* (New York: Threshold Editions, for Simon & Schuster, 2009), p. 198.

[4] Ahmed Rashid, *Taliban: Militant Islam, Oil, and Fundamentalism in Central Asia* (New Haven: Yale University Press, 2nd edn., 2010).

[5] Philippe Sands, *Torture Team: Rumsfeld's Memo and the Betrayal of American Values* (New York: Palgrave, 2008), p. 31.

[6] Jane Mayer, *The Dark Side: The Inside Story of How the War on Terror Turned Into a War on American Ideals* (New York: Doubleday, 2008), p. 123. Geneva Convention III, Art. 5, requires such hearings in case of uncertainty about POW status in international armed conflicts.

[7] Myers, *Eyes on the Horizon*, p. 198. See also Karen Greenberg, *The Least Worst Place: Guantánamo's First 100 Days* (New York: Oxford, 2009), pp. 4–7. Some US officials understood that US detention facilities in Afghanistan were not ready for sizable numbers and that the Northern Alliance was a dangerous jailer. Other US officials were more interested in evading legal constraints and oversight, as explained in Chapter 3.

agreed in federal court not to pursue the subject of abusive treatment. (The Australian David Hicks, also fighting with the Taliban, made a similar agreement to get out of Guantánamo with a relatively light sentence to be served in his home country. He also was reportedly abused.[8])

The United States created a major military prison facility at the Bagram Air Force base, receiving prisoners from a detention site in Kandahar and other places in that country, but also including detainees from outside the country. Here prisoner abuse was pervasive in 2002–2004, particularly as directed by Capt. (later Col.) Carolyn Wood, the operations and chief interrogation officer from Summer 2003 until 2004, with at least three prisoners dying from various abusive techniques.[9] The abuse was apparently broad and sometimes mindless, in that virtually all prisoners were apparently subjected to it. Eventually several US military reports confirmed the widespread problems with the detention system, as per the various reports noted in annex B. The key assumption seemed to be that if a prisoner was not cooperative and forthcoming, it must be that he was well trained to resist and conceal; and so the pressures were ratcheted up. For unexplained reasons, the FBI might have protested abusive interrogation at Guantánamo and in the CIA Black Sites, but the FBI was apparently part of the system at Kandahar and Bagram early on, along with the CIA.[10] Interrogations might be by military or civilian personnel, with some contract workers among the latter. In addition to torture,

[8] Sands, *Torture Team*, p. 31. On the harsh treatment of Lindh, and the close involvement of the Pentagon in ordering and supervising that treatment, see Reed Brody, "The Road to Abu Ghraib: Torture and Impunity in US Detention," in Kenneth Roth *et al.*, eds., *Torture: Does It Make Us Safer? Is It Ever OK? A Human Rights Perspective* (New York: The New Press, for Human Rights Watch, 2005), pp. 147–148. Hicks was apparently sodomized with some type of object, short shackled, subjected to sensory deprivation, injected with drugs, and beaten. Raymond Bonner, "Detainee Says He was Abused While in US Custody," *New York Times*, March 20, 2007, p. A 10. See also Barton Gellman and Jo Becker, "Pushing the Envelope on Presidential Power," Washington Post blog, Web Q and A, June 25, 2007, http://blog.washingtonpost.com/cheney.chapters/pushing_the_envelope_on_presi/index.html. On the mistreatment of Lindh and Hicks, see also Andy Worthington, *The Guantánamo Files: The Stories of the 774 Detainees in America's Illegal Prison* (London: Pluto, 2007).

[9] Philip Gourevitch and Errol Morris, *Standard Operating Procedure* (New York: Penguin, 2008). Emily Bazelon, "From Bagram to Abu Ghraib," *Mother Jones*, March 1, 2005, www.motherjones.com/spring/16328. Also Worthington, *The Guantánamo Files*, especially on the key role of Carolyn Wood.

[10] See particularly Moazzam Begg, *Enemy Combatant: My Imprisonment at Guantánamo, Bagram, and Kandahar* (New York: The New Press, 2006). As

which was sometimes fatal, CID treatment was prevalent across the different types of interrogators. Among allied states, the British in particular were intimately and extensively involved in the process, as a number of detainees had British connections.[11]

Specific military orders were not issued for such techniques as severe beatings and sodomizing with hard instruments, although Wood authorized detailed abusive techniques that went far beyond previous US military practice. As noted in the Fay–Jones report commissioned by Rumsfeld after the Abu Ghraib prison scandal in Iraq, Woods authorized interrogation techniques such as use of stress positions, sleep deprivation, dogs to terrify, sensory deprivation, and more.[12] Tellingly, superior officers made it known that "actionable intelligence" should be

noted in Chapter 3, while the FBI distanced itself from much military and some CIA abuse, its review of the situation found that some FBI agents were involved in abusive interrogation during 2001–2004 in unspecified situations. See the FBI internal report at the National Security Archives on the web.

11 The head of British MI6, the equivalent of the CIA, denied UK complicity in US torture. John F. Burns, "Head of MI6 Denies Role of Agency in Torture," *New York Times*, August 11, 2009, www.nytimes.com/2009/08/11/world/europe/11britain.html. Such denials are sometimes a way of asserting that the abuse was "only" CID, not torture. This particular UK denial is contradicted by considerable circumstantial evidence and is inconsistent with other statements made by British officials. Amnesty International and the Council of Europe found extensive cooperation by European states with various prisoner policies during the Bush I Administration. Many facts remain to be established about British policy on this matter, with several British inquiries in progress at the time this book was being written. On the British playing a role in abusive interrogation after 9/11 in Central Asia and other places, see Craig Murray, *Dirty Diplomacy* (New York: Scribner, 2006, 2010). Murray was for a time British Ambassador in Uzbekistan and apparently a crusader against torture and other human rights violations. His book was also published as *Murder in Samarkand: A British Ambassador's Controversial Defiance of Tyranny in the War on Terror* (Edinburgh and London: Mainstream Publishing, 2006). In the Fall of 2010 the UK government agreed to a multi-million dollar payout to some fifteen detainees held by the United States at Guantánamo. Some of these prisoners with British connections had previously been held in Afghanistan and other places. The negotiated settlement was to avoid British litigation over charges of torture and other abuse. The government admitted no fault but claimed the settlement avoided costly trials that might result in disclosure of sensitive information. Among numerous sources on relevant events throughout 2010 see John Burns and Alan Cowell, "Britain to Compensate Former Guantánamo Detainees," *New York Times*, November 16, 2010, www.nytimes.com/2010/11/17/world/europe/17britain/html.

12 Fay–Jones Report, AR 15–6 Investigation, August 23, 2004. On file at the National Security Archives, and noted in annex B. See also Emily Bazelon, "From Bagram to Abu Ghraib," *Mother Jones*, March–April 2005, www.motherjones.

obtained, and they would not inquire closely about the techniques employed.[13] Lip service to the "principles of Geneva" was too vague to control the abuse. Some US military reports that documented homicides were either covered up or not followed up by higher authorities.[14] Thus those trying to restrain the abuse were not supported by the chain of command.

Eventually under the pressure of media and NGO reports, several dozen lower-level military personnel were later prosecuted for prisoner abuse, but never their commanding officers under the principle of command responsibility – through lack of proper training or negligence in proper oversight.[15] An Army criminal inquiry recommended that Wood be prosecuted for dereliction of duty in not providing proper oversight and control at Bagram. Instead, she was given a Bronze Star for her role, promoted, and her career advanced. She was sent to Iraq to advise on prisoner affairs there. She circulated within US military circles as an expert on prisoner matters. It was a general pattern to be repeated elsewhere. These awards showed official approval for authorization of, and supervision of, abuse.[16] Lower-ranking defendants could not document the permissive climate that permeated Bagram, even while superiors could point to some rules on paper supposedly limiting abuse.

(Some prisons or parts of prisons were run by the CIA rather than the Pentagon. Fatal abuse occurred in these locales. Certain CIA officers involved in the fatal abuse were later promoted.[17] In 2007 a federal

com/politics/2004/03/bagram-abu-ghraib. Also Gourevitch and Morris, *Standard Operating Procedure*, p. 38.

13 See "Along the Chain of Command, Confusion and Contradiction," *New York Times*, juxtaposing a series of comments by a General, a Colonel, two Captains, and a Sergeant pertaining to Afghanistan and prisoner affairs. The more one got down the chain of command, the more there was discussion of the *de facto* push for actionable intelligence, www.nytimes.com/imagepages/2005/05/20/international/20050520_ABUSE_Grap.

14 Gourevitch and Morris, *Standard Operating Procedure*.

15 See, for example, Eric Schmitt and David Rohde, "About 2 Dozen G.I.'s to Face Trial or Other Punishment in Deaths of 2 Afghan Prisoners," *New York Times*, September 2, 2004, p. A 8. Also Thom Shanker, "US Army Inquiry Implicates 28 Soldiers in Deaths of 2 Afghan Detainees," *New York Times*, October 15, 2004, p. A 12. More generally see Guenael Mettraux, *The Law of Command Responsibility* (Oxford and New York: Oxford University Press, 2009).

16 Tim Golden, "Bagram Detention Center," *New York Times*, April 2, 2009, updated when viewed April 13, 2009, http:///topics.nytimes.com/top/reference/timestopics/subjects/b/bagram_air_base_afghanistan.

17 Joseph Margulies, *Guantánamo and the Abuse of Presidential Power* (New York: Simon & Schuster, 2006), p. 136.

court sentenced a CIA contract interrogator to eight years of prison for killing a prisoner at Bagram in 2003.[18])

The ICRC did early prison visits at Kandahar and Bagram, the United States having stated that the situation constituted an international armed conflict, even as it tried to exempt Taliban and Al-Qaeda fighters from the application of Geneva Convention III (the POW Convention). But US military officials hid prisoners from the ICRC (there was a secret US prison in Kabul apart from Bagram, just as there was a secret CIA facility at Guantánamo) or otherwise tried to manipulate those visits rather than be fully transparent about prisoner interrogation and detention. A general problem for the ICRC, at Bagram as elsewhere, was that without decisive improvements in conditions, the ICRC ran the risk of being discredited in the eyes of detainees. Some prisoners at Bagram thought the ICRC was ineffective and powerless.[19] The systematic abuse continued for some time. It took the ICRC as much as six years to gain access to some other detention centers in the countryside, far from Bagram and sometimes in dangerous territory. The US military command was not always forthcoming in a timely way about where prisoners were being held and when the ICRC might visit, although Washington was not obligated to open each and every transition point for prisoners to ICRC visits.

The Bush Administration switched much attention and many resources to the question of Iraq, especially from the Summer of 2002, which reduced the attention given to Afghanistan – including for detainee affairs. A US Army report fits with various independent studies in concluding that the US military effort in Afghanistan during 2002–2005 was understaffed and underresourced – and poorly planned.[20] The British and others concluded that the Bush team basically decided

[18] *Human Rights Brief*, 14, 3 (Spring 2007), Center for Human Rights and Humanitarian Law, American University, p. 42.

[19] Margulies, *Guantánamo*. A PBS TV special "Taxi to the Dark Side," focusing on the abduction and death of Dilwar, an Afghan taxi driver, also conveyed the point of US manipulation of the ICRC and the latter's minor impact on events at Bagram, at least early on.

[20] James Dao, "Report Finds Early Missteps in Afghanistan: New Unpublished History Shows Effort Was Undermanned and Resourced," copyright *New York Times*, www.msnbc.msn.com/id/34634750/ns/world_news-the_new_york_times. The report can be found at http://documents.nytimes.com/a-different-kind-of-war, Donald P. Wright *et al.*, *A Different Kind of War: The United States Army in Operation Enduring Freedom (OEF) October 2001–September 2005* (Fort Leavenworth: Combat Studies Institute Press, for the US Army Combined Arms Center, 2009).

to invade Iraq at that time, although some evidence suggests that Bush decided to oust Saddam as early as February 2002. So the Bush Administration lost its focus on Afghanistan relatively early, not just in the run-up to the Iraqi invasion in March 2003.[21]

Because of Washington's shift to focus on Saddam, when NATO eventually became more involved in Afghanistan to help an increasingly beleaguered US force, attention to prisoners took on greater salience. Some European members of NATO, aware of the controversy about US treatment of prisoners in various locales, and also worried about turning prisoners over to Afghan forces, sought greater clarity about humane treatment of prisoners.[22] Regarding US abuse of prisoners, it seems the British remained the most systematically complicit of the Europeans in Afghanistan, posing questions and receiving answers via the American process of interrogation. In 2008, it became known that the British had seized two Pakistanis in Iraq and transferred them secretly to US authorities in Afghanistan for further interrogation, although the British had denied those facts for years. Here one finds the British turning over prisoners under their control for harsh and secret interrogation by US personnel.[23]

In Afghanistan, as was true at Guantánamo and in Iraq, US treatment of prisoners improved over time. This was probably because of a combination of media and NGO reports, changes in military leadership, pressure from some NATO allies, congressional and judicial push back, and eventually Barack Obama's victory in the 2008 presidential elections. In the meantime, and particularly in the early stages of the conflict, *de facto* US policy was one of systematic abuse, certainly constituting at times CID treatment, and sometimes rising to the level of torture – including some cases of fatal torture. At the time of writing there had been little to no accountability for any of the abuse, except for

[21] Among many sources see George Packer, *The Assassins' Gate: Americans in Iraq* (New York: Farrar, Straus & Giroux, 2005, 2006), pp. 45 and 61.

[22] Much informal military commentary in Denmark in 2008 (where the author held a research position) stressed that if Danish forces in Afghanistan killed opponents, one avoided the quandary about whether to give prisoners to the Americans or Afghans. According to informal but widespread Danish conversations in military circles, the word went out: make sure you don't let the Taliban fighter drop his weapon and surrender.

[23] Karen De Young and Del Quentin Wilber, "Britain Acknowledges 2 Detainees are in US Prison in Afghanistan," *Washington Post*, February 27, 2009, www.washingtonpost.com/wp-dyn/content/articles/2009/01/26/AR2009022601065.

the prosecution and conviction, or other sanctioning, of several dozen lower-ranking personnel who could not show that superiors had explicitly authorized what they had clearly been expected to do.

The ICRC continued to criticize some aspects of US military policy in Bagram as late as 2007, including "ghosting" and abusing prisoners.[24] It seems that the United States followed Israeli experience in that some prisoners were kept from the ICRC for two weeks under an apparent agreement with that organization, but the organization claimed that some prisoners were withheld from its representatives for months.[25] As the United States tried to close Gitmo and shut down CIA secret detentions (covered in Chapter 5), the Bagram prison facility and its offspring grew larger and more important.[26] Thus while much American media attention focused on Gitmo, Bagram and then a new facility became the main detention center for enemy prisoners linked to the US struggle against global terrorism. This led to various legal questions about the rights of the various types of detainees housed and interrogated in Afghanistan.

Guantánamo

When Guantánamo was opened for business in early January 2002, started up in a rush on the basis of inadequate planning,[27] it was run according to the usual military rule book: Military Police (MP) were in charge of security, and Military Intelligence (MI) ran the interrogations

[24] Fisnik Abrashi, AP, "Red Cross Faults Afghan Prison," *Boston Globe*, April 15, 2008, www.boston.com/news/world/middleeast/articles/2008/04/a5/red_cross-faults-afghanistan. See also Tim Golden, "Foiling US Plan, Prison Expands in Afghanistan," *New York Times*, January 7, 2008, www.nytimes.com/2008/01/07bagram.html.

[25] On the ICRC and visits to Palestinian detainees under Israeli control see David P. Forsythe, *The Humanitarians: The International Committee of the Red Cross* (Cambridge: Cambridge University Press, 2005), p. 71, where negotiations over secret detention are reviewed. On the fourteen-day limit regarding the United States in Afghanistan, see Golden, "Foiling US Plan." Gen. Petraeus of CentCom publicly declared in 2009 that all prisoners held by the United States in Afghanistan had to be reported to the ICRC within fourteen days. See further 1949 Geneva Convention IV, Art. 136, which sometimes served as a point of reference for the ICRC.

[26] Tim Golden and Eric Schmitt, "A Growing Afghan Prison Rivals Bleak Guantánamo," *New York Times*, February 26, 2006, www.nytimes.com/2006/02/26/internatonal/26bagram.html.

[27] The best treatment is by Greenberg, *The Least Worst Place*. Statements of fact not otherwise referenced about the early days of Gitmo are drawn from this source.

according to the Army field manual, presumed to be applicable in a Navy facility.

An early request by a US JAG to bring in the ICRC for its usual prison visits associated with war and other violent situations was rejected by Washington. This was logically consistent with the Bush plan to use coercive interrogation when "necessary" and to minimize any oversight. A second request for the ICRC went up the chain of command, based partly on the notion that the presence of the ICRC would undercut any claims from human rights groups. Without a reply to this second request, a mid-level legal officer, Col. Manuel Supervielle, with the support of the base commander, Brig. Gen. Michael Lehnert, and also the support of SouthCom, bypassing the Pentagon, invited the ICRC to conduct its usual detention visits associated with war or other violent situations. Later, apparently the Pentagon's Legal Counsel, William Haynes, and possibly others, while unhappy about these developments, did not want the embarrassment of kicking out the ICRC once invited. It is not known at present whether Secretary of Defense Rumsfeld reviewed the ICRC's presence. Surely he was informed. In any event the ICRC stayed and was to contest the abusive interrogation when it developed. Its presence was the product of mid-level military commitment to "Geneva" and tradition, but in the context of the confused and haphazard way that Gitmo got started. At first the ICRC helped identify the prisoners and their country of origin, since amazingly the Gitmo authorities had no idea who the prisoners were and lacked the translators to find out.

Despite Vice President Cheney's earlier comments about "going to the dark side," and despite comments by security managers that after 9/11 the "gloves came off," already noted, much of the US uniformed military tried to carry on as usual. The early assumptions were to treat the prisoners arriving after "screening" in Afghanistan as if they were POWs. The point was stable and humane detention, as in other wars. The doctors worked to provide proper medical care. The psychologists were also oriented toward the welfare of the prisoners.

In early February, however, President Bush read a position paper prepared by his lawyers saying no one at Gitmo was covered by the rules of "Geneva."[28] This was consistent with what Rumsfeld had already

[28] A very accurate and useful overview, contesting the Bush Administration view and delving into various Gitmo issues, was eventually provided by five UN human rights rapporteurs, operating initially under the aegis of the UN Human

told the Joint Chiefs in a *fait accompli*, namely that anyone at Gitmo could be harshly interrogated because of military necessity, regardless of the principles of "Geneva."[29] So US policy asserted that the precise rules of Geneva Conventions III and IV did not apply at Guantánamo, but no one knew what rules did. If the principles of "Geneva" were to apply but not the precise rules, what did that mean on the ground? If "military necessity" could trump humane principles on occasion, when did that kick in?

Particularly commander Lehnert and his senior legal advisor Supervielle from CentCom continued to work for humane detention and interrogation while waiting for clarification about when the usual rules should be altered. To them it was a question of military honor and an awareness that abusive detention could rebound against the national interests of the United States. The negatives outweighed any anticipated positives. Lehnert told one interviewer about abusive interrogation at Gitmo early on: "The juice was not worth the squeeze."[30] He later said that in abusing prisoners on the Cuban island, the US lost the high moral ground in the struggle against terrorism, without getting much in return by way of important intelligence.[31]

In general, on prisoner affairs in the military as on many other issues, Rumsfeld and his assistants like Douglas Feith and Stephen Cambone and Paul Wolfowitz established prisoner policy, not JCS Chairman General Richard Myers and the rest of the Joint Chiefs. As previously noted, Myers tried to present himself as a great champion of "Geneva," but he seems not to have understood that lip service to the "principles of Geneva" while exempting prisoners from their precise rules opened the door to widespread abuse unrelated to any "ticking time bomb" scenario.[32] Moreover Rumsfeld tolerated little dissent and adversely affected the careers of those who dared to voice an independent

Rights Commission, "Situation of Detainees at Guantánamo Bay," UN Doc. E/CN.4/2006/120, 15 February 2006, noted in annex B.

29 Greenberg, *The Least Worst Place*, p. 121.

30 *Ibid.*, p. 138.

31 AP, "Marine who Built Gitmo: US Lost Moral High Ground," www.boston.com/news/nation/articles/2009/09/25/marine_who_built_gitmo_us_lost.

32 Myers' memoirs, *Eyes on the Horizon*, presents the picture of a thinker who was less than a heavyweight in that respect. This is confirmed by Sands, *Torture Team*. It is also confirmed by Feith's memoirs, *War and Decision*, cited in Chapter 2.

view.[33] The JCS did not oppose Rumsfeld regarding harsh interrogation at Gitmo. Cheney, and David Addington his point man on prisoner issues, also played hardball with those who had independent views. Given the weakness of Rice *vis-à-vis* Cheney and Rumsfeld, noted in Chapters 2 and 3, President George W. Bush did not get a wide range of opinion on prisoner and other security matters. For those with an eye on their future careers, it could be dangerous to contest the clear emphasis on abusive interrogation coming from Cheney and Rumsfeld.

Guantánamo, according to widely noted assertions, was supposed to hold the worst of the worst, the really bad guys, mainly from Afghanistan. It would turn out to be the case, however, that some Gitmo prisoners were seized in Gambia and other places far from the battlefields of Afghanistan and the neighboring Pakistan Tribal Areas. If Gitmo held the worst of the worst, it was then rather hard to rationalize the prisoner abuse that was on-going in Afghanistan (see pp. 97–103) or soon in CIA hands (as covered in Chapter 5).

In fact, many of the arrivals at Gitmo, transported in an inhumane process involving an intentionally abusive and degrading air flight,[34] had no actionable intelligence to offer up and were little threat to US security. The United States had offered cash rewards for enemy prisoners turned over to its forces in Afghanistan. Over time it became clear that some prisoners were offered up to the Americans to settle family or tribal or clan scores, or just to collect the money. Very few prisoners at Gitmo were captured by US forces. In 2004 Brig. Gen. Martin Lucenti was quoted as saying that of the 550 prisoners then held at Gitmo, "most of them, the majority of them … weren't fighting. They were

33 See especially Packer, *The Assassins' Gate*, pp. 244–246. When General Shinseki said that the United States would need many more troops to control Iraq than Rumsfeld and Wolfowitz were then indicating, his career was sent into a detour toward a dead end until brought back by President Obama to head Veterans Affairs some years later. See also Bradley Graham, *By His Own Rules: The Ambitions, Successes, and Ultimate Failure of Donald Rumsfeld* (New York: Public Affairs, 2009), on the arrogance and intolerance of Rumsfeld.

34 See Begg, *Enemy Combatant*, among other sources. Even in his memoirs, Gen. Myers does not back away from his controversial statement that airborne prisoners might have chewed through airplane cables to bring down the plane, thus meriting being tied down in uncomfortable positions and other abuses during the transatlantic flight. How they might have damaged a plane while humanely restrained under armed guard is difficult to fathom. See further Center for Constitutional Rights, "Report on Torture and Cruel, Inhuman, and Degrading Treatment of Prisoners at Guantánamo Bay, Cuba," July 2006.

running."[35] Maj. Gen. Michael Dunlavey, an early hard line officer at Gitmo, said that many prisoners there, perhaps half, were of little intelligence value.[36] His deputy echoed that view.[37] A CIA agent with experience at Gitmo said in 2004 that only 10 percent of the prisoners there were dangerous.[38] The large number of Gitmo detainees who would be eventually released suggested that he was accurate.[39] One academic report in 2006 found that over half of the Gitmo detainees had committed no hostile act against US personnel or facilities, that most detainees were captured by other parties, and that perhaps 8 percent of those at Gitmo were associated with Al-Qaeda.[40] President Obama commissioned a study of the 240 prisoners remaining at Gitmo in 2009. That report found that only about 10 percent were important for US security and that 5 percent could not be categorized at all due to lack of information. Most prisoners were low-level fighters, some with little interest in attacking the United States.[41]

Some prisoners at Gitmo throughout time were dangerous to Americans and US security and did believe in total war, including attacks on civilians. When released, some did return to the fight, or take up the fight, against US interests around the world.[42] Thus the

[35] Mark Huband, "US Officer Predicts Guantánamo Releases," *Financial Times*, October 4, 2004, http://news.ft.com/cms/s/192851d2-163b-11d9-b835-00000e2511c8.html.

[36] See Margulies, *Guantánamo*, p. 65. See also Sands, *Torture Team*, p. 43.

[37] Sands, *ibid.*

[38] Margulies, *Guantánamo*, pp. 209–210. For more on this CIA report indicating that the United States had mostly the wrong detainees at Gitmo, and expressing concern about abusive interrogation, see Seymour Hersh, *Chain of Command: The Road from 9/11 to Abu Ghraib* (New York: HarperCollins, 2004), pp. 2–3.

[39] Greenberg, *The Least Worst Place*, pp. 160–161, confirms the weak intelligence value of the early prisoners at Gitmo. See also Greenberg, *ibid.*, p. 107.

[40] Mark Denbeaux and Joshua Denbeaux, "Report on Guantánamo Detainees," http://law.shu.edu/news/Guantánamo_report_final_2_08_06.pdf.

[41] For a short summary see Peter Finn, "Most Guantánamo Detainees Low-level Fighters, Task Force Report Says," *Washington Post*, May 29, 2010, p. A 03. www.washingtonpost.com/wp-dyn/content/article/2010/05/28/AR2010052803873. For the larger report see Guantánamo Review Task Force, "Final Report," January 22, 2010, http://media.washingtonpost.com/wp-srv/nation/pdf/Gitmotaskforcereport_052810.pdf.

[42] See Greenberg, *The Least Worst Place*, p. 107. In 2009 the Pentagon reported that of released prisoners, one in seven had taken hostile action against the United States. Elisabeth Bumiller, "1 in 7 Freed Detainees Rejoins Fight, Report Finds," *New York Times*, May 21, 2009, www.nytimes.com/2009/05/21/us/politics/

Obama task force on Gitmo recommended some trials and some continued administrative detention for about eighty-five detainees.

Returning to our chronology, we find that as 2002 progressed Rumsfeld became dissatisfied with the lack of actionable intelligence coming out of Gitmo, no doubt because many of the detainees were not high-level Al-Qaeda or Taliban operatives. In mid-February Gen. Dunlavey was put in charge of interrogations, undercutting Lehnert. The point of the change was not in doubt. Rumsfeld wanted more information out of the Gitmo prisoners. It was up to Dunlavey to figure out how to get it. The trend toward abusive interrogation was made even clearer when in mid-March Rumsfeld replaced Lehnert with Brig. Gen. (reserves) Rick Baccus as camp commander, even if Baccus was eventually regarded at the Pentagon as not tough enough. In the mid-Fall of 2002, the tougher Dunlavey became acting commander for a time. This was the period when, as noted in Chapter 3, key Washington players like Addington and Haynes went to the island and encouraged the local JAG, Diane Beaver, to draft harsh interrogation rules for Dunlavey, who sent the memo on to SouthCom, where General Hill flagged it for further review in Washington. Neither Dunlavey nor Hill were going to oppose what Rumsfeld wanted, although Hill clearly had his doubts about the legality of some of the harsh methods in the memo.[43]

Some of these Gitmo decisions were probably affected by other developments. Rumsfeld was likely stimulated by reports that the CIA was getting important information from some HVDs it was holding in its own prisons, certainly from about April 2002 if not earlier. He reportedly did not like to be upstaged by Tenet and the CIA.[44] Also, there were various legal memos authorizing abusive interrogation techniques from early August 2002 for the CIA. If approved for the CIA, why not for the military, especially if various DOJ lawyers gave the green light? "Geneva" could supposedly be trumped by "military necessity." This trend transpired despite the fact that in August 2002, US

21gitmo.html? But the data were often imprecise, as discussed later. A US report in 2010 put the number of released Gitmo detainees who had returned to anti-American action as one in four, but the claims about confirmed or suspected action remained fuzzy. Charlie Savage, "Some Ex-detainees Still Tied to Terror," *New York Times*, December 7, 2010, www.nytimes.com/2010/12.08/world/americas/08gitmo.html.

[43] Sands, *Torture Team*, p. 83. [44] Mayer, *The Dark Side*.

internal reports confirmed earlier judgments that no big fish were at Guantánamo.[45]

To make absolutely sure that traditional, that is, humane, military detention and interrogation did not carry the day at Gitmo, the Secretary of Defense dispatched a new Gitmo commander, Lt. Gen. Geoffrey Miller as of September 2002 (who remained head of Gitmo until March 2004). He had no training in detention and interrogation, but he was known to be tough. Miller integrated the MP with MI, and gave the MP the job of softening up the prisoners for interrogation by MI. Thus intentional abuse became standard operating procedure for some prisoners at Guantánamo. Gitmo's Standard Operating Procedure (SOP) was detailed in a bureaucratic handbook that contained provisions about how to micromanage ICRC visits and hide prisoners from that agency.[46]

In an email summarizing a meeting of US officials about how to manage Gitmo in October 2002, legal advisor Beaver confirms that prisoners have been hidden from the ICRC as well as the intention to continue the practice. Others in the meeting confirm the policy of stopping abuse short of fatalities, which would bring negative attention and serious legal problems. The participants in this meeting were aware of the controversial nature of what was transpiring and the need for legal cover.[47] They were worried about the ICRC presence and what might happen if the organization left in protest.

Events were greatly affected when US authorities discovered that one of the prisoners at Gitmo was Mohammed al-Qahtani, supposedly one of the intended hijackers on 9/11. Rumsfeld then authorized, and closely followed, the concentrated abuse of al-Qahtani. The military kept detailed records of his abusive interrogation, which actually started before Rumsfeld officially approved it and which eventually leaked to the media. These abusive techniques were confirmed by the official Schmidt report of June 2005.[48] Used against al-Qahtani in

[45] Greenberg, *The Least Worst Place*, pp. 67–68.

[46] Gourevitch and Morris, *Standard Operating Procedure*, pp. 90–91. The 2003 manual for Camp Delta, part of Gitmo, can be viewed at www.wired.com/print/politics/onlinerights/news/2007/11/gitmo. Regarding ICRC visits, prisoners were put into four categories, from full access to no access.

[47] "Counter Resistance Strategy Minutes," National Security Archives, http://dspace.wrlc.org/doc/bitstream/2041/70969/00420_021002_001display.pdf.

[48] "Army Regulation 15–6: Final Report," available on the internet, including at the National Security Archives, noted in annex B. This report was commissioned by

combination were: sleep deprivation, manipulation of extreme temperatures, restriction in stress positions, humiliation through commands to bark like a dog and wear women's underwear, solitary confinement interspersed with long interrogation sessions, having cold war poured over him, etc. At times he was taken for medical treatment to ensure he was able to continue with interrogation, thus implicating US medical personnel in abetting abuse. At times he was clearly psychotic from the prolonged and concentrated abusive interrogation methods.[49]

Various military officials claimed that the United States gained valuable information from the abusive interrogation of al-Qahtani.[50] This has yet to be confirmed by independent sources. Schmidt, in his official Army report, claimed that the treatment of al-Qahtani was neither torture nor inhuman, a view vigorously contested by various human rights groups and independent lawyers and not sustained by any logical reading of the logs documenting abuse. In 2008 a US official, Susan Crawford, characterized his treatment as torture, which constituted grounds for dropping legal charges against him.[51]

Other prisoners have reported, after their release or through their lawyers, similarly abusive treatment such as being: "intimidated by dogs; stripped naked, hooded, and blindfolded; exposed to extreme heat and cold; denied basic necessities, such as blankets, clothing, or soap; routinely 'short shackled' or chained in a 'hog-tie' position or

the US SouthCom in response to FBI reports of harsh interrogation at Gitmo. On the one hand the report dismisses much abuse by simply stating that many techniques were consistent with instructions from Washington, with three exceptions. On the other hand Lt. Gen. Randall M. Schmidt, the principal author, himself gave an interview indicating that he was troubled by the use of combined techniques without time limits. See Michael Scherer and Mark Benjamin, "What Rumsfeld Knew," www.salon.com/news/feature/2006/04/14/rummy. The report itself is largely a white wash of abusive interrogation, similar to the Church report. The Schmidt report asserts that short shackling had been stopped at Gitmo by 2005.

49 For an overview and many references see Sands, *Torture Team*, whose book focuses on the al-Qahtani interrogation.

50 See for example Josh White, "Abu Ghraib Tactics Were First Used at Guantánamo," *Washington Post*, July 14, 2005, p. A 1.

51 On the treatment of al-Qahtani see especially Philippe Sands, *Torture Team*. On the comments of Susan Crawford, a retired judge who was politically appointed to serve as convening authority for the military commissions, asserting that his treatment rose to the level of torture, see Bob Woodward, "Detainee Tortured, US Official Says," *Washington Post*, January 14, 2009, www.msnbc.msn.com/id/28649218. Also William Glaberson, "Case Against 9/11 Detainee Is Dismissed," *New York Times*, May 14, 2008, p. A 19.

otherwise forced into painful stress positions for hours and even days during interrogations; sprayed with pepper spray; stripped; forcibly shaved of their hair and beards; given forcible body cavity searches; threatened with rendition to third countries where they would be subjected to torture; denied the use of toilet facilities during interrogations in order to force them to soil themselves; subjected to loud music for lengthy periods; deprived of rest or sleep; deprived of food or water; subjected to total isolation and sensory deprivation for prolonged periods; sexually humiliated; raped or threatened with rape, subjected to mock drownings, and deprived of medical treatment."[52] Some prisoners were slammed to the floor with such force that an Army interrogator feared internal injuries.[53] Other prisoners also reported excessive force in maintaining order. They reported excessive force and humiliation in use of restraint chairs for the purpose of forced feeding in response to hunger strikes.[54] It is possible that while some abuse was often limited and controlled during interrogations, considerable abuse was tolerated "after hours" and via the Emergency Response Teams who "subdued" prisoners on various pretexts.[55]

As we will see, many of these same techniques were widely used in Iraq. They were also used in Afghanistan. Abusive interrogation techniques often move horizontally and informally, and do not have to be taught vertically and officially by US officers[56] (who themselves often talk informally with security officials from various countries).

An abstract list of abusive techniques may not fully convey the processes used. Here is an FBI account of a Gitmo interrogation that military personnel tried to conceal:

> The detainee was shackled and his hands were cuffed to his waist. [The FBI agent watching through a two-way mirror] observed Sgt. Lacey [the female

[52] Barbara Olshansky, *Democracy Detained: Secret Unconstitutional Practices in the US War on Terror* (New York: Seven Stories Press, 2007). See also Jameel Jaffer and Amrit Singh, *The Administration of Torture: A Documentary Record from Washington to Abu Ghraib and Beyond* (New York: Columbia University Press, 2007), pp. 16–17, which focuses on 2003–2004, or the post-Qahtani period.

[53] Jaffer and Singh, *The Administration of Torture*, p. 16.

[54] The way restraint chairs were used in the feeding of prisoners on hunger strikes, and the way a wide feeding tube was used, probably constituted further abuse. See Margulies, *Guantánamo*, p. 250.

[55] Worthington, *The Guantánamo Files*.

[56] Darius Rejali, *Torture and Democracy* (Princeton: Princeton University Press, 2006).

military interrogator] apparently whispering in the detainee's ear, and caressing ... his arms ... On more than one occasion the detainee appeared to be grimacing in pain, and Sgt. Lacey's hands appeared to be making some contact with the detainee. Although [the FBI agent] could not see her hands at all times, he saw them moving towards the detainee's lap. He also observed the detainee pulling away and against the restraints ... [The FBI agent] asked [a marine] what had happened to cause the detainee to grimace in pain. The marine said Sgt. Lacey had grabbed the detainee's thumbs and bent them backwards and indicated that she also grabbed his genitals. The marine also implied that her treatment of that detainee was less harsh than her treatment of others by indicating that he had seen her treatment of other detainees result in detainees curling into a fetal position on the floor and crying in pain.[57]

Some FBI agents withdrew from Guantánamo rather than become complicit in the prevailing abuse, and we have already noted that the Schmidt report was undertaken in response to FBI complaints.[58] The Gitmo abuse was significant enough for a MI officer to go public with what he had observed.[59] A military chaplain did likewise.[60] By the Summer of 2004, despite the 2003 Walker report (noted in Chapter 3) supposedly limiting abuse in military facilities, major abuse continued at Gitmo. According to excerpts from a confidential ICRC report to the United States presumably leaked by dissidents in the Administration, the ICRC found widespread abuse at Guantánamo, abuse that was "tantamount to torture."[61] This was even after the scandal broke about abuse at Abu Ghraib in Iraq.

A number of released Gitmo prisoners, such as the "Tipton Three" (three British residents from Tipton) claimed to have been abused,

[57] Quoted in Margulies, *Guantánamo*, pp. 5–6.

[58] See Hersh, *Chain of Command*, pp. 6–7, 14.

[59] Erik Saar and Viveca Novak, *Inside the Wire: A Military Intelligence Soldier's Eyewitness Account of Life at Guantánamo* (London and New York: Penguin Press, 2005). See also Saar's interview on the subject with Onnesha Roychoudhuri, "Inside the Wire: An Interview With Erik Saar," *Mother Jones*, May 24, 2005, www.motherjones.com/cgi=bin/print_article.pl.

[60] James Yee and Aimee Molloy, *For God and Country: Faith and Patriotism Under Fire* (New York: Public Affairs, 2005).

[61] For an overview, see Neil A. Lewis, "Red Cross Finds Detainee Abuse in Guantánamo," *New York Times*, November 30, 2004, http://select.nytimes.com/gst/abstract.html?res=F30910FF3A5A0C638FDDA80994DC404. Also Josh White and John Mintz, "Red Cross Cites 'Inhumane' Treatment At Guantánamo," *Washington Post*, December 1, 2004, lexis-nexis: m=219e4fl0abd98498a.

including through use of prolonged solitary confinement, in cases of mistaken identity.[62] Another British resident at Guantánamo, Moazzam Begg, was also released without charge and also made claims of repeated abuse after traversing Kandahar, Bagram, and Gitmo.[63] The same process unfolded in 2009 when another British resident, Binyam Mohamed, was released. He claimed to have been tortured, and this time the British legal authorities under the Gordon Brown government promised to investigate – a promise still playing out at the time of writing. Human rights groups compiled reports confirming that serious abuse was not limited to al-Qahtani. One source says that one in six Gitmo prisoners was seriously abused, citing mostly press reports.[64] This is also the figure used by another study.[65]

British representatives, and similar officials from perhaps twenty states, were apparently complicit in US abusive action at Gitmo. The British in particular were consistently present at Guantánamo throughout its operation from early 2002, knowledgeable about events there, and silent in public about the abuse. In fact the British government, apparently at the request of the Obama Administration in 2009, pressed British courts not to release information about Binyam Mohamed's interrogation that might upset British–US relations. It seems that on occasion the British government sought the release of certain prisoners as cases of mistaken identity, but still refused to comment in public about US abuse. The British government under both Tony Blair and Gordon Brown were almost certainly complicit in abusive interrogation in Afghanistan and at Guantánamo, and then dissembled about that fact when pressed by parliamentary circles and sectors of public opinion.[66] At the time of writing the David Cameron government had promised to investigate.

Other released prisoners, on the other hand, have reported that they were not abused during lengthy detention at Gitmo. Of fifty-five former

[62] See especially Margulies, *Guantánamo*, p. 42 and *passim*.
[63] Begg, *Enemy Combatant*.
[64] John T. Parry, *Understanding Torture: Law, Violence, and Political Identity* (Ann Arbor: University of Michigan Press, 2010), p. 187.
[65] Worthington, *The Guantánamo Files*.
[66] See, for example, Begg, *Enemy Combatant*. See also the comprehensive report by Amnesty International, "Europe: State of Denial," June 24, 2008. See further Center for Constitutional Rights, *Foreign Interrogators in Guantánamo Bay*, June 3, 2008.

detainees, thirty-one claimed abuse and twenty-four did not, according to one careful study based on interviews conducted in various places around the world.[67] The Danish government inquired carefully into the Gitmo detention of one of their residents, concluding that while it was another case of mistaken identity, the prisoner had no other grounds for complaint.[68] So as of the time of writing it remains unclear what percentage of the Gitmo population was abused, and at what level of coercion. As noted previously, whether because of their treatment at Gitmo or because of pre-existing views, some prisoners contested their detention by resisting the prison regime and harassing their guards.[69]

From at least October 2003 if not earlier the ICRC had publicly expressed concern about the mental health of some prisoners there.[70] There were four suicides reported; other prisoners might have joined that list absent the forced feeding via restraint chairs. According to one source there were forty-one suicide attempts by twenty-five prisoners through 2006.[71] The suicides and forced feeding were both controversial. Some claimed that the suicides were less the result of despair from unending and uncertain detention and more from a political strategy by hard core leaders among the detainees. On the other hand, some claimed that the forced feeding of prisoners on hunger strikes to block further suicides was unreasonably harsh.[72]

Over time improvements occurred at Guantánamo. This was confirmed by a public statement by the head of the ICRC, under pressure

[67] Laurel E. Fletcher and Eric Stover, *The Guantánamo Effect: Exposing the Consequences of US Detention and Interrogation Practices* (Berkeley: University of California Press, 2009), p. 62 and *passim*.

[68] Interviews, Copenhagen, Fall, 2008.

[69] See Tom Lasseter, "Taliban Ambassador Wielded Power within Guantánamo," McClatchy Newspapers, Yahoo.News, June 19, n.d., http://news.yahoo.com/s/mcclatchy/2970616.

[70] For one of many reports see AP, "Red Cross Finds Deteriorating Mental Health at Guantánamo," *USA Today*, October 10, 2003, www.usatoday.com/news/world/2003-10-10-icrc-detainees_x.htm.

[71] Kathleen T. Rhem, American Forces Press Service, "Skirmish With Guards, Two Suicide Attempts Test Guantánamo Procedures," May 29, 2006, www.defense.gov.news/newsarticle.aspx?id=15717.

[72] See further Eric Schmitt and Tim Golden, "Force-Feeding at Guantánamo is Now Acknowledged," *New York Times*, February 22, 2006, p. A 5. On the general despair of the detainees but also some calculated rebellion, see Mourad Benchellali, "Detainees in Despair," *New York Times*, June 14, 2006, www.nytimes.com/2006/06/14/opinion/14benchellali.html.

for not speaking out more about the situation there.[73] The early open-air cages were replaced by permanent structures. While the amenities of these new structures varied, so that the United States could reward cooperative prisoners while retaining a Spartan prison regime for those not fully cooperating, as judged by the United States of course, there were general improvements. Juveniles were separated from older prisoners, for example.

The improvements were decidedly affected by: (1) the US Detainee Treatment Act (DTA) of 2005, passed by large congressional majorities, requiring US military interrogations to conform to the non-abusive techniques noted in the US army field manual; and (2) the US Supreme Court Judgment in the *Hamdan* case of Summer 2006 holding that the 1949 Geneva Convention Common Article 3, prohibiting torture and CID, pertained to all those at Guantánamo. This ruling, while focused on Military Commissions, implied that no torture, or CID, or humiliating treatment and conditions, could legally obtain at Gitmo.

It is impossible for an outsider to characterize the impact of the ICRC. A few reports or parts of reports leaked to the press, and from these we know that the ICRC was often quite candid and critical in its understated way. Since we do not know the total number of reports, much less their contents, it is difficult to say much more. The US legal advisor Diane Beaver, who drafted an early memo authorizing abusive interrogation, warned her colleagues not to implement the memo in the presence of ICRC representatives, implying that the organization was diligent in contesting abuse. She warned that the ICRC presence was a "serious concern."[74] The few leaked reports, never attributed to anyone with the organization, frequently proved embarrassing to the Administration and generated progressive pressures for change. This did not alter the organization's commitment to discretion, as long as sufficient humanitarian progress was evident to it. It has never been clear to outsiders how much humanitarian progress there must be for ICRC discretion to continue.

73 "Guantánamo Bay Conditions have Improved – Red Cross," Reuters News, Geneva, April 27, 2006. Regarding the ICRC policy of discretion, and whether it should have spoken out more and earlier concerning US policies in the GWOT, see the discussion by Daniel Warner and David P. Forsythe in *Millennium*, 34/2 (2005), pp. 449–475.

74 James P. Pfiffner, *Torture as Public Policy: Restoring U.S. Credibility on the World Stage* (Boulder and London: Paradigm, 2010), p. 29.

In February 2009 a US military team sent by the new Obama Administration concluded that Gitmo was in substantial compliance with "Geneva."[75] That inquiry did not review previous years but only the 2009 situation. This was confirmed by a visit of Eric Holder, Attorney General in the new Administration. The same evaluation was presented by some books and TV programs that focused on Gitmo after Congress and the US Supreme Court required humane detention. These sources confirmed that Gitmo was now correct, but they did not emphasize or treat in depth the period of greatest abuse – which ran from 2002, and particularly from late 2002, until perhaps the end of 2005.[76]

Ironically, the United States reportedly decided not to release certain Gitmo prisoners because Washington could not guarantee that they would not be abused when returned to their country of origin – e.g. Saudi Arabia or China. This irony if not hypocrisy was not lost on various parties.[77] At least one prisoner objected to his release to Algeria, fearing a negative reception.

Until the photos of Abu Ghraib surfaced (covered on p. 129), Guantánamo rather than Bagram in Afghanistan became the iconic symbol of US prisoner abuse after 9/11 – although perhaps there was no fatal abuse at Gitmo (aside from several suicides). The same could not be said about fatal interrogation in Afghanistan and Iraq. Reports of fatal abuse at Gitmo from reliable sources did not lead to rigorous review, either by the mainstream media or Executive and Congressional authorities. Scott Horton, an activist attorney whose reputation for integrity had earlier led JAG officers to seek out his help, reported in 2010 that in 2006 three of the claimed suicides had actually been deaths resulting from beatings by US military personnel. His sources were US military persons with a troubled conscience. A military investigation was open to criticism, as Horton clearly showed. At the time of writing,

[75] Jane Sutton, "US says Guantánamo Complies with Geneva Treaties," Reuters, February 23, 2009, http://news.yahoo.com/s/nm/us_Guantánamo_review.

[76] See for example Gordon Cucullu, *Inside Gitmo: The True Story Behind the Myths of Guantánamo Bay* (New York: HarperCollins, 2009). The National Geographic TV Channel ran a two-hour special in April 2009 focusing on the US attention to prisoner safety and welfare, while noting prisoner attempts to harass the guards.

[77] Tim Golden, "US Says it Fears Detainee Abuse in Repatriation," *New York Times*, April 30, 2006, www.nytimes.com/2006/04/30/world/30gitmo.html.

the silence about Horton's article has been deafening.[78] It was as if the country, and certainly officials in Washington, could not bring themselves to confront any more bad news about US prisoner policy.

We do not know the total picture about deaths in the CIA Black Sites, or those held by the CIA and then transferred to other security services. This iconic if negative status for Gitmo was in part the product of media coverage, which overlapped with NGO reports and commentary by UN and other human rights officials. Gitmo also drew much attention because American legal teams from NGOs and law firms could petition US courts more easily and with more success than was true for Afghanistan and Iraq. It was also the case that much abuse at Gitmo was by policy design, whereas for Abu Ghraib there was controversy about policy design versus "a few bad apples." There was no general chaos at Gitmo, which meant that mostly what happened there happened because of policy – either about detention conditions and interrogation, or about the response to claims of abuse.

Not only was there little official effort to assign responsibility in response to reports of torture, even fatal beatings, at Guantánamo, but also little official action on the question of the role of medical personnel there. Medical and psychological teams had advised on interrogation, sometimes were present at interrogations, and in some cases had treated detainees so that harsh interrogation could continue.[79] The ICRC protested the use of medical records for interrogation purposes. One medical study showed lasting effects from the abuse on many prisoners.[80] A report by Physicians for Human Rights charged that US authorities, including medical and psychological personnel, had in effect conducted experiments on prisoners, compiling new information

[78] Scott Horton, "The Guantánamo 'Suicides': A Camp Delta Sergeant Blows the Whistle," *Harper's*, March 2010, http://harpers.org/archive/2010/01/hbc-90006368, an article which circulated in advance of publication. For a rare follow-up piece, see Dahlia Lithwick, "Too Terrible To Be True?," *Slate*, January 20, 21010, http://www.slate.com/toolbar.aspx?action=print&id=2241948.

[79] See especially Steven H. Miles, *Oath Betrayed: America's Torture Doctors* (Berkeley: University of California Press, 2009). On the role of BSCT psychological teams, see further Margulies, *Guantánamo*, p. 124. On the role of medical doctors see Sands, *Torture Team*. See also Neil A. Lewis, "Interrogators Cite Doctors' Aid at Guantánamo Prison Camp," *New York Times*, June 24, 2005, www.nytimes.com/2005/06/24/politics/24gitmo.html, regarding both doctors and psychologists.

[80] Fletcher and Stover, *The Guantánamo Effect*.

on the effects of abuse for use in subsequent interrogations.[81] On the one hand some participating personnel may have had the intention to stop the abuse short of torture. On the other hand and at the same time, that role may have inherently involved participation in CID techniques. A 2005 US Army study of detainee medical operations implausibly found few problems in Gitmo, Afghanistan, and Iraq, although it did acknowledge unspecified problems early on, and did recommend better training and some rethinking of the use of Behavioral Science Consultation Teams (BSCTs) (made up of doctors and psychologists) in interrogation. Where Army investigators found a few cases of military personnel not reporting cases of suspected abuse, criminal investigation officials were informed.[82] The overall thrust of this Army report does not square with numerous other credible reports compiling evidence of the participation of medical and psychological personnel in serious abuse of detainees.

It was relevant to ask how many Gitmo prisoners had been made even more hostile toward the United States because of their administrative detention and abusive treatment, and had then carried out further violence when released. According to the *Washington Post*, a prisoner from Gitmo was released to Kuwait, found not guilty of terrorism, but then became a suicide bomber in Iraq because of, presumably, the detention and abuse he had undergone at Guantánamo.[83] According to another report, a Gitmo prisoner had been running illegal drugs in Afghanistan. After his stay on the Cuban island and then his release, he joined the Taliban.[84] It was difficult to say exactly how many released

[81] *Experiments in Torture: Evidence of Human Subject Research and Experimentation in the "Enhanced" Interrogation Program* (Cambridge, MA and Washington, DC: Physicians for Human Rights, 2010).

[82] "Final Report: Assessment of Detainee Medical Operations," 2005, www.globalsecurity.org/military/facility/Guantánamo-bay_camp-refs.htm, noted in annex B.

[83] Rajiv Chandrasekaran, "After Gitmo, a 'Ticking Time Bomb' Goes Off," *Washington Post*, February 23, 2009, http://www.msnbc.msn.com/id 29341889. The reporter wisely leaves open the question of the prisoner's guilt or innocence, while showing a personality change toward more intense hostility toward the United States after Gitmo, as stoked by radical jihadist clergy in Kuwait. His suicide bombing mission in Iraq killed Muslims, albeit Muslims cooperating with the United States.

[84] Tom Lasseter, "Militants Found Recruits among Guantánamo's Wrongly Detained," McClatchy Newspapers, Yahoo.News, June 18, n.d., [2008], http://news.yahoo.com/s/mcclatchy/20080618/wl_mcclatchy/2969823.

detainees returned to hostile action against the United States given the vagueness of US government assertions about what constituted hostile action. It was also impossible to say to what extent the nature of detention and the extent of abuse contributed to any such militant activity, given the lack of reliable interviews with many of the persons in question.

At Guantánamo one finds a secure military facility, carefully controlled and supervised in detail by US civilian and military authorities, where: abusive interrogation becomes clear and systematic policy for a certain part (probably 15–20 percent) of the prison population at least until 2005; female military interrogators wearing provocative clothing straddle, rub against, smear fake menstrual blood on, and otherwise sexually torment Islamic male prisoners;[85] military doctors and psychologists facilitate abuse; high US authorities repeatedly misrepresent the abuse that transpires; and the situation continues for years.

To date there has been no legal accountability for those who authorized and ran this system out of the White House, the Office of the Vice President, the Office of the Secretary of Defense, and the JCS. As noted, Gen. Miller, Gitmo commander, despite being investigated for misconduct, an investigation which led to a recommendation for sanctions, upon retirement was given the Presidential Service Medal by President Bush. This situation obtained despite the fact that Miller had taken the military equivalent of the Fifth Amendment when testifying in Congress, lest he incriminate himself in criminal behavior. Guantánamo represents, among other things, the moral corruption of the US civilian and military command structure, as well as needless abuse for many prisoners. (The Schmidt report recommended that Miller be "admonished." Schmidt's complaint was that Miller did not supervise the interrogation of al-Qahtani so as to limit the process. Thus the complaint was not that Miller instigated, at Rumsfeld's demand, an abusive system of interrogation at Gitmo, but rather that he failed to limit the abuse.) The US SouthCom, then commanded by Gen. Bantz Craddock, followed the Rumsfeld line, supported abuse, and refused to sanction Miller, who of course had been appointed by Rumsfeld for the explicit purpose of making Gitmo harsh. It was not just the Joint Chiefs who caved to Rumsfeld. Military "careerism" contributed to military

[85] The use of sexual acts to humiliate prisoners is documented in the Schmidt report, including one incident in which a female interrogator took her shirt off.

abuse after 9/11. At least Bush was consistent. He also awarded the Distinguished Service Medal to Gen. Myers, Chair of the JCS, who endorsed abusive interrogation.

Iraq

According to the arguments of the Bush Administration, beyond the question of alleged WMD, the US invasion of Iraq in March 2003 was supposed to produce a quick, low-cost, and orderly transition to a stable pro-Western Iraqi government that would eventually be democratic and help democratize the rest of the Arab world. The Iraqis supposedly would be so happy to be rid of Saddam Hussein that they would gladly welcome the US military forces as liberators, unite behind Ahmed Chalabi or another of Washington's favorites and, with their considerable oil money, move nicely toward democratic capitalism. The Administration, while adopting a worst-case scenario about Saddam in the future, assumed a best-case scenario for the post-invasion situation.

Instead, upon the US military victory over Saddam's army, Iraq descended into first uncontrolled looting and other spontaneous disorder. Then Iraq slid into a prolonged and murderous insurgency against foreigners, cross-cut by civil war among various Iraq ethnic, religious, and political factions. Foreign fighters joined the fray. The Bush Administration, and particularly Secretary of Defense Rumsfeld, facilitated both the disorder and the insurgency by: (1) the lack of adequate numbers of ground troops to maintain order and deter opposition; (2) the purge of Baath party members from transition politics, and (3) the disbanding of the officer corps of the Iraqi army. The latter decision led not only to unemployment but unemployment within the Sunni minority by fearful and resentful elements with knowledge of – and possession of – weapons and explosives. The Bush team had no concrete and workable plans for realistic occupation and transition.[86]

[86] Two of the best works on this subject are Thomas E. Ricks, *Fiasco: The American Military Adventure in Iraq* (New York: Penguin, 2006), and Ali A. Alawi, *The Occupation of Iraq: Winning the War, Losing The Peace* (New Haven: Yale University Press, 2007). See also James Fallows, "Blind into Baghdad," *The Atlantic*, January–February 2004, www.theatlantic/issues/2004/01/fallows.htm; the Rand Corporation, *After Saddam: Prewar Planning and the Occupation of Iraq*, June 30, 2008; Larry Diamond, *Squandered Victory: The American Occupation and the Bungled Effort to Bring Democracy to Iraq* (New York:

The Bush Administration, unlike in Afghanistan and at Guantánamo, agreed that the Geneva Conventions fully applied to their invasion and occupation of Iraq from March 2003 until June 2004, the phase of international armed conflict and follow-on occupation. After the formal handoff from occupation to Iraqi sovereign control in June 2004, the United States endorsed the norms of "Geneva" as policy. There was no attempt by Bush lawyers to explain away Geneva Convention III (pertaining to POWs) or Geneva Convention IV (pertaining to civilians). But widespread prisoner abuse occurred, both because of lack of lawful, clear, and consistent instructions followed by oversight, and because of intentional efforts to transfer into Iraq the abusive systems of interrogation used in Afghanistan and Guantánamo. The command structure sometimes issued directives mandating some restraint in interrogations, which conflicted with other memos authorizing, e.g., use of dogs to terrify, but the real emphasis was increasingly for actionable intelligence by coercion.

In an important change from the 1991 US war to liberate Kuwait from Iraqi control, the Bush team did not assign JAG lawyers to monitor interrogation. In an understatement, the legal scholar John Norton Moore said of the Bush Administration on this issue, "Something happened with the significance with which law was taken."[87]

The prison of Abu Ghraib, notorious under Saddam and in disarray after the US invasion, was selected as the major interrogation center by the United States, where prisoners from much of the rest of the country were held. In the Summer of 2003 it was in an insecure area, subject to mortar attack by uncertain and unseen enemies. Abu Ghraib quickly became overcrowded and chaotic. Prisoners rioted, and force was often used to maintain a semblance of order. A reservist with limited experience, Brig. Gen. (reserves) Janis Karpinski (later demoted to Col.) was put in charge of MP for the fifteen Coalition prisons in Iraq. She was given meager resources, and reservists with no training or experience in detention or interrogation were often expected to "hold the fort." Interrogation might be by MI assigned to Abu Ghraib, other military

Time Books, 2005). All these sources, and others, are in general agreement on the nature of the US occupation and the reasons for its chaotic nature.

[87] Adam Liptak, "Legal Review Could Have Halted Abuse, Lawyer Says," *New York Times*, May 29, 2004, p. A 14. The story refers mostly to observations by Scott Horton of the New York City Bar Association, Committee on Human Rights.

personnel who came and went, CIA officials, FBI officials, or contract employees for this or that agency. Some were in civilian clothes and difficult to identify. Some prisoners where "ghosted" or kept secret from the ICRC. Abu Ghraib became a macabre circus. It was amateur hour.

Gen. Ricardo Sanchez, the top US general in Iraq after Tommy Franks and others moved on, was faced with growing violence in the country from the Summer of 2003. He was under pressure from Rumsfeld in Washington and others to get actionable intelligence so as to curtail the insurgency. He passed this sense of urgency down the line, particularly to Thomas M. Pappas, the Colonel in charge of MI at Abu Ghraib,[88] while failing to allocate to Karpinski the resources she would need to run an orderly and humane detention system.[89] Karpinski herself was less than fully dynamic, attentive, and assertive. Similar to Rumsfeld when dealing with Gitmo and al-Qahtani, Sanchez issued various orders regarding permitted interrogation techniques, including use of dogs to terrify prisoners, then rescinded some of what he had just issued.[90] Eventually Sanchez was officially criticized for failing to maintain clear authority and adequate oversight at the prison.[91] Lines of authority were unclear among Sanchez, Karpinski, Maj. Gen. Barbara Fast, who was in charge of MI in the Baghdad region, Pappas, and others.[92] It did not help that CIA agents took charge of certain prisoners at Abu Ghraib, thus blurring the lines of military jurisdiction and authority.

Despite abstract agreement on the applicability of "Geneva" in Iraq, the same abuse that had transpired at Bagram was played out at Abu Ghraib, only worse with less control. Despite the argument that

88 Douglas Jehl, "Officers Say US Colonel at Abu Ghraib Prison Felt Intense Pressure to Get Inmates to Talk," *New York Times*, May 19, 2004, p. A 11.

89 Gourevitch and Morris, *Standard Operating Procedure*, p. 55. Jaffer and Singh, *The Administration of Torture*, p. 31.

90 Gourevitch and Morris, *Standard Operating Procedure*, pp. 53–54. Jaffer and Singh, *The Administration of Torture*, p. 25. Parry, *Understanding Torture*, p. 190 and *passim*.

91 Senate Armed Services Committee, "Inquiry into the Treatment of Detainees in US Custody," available on the web.

92 On general command confusion at Abu Ghraib and with regard to the ICRC reports, see Eric Schmitt, "2 Generals Outline Lag in Notification On Abuse Reports," *New York Times*, May 20, 2004, p. A 1. At the time of congressional hearings about the prison and photos, no one took responsibility for what happened.

"Geneva" did not apply to Gitmo, the same techniques of interrogation used in the latter were applied at Abu Ghraib and elsewhere, only worse and with less control. At Abu Ghraib prisoners were beaten to death, hooded until they suffocated, shackled in uncomfortable positions until they died. The sexual abuse was worse than at Bagram and Gitmo.[93] The supervision was often non-existent. The reports were more falsified and doctored. The ICRC was more impotent in the short term, despite its diligent efforts. Sanchez's legal advisors, including Col. Marc Warren, were insensitive to ICRC reports and other reports of broad abuse.[94] As at Gitmo, many prisoners had no vital intelligence to cough up. Most prisoners at Abu Ghraib were deposited there after indiscriminate sweeps; most were not jihadists or leaders of the insurgency. Some, including children, were detained as leverage against other suspects.[95]

It was not just Abu Ghraib.[96] Some detainees were held at Camp Cropper near the international airport, kept in darkened isolation, and hidden for a time from the ICRC.[97] One of those abused at Camp

[93] Apparently the book, *The Arab Mind* by Raphael Patai affected US decisions. It depicted sexual fixations, especially homosexuality, as a great weakness in Arab cultures, hence something to be exploited by US interrogation by creating shame and humiliation. See further Seymour M. Hersh, "The Gray Zone," *The New Yorker*, May 17, 2004.

[94] Gen. George R. Fay and Lt. Gen. Anthony R. Jones, heads of another military investigation, noted in 2004 that ICRC reports were not believed and not properly investigated. The Fay–Jones report is noted in annex B and can be found at www.defenselink.mil/news/Aug2004/d20040825fay.pdf. Also ignored were other reports of abuse by US military investigators. Andrea Elliott, "Unit Says it Gave Earlier Warning of Abuse in Iraq," *New York Times*, June 14, 2004, www.nytimes.com/2004/06/14/world/reach-war-interrogations-unit-says-it-gave-earlier-warning.

[95] Jaffer and Singh, *The Administration of Torture*, p. 35.

[96] Regarding broad prisoner mistreatment in Iraq, see the leaked ICRC report of February 2004, posted on the web site of GlobalSecurity.org. See also BBC, "Iraq Prisoner Abuse 'was Routine,'" July 23, 2006, http://news/bbc.co.uk/go/pr/fr/-/1/hi/world/americas/5206908.stm. See also the comments of James Schlesinger, PBS NewsHour, confirming broad abuse in Iraq particularly at the point of capture. See also Jaffer and Singh, *The Administration of Torture*, pp. 29–30, 39, re broad abuse in Iraq even after early 2004. And see Human Rights Watch, "'No Blood, No Foul': Soldiers' Accounts of Detainee Abuse in Iraq" (New York: HRW, July 22, 2006).

[97] Douglas Jehl, "Some Iraqis Held Outside Purview of US Command," *New York Times*, May 17, 2004, p. A 1. Various ICRC reports to US authorities during 2003 documented much abuse at various locales, some of which the agency labeled as "tantamount to torture." For one overview, see AP, "Red Cross: 'Tantamount to Torture,'" May 11, 2004, www.msnbc.msn.com/id/4944094/. These few ICRC reports entered the public domain probably through leaks on the

Cropper was an American, a veteran and a whistle blower on corruption in Iraq.[98] Abuses in the field, especially just after capture, were rampant,[99] with soldiers sometimes making up interrogation abuse from the American television program "24," in part because they had been given no clear instructions or training in "Geneva."[100] Reportedly, there were special operations teams drawn from various military units that operated out of uniform and with instructions not only to fight but also to get intelligence on the insurgency any way they could.[101] In a 2006 military study of army and marine personnel in Iraq, about 10 percent admitted they had abused civilians, and over a third said they would use torture to get information about insurgents.[102] In 2006 the United States itself reported to the UN committee of independent experts that supervises the Convention against Torture that twenty-nine detainees had died in detention in Iraq and Afghanistan as a result of abuse.[103] The military was supposed to be adhering to "Geneva," but it was probable that the Bush team had established different CIA rules for Iraq.[104]

American side. Apparently most ICRC reports remained confidential. In a policy that seems to this author overly deferential, the ICRC does not demand or even expect a reply to its reports. Therefore often it is not clear what happens, if anything, to an ICRC report once submitted to detaining authorities.

98 Michael Moss, "American Recalls Torment as a US Detainee in Iraq," *New York Times*, December 18, 2006, p. A 1.

99 See the comments of Tony Lagouranis, interrogator in Iraq from early 2004 to early 2005, PBS Frontline, "The Torture Question," October 19, 2005, www.pbs.org.wgbh/pages/frontline/torture/interviews.

100 Mayer, *The Dark Side*, p. 264.

101 See Mayer, *The Dark Side*, pp. 244–245. See also Eric Schmitt and Carolyn Marshall, "In Secret Unit's 'Black Room,' a Grim Portrait of US Abuse," *New York Times*, March 19, 2006. www.nytimes.com/2006/03/19/international/middleeast/19abuse.html. Also Jaffer and Singh, *The Administration of Torture*, p. 27, and Eric Schmitt, "Pentagon Study Describes Abuse By Units in Iraq," *New York Times*, June 17, 2006, p. A 1. Also Hersh, "The Gray Zone."

102 Jim Mannion, Agence France-Presse, "One in Three US Combat Troops Condone Torture: Survey," May 4, 2007, lexis-nexis: 3868fd2b225e9f5806b. Also Thomas E. Ricks and Ann Scott Tyson, "Troops at Odds With Ethics Standards," *Washington Post*, May 5, 2007, p. A 1.

103 For a summary see Alexander G. Higgins, AP, "US Bars Use of Torture in Interrogations," May 8, 2006, http://news.yahoo.com/s/ap/20060508/ap-on-re-eu/un-us-torture.

104 When an Army interrogator was convicted of killing an Iraqi military prisoner, no one seemed to pay any attention to the fact that the prisoner had been beaten by CIA agents before transfer to military custody. Eric Schmitt, "Army

The fiasco that was the US occupation in Iraq, including the prisoner dimension, was too great to escape attention in Washington. Col. Wood was transferred from Afghanistan to Iraq in July to help manage Abu Ghraib, despite her role in abuse at Bagram.[105] By decision of Rumsfeld, through Stephen Cambone his deputy, and his assistant, the anti-Islamic Christian evangelical Lt. Gen. William Boykin, Gen. Miller and more than a dozen others who had managed harsh but orderly prisoner regimes at Gitmo and in Afghanistan were transferred to Iraq in late Summer 2003 (August 31 to September 10).[106] They were supposed to bring order out of chaos. The fact that "Geneva" applied to Iraq without question or reservation made no difference.

Wood scrapped the interrogation portions of the Army field manual and fell back on the same abusive techniques she had employed at Bagram, with the knowledge and approval of her superiors. It is possible that two sets of rules were implemented by Wood, one set posted and one set that circulated otherwise indicating that the "gloves were off" when it came to interrogation.[107] Miller made clear that what he wanted at Abu Ghraib was systematic and orderly abuse patterned on Gitmo.[108] He brought in contract interrogators who had been at Gitmo and Bagram where supposedly "Geneva" did not apply to prisoners. Whatever the details of their recommendations, widespread and horrific abuse continued at Abu Ghraib in the Fall of 2003. Given what Miller and Wood had implemented elsewhere, it could hardly be otherwise. Once again the key to Miller's approach was to integrate the MP with the MI personnel, and thus to use the MP to soften up the prisoners, to break them, so they would cooperate more with MI.[109] He was reported to have said that the

Interrogator is Convicted of Negligent Homicide in 2003 Death of Iraqi General," *New York Times*, January 23, 2006, p. A 17. Regarding questions about the CIA in Iraq see Jaffer and Singh, *The Administration of Torture*, p. 34. Also Parry, *Understanding Torture*.

105 Douglas Jehl and Eric Schmitt, "Afghan Policies on Questioning Taken to Iraq," *New York Times*, May 21, 2004, p. A 1.

106 John Barry, Michael Hirsch, and Michael Isikoff, "The Roots of Torture," *Newsweek*, May 24, 2005, www.msnbc.msn.com/id/4989422. Also Hersh, "The Gray Zone."

107 Parry, *Understanding Torture*, pp. 190–191.

108 See the excellent and detailed summary of events at www.historycommons.org/entity.jsp?entity=thomas_m._pappas.

109 The "Taguba" report (annex B) focused on the role of the MP in the abuses at Abu Ghraib. According to James Ross of Human Rights Watch, that report was the most analytical of all the military reports. See Ross, "Black Letter Abuse: The

Iraqi prisoners should be treated like dogs.[110] Col. Pappas testified under oath that Miller recommended to Sanchez that dogs be used to terrify prisoners.[111] Once again Wood issued vague and conflicting instructions: "Geneva" applied, but stress positions and dogs were allowed, if approved by Sanchez. Tight oversight did not follow.

Sanchez, following Miller's advice, eventually put Col. Pappas in overall *de facto* command of Abu Ghraib. Pappas was MI. While various rules existed on paper, a permissive attitude pervaded Abu Ghraib: get actionable intelligence to rein in the insurgency and keep American soldiers safe. There were, of course, no academic debates about a "ticking time bomb" threatening homeland security, or how to define a supreme emergency. Particularly after Miller's visit to Iraq, a climate of abuse existed at Abu Ghraib, as an Army report (the "Taguba" report) said.[112]

Such was the situation that in October the ICRC suspended its prison visits in protest and filed special, if discreet, reports with the US authorities. Supposedly some ameliorating changes began to occur, although in later testimony in the US Congress various military officials professed ignorance about the ICRC reports. As already noted, key military officers at Abu Ghraib discounted ICRC reports;[113] Red Cross

US Legal Response to Torture since 9/11," *International Review of the Red Cross*, no. 89 (September 2007), pp. 561–590. See also Hersh, "The Gray Zone." Gen. Taguba later said that US officials were responsible for war crimes in Iraq. Warren P. Strobel, "General who Probed Abu Ghraib Says Bush Officials Committed War Crimes," McClatchy Newspapers, Yahoo.News, June 18, 2008, www.mcclatchydc.com/2008/06/18v-print/41514.

110 On Miller's visit to Iraq, see especially the web site History Commons, which compiled information from official and unofficial sources, for example at www.historycommons.org/entity.jsp?entity=Thomas_m._pappas. Another good source for cumulative information is SourceWatch, as at www.sourcewatch.org/index.php?title=Thomas_M._Pappas. Janis Karpinski is the source for Miller's comment about treating Iraqi prisoners like dogs; *One Woman's Army: The Commanding General of Abu Ghraib Tells her Story* (New York: Miramax Books, 2005).

111 UPI, "Report: General Urged Dogs for Abu Ghraib," *Washington Times*, May 26, 2004, www.washingtontimes.com/upi-breaking/20040526-071342-5775r.htm. The Miller report is noted in annex B.

112 Antonio Taguba, "Article 15–6 Investigation of the 800th Military Police Brigade," March 2004. See also Seymour M. Hersh, "Torture At Abu Ghraib," *The New Yorker*, May 10, 2004, discussing that report, www.newyorker.com/printable/?fact/040410fa_fact. The report is noted in annex B.

113 Gourevitch and Morris, *Standard Operating Procedure*, pp. 170–171. This evidence is very damaging to the ICRC assertion that adequate progress was being made in humanitarian affairs and thus that it should not publicly blow the whistle on US behavior.

delegates on the scene wanted a public protest but the Geneva headquarters overruled.[114] Since the ICRC is not a fully transparent organization, especially regarding high-level policy making, we do not know why. Despite ICRC efforts, the abuse at Abu Ghraib continued into late 2003 and 2004.[115] It is reasonably clear that abuse of detainees in Iraq declined after the Abu Ghraib photos entered the public domain in Spring 2004, and after Congress passed the DTA in 2005. But before all that, ameliorative steps, especially from ICRC actions, are hard to see. James Schlesinger, no great admirer of the ICRC, said that the organization's confidential report of November 2003 should have led to US changes, but it did not.[116]

What was it like at Abu Ghraib? According to an MP who did as MI asked at Abu Ghraib: "You had stress positions, and you escalated the stress positions. Forced to stand for hours at a time. Stand on a box. Hold a box out straight. Hold bottles of water out to your sides. Do the electric chair, put your back to the wall, and bend your knees ninety degrees to hold yourself. Handcuffs behind their backs, high up, in very uncomfortable positions, or chained down ... Then you had the submersion. You put the people in garbage cans, and you'd put ice in it, and water. Or stick them underneath the shower spigot naked, and open a window while it was like forty degrees outside, and watch them disappear into themselves before they go into shock ... It was Gitmo from the get-go ... I didn't invent any of these things. They were presented to us. I didn't jump out of the bed in the morning saying, 'Hey, I want to go

[114] Farnaz Fassihi and Steve Stecklow, "US Abuse in Iraq Left Red Cross Team in a Quandary," *Wall Street Journal*, May 21, 2004.

[115] According to ICRC doctrine, discretion is not absolute but is contingent on the detaining authority making (unspecified) humanitarian progress over (unspecified) time in correcting any problems. Absent that progress in the wake of discreet diplomacy, if the ICRC judges public criticism to aid the prisoners, its doctrine allows it to go public. Then-Secretary of State Colin Powell said that in the Fall of 2003 ICRC views were discussed at high levels in the Bush Administration and "some corrective action was taken with respect to those concerns." Peter Yost, AP, "Abuse Scandal Focuses on Bush Foundation," *Anchorage Daily News*, May 16, 2004, www.adn.com/24hour/front/v-printer/story/1361275[-8692956c.html. A Swiss journal, *L'Hebdo*, often with good contacts inside the ICRC, reported that some humanitarian progress in 2003–2004 was occurring in the south at Umm Qasr, but not at Abu Ghraib; May 27, 2004.

[116] PBS NewsHour, August 24, 2004, transcript online at www.pbs.org/newshour/bb/military/july-dec04/abuughraib_8-24.html.

smack up a detainee,' or, 'Hey I want to throw ice on people,' or, 'I want to play loud music.' Who would have thought of something like that?"[117]

When one reviews the abusive interrogation of al-Qahtani at Gitmo, his being made to act like a dog and wear female underwear, plus all the stress techniques, and then one sees the photos of Abu Ghraib, the stress techniques, the prisoners being led around on a dog leash, the forced wearing of female underwear, etc., it is perfectly clear that abusive interrogation "migrated" as the Schlesinger report stated. Whether facilitated formally by the likes of Miller and Wood, or moving horizontally by word of mouth, they migrated. Rumsfeld and Sanchez and others wanted actionable intelligence to suppress the insurgency. And so the abusive techniques migrated. Lip service to "Geneva" in Iraq made absolutely no difference. The CIA, with its authorized abuse, was active at Bagram, at Gitmo, and in Abu Ghraib, among other places. Oversight of military interrogation, to ensure it was different from the CIA's, was largely absent.

Even after unauthorized photos of the Abu Ghraib abuses became public in the Spring of 2004, the "ghosting" of some prisoners continued at various places. Art. 5 of Geneva Convention IV (pertaining to civilians in international armed conflict and occupied territory), says that "a person under definite suspicion of activity hostile to the security of the Occupying Power shall . . . be regarded has having forfeited rights of communication under the present Convention." Detainees are to be "treated with humanity," and they are to be granted full rights under the Convention "at the earliest date consistent with the security of the State or Occupying Power . . ." The ICRC has negotiated this time with Israel concerning its interrogation of various Arab detainees (fourteen days, at one historical juncture, and Gen. Petraeus adopted the fourteen-day rule later in Afghanistan, as already noted).

The ICRC might believe that all of this subject matter is now regulated by API as customary international law, and that restrictions on ICRC visits and detainee communications with family now pertain only to spies. API, Art. 45(3) reads: "Any person who has taken part in hostilities, who is not entitled to prisoner-of-war status and who does not benefit from more favourable treatment in accordance with the Fourth Convention shall have the right at all times to the Protection of

[117] Gourevitch and Morris, *Standard Operating Procedure*, pp. 101–102.

Article 75 of this Protocol. In occupied territory, any such person, unless he is held as a spy, shall also be entitled, notwithstanding Article 5 of the Fourth Convention, to his rights of communication under that Convention."[118] But US detaining authorities in Iraq and Afghanistan still trotted out Art. 5 from time to time as justification for blocking ICRC visits to some prisoners, especially since the United States had never ratified API.

The big picture in Iraq was, in a way, reminiscent of Vietnam. "Geneva" was posted on the bulletin boards in Vietnam, but the reality was that the chain of command in the field tolerated much abuse of enemy prisoners in a very nasty war in which "Geneva" was ignored by the other side. And when disturbing pictures emerged of the massacre of unresisting and unarmed persons at My Lai, the response of many commanders, all the way to the top, was to dissemble and contain. The story broke through unauthorized disclosure of photos.[119] In fact, while many high military officials praise the US record of commitment to "Geneva" in Vietnam, evidence piles up regarding US unlawful brutality – brutality that did not immediately trigger a clear and broad recommitment to "Geneva" by particularly the US Army.[120] Over time, however, the Pentagon realized that unlawful behavior in the field created numerous problems and moved to improved training in "Geneva."

Something similar was true in Iraq. There was some general lip service to "Geneva," and some military memos made reference to that body of law. But off the record and especially in the shadows, the word went around that "the gloves were off" and the dominant concern was to get actionable intelligence even if you had to coerce it out of the prisoners. That is precisely why Rumsfeld, after the Abu Ghraib photos surfaced, commissioned numerous military investigations that were carefully constructed to avoid the issue of command responsibility. The various military reports were fragmented and carefully pointed downward. It was a cover-up designed to hold Congress at bay – to pre-empt congressional inquiries, not to deal honestly with the problem. Even Schlesinger, when he was not misrepresenting the ICRC,

[118] The ICRC understands "rights of communication" not only to include its own visits, but prisoner communication with family and others such as lawyers.

[119] See Gourevitch and Morris, *Standard Operating Procedure*, pp. 251–253.

[120] See Deborah Nelson, *The War Behind Me* (New York: Basic Books, 2009), based on Pentagon files that record the US military response to reports of atrocities.

sometimes tried to perpetrate the myth that Abu Ghraib was just "Animal House" (the movie) on the night shift. It was a local and "extracurricular" problem, having nothing to do with higher authority.[121] And yet in early 2004, before the Abu Ghraib photos, the military's own internal documents showed extensive abuse in Iraq, including fatalities, and yet no remedial action had been taken.[122]

The problem went all the way to the top. As far as the military lines were concerned, Rumsfeld, Miller, Wood, Abizaid (Commander of CentCom), Sanchez, Karpinski, etc. were all involved and responsible. Abizaid dissembled in his testimony to Congress in May 2004, asserting that prisoner abuse was not widespread and systematic in Iraq when ample evidence suggested otherwise. Institutionalized responsibility for abuse was documented by particularly the "Taguba" and Schlesinger reports, not to mention by careful media and NGO reporting. It may be recalled that Army reports recommended sanctions for both Carolyn Wood for her role at Bagram and Geoffrey Miller for his role at Guantánamo.

Later a widespread view was that both Sanchez and Karpinski were "in over their heads." Eventually Karpinski was officially criticized and demoted, and Sanchez forced into retirement – presumably so he would not have to testify before Congress.[123] Pappas was fined and demoted,

121 Comments made on the PBS Jim Lehrer NewsHour. Schlesinger's comments were inconsistent. On the one hand he characterized the problems at Abu Ghraib as just some army personnel running amok. On the other hand he said there was institutional responsibility. Furthermore, he claimed that the ICRC, which in his view was nothing more than an accounting agency for prisoners, was trying to be the high priest of humanitarianism and hold the United States to legal norms not accepted by Washington. In fact, US officials had said in print that legal concepts pertaining to prisoners as found in Protocol I to the 1949 Geneva Conventions had become part of customary international law, and thus binding on the United States despite its lack of ratification of that Protocol. See in particular Michael J. Matheson, *American University Journal of International Law and Politics*, 2 (1987), p. 434, as noted in Chapter 3. Other sources on this point were given earlier. Schlesinger, in an op ed piece, strangely found no US policy encouraging abuse of prisoners in Iraq, despite the fact that Miller and Wood and others had been sent to Iraq to create a more abusive prisoner regime. "The Truth About Our Soldiers," *Wall Street Journal*, September 9, 2004, p. A 16. Schlesinger was part of the effort to cover up the responsibility for Abu Ghraib at high levels in Washington.

122 Jaffer and Singh, *The Administration of Torture*, p. 29.

123 See Lt. Gen. Ricardo S. Sanchez, *Wiser In Battle: A Soldier's Story* (New York: Harper, 2008). He conveniently fails to mention his authorization of dogs for interrogation, and of course he never mentions the pressure he put on Pappas to

his military career basically terminated. His assistant, Lt. Col. Steven L. Jordan, answered to a court martial but was not convicted on any charge directly related to abuse.

It is true that detailed rules for interrogation by Rumsfeld, Sanchez, Miller, and Wood, *inter alia*, did not include forced group masturbation, stacking naked bodies on top of each other, simulated oral sex, and some other abuses practiced at Abu Ghraib. Those rules did not call for prisoners to be asphyxiated or suffocated with hoods or beaten to death. But ample studies have documented that many individuals will utilize a position of total control, and lack of clear instructions otherwise, to abuse prisoners when given the chance.

The well-known "Stanford prison experiment," for example, found that college students, playing the role of prison personnel in a simulation, would take advantage of their position of authority to abuse other students playing the role of prisoner. The experiment had to be prematurely terminated to protect the student prisoners.[124] Even though the student guards had been carefully screened to weed out those with evident deviant or violent tendencies, nevertheless, when in a position of total control, they utilized their authority to abuse. Contributing to the student guards' abuse was the fact that early in the process of simulated detention, the student guards had been instructed to humiliate the prisoners by shaving their heads, removing their clothing, and other degrading measures.

In Iraq a number of military personnel exceeded the official guidelines – guidelines that allowed some unlawful abuse to start with. But the context mattered. That context included: mostly confusing and

get actionable intelligence. He furthers the myth that the problems at Abu Ghraib were created by a few bad apples, while glossing over the culture of abuse his command tolerated. Sanchez does note (p. 150) that regarding late 2002 "there is irrefutable evidence that America was torturing and killing prisoners in Afghanistan. It occurred at the coalition's Bagram collection point located at Bagram Air Base, just north of Kabul." Then, inexplicably, he goes on to say nice words about Carolyn Wood, who supervised the torture and killing at Bagram. His basic criticism is of high Bush officials who undercut "Geneva," but he is less than forthcoming about what this meant for Abu Ghraib. He casts himself improbably as on the side of those struggling for more attention to "Geneva," but notes he undercut an ICRC effort to send its reports outside his chain of command to the State Department. His memoir is full of contradictions and unreliable assertions. Like the memoirs of former Chair of the JCS, Richard Myers, after the fact Sanchez wants to paint himself as devoted to the laws of war. Many facts are otherwise, in both cases.

124 See www.prisonexp.org.

unclear guidelines, systematic lack of proper supervision, often lack of proper response to cases of abuse that were reported, sometimes intrusion of CIA officials hiding and abusing prisoners, and general informal tolerance of a harsh quest for actionable intelligence. It is worth recalling that the Schmidt report found fault with Gen. Miller at Gitmo for not assuring that the harsh interrogation rules remained short of torture and inhuman treatment. Little wonder, then, that conditions turned out worse at Abu Ghraib given the chaos of the insurgency in Iraq.

Prosecutions for events related to Abu Ghraib also reminded one of Vietnam. Regarding Iraq, only lower enlisted personnel were charged (with the exception of Lt. Col. Jordan, who was acquitted of abuse charges). This was similar to My Lai in that only Lt. Calley (convicted but freed early) and Capt. Medina (never brought to trial) were charged for the killing of not less than 300 unresisting Asian civilians. (The actual death toll was probably higher.) At the eleven trials related to Abu Ghraib, the presiding military officer always excluded evidence suggesting systematic factors related to higher command.[125] The poisoned atmosphere at Abu Ghraib noted in one Army report (the Fay–Jones report) was excluded from trial evidence. Other reports documenting extensive abuse in Iraq, Afghanistan, and Guantánamo were excluded from trial evidence.

These trials played along with the fiction, established at high levels in Washington, that Abu Ghraib was the result of a few bad applies. Interestingly, none of those convicted in the courts martial had manifested a record of misbehavior in army life prior to Abu Ghraib. They may have been weak and exploitative in the abusively permissive system that was Abu Ghraib, but their overall military records were not troublesome or indicative of "bad apples." As the "Stanford prison experiment" makes clear, context could be expected to make a difference. The general context at Abu Ghraib was established and permitted by US senior officials, both civilian and military. It can be recalled that the publication *The Army Times*, which often reflects rank-and-file and traditional Army views, opined in May 2004 that the responsibility for Abu Ghraib went all the way to the top, and that Rumsfeld should resign.[126]

[125] S. G. Mestrovic, *The Trials of Abu Ghraib: An Expert Witness Account of Shame and Honor* (Boulder: Paradigm, 2007).

[126] CNN, "Army Times Calls for Rumsfeld's Departure," posted at cnn.com, November 6, 2006, www.cnn.com/2006/POLITICS/11/03/rumsfeld.resign/.

The few persons legally punished or administratively sanctioned for abusing prisoners were largely scapegoated in the sense that the most senior military and civilian officials who manifested some responsibility avoided accountability. For example, for abuse at Abu Ghraib the MP Cpl. Charles Granger got ten years' imprisonment for his role. But Capt. Christopher Brinson, who filed reports indicating Granger was doing a fine job, went unsanctioned and eventually became an aide to Rep. Mike Rogers, (R, AL).[127] Marc Warren, Sanchez's legal advisor at Abu Ghraib, who had discounted ICRC reports, was promoted. So was Maj. Gen. Walter Wodjakowski, also one of the officers responsible for that prison.[128] So was Barbara Fast, in charge of intelligence in Baghdad. We have already noted the advancement of Carolyn Wood and the medal given to Maj. Gen. Miller, both with responsibility for some of the abuse at Abu Ghraib. Sanchez, on the other hand, was denied a promotion and forced into retirement. So the Pentagon's response to prisoner abuse was anything but clear, systematic, and principled.

Nevertheless, the photos, but as best we can tell not the ICRC reports, made a difference over time. The Pentagon created a new Office of Detainee Affairs, and several officials from that office and elsewhere moved to rein in abuses.[129] Coercive interrogation by US special forces in Iraq were also reined in.[130] The situation did improve from 2005 to 2006.[131] "Overall, about 800 investigations of alleged detainee mistreatment in Iraq and Afghanistan have led to action against more than 250 service personnel, including 89 convicted at courts martial, US diplomats told the United Nations in May [2006]."[132]

127 "Talk of the Town: Comment – Interrogating Torture," *The New Yorker*, May 11, 2009, p. 33.

128 Eric Schmitt, "Army Moves to Advance 2 Linked to Abu Ghraib," *New York Times*, June 25, 2005, p. A 19.

129 Eric Schmitt, "Pentagon Officials are Hurrying to Correct Conditions in Iraqi Prisons," *New York Times*, September 9, 2004, p. A 14.

130 Mark Bowden, "How to Break a Terrorist: The Ploy," *The Atlantic*, May 2006, starting at p. 54. Abu Musab al-Zarqawi, the Jordanian who was the leader of Al-Qaeda in Iraq, was located and killed via clever and humane interrogation.

131 For an overview see Tom Farer, *Confronting Global Terrorism and American Neo-Conservatism: The Framework of a Liberal Grand Strategy* (New York: Oxford University Press, 2008).

132 Patrick Quinn, AP, "US War Prisons Legal Vacuum for 14,000," Yahoo. News, September 17, 2006, http://news.yahoo.com/s/ap/20060917/ap?on_re_mi_ea/in_american_hands.

Conclusion

When the Bush Administration threw away "Geneva," clearly for Taliban and Al-Qaeda personnel and for all at Guantánamo, and effectively did the same in Iraq, problems were bound to arise. When the Bush team then issued various and shifting lists of abusive interrogation techniques in the original hope they would be clear and compelling and fall short of torture, they embarked on a course that in the field led to torture and other major forms of cruelty. This was certainly true in the violent conditions of Afghanistan (Bagram) and Iraq (Abu Ghraib). Compounding the problem was that poorly trained reservists were sometimes put in charge of maintaining order in some prisons, then told effectively to soften up the prisoners.

Even at a controlled site like Gitmo the process did not lead to neat and tidy minor coercion, but to torture and situations that were tantamount to torture from the Winter of 2002–2003 until about 2005. The process spun completely out of control at Abu Ghraib. Given the large US military structure, a certain percentage of the military could be counted on to run amok in the absence of clear restraints and proper oversight. Some of these soldiers might be good killers in combat, but they were not the ones a professional and honorable military would rationally put in charge of detention and interrogation.

But the more general problem rested with commanders, both civilian and military. They threw away, intentionally in most cases, the clear rules of the 1992 Army field manual based on "Geneva" (the manual was revised in 2006 with an even stronger emphasis on IHL) and put in place a system of abuse which in the minds of top officials would fall short of torture. But it did not play out that way.

One doubts that the "actionable intelligence" gained from this abusive process of military interrogation offset the damage done to the US position at home and abroad. One wonders how many "terrorists" were motivated to violent action by what happened to them in US military prisons. One wonders how many "terrorists" and "insurgents" were motivated to violent action by their knowledge of particularly Bagram, Guantánamo, and Abu Ghraib.

There is considerable evidence that all of the US abuse might have done more harm than good. Several security sources indicated that US detention policies had inflamed a number of the armed parties on the other side. Despite abusive interrogation, the situation continued to deteriorate in Iraq until changes were made in many US policies. There is scant evidence that torture and CID played any significant role in the increased stability in Iraq from 2007 to the reduced US military role by 2009.[133] For example, the capture of Saddam did not result from abusive but rather humane interrogation. The same general pattern is true for Afghanistan as well. Widespread abuse of prisoners during 2001–2005 did not prevent that situation from deteriorating, especially after the Bush team prioritized Iraq. The central point here is that abusive interrogation did not produce major military and political gains anywhere it was employed by the military. Rather, it cost the United States much in political and security terms.

It was strange that the Bush Administration had such a tin ear about its own military abuse, and yet it repeatedly advised the Iraqis not to abuse prisoners but to work for humane detention and interrogation in the interests of broader political goals.[134]

The Bush Administration took a harsh and negative approach to detention and interrogation after 9/11, not on the basis of careful study but on the basis of intuition, if not panic. While particularly Cheney and Tenet trumpeted its success, other Americans from John McCain to General David Petraeus, the latter implementing a return to humane interrogation in Iraq from 2006, thought differently. Most of the evidence concerning the military was that, indeed, when one did a cost-benefits analysis, torture and other mistreatment of prisoners was not a panacea for US national security.

[133] It is not clear if the same two-track approach transpired in Iraq as in Vietnam, with official endorsement of "Geneva" but brutal methods in the shadows. In Vietnam, as noted in Chapter 1, there were US military limitations on interrogation based on "Geneva" at the same time that the Phoenix program of torture and murder went forward. In Iraq from 2007, while Gen. Petraeus emphasized "Geneva," Gen. Stanley McChrystal and his special forces may have used brutal interrogations. See the *New York Times* editorial, "Questions for General McChrystal," June 1, 2009, www.nytimes.com/2009/06/01/opinion/01mon2.html. In his congressional testimony of June 2, 2009, which featured soft questions on the issue, McChrystal distanced himself from harsh interrogation in Iraq and promised great attention to proper detainee treatment in Afghanistan.

[134] Eric Schmitt and Thom Shaker, "US Refuses to Give Iraq Control over Detainees," *International Herald Tribune*, December 25, 2005, www.iht.com/bin/print_ipub.php?file=/articles/2005/12/25/news/detain.php. Also John F. Burns, "To Halt Abuses, US Will Inspect Jails Run by Iraq," *New York Times*, December 14, 2005, www.nytimes.com/2005/12/14/international/middleeast/14abuse.html.

5 *The CIA: kidnapping, Black Sites, extraordinary rendition*

The ICRC ... has been informed ... that the objective of the CIA detention program was ... directed by President Bush. Currently ... both the interrogation plan and specific use of techniques must be approved by the Director or Deputy Director of the CIA.

(ICRC Report on the Treatment of Fourteen "High Value Detainees" in CIA Custody, February 2007, p. 38)

In parallel to the US military and sometimes intersecting with it, the CIA ran operations to seize persons who were suspected of hostile actions against the United States (or arranged for local authorities to seize them). Here we are talking first of all about state kidnapping in that persons are seized rather than arrested: they are held without due process of law and in denial of the internationally recognized right to be recognized as a person under law.[1] Held incommunicado (and without ICRC visits), they are either detained in Agency secret places (including parts of US military prisons and US military vessels), or they are transferred to states known for forced disappearances and torture. There would be no point to such a policy of forced disappearances except for abusive interrogation. Key to CIA doctrine on interrogation, as we noted in Chapter 1, is isolation and humiliation, total control, and abuse, as recorded in the Kubark manual and other documents.

A detaining authority that pays due respect to the 1949 Geneva Conventions and the 1984 UN Convention against Torture, among other international norms, and its own laws derived therefrom, creates

[1] Supporting more general provisions in international human rights law, the UN General Assembly adopted the Convention against Forced Disappearances on December 20, 2006. The Rome Diplomatic Conference that created the International Criminal Court (ICC) in 1998, in approving the Statute creating that criminal court, noted that forced disappearances could in some circumstances constitute a crime against humanity.

no policy space for kidnapping and "ghost detainees." One of the first things that the ICRC tries to do in armed conflict and other situations of violence is to register detainees so that they cannot be disappeared. The Torture Convention, to which the United States is a party, prohibits the transfer of persons to a state where there is a likelihood of torture, and often the first step toward torture is to engage in enforced disappearance.

Kidnapping

The United States has long practiced what might be called "rendition to justice." On occasion US agents or bounty hunters working for Washington will seize persons abroad who are wanted for crimes in the United States and "render" them for legal justice in the United States. US courts have adopted the Ker doctrine under which they will not inquire into the process by which a defendant appears before them. The practice has been upheld even in cases in which there is an extradition treaty between the United States and another state, but in which a US snatch operation transpires anyway.[2] Other states have operated in similar fashion, with France seizing "Carlos the Jackal" in Sudan and Israel seizing Adolf Eichmann in Argentina in roughly analogous ways. Israel apologized for the violation of Argentine sovereignty involved in the seizure of Eichmann, then proceeded to try, convict, and execute him. In this practice, illegal action (impermissible intervention in the domestic affairs of another state) does not preclude national legal proceedings. In some situations the kidnapping occurs with the consent of the local authorities.

Extraordinary rendition is different. Apparently practiced by the Clinton Administration on a small scale, perhaps to render to legal justice in other countries, it involves the seizure of a person and transfer abroad to avoid normal US legal protections.[3] According to Human

[2] See the Alvarez-Machain case: *U.S.* v. *Alvarez-Machain* 504 US 055.

[3] Among many sources see Michael Scheuer, "A Fine Rendition," *New York Times*, March 11, 2005, p. A 23, who defends the program – in part because he ran it for the CIA for forty months. On the other hand, former Secretary of Defense Melvin Laird criticized renditions leading to torture, and other forms of US abuse, for putting the country "on a slippery slope toward the inhumanity that we deplore." As quoted by David Broder, "Powerful Words on Iraq, Vietnam," reprinted in the *Lincoln Journal Star*, October 16, 2005, p. F-4. The argument that the United States obtained "diplomatic assurances" that rendered persons would not be

Rights Watch, even before 9/11 a number of countries were seizing persons and sending them to Egypt, known for its torture and mistreatment, to be interrogated.[4] As practiced by the Bush Administration, while some type of legal or quasi-legal proceeding might eventually obtain (as, for example, in Military Commissions), the primary purpose of the operation is not to render to justice but to obtain actionable intelligence by means that are legally controversial if not clearly prohibited. Given that kidnapped persons are often abused, the detaining authority is not really interested in normal legal justice subsequent to seizure. One of the well-founded criticisms about Bush policies of abuse is that it inherently complicates the prospects of proper legal justice for the perpetrators of 9/11 and other attacks on US persons and properties.[5] (More on this in Chapter 6.)

After 9/11 the seizure and secret transport of persons by the CIA was reasonably well documented by enterprising journalists and human rights NGOs. The CIA, working with a Navy office in the Pentagon, and using private corporations for flight services, moved these persons from the point of seizure to other locales – sometimes foreign prisons, sometimes CIA prisons, and sometimes US military prisons.[6] Often there was a dizzying mix of routes and locales. According to various human rights organizations, journalists, and the ICRC, some of these detainees are unaccounted for at the time of writing. Somewhere in the range of one hundred persons, as noted below, seem to have been held by the CIA in secret, but not eventually transferred to Guantánamo or acknowledged to be in other US military prisons. Their numbers and fates remain unknown at the time of writing.[7]

tortured has been subjected to careful comparative study, with the conclusion being that Canadian and European use of diplomatic assurances in transfers has been much more rigorous, with tighter court oversight, than in the United States. See Ashley Deeks, "Promises Not to Torture: Diplomatic Assurances in US Courts," American Society of International Law Discussion Paper, December 2008, www.asil.org/files/ASIL-08-DiscussionPaper.pdg.

4 Human Rights Watch, "Black Hole: The Fate of Islamists Rendered to Egypt," May 10, 2005. Also David Johnston, "Terror Suspects Sent to Egypt by the Dozens, Panel Reports," *New York Times*, May 12, 2005, p. A 4.

5 See, e.g., Mark Danner, "The Red Cross Torture Report: What It Means," *The New York Review of Books*, 56/7 (April 30, 2009), p. 14.

6 Seth Hettena, AP, "Navy Office Contracted Planes used in 'Renditions,'" *Lincoln Journal Star*, September 25, 2005, p. A-3.

7 Jane Mayer, "Ten Unsolved Mysteries in the 'War on Terror,'" *The New Yorker*, December 16, 2009, www.newyorker.com/online/blogs/newsdesk/2009/12/unsolved-mysteries. Michael Isikoff and Mark Hosenball, "The Disappeared:

Because of the CIA practice of using private aircraft, even if coordinated through a Pentagon office, law suits have been filed against Boeing and other aircraft corporations that provided the planes through their subsidiaries. Plaintiffs have tried to use the US Alien Tort Claims Statute, under which foreign individuals may use US courts to file a claim against private actors for torts, or wrongful damage, that stems from a violation of "the law of nations." Hence, in a civil action, private plaintiffs have tried to sue private defendants, namely US corporations, for damages stemming from torture. The ultimate outcome of this legal challenge is not yet clear.

At the time of writing, US district and appellate courts, at the request of the Obama Administration, had used the "state secrets doctrine" to dismiss the charges against Jeppesen Dataplan, a subsidiary of Boeing, brought by Binyam Mohamed and other former detainees held by the United States and who allege they were tortured.[8] The state secrets doctrine was created by the courts in 1953 to avoid ruling on legal issues that might involve disclosure of sensitive national security information. In that 1953 case the doctrine was used to cover up negligence by the US Air Force in the crash of a military plane, rather than to protect genuine sensitive information vital to national security. The doctrine remains controversial precisely because of its potential to be used to protect governmental wrong doing. Nevertheless, in the case of Jeppesen Dataplan, even though corporation executives referred to their role as running torture flights, the courts refused to adjudicate whether illegal action had been inflicted on the plaintiffs because of their treatment by US and Moroccan officials as facilitated by the American corporation. American NGOs like the American Civil Liberties Union

What Happened to Terror Suspects Washington Turned Over to Foreign Governments?," *Newsweek*, April 8, 2009, www.newsweek.com/id/193107.

8 *Mohamed et al.* v. *Jeppesen Dataplan*, US Court of Appeals for the 9th Circuit, en banc, filed September 8, 2010, opinion no. 08–15693 ("en banc" means that a case is so important that the judicial panel consists of the entire group of judges comprising the court whereas usually a case on appeal will be assigned to just three judges). For background see Charlie Savage, "Court Allows Civil Torture Case to Proceed," *New York Times*, April 29, 2009, www.nytimes.com/2009/04/29/us/29secrets.html. For an overview see Daphne Eviatar, "Appeals Court Reinstates Torture Case Previously Dismissed on 'State Secrets' Grounds," *The Washington Independent*, April 28, 2009, http://washingtonindependent.com/40873/appeals-court-reinstates. For a *New York Times* editorial lamenting the split Appellate decision, see "Shady Secrets," September 29, 2010, www.nytimes.com/2010/09/30/opinion/30thul.html.

(ACLU) and the Center for Constitutional Rights, which had worked with the plaintiffs, were bitterly disappointed. Unless the US Supreme Court decided to take up the case, national legal review of the alleged kidnapping and torture seemed to be at an end.

The persons targeted for US kidnapping may have been seized in Afghanistan or Pakistan, or in the Balkans or Italy, or in the Middle East or Africa or Asia. The range of US snatch operations has been very wide, including Djibouti, Thailand, Indonesia, and Dubai. The persons may have been transported through Ireland, or the United Kingdom, or Germany, or Poland or Romania or Latvia, or Thailand, or the island of Diego Garcia (British), or some other place. East Africa became the scene of increased seizures and transport as US attention refocused on the failed state of Somalia and the presence of Muslim extremists in that area.

Many countries have cooperated with the United States in this practice. The Council of Europe (CoE) launched a probe into the role of European states in extraordinary rendition, disappeared persons, and secret prisons on European territory. Given that European and US security managers were not forthcoming in replies to this CoE investigation, the resulting report was built on circumstantial evidence rather than official documents and testimony. The report concluded that there was probable European violation of European and global human rights standards, with Poland and Romania being prime suspects for hosting CIA detention and interrogation facilities.[9] Later, Lithuania was added to this list. Certainly the security managers of these nations knew what was transpiring. It is a more complex question to ask what high governmental officials definitely knew and how one proves that knowledge (given that authorization and information may pass orally, or with a wink and a nod, or by unrecorded phone conversations). Press accounts reported that political leaders in Lithuania were unaware that their

[9] Report, Committee on Legal Affairs and Human Rights, Parliamentary Assembly, Council of Europe, Doc. 11302 rev., "Secret Detentions and Illegal Transfers of Detainees Involving Council of Europe Member States: Second Report," June 11, 2007. See also Amnesty International, "State of Denial: Europe's Role in Rendition and Secret Detention," 2008, AI web site. According to one web source, twenty-eight states were involved in US kidnapping, secret detention, and renditions. Sherwood Ross, "28 Countries Helped US Detain War on Terror Suspects," *Antemedius*, March 30, 21010, www.antemedius.com/print/content/28-countries.

security officials cooperated with US secret interrogation policies.[10] It was not unheard of for foreign courts and/or parliaments to criticize US extraordinary renditions that were quietly facilitated by the security services of the state in question. One could document some US officials saying that allies were objecting to Bush's detention policies, yet at the same time many were quite complicit in those policies. It was not entirely clear which allies were supportive and which were critical, given the public posturing on the subject.[11]

US kidnapping, and complicity in this practice by many strategic partners, some of them also liberal democracies, is not really open to question. The United States has thus engaged in the policy of forced disappearances, prohibited by international law. It was a policy loudly condemned by Washington when practiced by South American authoritarians in the 1970s and 1980s, particularly in Pinochet's Chile and the junta's Argentina.[12] Whatever the Clinton record and that of the Reagan Administration, the George W. Bush Administration adopted state kidnapping and secret detention on a broad scale after 9/11. According to one source, the CIA seized more than 3,000 persons in the first year after 9/11, releasing many of them relatively quickly.[13] According to Bush's last CIA Director, Michael Hayden, between 2002 and 2006 the CIA secretly detained 100 persons for varying lengths of time, subjecting about thirty or so to "enhanced interrogation techniques."[14] Since only about eighteen CIA "HVDs" have been formally accounted for, questions continue regarding the whereabouts of the others, as noted above.

The British government of Tony Blair was arguably the closest ally of the George W. Bush Administration. Blair was a crucial partner in the

[10] Clifford J. Levy, "US Put Jails in Lithuania, Premier Says," *New York Times*, December 23, 2009, www.nytimes.com/2009/12/23/world/europe/23lithuania.html.

[11] For example, many CIA flights went through the Shannon airport, yet at one point the then-Irish Prime Minister, Bertie Ahern, joined the European public cry for closing Guantánamo. Polish leaders repeatedly denied the presence of CIA secret facilities on Polish soil, but the CoE believed differently, and strong circumstantial evidence suggested otherwise.

[12] See further Rebecca Evans, "South American Southern Cone: National Security State, 1970s and 1980s," in David P. Forsythe, ed., *Encyclopedia of Human Rights* (New York: Oxford University Press, 2009).

[13] Tim Weiner, *Legacy of Ashes: The History of the CIA* (New York: Doubleday, 2007), p. 485.

[14] Joby Warrick, "Senate Panel to Examine CIA Detainee Handling," *Washington Post*, February 27, 2009, www.washingtonpost.com/wp-dyn/content/article/2009/10/26/AR2009022603282.

2003 invasion of Iraq, and there is considerable evidence that his government supported Bush's harsh policies pertaining to detention and interrogation. According to a British parliamentary report in 2007, British security managers only began to distance themselves in 2003–2004 from US extraordinary rendition that led to torture in foreign countries.[15] It is likely that from 2001 to 2003–2004, British representatives were involved in abusive interrogation in places like Afghanistan and elsewhere, at a minimum in posing questions for US personnel to pursue in abusive interrogation of detainees with British connections.[16] In 2004 a British diplomat, Craig Murray, criticized the British record of complicity regarding US-sponsored torture in Uzbekistan, as noted on p. 99.[17] British representatives were often present at Guantánamo and other US detention centers. So there is growing evidence that British security managers were not squeamish for a time about US abuse of detainees after 9/11. Moreover, their own interrogations in Northern Ireland and elsewhere had not shown great respect for prisoner rights, as noted in Chapter 1. As will be noted in Chapter 7, a new government in Britain in 2010 promised an investigation into the British record on torture after 9/11. We have already noted the decision of the British government to agree an out-of-court settlement with several ex-Gitmo detainees who charged British complicity in torture. The settlement left open the question of whether the government was trying to avoid embarrassing information about its role in US interrogations.

CIA Black Sites

In the Fall of 2005, Dana Priest of the *Washington Post* broke the story of a system of secret CIA detention centers abroad.[18] President Bush

[15] www.cabinetoffice.gov.uk/intelligence. And see Raymond Bonner and Jane Perlez, "British Report Criticizes US Treatment of Terror Suspects," *New York Times*, July 28, 2007, p. A 5.

[16] See for example, Moazzam Begg, *Enemy Combatant: My Imprisonment at Guantánamo, Bagram, and Kandahar* (New York: The New Press, 2006). At the time of writing, British authorities had promised to release information, under a court order, regarding the British role in the treatment of Binyam Mohamed, another detainee claiming British complicity in his torture.

[17] Don Van Natta, Jr., "U.S. Recruits a Rough Ally to Be a Jailer," *New York Times*, May 1, 2005, pp. A 1, A 12, which supplements Murray's books cited earlier.

[18] Dana Priest, "CIA Holds Terror Suspects in Secret Prisons," *Washington Post*, November 2, 2005, www.msnbc.msn.com/id/9890829.

finally confirmed the veracity of her reporting when in September 2006 he acknowledged the transfer of fourteen HVDs from these Black Sites to Guantánamo. Later, other HVDs were transferred. Hayden said in 2007 that of about 100 persons who had passed through the CIA system, three had been subjected to waterboarding.[19] Despite a Court order otherwise, the CIA destroyed videotapes of some of this torture and other abuse. Reportedly Porter Goss, then head of the Agency, agreed with the destruction. Apparently the dominant view by those who took the action was that it was better to destroy the tapes than have the public and Congress eventually see official action that "shocked the conscience" and thus violated the Constitution (as well as international law).[20] The Bush Administration asserted in 2006 that no other prisoners were then being held in Black Sites, but it reserved the right to reactivate the practice as needed. Distinct CIA prisoners can be distinguished from "ghost detainees" in CIA sections of military resources – including ships. The ICRC has reported its concerns about the fate of certain disappeared persons who have not resurfaced and whose fate is unknown to the organization. Earlier the ICRC had "deplored" its lack of access to secret US prisons."[21]

With the capture of supposedly top Al-Qaeda operatives from the Spring of 2002, the question of CIA secret detention and interrogation demanded high-level attention. The reasons for relying on the CIA in this role have yet to be officially explained. It has been asserted that Tenet got Bush to give the HVDs to the CIA mainly to circumvent the FBI approach that was relatively careful about abuse because of having an eye on criminal justice at the end of the process. Reportedly Rumsfeld agreed to the CIA role, not wanting the DOD to be the world's jailer, although Guantánamo had already been selected to hold, in one hyperbolic description, the "worst of the worst."[22] It was not at all clear why both the CIA and the Pentagon should have been in the business of

19 Michael Hayden, in the *Washington Post*, November 2, 2005, at n. 14.

20 Among many sources see the AP report by Matt Apuzzo and Adam Goldman, "Destruction of Videotapes Documented in CIA e-mail," Yahoo.News, April 16, 2010, http://news.yahoo.com/s/ap/20100416/ap_on_pr_wh/us_cia_videotapes. Supposedly the tapes showed CIA abuse that went beyond approved guidelines, as indicated by a later CIA report, the 2004 Helgerson report.

21 ICRC Press release no. 06/43, 12 May 2006.

22 Michael Isikoff and David Corn, *Hubris: The Inside Story of Spin, Scandal, and the Selling of the Iraq War* (New York: Crown, 2006), p. 121.

secret, abusive interrogation of supposedly important enemies. But then much US policy in this realm was not based on carefully considered judgments as compared to personal intuitions and gut reflexes.

The CIA had little experience in managing prisons, or for that matter in directly interrogating foreign-speaking prisoners after the Cold War. (Yet in the early stages of the US military operation in Afghanistan in the Fall of 2001, it was CIA agents, not military officers, who went to a makeshift prison run by the Northern Alliance to interrogate detainees at Qala-i-Jangi near Mazar-e-Sharif.[23]) In a damning comment, the then-CIA number three, A. B. Krongard, told a reporter that the Agency not only had to create an interrogation program "from scratch," but also that it consulted with Egypt, Israel, and Saudi Arabia, all known for their abuse of detainees, regarding what to do after 9/11.[24] More than five years after 9/11, the CIA still did not have an extensive training program in interrogation.[25] According to the US Science Intelligence Board (SIB), the CIA has never made a careful comparison of the effectiveness of abusive versus non-abusive interrogation techniques.[26] And there were always those in the US security community, or close to it, that opposed a role for the CIA in detention and interrogation, believing – correctly as it turned out – that the matter was a hornet's nest sure to eventually greatly complicate the life of the Agency.[27]

For whatever reasons, a dual system emerged, with both the military and the CIA in the business of detention and abusive interrogation in the so-called GWOT. Institutional lines were blurred. In Afghanistan, sometimes CIA and military special operations personnel acted together regarding prisoners. We have already noted (p. 84) that some trainers in

23 Richard B. Myers, with Malcolm McConnell, *Eyes on the Horizon: Serving on the Front Lines of National Security* (New York: Threshold Editions, for Simon & Schuster, 2009), p. 198.

24 Scott Shane and Mark Mazzetti, "Advisers Fault Harsh Methods in Interrogation," *New York Times*, May 30, 2007, http://select.nytimes.com/search/restricted/article?res=F60B11F83F540C638FddAC0894. The CIA Inspector General, John Helgerson, confirmed in his report on CIA secret interrogations after 9/11 that the Agency was unprepared to directly manage interrogations. A heavily edited version of the Helgerson report is available on the internet at various web pages, such as that of the London *Times* or the ACLU. See annex B.

25 Shane and Mazzetti, "Advisers." 26 *Ibid.*

27 See further Robert Baer, "The CIA and Interrogations: A Bad Fit from the Start," *Time*, August 8, 2009, www.time.com/time/printout/0,8816,191406,00.html.

the SERE program advised or taught both CIA and military personnel. James Mitchell and Bruce Jessen, former military persons with SERE experience, formed their own consulting company, contracted with the CIA, and helped devise the abusive interrogation schemes in the Black Sites. They had conducted no interrogations prior to that of Abu Zubaydah, an early CIA prisoner presumed to be a HVD, and were not experts on the Arab–Islamic world, but parlayed their SERE experience into a multi-million-dollar consulting enterprise with the government and corporations.[28] This consulting company was fired by CIA Director Leon Panetta of the Obama Administration, and in general that Administration seemed more skeptical about contract personnel in the CIA.[29]

When moved from the Black Sites to Gitmo, fourteen supposed HVDs were interviewed individually by the ICRC. The subsequent ICRC report, listing what the humanitarian organization labeled as sometimes torture and sometimes CID treatment, was leaked to the public domain – most probably by dissidents in Washington.[30] It is reasonable to assume that ICRC representatives had learned of many of the same abusive techniques when interviewing prisoners at Guantánamo, Abu Ghraib, and other places visited. And, in the last analysis, the ICRC's report is entirely consistent with the "Bybee torture memo" of August 1, 2002, meaning that what was authorized was implemented – and more.[31]

After a summary of the ICRC report appeared in the press, the journalist Mark Danner was eventually given a copy of the actual report. A fair reading of the report leaves no doubt but that the United States carried out torture against certain detainees – not only via waterboarding, but by such other methods as holding a prisoner in a coffin-like box, repeatedly slamming the prisoner into a wall, prolonged isolation,

[28] Scott Shane, "2 U.S. Architects of Harsh Tactics in 9/11's Wake," *New York Times*, August 12, 2009, www.nytimes.com/2009/08/12/us/12psychs.html.

[29] Walter Pincus, "CIA Fired Firms Aiding Questioning," *Washington Post*, June 15, 2009, www.washingtonpost.com/wp-dyn/content/article/2009/06/14/AR2009061402819.

[30] Strictly Confidential, "ICRC Report on the Treatment of Fourteen 'High Value Detainees' in CIA Custody," February 2007, transmitted by the Washington office of the ICRC to John Rizzo, Acting General Counsel of the CIA. Available on the internet via, e.g., the web site of the *New York Review of Books*.

[31] The Helgerson report indicated that some CIA interrogators exceeded authorized procedures.

prolonged sleep deprivation, and so on in a litany of *combined* methods already largely discussed in Chapter 4 in relation to Gitmo and Abu Ghraib. The ICRC is a very conservative organization, not at all prone to hyperbole.[32]

Some of the report's contents are worth quoting verbatim: "Throughout the entire period during which they were held in the CIA detention program – which ranged from sixteen months up to almost four and a half years and which, for eleven of the fourteen was over three years – the detainees were kept in continuous solitary confinement and incommunicado detention." Increasingly it is accepted that prolonged solitary confinement in and of itself is fundamentally injurious to a person's mental wellbeing and can reasonably be said to sometimes create severe mental pain within the meaning of the Convention against Torture.[33] (When the US legal resident Ali Saleh Kahlah al-Marri, who eventually confessed to being a sleeper agent for Al-Qaeda, was held in total isolation for a prolonged period in a Navy brig in Charleston, South Carolina, he developed such a "mental health emergency" that some of his US military captors began to befriend him.[34])

The ICRC report on the fourteen HVDs continues:

[32] See David P. Forsythe, *The Humanitarians: The International Committee of the Red Cross* (Cambridge: Cambridge University Press, 2005). Very rarely in the 150-year history of the organization can one find examples of mistaken statements, and almost always they occurred because of repeating some statement by others that was not sufficiently checked out. There are apparently no cases of its representatives making false statements about prison conditions. Jane Mayer of *The New Yorker Magazine* referred to the ICRC as "known for its credibility and caution." *The New Yorker*, "Reporter at Large: The Black Sites," August 13, 2007, www.newyorker.com/reporting/2007/08/13/070813fa_fact_mayer.

[33] See Peter Scharff Smith, "The Effects of Solitary Confinement on Prison Inmates: A Brief History and Review of the Literature," *Crime and Justice*, 34 (2006), pp. 441–528; also Scharff Smith, "Prisons and Human Rights: The Case of Solitary Confinement in Denmark and the US from the 1820s until Today," in S. Lagoutte, H.-O. Sano, and P. Scharff Smith, eds., *Human Rights in Turmoil* (The Netherlands: Brill, 2007), pp. 221–248. The International Psychological Trauma Symposium in Istanbul, December 2007, adopted a statement on the dangerous effects of solitary confinement for many prisoners. This Statement was mentioned in a UN General Assembly resolution on human rights, adopted in the Fall of 2008.

[34] Jane Mayer, "The Hard Cases," *The New Yorker*, February 23, 2009 starting at p. 38. Al-Marri agreed to a plea bargain in which he admitted being a sleeper agent and was sentenced to prison.

The methods of ill-treatment alleged to have been used include the following:

- Suffocation by water poured over a cloth placed over the nose and mouth, alleged by three of the fourteen.
- Prolonged stress standing position, naked, held with the arms extended and chained above the head, as alleged by ten of the fourteen, for periods from two or three days continuously, and for up to two or three months intermittently, during which period toilet access was sometimes denied resulting in allegations from four detainees that they had to defecate and urinate over themselves.
- Beatings by use of collar held around the detainees' neck and used to forcefully bang the head and body against the wall, alleged by six of the fourteen.
- Beating and kicking, including slapping, punching, kicking to the body and face, alleged by nine of the fourteen.
- Confinement in a box to severely restrict movement alleged in the case of one detainee.
- Prolonged nudity alleged by eleven of the fourteen during detention, interrogation and ill-treatment; this enforced nudity lasted for periods ranging from several weeks to several months.
- Sleep deprivation was alleged by eleven of the fourteen through days of interrogations, through use of forced stress positions (standing or sitting), cold water and use of repetitive loud noise or music. One detainee was kept sitting on a chair for prolonged periods of time.
- Exposure to cold temperature was alleged by most of the fourteen, especially via cold cells and interrogation rooms and, for seven of them, by the use of cold water poured over the body or, as alleged by three of the detainees, held around the body by means of a plastic sheet to create an immersion bath with just the head out of the water.
- Prolonged shackling of hands and/or feet was alleged by many of the fourteen.
- Threats of ill-treatment to the detainee and/or his family, alleged by nine of the fourteen.
- Forced shaving of the head and beard, alleged by two of the fourteen.
- Deprivation/restricted provision of solid food from three days to one month after arrest, alleged by eight of the fourteen.

According to the ICRC report, all the techniques listed above were used on one detainee, Abu Zubaydah. According to a separate account, Zubaydah was severely abused by the CIA early on, against the judgment of the FBI, and before the "Bybee torture memo" of August 1, 2002 noted in Chapter 3.[35] The emerging conventional wisdom is that

[35] David Johnston, "At a Secret Interrogation, Dispute Flared Over Tactics," *New York Times*, September 10, 2006, www.nytimes.com/2006/09/10/washington/10detain.html.

Zubaydah was not a very high-level Al-Qaeda operative, had mental problems, and was made at least temporarily psychotic by his CIA treatment. Apparently he gave up the name of KSM (Khalid Sheikh Mohammed) in non-abusive interrogation, but clammed up after abuse was started. An FBI agent involved in the case, who was withdrawn because of the abusive treatment, testified that in this case the abuse was unnecessary and counter-productive.[36]

According to the ICRC report, an amputee was required to stand for long periods on his one good leg, which led to such swelling that his treatment was periodically stopped. According to the ICRC, a special collar was fashioned so that detainees could be slammed into a wall.

The report noted the participation of health care personnel in the process. The ICRC seems entirely correct in its judgment that the primary purpose of such a role was to facilitate abusive interrogation, not primarily to care for the individual. The organization termed this situation a gross violation of medical ethics, citing authorities on the subject.[37] This part of its report inherently recalled the role of Nazi doctors in facilitating gross abuse and even death during the Holocaust.[38] One can also recall the participation of Argentine health personnel in the torture of Jacobo Timerman and others in the 1970s and 1980s.[39] And one can observe that the United States has now joined a very broad trend toward the participation of health personnel in torture and other forms of severe abuse.[40]

Given that torture and CID treatment are absolutely illegal under international law in any and all circumstances, with torture and the most severe forms of cruel and inhuman treatment being a crime with individual responsibility under US law, the only possible justification for such measures is consequentialist. That is, given the obvious

[36] Ali H. Soufan, "My Tortured Decision," *New York Times*, April 23, 2009, www.nytimes.com/2009/04/23/opinion/23soufan.html.

[37] See also Steven H. Miles, *Oath Betrayed: Torture, Medical Complicity, and the War on Terror* (New York: Random House, 2006), who focuses mainly on the US military.

[38] E.g. Robert J. Lifton, *Nazi Doctors: Medical Killing and the Psychology of Genocide* (New York: Basic Books, 1986).

[39] Jacobo Timerman, *Prisoners Without a Name, Cell Without a Number* (Madison: University of Wisconsin Press, 2002, new edn.).

[40] For an overview see Eric Stover and Elena Nightingale, *The Breaking of Bodies and Minds* (Washington, DC: American Association for the Advancement of Science, 1985).

illegality, the only possibly persuasive argument is political – that the information gained from illegal interrogation materially contributed to the security of the United States, and absent that information catastrophic damage would have been inflicted on the country. (Of course the government attorneys like John Yoo, as noted in Chapter 3, tried to define torture as akin to producing organ failure, and otherwise tried to lawyer the legal prohibitions out of existence.) It is then little wonder that CIA Director George Tenet defended these "enhanced interrogation techniques" in his memoirs as vital to national security, or that Vice President Cheney asserted that these measures led to a windfall of intelligence. President Bush in his memoirs followed the Cheney and Tenet arguments in asserting a treasure trove of useful intelligence from high abusive interrogation. Since they were among the principal architects of the policy, with the CIA Director or his designated replacement among those who supervised its application, they can hardly be expected to argue otherwise. (National Security Advisor Rice, with perhaps more creativity, argued that since the measures were derived from SERE training for some US military personnel, they fell short of either torture or CID treatment.[41] But in SERE training, US military personnel were not held in solitary confinement for months, heads were not slammed into walls, persons were not waterboarded dozens of times, etc.)

CIA Inspector General John L. Helgerson compiled a report in May 2004 that was released by the Obama Administration in heavily redacted form.[42] This report noted that Bush interrogation policies deviated from those standards regarding treatment of prisoners publically endorsed by other democratic officials, including US officials in the past. The report showed both tight supervision of interrogation by officials in Washington, as well as an excess of zeal by certain CIA personnel or contractors. Some prisoners were threatened with mock execution, with sexual abuse of their relatives, with harm to their children. Prisoners were threatened with a weapon, and with a power drill. There was on occasion extensive sleep deprivation, extensive shackling, extensive wall slamming, and other systematic and severe

[41] US Senate, "Report on Detainees" and Mark Mazzetti, "Bush Aides Linked to Talks on Interrogations," *New York Times*, September 25, 2008, www.nytimes.com/2008/09/25/washington/25detain.html.

[42] Available on the ACLU web site: http://luxmedia.vo.llnwd.net/o10/clients/aclu/IG_Rep.

abuse including extensive waterboarding of two of the three prisoners who underwent that process. The Helgerson report basically fitted with the findings of the ICRC report, in that both stressed probable CID behavior, with some torture. His conclusions and recommendations for change were blacked out by Obama officials. Scott Horton, a lawyer who tracked many of the details of the CIA (and military) abuses, argued that despite the heavy redactions, one could see the role of the Office of the Vice President, and the attempts by various parties both to object to the CIA program and to sidetrack efforts to bring it back into legal compliance.[43]

The Inspector General's report confirmed that Zubaydah and KSM had been waterboarded numerous times – apparently a combined 226. Use of "the waterboard" has been considered a crime by the United States for a long time, was suppressed when it became known to be used against Filipino insurgents after the Spanish–American War, and was certainly protested when used by the Japanese against US POWs during the Second World War.[44] As noted already, waterboarding is considered a war crime by US legal authorities in the military.

But waterboarding was not the only controversy in CIA interrogations. It is the combined techniques that have to be considered. According to one account: "As the session begins, the detainee stands naked, except for a hood covering his head. Guards shackle his arms and legs. They slip a small collar around his neck. The collar will be used later; according to CIA guidelines for interrogations, it will serve as handle for slamming the detainee's head against a wall. After removing the hood, the interrogator opens with a slap across the face ... followed by other slaps, the guidelines state. Next comes the head slamming, or 'walling,' which can be tried once 'to make a point,' or repeated again and again. 'Twenty or thirty times consecutively' is permissible, the guidelines say, 'if the interrogator requires a more significant response to a question.' And if that fails, there are far harsher techniques to be tried."[45]

43 Scott Horton, "Seven Points on the CIA Report," Harpers Magazine on-line, August 20, 2009, www.harpers.org.archive/2009/08/hbc-90005599.

44 Evan Wallach, "Waterboarding Used to Be a Crime," *Washington Post*, November 4, 2007, www.washingtonpost.com/wp-dyn/content/article/2004/11/02?AR2006110201170.

45 Joby Warrick, Peter Finn, and Julie Tate, "CIA Releases Its Instructions For Breaking a Detainee's Will," *Washington Post*, August 26, 2009, www.washingtonpost.com/wp-dyn/content/article/2009/08/25/AR2009082503277.

From a variety of documents released by the Obama team, including but not limited to the Helgerson report, it seems that KSM in particular yielded considerable actionable intelligence. It seems that he became a kind of CIA consultant on Al-Qaeda matters.[46] There remains uncertainty about whether all of his statements were true, whether humane interrogation could have achieved the same results, and whether the information he gave stopped any imminent attacks.[47] There appears to be no "ticking time bomb" scenario in his case, often used to justify torture in general argumentation. Conventional wisdom holds that he gave up useful information on Al-Qaeda's structure and functioning, names of other operatives, and some future plans. Ali Soufan, an FBI expert involved in the early interrogation of Zubaydah, maintained that the US intelligence gains from KSM and others have been vastly overstated.[48]

There is no way for an outsider to evaluate the competing views about the usefulness of torture and CID until some independent review panel is given access to the information existing in CIA and other records. As the journalist Mark Danner has written, "What is needed is . . . a broadly persuasive judgment, delivered by people who can look at all the evidence, however highly classified, and can claim bipartisan respect on the order of the Watergate Select Committee or the 9/11 Commission, on whether or not torture made Americans safer."[49]

It has often been said by those opposed to torture and inhuman treatment that the information gained from the process is unreliable; those tortured will say anything to stop the torture. It is highly probable that some misinformation transpires, and the case of Ibn al-Shaik al-Libi is covered on p. 158. The CIA had a "truth squad" in operation to check the assertions emanating from Zubaydah, KSM, and others. But it is also true that on occasion torture does yield accurate information;

[46] Peter Finn, Joby Warrick, and Julie Tate, "9/11 Planner becomes Key Asset for CIA," *Washington Post*, August 29, 2009, www.msnbc.msn.com/id/32605529/ns/us_news-washington.

[47] "The Red Cross Report: What It Means," *New York Review of Books*, April 30, 2009, p. 15, www.nybooks.com/articles/22614.

[48] Ali H. Soufan, "What Torture Never Told US," *New York Times*, September 6, 2009, www.nytimes.com/2009/09/06/opinion/06soufan.html. See also his testimony before the US Senate, Committee on the Judiciary, http://judiciary.senate.gov/hearings/testimony.cfm?id=3842&wit_id=7906.

[49] Danner, "The Red Cross Torture Report," p. 15.

"it periodically does work . . ."[50] In Ethiopia a CIA agent, David Wells, was seized, tortured, and coughed up considerable information about US covert operations in the Horn of Africa.[51] In Lebanon, a CIA agent, William Buckley, was also seized, brutally tortured, and divulged much accurate information before his death.[52] Sometimes cited is the Filipino brutal interrogation of Abdul Hakim Murad, a leader in the violent Abu Sayyaf movement, and how it led to important information that disrupted hijacking plans; but Rejali questions this conclusion.[53] It is certainly possible that KSM yielded both accurate and inaccurate information after he was waterboarded and otherwise abused.

When and if accurate information is gained through torture or inhuman treatment, a consequentialist analysis must also take into account any damage to national interest that stems from the process. Suppose the torture of Zubaydah and KSM, among others, did yield some actionable intelligence that led to the capture of other terrorists and/or disrupted planning for future terrorist attacks. But suppose that information was accompanied by reports of their abusive treatment along with other factors like reports about Gitmo and Abu Ghraib which mobilized some Muslims to join terrorist networks and accept suicide missions. On balance, was the juice worth the squeeze, to recall the phrase of a commander at Guantánamo who was supportive of humane interrogation at least partly on expedient grounds (in addition to military order and respect for law)? Did the gains from abusive interrogation off-set the mobilization of further terrorists, not to mention increased divisions at home? And could the same information have been gained by more patient and humane means?

Consequentialist arguments aside, the one thing that is clear about the CIA Black Sites is that they constituted an egregious violation of various norms on international human rights and humanitarian law. No leading independent international lawyer claims that the combined methods used on Zubaydah, KSM, and others fell short of the

50 Robert D. Kaplan, "The 'Interrogators' and 'Torture': Hard Questions," *New York Times*, January 23, 2005, www.nytimes.com/2005/01/23/books/review/23KAPLAN.html?.

51 Weiner, *Legacy of Ashes*, pp. 395–396.

52 Gordon Thomas, *Gideon's Spies: The Secret History of the Mossad* (New York: St. Martin's, 1995).

53 Darius Rejali, *Torture and Democracy* (Princeton: Princeton University Press, 2006), p. 507.

proscriptions found in the Torture Convention and Common Article 3 of the 1949 Geneva Conventions. The Bush Administration initially argued that the abuse was reasonable in context and certainly fell short of torture and inhuman treatment. (Humiliating treatment is not now a crime under the US War Crimes Act [WCA], after the revised definitions found in the Military Commissions Act [MCA] passed by Congress in 2006.) But the consensus view among independent lawyers is that US treatment was indeed sometimes torture and sometimes cruel and inhuman. (The Bush Administration's legislative maneuvers in 2006 indicated an admission that what it had done was at least humiliating – hence the need to say via congressional legislation that such behavior was no longer a war crime in US law.)

When it is recalled that many of these techniques were used in combination over a prolonged period, there is little doubt that in a number of cases treatment rose to the level of torture. As noted, Zubaydah and KSM were waterboarded a total of 226 times.[54] For the others, given the totality of how they were treated from seizure to transfer, there can be little reasonable quibble with the ICRC's characterization of that process as, at a minimum, cruel, inhuman, and degrading. Helgerson, like the 2005 Schmidt report on the military side, had raised questions about the status of combined and extended techniques of abuse.[55] To repeat, perhaps about thirty of 100 CIA "ghosted" prisoners were tortured or subjected to CID techniques, even if only three were waterboarded.[56]

Bush early policies on detention and interrogation via the CIA eventually unraveled in a chaotic process. Just after the Helgerson report Tenet insisted on further authorization and legal clearance for the harsh techniques employed, which he received in 2005 via both the White House and the DOJ, with Steven G. Bradbury playing the key legal role. Bradbury issued a secret memo reaffirming, in his view, the legality of CIA harsh interrogation.[57] On the Hill, Cheney continued to fight

[54] Scott Shane, "Waterboarding Used 266 Times on 2 Suspects," *New York Times*, April 20, 2009, www.nytimes.com/2009/04/20/world/20detain.html.

[55] Douglas Jehl, "Report Warned On C.I.A.'s Tactics in Interrogation," *New York Times*, November 9, 2005, p. A 1. See also Shane and Mazzetti, "Advisers."

[56] Scott Shane, "C.I.A. to Close Secret Prisons for Terror Suspects," *New York Times*, April 10, 2009, www.nytimes.com/2009/04/10/world/10detain.html.

[57] Scott Shane, David Johnson, and James Risen, "Secret U.S. Endorsement of Severe Interrogations," *New York Times*, October 4, 2007, www.nytimes.com/2007/10/04/washington/04interrogate.html.

Senator McCain and others for an exemption for the CIA in any legislative effort to restrict abusive interrogation. But Secretary of State Rice stated toward the end of 2005 that the prohibition on torture and CID found in international law pertained to all US actions abroad, which pointedly if implicitly included the CIA.[58] It seems clear enough in retrospect that Rice and her closest confidants were battling Cheney and the DOJ lawyers, the former trying to rein in the CIA, the latter trying to carve out continuing space for major abuse.

President Bush, apparently yielding to political reality, formally signed the 2005 Detainee Treatment Act (DTA) which prohibited not just torture but also CID at least when practiced by the military and (by the CIA) in military facilities.[59] However, when he signed the bill, which had passed the Senate 90–9 and the House 308–122, which meant a presidential veto could be overridden, he issued a "signing statement" which seemed to suggest that he might disregard the new law if in his judgment as Commander in Chief he found a contrary policy necessary for national security.

Administrative statements to the public, ranging from the President to CIA officials, repeated the mantra that the United States did not torture. In general there is persuasive evidence that all administrations, not just the Bush team, misrepresent when trying to sell contested security policies to Congress, the American public, and the world.[60] But the Bush misrepresentations were increasingly seen as unpersuasive – as they were also eventually with regard to justifications for invading Iraq. It was increasingly difficult to rely on controversial legal memos from John Yoo, Steven Bradbury and others in the Bush DOJ asserting the legality of waterboarding, wall slamming, and other techniques. It is well to recall that these memos, carefully kept secret for as long as possible, led to an ethics investigation by the DOJ, and some of them were so egregious that they were withdrawn by subsequent Bush officials like Jack Goldsmith – particularly regarding the definition of

[58] Brian Knowlton, "Rice Seems to Shift Policy on Prisoners," *International Herald Tribune*, December 8, 2005, www.iht.com/bin/print_ipub.php?file=articles/2005/12/07/news/torture.php.

[59] Josh White, "President Relents, Backs Torture Ban," *Washington Post*, December 16, 2005, p. A 1, www.washingtonpost.com/wp-dyn/content/article/2005/12/15/AR2005121502241.

[60] Jon Western, *Selling Intervention & War: The Presidency, the Media, and the American Public* (Baltimore: Johns Hopkins University Press, 2005).

torture. One test of veracity is whether national legal arguments are accepted by independent international lawyers. In this light, many of the legal arguments by Bush lawyers were clearly dubious.

While new rules for CIA interrogations were reportedly established in 2007, they remain classified.[61] In President Bush's executive order of July 20, 2007 ostensibly ordering the CIA to comply with the strictures of Geneva Convention Common Article 3, he and his lawyers still played word games to the detriment of humane values. What they prohibited was any infliction of "personal abuse" but "done for the purpose of humiliating or degrading the individual . . . or for the purpose of humiliation . . ."[62] Logically not prohibited was abusive interrogation for the purpose of obtaining information for national security. Such word games transparently called into question the veracity and integrity of that Administration. It was a continuation of the effort to say that if an interrogator did not intend to inflict intense pain, but only intended to obtain information, then the legal prohibitions did not apply.

Beyond the ICRC report about the fourteen HVDs, the case of Khaled al-Masri shows more of the brutalities, and some of the gross injustices, of CIA forced disappearances.[63] Al-Masri, a German national with a fairly common family name in some circles, was seized in the Balkans in 2003. Beaten at the point of handover from Macedonian to CIA teams, he was transported to a secret CIA facility in Afghanistan where he was abused further, including being injected with drugs. Medical personnel were involved in the abuse. It eventually became clear that the CIA had the wrong person. After about half a year of CIA debate, confusion, and bureaucratic wrangling, with an ill al-Masri going on a hunger strike which resulted in forced feeding, he was eventually released in an

[61] Mark Mazzetti, "Rules Lay Out C.I.A.'s Tactics in Questioning," *New York Times*, July 21, 2007, p. A 1.

[62] The White House, Office of the Press Secretary, "Executive Order: Interpretation of the Geneva Conventions Common Article 3 as Applied to a Program of Detention and Interrogation Operated by the Central Intelligence Agency," July 20, 2007, www.whitehouse.gov/news/releases/2007/07/print/20070720-4.html.

[63] Among various sources, see Jane Mayer, *The Dark Side: The Inside Story of How the War on Terror Turned Into a War on American Ideals* (New York: Doubleday, 2008), pp. 282–288. Also Dana Priest, "Anatomy of a CIA 'Rendition' Gone Wrong," *Washington Post*, December 4, 2005, www.msnbc.msn.com/id/10316560. She suggests that many mistakes were made in the US rendition program. Concerning erroneous foreign renditions see further Katherine Shrader, AP, "Terrorism Renditions Raise Questions," *Lincoln Journal Star*, December 28, 2005, p. 7-A.

unceremonious – which is to say abrupt – fashion, made to find his own way to safety in Germany. When human rights groups helped al-Masri press the German courts for legal justice and reparations, the German authorities stonewalled, probably at the urging of the United States.[64] When he then turned to legal action in the United States, his case was dismissed on grounds of "state secrets."[65] The CIA officer in charge of the bungled case was promoted.

While those who authorized and managed the Black Site program with its "enhanced interrogation techniques" operated with apparent impunity for torture and CID, including those who obstructed justice by destroying the videotapes contrary to a court injunction, lower-level operatives might occasionally be held accountable for exceeding instructions. David Passaro, a contract employee for the Agency, fatally assaulted a prisoner in a secret Afghan prison called the Salt Pit in 2003. He was convicted in federal court and sentenced to eight years in prison.[66] This prosecution reflected the philosophy that if the prisoner dies, the interrogation was done wrong. The policy was designed to abuse, sometimes in major ways, but without being fatal. On the other hand, when CIA operatives doused a prisoner, Gul Rahman, with cold water and left him in cold temperatures overnight, he died. This was in

[64] In 2010 unauthorized release of secret State Department cables via "Wikileaks" confirmed that US officials had warned the German authorities not to look too closely into the al-Masri affair lest US–German relations should be harmed. Regarding German–US affairs there is also the very strange case of "Curveball," an Iraqi defector under the control of the Germans who said that Saddam Hussein had mobile labs for germ warfare. There was a tug of war between the two states over both the person and the information coming out of his interrogation. Curveball's claims circulated at high levels and no doubt fed into US arguments about Saddam's military capabilities and intentions. Curveball turned out to be a screwball who manufactured false "information." But for present purposes his case showed the tight interaction of the two states on security affairs, even if tensions were also present. See Bob Drogin, *Curveball: Spies, Lies, and the Con Man Who Caused a War* (New York: Random House, 2007). Also, it has been reported that German intelligence agents were part of an extraordinary rendition involving torture in Morocco. Further, it is very clear than many CIA rendition flights traversed Germany.

[65] Adam Liptak, "U.S. Appeals Court Upholds Dismissal of Abuse Suit Against C.I.A., Stating Secrets Are at Risk," *New York Times*, March 3, 2007, p. A 6.

[66] Joseph Finder, "The C.I.A. in Double Jeopardy," *New York Times*, August 30, 2009, www.nytimes.com/2009/08/30/opinion/30finder.html. Julian E. Barnes, "CIA Contractor Guilty in Beating of Detainee," *Los Angeles Times*, August 18, 2006, http://articles.latimes.com/2006/aug/18/nation/na-abuse18.

the Afghan Salt Pit in 2002. Those in charge of Rahman were not prosecuted, and it is not clear that they were subjected to Agency sanctions.[67] Some reports said that the CIA officer in charge was subsequently promoted, but the case is shrouded in secrecy. Other lower-level CIA personnel were apparently given administrative sanctions for other unauthorized abuse.[68] It was said in some circles that Obama chose Leon Panetta, who had no background in intelligence matters, to be CIA Director because of his management skills and the need of the Agency for precisely those qualities.

Renditions abroad

In a number of instances it is now well known that the CIA transported persons to foreign governments for abusive interrogation. It has yet to be made clear why the Agency decided to torture and otherwise mistreat some prisoners itself and why it decided occasionally to outsource this process to others. Still further, it is not at all clear why the CIA abused some prisoners in US military facilities rather than moving them to other locales, whether its own or foreign. But then US policy toward enemy prisoners after 9/11 was not characterized by clear, systematic thought. One recalls the confusions about military interrogation in Afghanistan, Guantánamo, and Iraq as demonstrated in Chapter 4.

The case of Maher Arar is illustrative of the problem of mistaken identity in the extraordinary rendition process. Arar, a Canadian of Syrian descent, was seized at JFK airport in New York on information supplied by Canadian intelligence. Denied legal due process in New York, he was shipped off to Syria without notice to his family. Despite the fact that the Syrian government was highly repressive at home, brutally and illegally interventionist in Lebanon, not entirely cooperative regarding Iraq, and definitely not historically cooperative regarding an accommodation with Israel, the Bush Administration sought its help in the torture of Arar. To

[67] Adam Goldman and Kathy Gannon, "Salt Pit Death: Gul Rahman, CIA Prisoner, Died of Hypothermia in Secret Afghanistan Prison," *Huffington Post*, March 28, 2010, www.huffingtonpost.com/2010/03/28/salt-pit-death-gul-Rahman_n_516559.html. The same writers posted similar stories with the Associated Press and with Yahoo.News. For a critique of poor management and inconsistent policies at the CIA, see Charles Faddis (a former agent), *Beyond Repair: The Decline and Fall of the CIA* (Guilford: Lyons Press, 2009).

[68] Faddis, *Beyond Repair*.

emphasize, it is not at all clear why the Bush Administration sought to work closely with a rogue regime like Bashar al-Assad's Syria. But then it also worked with Uzbekistan in the abuse of prisoners, another authoritarian rogue regime with a terrible human rights record.

After severe abuse but with no intelligence gains, because again, as with al-Masri, the CIA had abducted the wrong person, Arar was released. Upon return to Canada, he eventually gained an apology from the government and sizable reparations (the Canadian intelligence had been faulty). When he sought legal relief in the United States, the Bush Administration urged the US court system to drop the case on grounds of national security and state secrets, which is precisely what happened. So even though the Arar events are public knowledge, a US judge refused to allow the case to proceed. The US Supreme Court refused further legal review, being advised to do so by the Obama Administration. In certain circles the US record was "disgraceful," with Obama being urged to emulate the Canadian response.[69]

Then there was the case of Ibn al-Shaik al-Libi. Abducted by the CIA from Pakistan in late 2001, before the CIA had its secret detention system fully in place, he was sent to Egypt where he was reportedly tortured. One of the reported statements he made, under torture, was that Saddam Hussein had links with Al-Qaeda. This was reported to the highest levels of the Bush Administration, contributing to the claims by the President, Vice President, and others that Saddam was in some way involved in 9/11. Al-Libi, upon his release from Egypt, recanted what he was reported to have said under torture. It is likely that CIA rendition and Egyptian torture in this case contributed to one of the several myths advanced by the Bush Administration, namely that there were operational links between Saddam and Bin Laden's network. If conventional wisdom about this case proves to be true, one sees the dangers that can arise from torture that leads to false statements.[70] Proving the facts of

[69] Editorial, "No Price to Pay for Torture," *New York Times*, June 15, 2010, www.nytimes.com/1010/06/16/opinion/16wed2.html.

[70] The al-Libi case has been covered in various sources including John Diamond, *The CIA and the Culture of Failure: US Intelligence from the End of the Cold War to the Invasion of Iraq* (Stanford: Stanford University Press, 2008), pp. 405–409. See also Brian Ross and Richard Esposito, "CIA's Harsh Interrogation Techniques Described," ABC News, November 18, 2005, http://abcnews.go.com.WNT/WNT/print?id=1322866. Also Douglas Jehl, "Qaeda–Iraq Link US Cited is Tied to Coercion Claim," *New York Times*, December 9, 2005, p. A 1, also at www.nytimes.com/2005/12/09/politics/09intel.html.

this case may in fact prove difficult, as al-Libi reportedly committed suicide while in detention in Libya.

The case of Muhammad Saad Iqbal demonstrates the intersection of CIA rendition, CIA detention, military detention, and abuse of a prisoner before his release. Seized in Indonesia in 2002, he was rendered by the CIA to Egypt where he claims to have been tortured. He was then transferred to Bagram where he again claims that abuse transpired. He was finally sent to Guantánamo where, six years after his kidnapping, he was released to Pakistan where he was living before his travels to Indonesia. When interviewed, he was found to have multiple physical and psychological problems that he attributed to his captors, and he was addicted to various drugs.[71] US officials would not candidly discuss his case.

Abu Omar (Hassan Mustafa Osama Nasr) was seized in 2003 in Italy, a democratic ally, possibly with the participation of Italian secret security agents.[72] He was associated with a violent Islamic movement focused mainly on Egyptian affairs. Flown to Egypt, he reportedly was tortured.[73] Released in 2007, he recanted his confessions. In the meantime the Italian courts began a court case involving the trial *in absentia* of more than twenty CIA agents, who were duly convicted of violation of Italian laws. The proceedings were something of a circus, and no penalties had been applied at the time of writing, the defendants apparently being careful to stay away from Italian jurisdiction.[74]

Conclusion

Most states are hypocritical in the sense that they profess commitment to the norms of public international law, whether pertaining

[71] Jane Perlez, Raymond Bonner, and Salman Masood, "An Ex-Detainee of the U.S. Describes a 6-Year Ordeal," *New York Times*, January 6, 2009, www.nytimes.com/2009/01/06/world/asia/06iqbal.html.

[72] Former CIA agent Robert Seldon Lady admitted to the Italian events while down playing his own role. He argued that events constituted not a "criminal act" but a "state affair." Human Rights First, "Law and Security News," July 2, 2009, electronic message. For one overview see Mark Mazzetti, *Spy vs. Spy: A Kidnapping in Milan* (New York: W. W. Norton, 2010).

[73] Elisabetta Povoledo, "Egyptian Says he was Tortured After Being Kidnapped in Milan," *New York Times*, November 11, 2006, p. A 7.

[74] Amnesty International, "Convictions in Abu Omar Rendition Case a Step Toward Accountability," November 5, 2009, www.amnesty.org/en/news-and-updates/news/convictions-abu-omar-rendition.

to non-intervention in the internal affairs of other states or non-abuse of detainees. At the same time, all states manifest secret intelligence services whose *raison d'être* is to act covertly outside the law, or at least outside the bounds of international law as traditionally understood as directed by their national authorities. Outsiders are never sure at a given moment what these agencies are doing, and whether they are under national control as compared to freelancing. Outsiders are never sure if accounts of their deeds and misdeeds are accurate, particularly when documentary support is absent. Intelligence agencies are in the business of deception and misrepresentation, so even their public statements and off-the-record interviews are properly suspect (not that the State Department and Pentagon are totally different in this regard).

In liberal democratic states with a free press and independent courts, the truth usually gets out – even if not necessarily in a timely way. The press can be deferential and too patriotic (even jingoistic) at times. And courts do not often like to challenge the Executive on national security matters. But even so, over time it is hard to keep secrets forever in a liberal democracy. This is certainly true in Washington. Those in the know but opposed to a policy can easily find a reporter to talk to. Leaks eventually occur in an effort to sabotage policy. Judges can sometimes eventually exhaust their patience, even with those who appointed them, and at least occasionally demonstrate a strong commitment to the rule of law. Human rights groups nudge the process along on both fronts, probing into the dark corners of state policy and funneling information to the media, while also working with plaintiffs in legal challenges.

We know enough about the CIA after 9/11 to know that it was an important part of the "forward leaning" strategy of the United States in dealing with terrorism, as broadly defined by the Bush team. We know that, as instructed by the highest authorities, it sometimes engaged in torture and inhuman treatment in various detention centers – its own and those belonging to the military. We know that it colluded with various unsavory foreign governments, as well as democracies, in order to try to get "actionable intelligence" without lawful limitations on the methods employed. We do not yet know the quality of the information obtained in all cases, and in particular whether the Agency shrewdly controlled the process so as to cull truth from fiction, actionable intelligence from wild goose chases and dead ends. We do not yet know its contribution to US security, and how to balance that against US loss of reputation and soft power from CIA kidnapping,

Black Sites, extraordinary rendition, and abuse. We do know that rather often, maybe 10 percent of the time would be a reasonable guess, the CIA seized and abused the wrong person, which casts a serious shadow over the entire process. (The military rate of mistaken detention is much higher, maybe 60–80 percent, given their broad sweeps and indiscriminate detention.)

Throughout the course of events after 9/11 there were always two schools of thought among security managers about CIA (and military) interrogation. What might be called the "Dick Cheney" school, with apparently quite a few members in the CIA, advocated abusive interrogation, even if a large component of this was supposed to be "no touch torture" or mostly self-infliction of mental pain and suffering. (Even the Kubark manual and successor CIA documents expressed caution about the utility of physical torture.) Psychological harassment and "messing with the mind," however, can rise to torture and other inhuman treatment no less than restraining in uncomfortable positions, beatings, and slamming bodies into walls. Of course the CIA did the latter as well as the former, whatever its official doctrines. On the other hand, what might be called the "Geneva" school, with lots of followers in the military (and FBI), advocated non-abusive interrogation built on establishing rapport with prisoners and persistent questioning over time with detailed knowledge of the person and his social or cultural context. One clear advantage of the latter was that it preserved the option of legitimate criminal justice after interrogation. We turn to that subject in Chapter 6.

6 *Due process: detention classification, Military Commissions*

Whoever says war, says law of war.

(Patrick Jarreau, *Le Monde*, June 30, 2004[1])

[To claim that] the president has all the powers of a normal war yet few of its restraints, that the whole world is his battlefield, and that this state of affairs goes on in perpetuity is really akin to claiming a kind of worldwide martial law. It only stood to reason that the public – and the courts – would eventually grow uneasy.

(Benjamin Wittes, *Law and the Long War: The Future of Justice in an Age of Terror*, New York: Penguin Press, 2008, p. 64)

By now it should be evident that the George W. Bush Administration not only tried to deconstruct the international legal regime designed to protect prisoners in war and other national emergencies, certainly in Afghanistan and at Guantánamo, a legal regime incorporated into US law for the most part. But also it tried to keep other authorities, primarily the US courts, from reviewing any of its decisions related to prisoner matters. President Bush asserted an unlimited authority to engage in endless administrative detention; a unilateral authority to declare persons, even American citizens, "unlawful enemy combatants" who, *ipso facto*, had forfeited all legal rights, including a right to legal counsel and a right to habeas corpus; an absolute authority to avoid review of any of its decisions pertaining to alien prisoners held outside the United States; and a unilateral authority to establish Military Commissions to try enemy prisoners whose rules would be determined by the Executive alone.

[1] "Qui dit guerre dit droit de la guerre et, par consequent, respect des conventions de Genève," *Le Monde* special feature, "Au coeur de l'argumentaire americain" (At the Heart of the American Argument).

On the one hand, as we saw in Chapter 3, Bush officials made extensive legal arguments in order to circumvent the law. On the other hand, and at the same time, deep down they were worried that some of these claims would come back to bite them in the form of personal legal liability. From the start, high Bush officials were worried about being charged with war crimes, both at home and abroad. According to then-White House legal counsel Alberto Gonzales, by denying POW protection to Taliban fighters and by declaring that no one at Gitmo was covered even by Common Article 3 of the 1949 Geneva Conventions (pertaining, *inter alia*, to non-state parties), that "would create a reasonable basis in law" that the US War Crimes Act (WCA) "does not apply, which would provide a solid defense to any future prosecution."[2] Moreover, as already noted, the Bush strategy was to argue: we do not torture, we do not even use cruel techniques; we might have to humiliate some enemy prisoners to protect the country, but humiliating treatment is no longer a war crime in US law.

Obviously these legal claims were driven by the underlying desire of the Bush Administration to have a free hand in dealing with enemy prisoners and many other security matters, and equally by the desire to build up the authority of the Executive in its dealings with Congress and the Courts. To reiterate, what some saw as a dangerous imperial presidency, Vice President Dick Cheney and some others saw as a restored powerful presidency after unwise restrictions imposed particularly by the Congress in the wake of Vietnam and Watergate. It was not a misunderstanding for Jack Goldsmith to say of John Yoo and some other Bush Administration officials that they saw the wartime presidency as possessing all the legal powers of George III of England.[3]

This chapter returns to the subject of law, and in particular the matter of legal justice. What legal rights did detainees have, and what authorities were entitled to apply legal justice to them?

[2] Memo of January 25, 2002, as reproduced in Karen J. Greenberg and Joshua L. Dratel, eds., *The Torture Papers: The Road to Abu Ghraib* (New York: Cambridge University Press, 2005).

[3] Jack Goldsmith, *The Terror Presidency: Law and Judgment inside the Bush Administration* (New York: W.W. Norton, 2007), p. 97.

Lawfare and the Red Cross

In Chapter 2 we observed how the so called "neo-cons" held a dim view of international law and organization in general, compared to American virtue and prerogatives. In Chapter 3 we reviewed how John Yoo and other lawyers in the Bush Administration deconstructed the legal protection of prisoners that is based in international law. Here we emphasize what this meant for international human law (IHL) and humanitarian law and for the ICRC which is linked to IHL.

More than one high Bush official saw IHL and humanitarian law, and the international organizations that sought to apply it, as actually in league with the enemy. What some others thought normal defense of normal law, and indeed progressive steps, Secretary of Defense Rumsfeld and some others saw as "lawfare," the pursuit of an anti-American (and anti-Rumsfeld) agenda by enemies. Human Rights Watch, for example, taking a cosmopolitan approach to the subject of war crimes, meaning that the organization viewed American offenders as subject to the law like any other nationality, published a report detailing leading war crimes suspects in the United States, including Rumsfeld.[4]

As Jack Goldsmith has accurately recounted: "[According to Rumsfeld] the weak 'enemy' using asymmetric legal weapons was not al Qaeda, but rather our very differently motivated European and South American allies and the human rights industry that supported their universal jurisdiction aspirations. Rumsfeld saw this form of lawfare as a potentially powerful check on American military power. He also saw it in more personal terms."[5] For two Bush supporters who were close to Pentagon and DOJ officials in the Bush era, "the ICRC has become the leading practitioner of 'lawfare' ..."[6]

Certain Bush officials did not have a monopoly on ultra-nationalist or non-cosmopolitan views. Some Republican congressional circles, led by Senator Jon Kyl of Arizona, circulated a position paper advocating the restructuring of the ICRC so as to get a sizable number of Americans on

4 Human Rights Watch, "Getting Away with Torture?: Command Responsibility for the US Abuse of Detainees," April 2005.

5 Goldsmith, *The Terror Presidency*, p. 58.

6 David B. Rivkin, Jr. and Lee A. Casey, "Friend or Foe?," *Wall Street Journal*, April 11, 205, p. A 23. See also their "Double-Red-Crossed," *The National Interest*, Spring 2005, pp. 63–69.

the Assembly, or governing board.[7] If the United States voluntarily contributed about one-quarter of the ICRC's budget, so his thinking went, Americans should constitute a proportional number of the Assembly. This reaction was triggered primarily by the fact that the ICRC had dared to publically criticize detention at Gitmo without a proper legal framework and the effect it had on the mental health of detainees. ICRC arguments about how lack of a clear legal framework at Gitmo contributed to debilitating stress and anxiety were seen by the American right wing as anti-American statements. Lost in the political shuffle was settled ICRC doctrine: that its discretion was limited, and if its discreet efforts over time did not bear humanitarian fruit, it reserved the right to make public commentary.

The proposed restructuring was highly unlikely since the ICRC Assembly has been drawn from only Swiss nationals since 1863, as decided by cooptation of that body. The American Red Cross and other national Red Cross/Red Crescent societies have no say in the matter. These rules and traditions had been endorsed by the International Conference of the Red Cross and Red Crescent Movement. Voting members at the Conference include states that have ratified the Geneva Conventions for War Victims. And the proposed restructuring was widely seen by many if not most experts as unwise, as happily even some Bush officials understood, since the all-Swiss Assembly contributes to the image of ICRC neutrality. Would an ICRC Assembly with any significant part of its membership comprising Americans be seen as neutral, especially in conflicts involving Washington? How could the ICRC continue to play the role of neutral intermediary if it were seen as heavily influenced by nationals of one of the major states? What would be the reaction in Washington if a sizable part of the Assembly were made up of Iranians, or even French?[8] Would not a restructuring of the

[7] Republican Policy Committee, US Senate, "Are American Interests Being Disserved by the International Committee of the Red Cross?," June 13, 2005.

[8] On the ICRC and the Red Crescent Movement see further David P. Forsythe, *The Humanitarians: The International Committee of the Red Cross* (Cambridge: Cambridge University Press, 2005). The last major discussion about changing the composition of the ICRC's Assembly occurred after the Second World War when the Swedish Red Cross, under the leadership of Count Bernadotte, and anxious to play a larger role in the Red Cross Movement, wanted to internationalize the board. But Bernadotte changed his mind, precisely because of the matter of the ICRC's neutral image which from 1863 has been tied to the permanent neutrality of the Swiss state.

ICRC Assembly actually reduce the chances that the organization would get to visit detained US personnel in the future, since its reputation for neutrality would have been compromised? In any event moderate Republicans and Democrats were able to beat back this trial balloon by those like Senator Kyl.

Nevertheless others on the far right repeatedly attacked the ICRC on various grounds. Republican activists David Rivkin, Jr. and Lee Casey spearheaded the press campaign. They castigated the ICRC for referring to a part of 1977 Additional Protocol I, namely Art. 75, which lays out protections for prisoners that go beyond the 1949 law, as binding on the United States.[9] They failed to note that several US officials had written that the disputed Art. 75 was indeed now part of customary international law. Regardless, to them the ICRC was biased against the United States.[10] Similar criticisms were attributed to unnamed Pentagon officials.[11] James Schlesinger, a former Secretary of Defense who headed one of the investigations after the Abu Ghraib scandal, was also critical of the ICRC. He, too, failed to mention statements about customary international law by US officials when attacking the ICRC for seeing themselves as "the supreme court of humanitarian law" and trying to get the United States to abide by norms it had not consented to.[12]

Clearly there was a determined effort in some American political circles to discredit the ICRC, despite the fact that historically it had been widely recognized as mostly neutral and certainly discreet. During the Cold War if it had strayed from neutrality in places like Korea and Southeast Asia it had tilted toward the West. During the George W. Bush era it was actually still quite conservative (it was repeatedly criticized in certain circles for not speaking out *more* about Gitmo), but

[9] Lee A. Casey and David B. Rivkin, Jr., "Reading the Fine Print," *Washington Times*, June 16, 2004, www.washingtontimes.com/news/2004/jun/16/20040616-09241.

[10] See also their attack on the organization in "Not Your Father's Red Cross," National Review Online, December 20, 2004, www.nationalreview.com/comment/rivkin_casey_delaquil200412200800.asp.

[11] See Rowan Scarborough, "Pentagon, Analysts Hit anti-US Bias at Red Cross," *Washington Times*, December 1, 2004.

[12] PBS NewsHour, "Chaos at Abu Ghraib," August 24, 2004, www.pbs.org/newshour/bb/military/july-dec04/abughraib_8-24.html.

certain American circles of opinion viewed it as just another left-wing European human rights organization.[13]

Be all that as it may, and despite some defenders of the ICRC, it remains true that there were quite a few in the George W. Bush Administration who saw international law, human rights law, and humanitarian law in essentially negative terms. Likewise, they saw the development of international criminal courts and public prosecutors not as a progressive development for the enforcement of law but as an undesirable complication for American power and virtue.[14] They were especially dismissive of the principle of universal jurisdiction, which allowed any state to prosecute for certain crimes like genocide and grave breaches of IHL, such as torture and cruel treatment, without regard to the nationality of the defendant or location of the alleged crime.[15]

Goldsmith, who as already noted became head of the OLC in the DOJ for a short time in the first George W. Bush Administration, argued that in pushing so hard for unlimited Executive power, the Bush team unnecessarily provoked a push back by especially the US Supreme Court.[16] Some would add also by the Congress. There was also foreign criticism of Bush arguments and policies. This chapter examines the

[13] Later in this chapter it is noted that several Supreme Court Justices in the various *Hamdan* opinions (2006) referred to API, Art. 75 as having passed into customary international law. The ICRC followed these debates and decided not to press the argument about US officials having endorsed API, Art. 75 as part of customary international law, fearing that Bush officials would repudiate these earlier US statements. Senator McCain, NSC Advisor Rice, Secretary of State Powell, and others rose to the defense of the ICRC. See McCain's comments in *Wall Street Journal*, June 1, 2004. For another example of support for the ICRC by an official in the Bush Administration, see William H. Taft, IV, "Accounting for the Detainees," *Washington Post*, September 27, 2006.

[14] Jack Goldsmith is actually among these. He attributes great power to the human rights lobby, but he prefers to prioritize the decisions of democratically elected national leaders. He does not address the question of what to do when democratically elected national leaders violate international law or otherwise take wrong decisions. Two of the major sources of legitimacy for public policy are: (1) being the product of freely elected governments; and (2) being in conformity with international law. It is not clear what happens to the amorphous idea of legitimacy when the two are in conflict. See further Seyla Benhabib, *Another Cosmopolitanism* (Oxford and New York: Oxford University Press, 2006). She provides a sophisticated discussion of the conflict between legality and democratic legitimacy, but no resolution of the clash.

[15] See further Henry Kissinger, "The Pitfalls of Universal Jurisdiction: Risking Judicial Tyranny," *Foreign Affairs*, 19, 4 (July–August, 2001), from p. 86.

[16] Goldsmith, *The Terror Presidency*.

Goldsmith argument in slightly broader form. It suggests that the extensive Executive claims were detrimental not only to presidential power but to US national interests. By asserting US and presidential exemptionalism from law as normally understood, both internationally and nationally, the Bush team actually brought about some reassertion of traditional limits on the United States and its President. Along the way, its revolutionary claims created much criticism and opposition. At the time of writing the Barack Obama Administration had reasserted some of the same Bush claims to Executive prerogative, even while scaling back or altering other Bush legal arguments and related policies.

Debates about detention classification

In the most general terms, 9/11 raised the question of whether those taking violent action against the United States should be seen through the war model or the law enforcement model. Were members of Al-Qaeda (and their supporters) some type of combatant or some type of criminal? Should one respond with military measures or judicial measures as far as retributive justice was concerned? Similar questions had faced the British when dealing with "the troubles" in Northern Ireland, with London responding with hybrid and shifting measures entailing both the war model and the enforcement model, depending on which years were concerned.[17] In general over time, the British tended to shift from the war model to the enforcement model. The US record was to prove similar, but not completely so.

In general, the war model tends to undercut and lower human rights standards normally at play in the law enforcement model. As one author argues: "the claim that a state's responses to terrorism fall within international humanitarian law broadens the idea of war in ways that will not enhance human rights . . . Applying the Geneva Conventions to terrorism in general would thus entrench the idea that armed conflict is normal and routine. Indeed, if efforts to combat terrorism in general always involve an armed conflict, then ... it is a conflict with no boundaries in time or space. It takes place everywhere, has no logical

[17] Timony Shanahan, *The Provisional Irish Republic Army and the Morality of Terrorism* (Edinburgh: Edinburgh University Press, 2009).

culmination, and irrevocably blurs the distinctions between civilian and combatant that are so important to the Geneva Conventions."[18]

In traditional wars among states such as the Second World War, states owed legal obligations to each other as per their treaty commitments and via customary international law, but individual prisoners of war and other war detainees such as civilians in occupied territory were said to have no rights of legal action themselves.[19] Legal instruments such as the 1929 Geneva Convention on Prisoners of War were implemented, more or less, by the workings of state reciprocity and with the help of Protecting Powers (neutral states designated by the belligerents to help with treaty implementation). The ICRC made its traditional contributions to the process by visiting detainees, tracing missing persons, and organizing humanitarian assistance and family contacts. As already noted, the ICRC did not gain an explicit right of access to detainees in international armed conflict until 1949. Prisoners of war could be held for the duration of the conflict. Regular criminal courts had little role to play. Military Commissions were sometimes used.

Bush Administration claims that it was fighting a Global War on Terror (GWOT) but without the full application of the laws of war caused a number of organizations such as the American Civil Liberties Union (ACLU) and the Center for Constitutional Rights, among others, to challenge the Bush paradigm through court cases in civil proceedings. The Bush Administration's attempt to hold Al-Qaeda and Taliban detainees, and others, in unlimited and undefined administrative detention, with no supervision by courts, caused these organizations to work with various persons seen by Washington as enemy prisoners to test the Bush arguments. The context was characterized primarily by: (1) the lack of a UN human rights court; (2) the inability of private parties to gain access to the International Court of Justice at the Hague (ICJ, aka the World Court, where only states are parties to binding judgments, and only those states that have so consented can be sued there); and (3) the lack of US ratification of the Rome Statute regarding the International Criminal Court (ICC). Hence plaintiffs and their legal

[18] John T. Parry, *Understanding Torture: Law, Violence, and Political Identity* (Ann Arbor: University of Michigan Press, 2010), p. 25, and the source on which he relies, Helen Duffy, *The "War on Terror" and the Framework of International Humanitarian Law* (New York and Cambridge: Cambridge University Press, 2005).

[19] US Supreme Court, *Eisentrager* case: 339 US 763.

counsel focused primarily on US courts (although they sought to engage other national courts as well, such as in Germany and Spain). They also focused first on Guantánamo rather than Afghanistan or Iraq. Plaintiffs were convinced that miscarriages of justice were being carried out there by the United States, both with regard to who was being detained and how detainees were being treated.

Geneva Convention III of 1949 (pertaining to POWs), states that if in an international armed conflict question arises as to the legal status of someone suspected of hostile action, a "competent tribunal" shall be created to determine the proper status of the individual. In Vietnam, despite controversy over the correct legal characterization of that conflict and the legal status of various parties involved there, the United States had held a number of "Art. 5 hearings" in a good faith effort to determine the status and rights of the person in question. In other armed conflicts the US military had likewise held Art. 5 proceedings in order to try to properly classify those it had captured.[20] The Bush team refused to hold Art. 5 hearings regarding those held at Gitmo and in Afghanistan, preferring to make blanket and *a priori* determinations.

(The United States formally accepted the traditional understanding of IHL in Iraq from March 2003 until the official end of US occupation in Summer 2004, meaning for present purposes that even Iraqi "terrorists" had the right not to be tortured or otherwise abused, being civilians under Geneva Convention IV [which pertained to international armed conflict and resulting occupation]. Washington, however, never did fully accept this as the proper legal paradigm for Afghanistan from October 2001, as we noted in Chapter 2. With regard to Iraq, Washington maintained that non-Iraqi detainees, such as foreign jihadists from, say, Algeria, did not benefit from "Geneva" protections.[21])

The Bush team proceeded with detention early on after 9/11 without a careful and reliable system for reviewing the validity of its seizures. It also made no study of the effectiveness of coercive versus non-coercive interrogation. On the basis of its suspicions, it made a sweeping and *a priori* judgment that those under its control were "unlawful enemy combatants." This term is not found in international law but was

[20] Maj. James F. Gebhardt, *The Road to Abu Ghraib: US Army Detainee Doctrine and Experience*, Global War on Terror Occasional Paper 6 (Fort Leavenworth: Combat Studies Institute Press, n.d.).

[21] See Goldsmith, *The Terror Presidency*.

more or less deduced from that law: if POWs were privileged combatants, then other detained combatants must be unlawful. As noted previously, the Bush Administration overruled initial military inclinations to hold Art. 5 hearings, leaving prisoners with no recourse in challenging the validity of their seizure and detention. (We have already noted that Iraq was supposed to be different regarding the treatment of prisoners but was not during 2003–2005.) After 9/11, persons could theoretically be held in administrative detention forever, given that the US GWOT might last forever. Under the Bush version of the war model, prisoners at Gitmo in particular had no clear status in international law, no way to challenge their detention, and no sure prospect of release. It was this condition that prompted the ICRC to comment publicly on the link between the lack of an agreed legal framework and the mental health of detainees.

In a series of civil law cases that wound their way to the US Supreme Court, that body ruled that: Guantánamo was within the *de facto* jurisdiction of the United States (*Rasul* v. *Bush* and *Hamdi* v. *Rumsfeld* cases); prisoners there did have the right of habeas corpus or some equivalent thereof (the right to challenge the reasons for detention) (*Rasul* v. *Bush* and *Hamdi* v. *Rumsfeld* cases); the Congress even though so requested by the President could not terminate the right of habeas for those prisoners who had already filed petitions of challenge (*Hamdan* v. *Rumsfeld* case); and finally, indeed, prisoners could have access to US federal courts to determine the validity of the government's detention program (*Boumediene* v. *Bush* case).[22]

Nine days after *Rasul* and *Hamdi* in 2004, the Bush Administration instituted at Gitmo the Combatant Status Review Tribunals (CSRT) system. This system, comprising US military personnel, was to review the designation of "unlawful enemy combatant." Prisoners had no right to an attorney and were not allowed to see the full information that had led to their seizure and detention. Lt. Col. Stephen Abraham, assigned to the CSRT system for some six months during 2004–2005, said that he was asked to ratify vague US statements lacking reliability.[23] In 570

[22] For early overviews see Richard M. Pious, *The War on Terrorism and the Rule of Law* (New York and Oxford: Oxford University Press, 2006); and H. L. Pohlman, *Terrorism and the Constitution: The Post 9/11 Cases* (New York: Rowman & Littlefield, 2007).

[23] Ben Fox, AP, "Army Officer Says Gitmo Panels Flawed," *Washington Post*, June 23, 2007, www.washingtonpost.com/wp-dyn/contents/articles/2007/06/23/AR2007062300398.html.

tribunal reviews between 2004 and 2007, only thirty-eight persons were held to be wrongly detained and classified.[24] If the US authorities did not get the determination they wanted in a first CSRT, they were free to convene a second or third review until they got the judgment they wanted. Little wonder, then, that the CSRT system was vigorously criticized by various human rights organizations. One might recall statements by various US authorities, both military and CIA, that most of the CIA detainees did not belong there (yet the CSRT system gave Washington the determinations that higher authorities wanted). The ICRC continued to say – sometimes publicly – that the lack of a proper legal framework for the Gitmo regime of detention, and the prospect of indefinite detention, was a serious humanitarian problem.

The CSRT system was supplemented in 2005 by an Administrative Review Board that annually reviewed whether detainees might be released or transferred, whatever the original judgment by the CSRTs. These boards made a number of recommendations that certain prisoners be released or transferred to other national authorities because of being a low security threat. But the overall dual system review of detention remained "anemic" in terms of due process.[25]

It seems to be the case that with regard to at least 60 percent or more of those held at Gitmo over time, the United States lacked clear and compelling information showing violent action against the country or its personnel abroad.[26] Most of those prisoners were therefore eventually released to their countries of origin, or to another destination, where often the local authorities either refused to prosecute or failed to obtain a conviction for criminal action. (Some prisoners were cleared but not released, due to the difficulty of finding a reliable or safe haven.) Of those so released, the percentage subsequently engaging in violent action against persons or installations of the United States is difficult to say, Pentagon figures on this point being debatable.[27] Clearly, some

[24] Human Rights First (HRF), "Tortured Justice" (April 2008), HRF web site.
[25] See Benjamin Wittes, *Law and the Long War: The Future of Justice in an Age of Terror* (New York: Penguin Press, 2008) for details.
[26] See Wittes, *Law and the Long War*, p. 99.
[27] See Peter Bergen and Katherine Tiedemann, "Inflating the Guantánamo Threat," *New York Times*, May 29, 2009, www.nytimes.com/2009/05/29/opinion/29bergen.html. A study of this subject based at Seaton Hall University and another at the US Military Academy at West Point reached different conclusions. See also Elisabeth Bumiller, "Many Ex-Detainees Said to Be Engaged in Terror,"

who were detained for lengthy periods were detained in error; and some who were released probably should not have been because of security considerations. One released detainee became a high Taliban operative in Afghanistan.[28] Another former Gitmo prisoner returned to militancy in Yemen.[29] Yet another, having been detained in error for seven years, returned to being a journalist; working for Al Jazeera, which is oriented primarily to the Arab-speaking world, he did not hide his criticism of US detention policies.[30]

In 2005, when a Republican Congress passed the Detainee Treatment Act (DTA), a section of that otherwise progressive legislation tried to eliminate habeas for Gitmo detainees. This is what prompted part of the *Hamdan* judgment in 2006, in which a plurality of the justices on the Supreme Court agreed that the DTA legislation did not block the Court's review of legal petitions already filed. So a controlling group of justices (Ginsberg, Souter, Stevens, Breyer – and sometimes Kennedy) was determined to review Executive authority on the matter of classification of enemy prisoners.

At about the time of the passage of the DTA in 2005, the bipartisan members of the 9/11 Commission, continuing as the 9/11 Public Discourse Project, criticized the Bush Administration for not having come up with a responsible and workable legal framework for detention. The ICRC had been raising precisely this point for some time, publicly since May 2003. The Commission/Project members urged the application of the 1949 Geneva Conventions as the proper framework.[31]

In 2006, when a Republican Congress passed the Military Commissions Act (MCA, dealt with further on p. 184), it again denied the right of habeas to Gitmo prisoners, a legislative reaction to

New York Times, January 7, 2010, www.nytimes.com/2010/01/07/us/politics/07gitmo.html.

28 For the Associated Press, Kathy Gannon and Pauline Jelinek, "Officials: Ex-Gitmo Detainee Now Running Afghan Battles," *Lincoln Journal Star*, March 4, 2010, p. A-5.

29 For the Associated Press, Mike Melia and Sarah El Deeb, "One-time Gitmo Detainee Now al-Qaida Leader," *Lincoln Journal Star*, January 1, 2010, p. A-8.

30 Brian Stelter, "From Guantánamo to Desk at Al Jazeera," *New York Times*, December 23, 2009, www.nytimes.com/2009/12/23/world/middleeast/23jazeera.html.

31 Jonathan Weisman, "Senators Agree on Detainee Rights," *Washington Post*, November 15, 2005, p. A 1; and Human Rights First, "U. S. Law and Security Digest," no. 73, November 17, 2005.

countermand *Hamdan*. In the view of Wittes, a view widely shared, this was "a partisan bill hastily cobbled together and pushed through on the eve of the midterm elections."[32]

So on the question of detention and classification at Gitmo, the Bush Administration's unilateral claims led to a tripartite struggle between the Executive, the Legislature, and the Judiciary as to proper prisoner status and process. A majority on the Court was willing to challenge several aspects of presidential claims, but the Bush Administration continued to rely on a deferential Republican Congress to try to get what it wanted – at least until Democrats won control of both houses in November 2006.[33]

In the *Boumediene* case of June 2008, the Supreme Court reversed itself in order to once again take up the subject of habeas. Having refused to grant *certiorari* when Boumediene first appealed, the Court then learned of the experience of Lt. Col. Stephen Abraham, as noted above, who experienced pressure to sign off on unreliable evidence in the CSRT process. Upon reconsideration, which was quite unusual (it had been some sixty years since the Court refused *certiorari* and then turned around and granted it), by a 5–4 vote the Court again reaffirmed that Gitmo prisoners had the right of habeas corpus. Justices Scalia, Thomas, Alito, and Roberts were sympathetic to Executive discretion, especially when endorsed by congressional action, whereas Kennedy, Ginsberg, Souter, Breyer, and Stevens were concerned about possible arbitrary detention – even for aliens said to be associated with the so-called GWOT.

In the wake of *Boumediene* that endorsed habeas at Gitmo, several courts ordered the release of Gitmo detainees, holding that the government's allegations were not supported by reliable evidence. One judge to so rule was not supportive of the Supreme Court's judgment and remarked about the lack of wisdom entailed in projecting courts into intelligence matters, but felt bound to implement what the Supreme

[32] Wittes, *Law and the Long War*, p. 69. On the response of President Bush to *Hamdan*, featuring political maneuvers rather than concern for due process, see David A. Martin, "Judicial Review and The Military Commissions Act: On Striking the Right Balance," *American Journal of International Law*, 101, 2 (April 2007), pp. 344–362.

[33] For an accurate and concise review, see Robert Lallitto, "The Legacy of the Magna Carta in Recent Supreme Court Decisions on Detainees' Rights," *PS*, 43, 3 (July 2010), pp. 483–486.

Court had decreed.[34] But especially since Congress was unable to establish a clear legal framework for detention related to terror, a series of habeas judgments ensued, with much inconsistency. With perhaps some 200 habeas petitions anticipated (because of the number of Gitmo detainees remaining) at one point the government had lost thirty of thirty-eight early habeas cases.[35] Slightly later the count was thirty-six lost out of fifty-one.[36] A study by authors at the Brookings Institution showed that the probability of a Gitmo detainee winning his habeas proceedings was greatly affected by which judge ruled on his case.[37] Common standards and perspectives were few.[38] Sometimes lower court judgments were reversed by appellate courts, showing how the same factual record could be read differently by different judges, perhaps with different philosophies about the interplay of national security and individual rights.

The Obama Administration discussed a statutory framework with Senator Graham (R, SC) in particular, but finally abandoned the project and decided to continue to rely on the vague and controversial congressional Authorization to Use Military Force (AUMF, 2001), as had its predecessor.[39] The AUMF was so vague that in effect it posed almost no limits on Executive decisions. When, for the Obama Administration, the State Department Legal Advisor, Harold Koh, asserted to the American Society of International Law that the Obama team was relying on the AUMF as informed by the principles of the laws of war, that assertion remained devoid of specific limitations on Executive decisions.[40]

[34] William Glaberson, "Judge Declares Five Detainees Held Illegally," *New York Times*, November 21, 2008, www.nytimes.com/2008/11/21/us/21Guantánamo.html.

[35] Peter Finn, "Administration Won't Seek New Detention System," *Washington Post*, September 24, 2009, www.washingtonpost.com/wp-dyn/content/article/2009/09/23/AR2009092304427. Of the thirty ordered released, twenty were still held at Gitmo because no state agreed to take them.

[36] Charlie Savage, "Reversal Upholds Detention of Yemeni at Guantánamo," *New York Times*, July 13, 2010, www.nytimes.com/2010/07/14/nyregion/14detain.html.

[37] Benjamin Wittes, Robert Cheney, and Rabea Benhalim, "The Emerging Law of Detention: The Guantánamo Habeas Cases as Lawmaking," *Governance Studies*, January 22, 2010.

[38] See also Jack Goldsmith and Benjamin Wittes, "No Place to Write Detention Policy," *Washington Post*, December 22, 2009, p. A 19.

[39] Finn, "Administration Won't Seek New Detention System."

[40] "The Obama Administration and International Law," March 25, 2010, US Department of State, www.state.gov/s/l/releases/remarks/130110.htm.

Senator Graham continued to push for a legislative framework to avoid both controversial Executive decisions and inconsistent judicial pronouncements, but agreement remained elusive at the time of writing.[41] One close student of these matters vigorously criticized the Obama team for not crafting a statutory framework that would constitute a compromise between liberals and conservatives, and in the process improve on the Bush record while acknowledging that relying on the federal courts alone and avoiding all administrative detention was not politically feasible.[42] A central problem was that President Obama and his Attorney General Eric Holder wanted to use the federal courts as much as possible, whereas Senator Graham was firmly opposed to trying leading Al-Qaeda operatives like Khalid Sheikh Mohammed in those courts.[43] The Administration wanted to minimize Military Commissions and Senator Graham wanted to maximize them.

The Supreme Court gave the Bush Administration endorsement of some of its claims, namely that the United States was indeed involved in a global war against Al-Qaeda even though the latter was a non-state actor, and that the President could designate persons as "unlawful enemy combatants."[44] This latter judicial position involved a broad reading of the congressional AUMF, since the Congress in its rush to give the President broad authority for responding to 9/11 had never been clear on this point. Moreover, two of the detainees, Hamdi (held at Gitmo) and José Padilla (held in a military prison in South Carolina) were American citizens. Ali Saleh Kahlah al-Marri, the sleeper agent in the American Midwest, was a legal resident alien (also held in South

[41] Charlie Savage, "Senator Proposes Deal on Handling of Detainess," *New York Times*, March 3, 2010, www.nytimes.com/2010/03/04/us/politics/04commissions.html. Senator Graham wanted high-level terror suspects tried in Military Commissions, which was opposed by a number of supporters of the Obama Administration who favored trials in federal courts. He also wanted to legalize open-ended administrative detention, which again was opposed by many Democrats and human rights groups.

[42] Benjamin Wittes, "Obama's Dick Cheney Moment," *Washington Post*, September 29, 2009, www.washingtonpost.com/wp-dyn/content/article/2009/09/28/AR2009092802492.

[43] Peter Finn, "Sen. Graham: U.S. is 'punting' on national security issues," *Washington Post*, September 20, 2010, www.washingtonpost.com/wp-dyn/content/article/2010/09/20.

[44] The UN Security Council had already decided by unanimous vote in 2001 that the United States was justified in using forceful self-defense after the armed attacks by Al-Qaeda.

Carolina). The notion that the President could unilaterally declare American citizens or legal residents to be unlawful enemy combatants and stripped of at least some of their constitutional rights was deeply troubling to many who followed these matters. (One of the Nazis who appeared before FDR's Military Commission in the Second World War, however, was a US citizen.) There was no explicit and specific legal framework to guide or restrain presidential decisions on this matter.

Padilla, having been seized on American soil far from any battlefield (Chicago), was locked away in solitary confinement in South Carolina for long periods and denied access to legal counsel and habeas. He claimed other abuse as well. On the eve of a court ruling regarding his rights, the Bush Administration dropped charges about his being an enemy agent bent on setting off a "dirty bomb" and transferred him to the federal court system where he was eventually convicted of helping to finance Al-Qaeda.[45] He did not receive a life sentence but rather seventeen years, the judge taking into account, *inter alia*, the harsh conditions of his detention.[46] The Bush team thus avoided a Supreme Court judgment on the rights of an American who had been labeled an unlawful enemy combatant, a judgment they no doubt feared would restrict Executive authority. Padilla may have been a dangerous thug, but here we find an American citizen being held incommunicado on American soil solely based on Executive information, and then denied any right to contest that view. For a certain number of other detainees, the Executive had been mistaken about the nature of the prisoner – as we showed in Chapters 4 and 5. It appears to be the case that at least seven persons were wrongly "rendered" abroad for abusive interrogation. Al-Marri, who pleaded guilty in the federal courts, also received a reduced sentence because of his severe mistreatment in detention.

By comparison Daniel Maldonado, another American citizen, who was seized by Kenya because of his activities with Muslim extremist groups in Somalia and transferred to the United States, unlike Padilla was never held as an "unlawful enemy combatant." Rather he was charged in the US federal court system (like John Walker Lindh) and

[45] For a summary of the Padilla case see Peter Jan Honigsberg, *Our Nation Unhinged: The Human Consequences of the War on Terror* (Berkeley: University of California Press, 2009), *passim*.

[46] Kirk Semple, "Padilla Gets 17-Year Term For Role in Conspiracy," *New York Times*, January 23, 2008, p. A 14.

eventually convicted of material support of terrorism (like Padilla). Apparently he had been held in prolonged solitary confinement. Comparing Padilla and Maldonado, both American citizens, shows the arbitrary nature of the Bush classification system. In fact, there really was no system. Moreover, whereas the Padilla case got considerable media attention, the Maldonado case got very little.

At the time of writing there was still controversy about who might be detained at Guantánamo and what rights they possessed. The change from Bush to Obama had not led to clarity on these issues, even if the latter administration had dropped the concept of "unlawful enemy combatant" in favor of the more traditional notion of "unprivileged combatant." (As explained previously, prisoners of war are privileged combatants, whereas other combatants taking up arms but not meeting the terms of Geneva Convention III are, when detained, unprivileged combatants. In the view of the ICRC they are still covered by IHL, either the full Geneva Convention IV or at least its Common Article 3, even though not protected by Geneva Convention III covering POWs.)

For example, in 2010 a US federal appeals court ruled that a Gitmo detainee, Bensayah Belkacem from Algeria, was not an active participant in Al-Qaeda. The Administration, and a lower court, had seen the detainee as facilitating travel to Afghanistan for those wanting to fight for the terrorist organization, and thus effectively a member of the terrorist organization. But the appellate court held that the prosecution had failed to show that Bensayah had any direct connection to Al-Qaeda.[47] Thus one issue was whether indirect supporters of terrorism could be held in the same way as active participants. How broad was the concept of combatant? Did it include various types of supporters? Another question in the Bensayah case focused on the quality of the government's evidence.

Similar issues about the US right to detain, and prisoner rights to challenge that detention, arose in the context of Afghanistan. As the Obama Administration tried to reduce the number of prisoners at Gitmo it expanded detention at the new facility at Parwan. The prison

[47] For a summary see Charlie Savage, "Appeals Court Sides With Detainee," *New York Times*, July 3, 2010, www.nytimes.com/2010/04/04/us/04gitmo.html. For coverage of debates inside the Obama Administration on these and related issues, see Charlie Savage, "Obama Team is Divided on Tactics Against Terrorism," *New York Times*, March 28, 2010, www.nytimes.com/2010/03/29/us/politics/29force.html.

at Bagram was associated with abuse, and US authorities knew it. They did not want other symbols like Guantánamo and Abu Ghraib to hinder their relations with the Muslims they were trying to win over. At Parwan the US military was holding a number of detainees seized not only in Afghanistan but also in various parts of the world. The Obama team did not want the prison to become a recruiting ground for Islamic extremists, and so there were efforts at improved review, timely release, and transfer to the Afghan court system (itself underdeveloped).[48]

Similar to the Bush Administration, however, the Obama team fought judicial review of its policies there, even as it instituted some improvements in detention and interrogation.[49] A federal lower court, perhaps looking to Guantánamo, held that foreign prisoners at Bagram did have a right of habeas.[50] But a federal appeals court ruled in 2010 that detainees held in Afghanistan did not have the right of access to US courts to review their detention.[51] This judgment was hailed by those who, like Senator Graham, thought it unwise for US courts to review detention in zones of armed conflict, while criticized by those who noted that some detainees in question were not from Afghanistan but had been seized in other countries. The critics wondered how erroneous detention was to be properly and surely corrected.

Debates about Military Commissions

In November 2001 President Bush declared an intention to try "unlawful enemy combatants" in Military Commissions. Such commissions

[48] Alissa J. Rubin, "U.S. Frees Detainees, but Afghans' Anger Persists," *New York Times*, March 19, 2010, www.nytimes.com/2010/03/20/world/asia/20kabul.html. Also Eric Schmitt, "U.S. Moves to Overhaul Jails that Breed Insurgents in Afghanistan," *New York Times*, October 8, 2009, www.nytimes.com/2009/10/08/world/asia/08detain.html. According to one report in the author's possession, at one point the United States was holding some 600 prisoners in Afghanistan, 400 of which were *not* high-level enemy combatants.

[49] Editorial, "Back to Bagram," *New York Times*, September 20, 2009, www.nytimes.com/2009/09/21/opinion/21mon2.html.

[50] Charlie Savage, "Judge Rules Some Prisoners at Bagram Have Right of Habeas Corpus," *New York Times*, April 3, 2009, www.nytimes.com/2009/04/03/washington/03bagram.html.

[51] Charlie Savage, "Detainees Barred From Access to U.S. Courts," *New York Times*, May 21, 2010, www.nytimes.com/2010/05/22/world/asia/22detain.html. The case was *Al Maqaleh* v. *Gates*.

have a rather long and controversial position in US history,[52] being associated with "rough justice."[53] The primary reason for their use in modern times is to abbreviate the due process requirements of US federal law and even of US military law. Their real central purpose is to make it easier for the prosecution to gain convictions, taking into account such things as the difficulty of making a crime scene out of the amorphous "battlefield" in places like Afghanistan and the desire to protect sensitive sources of information. In the case of the Bush Administration, the initial proposal was to allow the death penalty, perhaps via information gained by abuse, with hearsay being admissible, without the defendant being allowed the legal counsel of his choice or to cross-examine any witnesses – and all by fiat of the Executive.[54] For the Gitmo prisoners, maybe sixty-five to seventy-five trials were foreseen. In the prolonged debate that ensued, two questions were central: (1) were Military Commissions needed after 9/11, or could federal courts or military courts-martial try foreign enemy prisoners; and (2) if Military Commissions were needed, how much due process was enough to satisfy US and international law?

A core problem during the Bush Administration was that the system of Military Commissions was not independent but firmly under the control of the Pentagon. The system was overseen by the Office of the Secretary of Defense (first Rumsfeld and then Robert Gates in the Bush and Obama Administrations), through a Deputy Secretary of Defense (Gordon England toward the end of the Bush era) and the DOD General Counsel (first William Haynes). Haynes is reported to have indicated that he wanted convictions and that acquittals would not be a good thing.[55] There was a Convening Authority, the most well known of which was perhaps Susan Crawford, for mid-level oversight. She decided to drop charges against al-Qahtani, given his torture, which she characterized in those terms, as we have noted already. For some time

[52] For a quick overview see Eugene R. Fidell, "The Trouble With Tribunals," *New York Times*, June 14, 2009, www.nytimes.com/2009/06/14/opinion/14fidell.html. See also Pierce O'Donnell, *In Time of War* (New York: The New Press, 2005).

[53] Wittes, *Law and the Long War*, p. 176.

[54] For a critical overview see Amnesty International (AI), "Guantánamo's Military Commissions: A Travesty of Justice," 51/184/2006, AI web site.

[55] *Democracy Now*, July 16, 2008, www.democracynow.org/2008/7/16/fmr_chief_Guantánamo_prosecutor_Says_military.

her legal advisor was Thomas Hartmann, who was actually barred from further action in a case because of efforts to exert undue influence to get a conviction.[56] Hartmann was in favor of allowing convictions on the basis of confessions obtained by waterboarding and other forms of severe abuse.[57] There was also an official in charge of prosecutions. One of the officers who held this post, Col. Morris Davis, resigned to protest what he considered an unfair process. He repeatedly had differences of opinion particularly with Haynes and Hartmann. A prosecutor, Lt. Col. Darrel Vandeveld, was one of six who resigned in protest. He objected to, among other defects, the fact that critical information was withheld from the defense.[58] Most of the remaining personnel were US military officials also: prosecutors, one military judge per Commission, four military staff serving alongside each judge, and many defense attorneys. These latter were sometimes joined by civilian attorneys who volunteered their services in a *pro bono* capacity.

The system was plagued by slowness and controversy. At the time of the election of President Obama, two persons had been tried and convicted in this system. One was Salim Hamdan, a driver for Osama bin Laden and Al-Qaeda, who was given a relatively light sentence of five months, widely interpreted as a slap on the wrist. He was then deported. The second was Ali Hamza al-Bahlul, a propaganda operative for Al-Qaeda, who refused to cooperate with the Commission system and who received a life sentence. (The Australian David Hicks had agreed to a plea bargain to avoid Commission trial, and received a relatively light sentence to be served in Australia.) At that point Obama suspended proceedings in order to evaluate the system. At the time of writing, while Obama had changed positions and indicated support for a reformed Military Commission system, it remained controversial and had produced one further conviction: Ibrahim al-Qosi, a cook and general assistant for bin Laden, who pleaded guilty to conspiracy and material support for terrorism.

[56] *Ibid.*

[57] Morris Davis, "Unforgivable Behavior, Inadmissible Evidence," *New York Times*, February 17, 2008, www.nytimes.com/2008/02/17/opinion/17davis.html.

[58] Human Rights Watch (HRW), "Confessions of a Former Guantánamo Prosecutor," October 26, 2008, HRW web site. Also Davis, "Unforgivable Behavior."

One central issue was the same as for Padilla. Even if a person was highly likely to be a security threat, was he entitled to a fair treatment and trial? Col. Davis, mentioned above, put it this way:

> I've seen it reported a number of times that I testified on behalf of Salim Hamdan. You know, I've seen the evidence against Mr. Hamdan, and I have little doubt in my mind that he's – as I think it is well known, he was captured with surface-to-air-missiles in the back of his car, and the only thing flying in Afghanistan at that time were geese and us. So I have little doubt about his guilt. And so, I don't believe I'm testifying for Salim Hamdan, but what I am testifying for is that Mr. Hamdan and all of the detainees that will face military commissions are entitled to a fair trial.[59]

After all, if one of the primary purposes of a trial, of some kind of legal justice even if under military supervision, is expressive – to convey to everyone your standards, your humanity, your civilization, your values – then blatantly unfair proceedings are not going to accomplish that objective.[60] Other objectives might be achieved even by unfair trials, such as taking dangerous people "off the streets."

Certainly from the point of view of many US military lawyers assigned as defense counsel, the system was unfair. They did not have full confidentiality with the prisoners, they had great difficulty in obtaining access to the full dossier used by the prosecution (indeed, key exculpatory evidence was sometimes withheld), their efforts to call witnesses for the defense were made difficult or denied, and so on. Many protested, at the risk of their military careers. By and large the military defense counsels were much more independent and determined to properly represent the clients assigned to them than most expected at the start.[61] Civilian defense counsels for Gitmo defendants were also highly praised in some circles, although other circles stirred controversy by

59 *Democracy Now*, July 16, 2008.

60 For a clear, short exposition see Mark A. Drumbl, "The Expressive Value of Prosecuting and Punishing Terrorists: *Hamdan*, the Geneva Conventions, and International Criminal Law," *The George Washington Law Review*, 75, 5–6 (August 2007), pp. 1165–1199. See also his longer study, *Atrocity, Punishment, and International Law* (Cambridge and New York: Cambridge University Press, 2007).

61 See Tim Golden, "Administration Officials Split Over Stalled Military Tribunals," *New York Times*, October 25, 2004, www.nytimes.com/2004/10/25/international/world.

referring to such legal teams as un-American that should be denied further legal business.[62]

Lt. Comm. William C. Kuebler, representing the youthful Canadian Omar Khadr, asserted that the system worked to get convictions on the basis of "no real evidence." He also charged that officials on the government side "launder evidence derived from torture."[63] Any trial for Khadr produced controversy, since he was fifteen years of age when he allegedly threw a grenade that killed a US soldier in Afghanistan. He was also abused in detention.[64] International standards and US federal law both made special provisions for legal charges against those under eighteen. The Obama team allowed the Khadr case to proceed in a Military Commission.[65] Eventually a deal was reached in which Khadr, then twenty-four years of age, confessed to taking violent actions against Americans in Afghanistan, in return for which he received a limited sentence of several years, to be served in his native Canada.[66]

Vanderveld, mentioned above, was also outspoken about Mohammed Jawad, seized in Afghanistan when perhaps somewhere in the range of twelve to sixteen years old for throwing a grenade at US soldiers, and who was also abused in detention, including being pushed down stairs while hooded and shackled. He was also subjected to sleep deprivation, being moved eight times a day for fourteen days. By 2009 he had

[62] For a positive view of Gitmo defense teams see Mark P. Denbeaux and Jonathan Hafetz, eds., *The Guantánamo Lawyers: Inside a Prison Outside the Law* (New York: NYU Press, 2010). For coverage of Lynne Cheney's effort to deny legal business to civilian defense teams at Gitmo, see John Schwartz, "Attacks on Detainee Lawyers Split Conservatives," *New York Times*, March 9, 2010, www.nytimes.com/2010/03/10/us/politics/10lawyers.html. A number of conservative circles, including *Forbes Magazine*, saw the Cheney attacks as a new form of McCarthyism.

[63] William Glaberson, "An Unlikely Antagonist in the Detainees' Corner," *New York Times*, June 19, 2008, www.nytimes.com/2008/06/19/us/19gitmo.html. On the independent and important role of JAGs, whether as defense counsel or in other roles, see especially Mark Osiel, *The End of Reciprocity: Terror, Torture, and the Law of War* (New York and Cambridge: Cambridge University Press, 2009), particularly Chapter 12.

[64] Editorial, "Tainted Justice," *New York Times*, May 23, 2010, www.nytimes.com/2010/05/24/opinion/24mon1.html.

[65] Peter Finn, "Former Boy Soldier, Youngest Guantánamo Detainee, Heads Toward Military Tribunal," *Washington Post*, February 10, 2010, p. A-1.

[66] Charlie Savage, "Deal Averts Trial in Disputed Guantánamo Case," *New York Times*, October 25, 2010, www.nytimes.com/2010/10/26/us/26gitmo.html.

already been held for almost seven years.[67] At the end of July 2009, a federal judge ordered Jawad's release, noting the weakness of the government's case and that the detainee had been abused.[68] He was indeed released and returned to Afghanistan, where the authorities had earlier threatened to kill him and his family.[69]

In the Summer of 2006 the Supreme Court held in *Hamdan* that the then-existing system did not meet the standard of Geneva Convention Common Article 3, which was held to be the minimum standard of law applicable in all armed conflicts, and which required "judicial guarantees indispensable to civilized nations." These were not specified in the treaty. The Court referred to API, Art. 75, that listed a number of guarantees. Some judges considered this Article to be part of customary international law. The Court emphasized the narrow, procedural US requirement that the President alone could not establish Military Commissions but required congressional approval. If the Court majority was hoping for congressional help in improving the process, they were to be disappointed. As already noted, a Republican Congress quickly gave President Bush much of what he wanted while taking a slap at the Court's *Hamdan* majority in the 2006 MCA. We have also already noted the follow-on *Boumediene* case, in which continuing turmoil in the Military Commission system caused the Supreme Court to reverse its denial of *certiorari* so as to exercise further judicial oversight over the system. The Court reaffirmed that Gitmo prisoners had the right to habeas.

Candidate Obama, despite having criticized Military Commissions under President Bush, had come around to seeing them as a political necessity by the Fall of 2009. He worked with Congress to produce a new law, the MCA of 2009, which revised the extant system by: focusing on unprivileged combatants, reducing the scope for coerced and hearsay evidence, providing for experienced defense counsel in capital cases, and broadening defense access to witnesses and evidence. Still, much controversy remained, with leading human rights groups like Amnesty International and Human Rights Watch still

[67] Bob Herbert, "How Long Is Long Enough?," *New York Times*, June 30, 2009, www.nytimes.com/2009/06/30/opinion/30herbert.html.

[68] William Blaberson, "Judge Orders Guantánamo Detainee to Be Freed," *New York Times*, July 31, 2009, www.nytimes.com/2009/07/31/us/31gitmo.html.

[69] AP, "Guantánamo Detainee Released," August 25, 2009, www.nytimes.com/2009/08/25/world/asia/25gitmo.html.

arguing that the Commissions failed to meet international standards of due process.[70]

It certainly remained unclear under Obama, as it was under Bush, as to which detainees would be tried in the federal courts and which in the Military Commissions. Clearly the Obama Administration leaned toward greater use of the courts. But the decision to try KSM (Khalid Sheikh Mohammed, the self-styled brains behind the 9/11 attack) in a federal court in New York City produced a strong domestic backlash. Attorney General Eric Holder had asserted that those responsible for foreign attacks should be tried in Military Commissions, using the courts for the others like KSM. This vision was supported by certain Republican legal experts,[71] but that did not dampen the domestic critics driven both by continuing hatred of those associated with 9/11 and by partisan opportunism to embarrass the Obama Administration. It was a fact that under both Bush and Obama, and even before, a large number of terror suspects had been convicted in federal courts, with the courts having devised rules for handling sensitive security and other information.[72] It was also true that the legitimacy of Military Commissions remained in question, both at home and abroad. Despite this ambiguity if not confusion over the proper forum for proceedings, a number of persons, including former Bush security officials, argued for the utility of a dual approach – using both courts and Commissions – for retributive justice in the name of pragmatism and flexibility.[73]

[70] See for example, Amnesty International, "Trials in Error: Military Commissions," October 12, 2009, www.amnesty.org.au/hrs/comments/21836 and the reports cited there; and Human Rights Watch, "US: New Legislation on Military Commissions Doesn't Fix Fundamental Flaws," October 8, 2009, www.hrw.org/en/news/2009/10/08/us-new-legislation-military-commissions.

[71] Jim Comey and Jack Goldsmith, "Holder's Reasonable Decision," *Washington Post*, November 20, 2009, www.washingtonpost.com/wp-dyn/content/articles/2009/11/10/AR2009111903470.

[72] The exact number of terror convictions in federal courts is open to debate because of such parameters as foreign versus domestic terrorism, major versus minor convictions and plea agreements, etc. After 9/11 numbers range from perhaps a dozen major convictions related to radical Islam, to 195 international terror convictions, to 523 total terror convictions. See further the respected *St. Petersburg Times*' "Truth-O-Meter: Obama Claims Bush Administration got 190 Terrorism Convictions in Federal Court," February 12, 2010, www.politifact.com/truth-o-meter/statements/2010/feb/12/barack-obama/obama-claim.

[73] Charlie Savage and Scott Shane, "Experts Urge Keeping Two Options for Terror Trials," *New York Times*, March 8, 2010, www.nytimes.com/2010/03/09/us/politics/09terror.html.

As the Obama team tried to show that federal courts could handle terrorism cases, further controversy arose. In 2010 it moved to try Ahmed Khalfan Ghailani, who had been detained at Gitmo after being held by the CIA. He was alleged to have been, and probably was, involved in the 1998 attacks on US embassies in east Africa. The court barred the government from calling a witness who had been identified by Ghailani while being interrogated during CIA custody. The witness was prepared to testify that Ghailani had purchased explosive material. While the judge did not rule on the defendant's claim that he had been tortured by the CIA, the judge did rule that the circumstances of his CIA detention made it likely that information had been obtained under coercion, hence "poisoned" testimony would not be allowed. It is settled US judicial doctrine that "fruits of the poisoned tree" are not allowed in court.[74] When in 2010 Ghailani was convicted on one count of conspiring to destroy American property and faced a significant prison sentence, critics were incensed that he had been acquitted on a large number of murder charges. Supporters stressed the problem of torture in fair trials, while critics seized the opportunity to criticize the Obama Administration and push for Military Commissions. While those who championed due process and fair trials cheered the ruling, others castigated it. Some of the critics argued that events demonstrated the value of Military Commissions, with their supposed more relaxed rules of evidence. Some also pointed out that even if Ghailani had been acquitted on all charges, he might still have been held by the Executive in administrative detention, making the federal trial a political show trial. Some argued for no trials either in federal court or Military Commission but rather for administrative detention under the law of war principle that combatants could be detained for the duration of the conflict.[75]

Once again, a national consensus on how to process enemy prisoners proved elusive.

[74] Charlie Savage, "Deal Averts Trial in Disputed Guantánamo Case," *New York Times*, October 25, 2010, www.nytimes.com/2010/10/26/us/26gitmo.html. See Benjamin Weiser, "Ghailani Case Ruling Spurs Debate on Trial's Value," *New York Times*, October 7, 2010, www.nytimes.com/2010/10/08/nyregion/08terror.html.

[75] See Jack Goldsmith, "Don't Try Terrorists, Lock Them Up," *New York Times*, October 8, 2010, www.nytimes.com/2010/10/09/opinion/09goldsmith.html.

Two categories of Gitmo detainees were especially problematic when it came to trials. The first comprised those who had been tortured or inhumanly treated, as demonstrated in the *Ghailani* case. Apparently Attorney General John Ashcroft recognized this problem in the Fall of 2001 but came down on the side of preventing any more terrorist attacks by abusive means, even if this made legal justice for the attackers unlikely.[76] It was reported that in later meetings at the White House others in the Executive branch reiterated the point that abusive interrogation undercut punishment via legitimate criminal justice, but to little avail.[77] One can recall, among several relevant cases, in addition to the *Ghailani* case, that charges in the Military Commission system were dropped against al-Qahtani who was tortured at Gitmo, and that the sentences against José Padilla and Ali Saleh Kahlah al-Marri were reduced because of government mistreatment in a military prison in South Carolina. Yet prosecutors may try to pursue charges different from charges linked to abuse, or may try to obtain the same information by non-abusive methods. Then courts have to determine whether the untainted evidence is too close to tainted evidence.[78]

The second group of highly problematic cases comprised prisoners who were probably dangerous to US security, but where the evidence for that status might not stand up to judicial scrutiny, particularly if sensitive sources of information were to be protected. Certainly Presidents, facing domestic political pressures, could be expected to be sensitive to the problem of released prisoners returning to active hostility against US persons and property. (Moreover, there were the abused prisoners against whom the evidence was presumably solid. KSM had been tortured, but he continued to manifest hatred of Americans; no responsible President could simply release him because of past governmental misconduct. At the time of writing it was still undecided where KSM should be tried, or if he should be tried or just placed in administrative detention.)

[76] Human Rights Watch (HRW), "Tortured Justice," April 2008, HRW web site, relying on the book by Bob Woodward, *Bush At War* (New York: Simon & Schuster, 2002).

[77] Carrie Johnson and Josh White, "Interrogation Tactics Were Challenged at White House," *Washington Post*, May 22, 2008, p. A-7.

[78] Key cases are *Nardone* v. *United States* (1939) and *Wong Sun* v. *United States* (1963).

The position of Human Rights Watch, Human Rights First, Amnesty International, and the ACLU, *inter alia*, to try the prisoners in federal courts or release them, did not, to most US officials, adequately protect US security interests for these two problematic categories of detainees – those that had been abused but remained hostile to the United States, and those who were probably hostile but where the evidence was not ironclad. The position of most human rights groups was that federal courts had rules in place to deal with sensitive security issues, and that they had demonstrated a record of being able, in fair proceedings, to convict Al-Qaeda operatives like Richard Reid, Ramzi Yousef, Zacarius Moussaoui, and others. The advocacy groups contrasted the complexities and controversies of the Military Commissions with the on-going record of the federal courts in handling various terrorism cases, both foreign and domestic.[79] But however well grounded this view was in judicial specifics, there were still strong political currents opposed to it – in part because of fear of released detainees returning to the fight. For the human rights groups, due process was trump. For the defenders of Military Commissions and extended administration detention, US security was trump. Candidate Obama had been sympathetic to the first view. President Obama came around to the necessity of accepting the second view, but with some alterations to the policies of the Bush era.

Conclusion

With regard to categories of detainees and the role of Military Commissions during the Bush era, one can only agree with Benjamin Wittes:

> the system is in total disarray. While the vast majority of aliens who fought for or conducted operations on behalf of Al Qaeda have ended up in military detention, some – like attempted shoe-bomber Richard Reid – have ended up

[79] Even as controversy continued in political circles about trials for KSM and Ghailani, other terrorist trials in federal courts continued as usual, with citizens in the locus of court proceedings apparently unconcerned. Thus the trial and sentencing of Faisal Shahzad for attempting to set off a car bomb in Times Square in New York City played out without incident. There was great inconsistency in political debates and public reactions. See Clyde Haberman, "Outside Court, a Failure to be Fearful," *New York Times*, October 7, 2010, www.nytimes.com/2010/10/08/nyregion/08nyc.html.

facing indictment as civilians in federal court. One American citizen – John Walker Lindh – who allied himself with the Taliban was prosecuted and pleaded guilty in federal court and sentenced to twenty years in prison. Another, Yaser Esam Hamdi, did substantially the same thing yet was held for three years in military detention and was then, after the Supreme Court decision that bears his name, sent home to Saudi Arabia … Meanwhile, the so-called Lackawanna Six [from New York state who trained for violence in Afghanistan] … pleaded guilty in federal court [to conspiracy but not violent action] and received sentences ranging from seven to ten years. Australian former Guantánamo detainee David Hicks pleaded guilty before a military commission. Alleged twentieth hijacker Mohammad Al-Qahtani was detained at Guantánamo for years without charge before facing military commission charges … [which have been dropped because he was tortured]. Alleged twentieth hijacker Zacarias Moussaoui went through a circus of a trial in federal court in Virginia. And alleged twentieth hijacker Ramzi Binalshibh was held and interrogated by the CIA in its secret prison [*sic*], then transferred to Guantánamo and ultimately charged alongside Qahtani. Jose Padilla faced detention first in civilian custody and then in military custody for three years, and he then faced trial and conviction in federal court. There is no rhyme or reason to who ends up in what system, save the convenience of the executive branch at any given time.[80]

During the Bush years the process of seizing persons and placing them in various categories and places of detention was unreliable. Many mistakes were made due to factors already noted. Central to these was the failure to hold Art. 5 hearings for those detained in Afghanistan in particular. There was also just simple incompetence as US authorities accepted at face value erroneous claims from various parties ranging from an Afghan clan settling local scores to misinformed Canadian security forces (as per the *Arar* case). From the opening of Gitmo in early 2002 to the occupation of Iraq from the Summer of 2003, US authorities made broad sweeps and dumped numerous prisoners on unprepared detention and interrogation personnel. The Bush Administration simply was unable to come up with a reliable and dependable process for rational and humane detention. One sees this situation clearly when one compares the CSRT system that certified proper detention at Gitmo, for the most part, with the number of habeas cases out of Gitmo that the government lost once independent courts began to get involved.

[80] Wittes, *Law and the Long War*, pp. 155–156.

The process for legal justice was no better, with unsystematic reference to federal courts, Military Commissions, and administrative detention. It fell to the Obama Administration to try to restore some respect for the rule of law while trying to protect US security interests. The Obama team struggled with this dialectic, even as it recognized the loss of US reputation and soft power from decisions of the previous regime. But once torture and lesser forms of mistreatment occur, and once persons are locked up for years in error without recourse to legitimate procedures to challenge their status, most forms of legal justice become tainted. At that point the wisest course of action is not so easy to establish on the basis of consensus or broad support. Once the shock of 9/11 wore down, political elites in Washington could not reach agreement on how to proceed on most of these issues.

The Supreme Court pushed back against Executive claims to have a free hand in detainee affairs, as shown by principally *Rasul, Hamdi, Hamdan*, and *Boumediene*. In one memorable line out of *Hamdi*, Justice Sandra Day O'Connor wrote that "a state of war is not a blank check for the President . . ."[81] Under the ruling in *Boumediene*, at the time of writing in about 75 percent of habeas proceedings out of Gitmo, the Executive lost, as the courts ordered the release of the petitioner. This ruling did not, in fact, always result in the release of the prisoner, since the Executive still had to find a reliable or safe haven. Particularly difficult to deal with were apparently innocent Yemenis at Gitmo, since their native country was unstable with an active Al-Qaeda affiliate.[82]

Clearly issues were not always addressed in a dispassionate way on the legal and logical merits. The Congress went on record as opposing prisoner abuse by principally the military via the DTA, and more than one security official testified to Congress that Guantánamo had proved such an inducement to terrorist recruiting that it should be closed. Yet Congress opposed Obama's plan to close Guantánamo and transfer some detainees to an enhanced security prison in Illinois, as if US authorities were somehow incapable of restraining persons with violent intent. The record was that no one had ever escaped from a US

[81] *Hamdi* v. *Rumsfeld*, June 28, 2004.

[82] Scott Shane, "Detainee's Case Illustrates Bind of Prison's Fate," *New York Times*, October 4, 2009, www.nytimes.com/2009/10/04/world/middleeast/04gitmo.html.

maximum security prison. Still, a bipartisan group in Congress made it impossible for Obama to close Gitmo. Likewise, the record showed that federal courts were quite able to process terrorism cases, especially away from battlefield conditions, even if some grandstanding and obstructionism occurred from defendants. Yet a number of important Washington figures demanded the use of Military Commissions, which inherently raised questions of fairness at home and abroad.

Such were the complexities, as much political as legal, with regard to legal justice after 9/11. We shall return to these issues in Chapter 7.

7 *Prisoner abuse and the politics of transitional justice*

Torture, its practice, its rationalization and legal justification, is one of the great moral issues of our time.

(Jorge Heine, "Closing Guantánamo," *The Hindu*, May 27, 2009)

The terrorist with weapons of mass destruction may very well put an end to our dream of a global community of human rights.

(Paul W. Kahn, *Sacred Violence: Torture, Terror, and Sovereignty*, Ann Arbor, University of Michigan Press, 2008, p. 178)

Transitional justice (TJ), the process of establishing the proper and principled response to gross violations of human rights and humanitarian law, became a growth industry after the Cold War. Designed for small and weak states emerging from authoritarian brutalities or armed conflicts, it bedeviled the Obama Administration from 2009. International TJ developments created a context in which pressure built on Obama to deal with the abuses of the Bush era. When in 2010 the new UK government agreed to investigate the British role in US rendition and torture allegations, it was difficult to insulate US policy making from that inquiry.[1] On the other hand, certain circles of opinion in Washington and the country itself could be quite insular and parochial, ignoring international trends and emphasizing strictly American perspectives – especially those prioritizing national security.

[1] Patrick Wintour, Nicholas Watt, and Ian Cobain, "Torture Claims Investigation Ordered by William Hague," *The Guardian*, May 20, 2010, www.guardian.co.uk/law/2010/may/20/torture-william-hague-terrorism. Also John F. Burns, "Britain Pledges Inquiry Into Torture," *New York Times*, July 6, 2010, www.nytimes.com/2010/07/07/world/europe/07britain.html. At the time of writing it was not clear what information would become public, and how any released information would affect the relations between the two states. It appeared that legal immunity would be offered to those who testified.

This chapter argues that: (1) major states like the United States, not being subjected to powerful outside pressure (as compared to weak transnational criticism), tend not to engage in TJ for a considerable time – if ever – after gross violations of human rights; (2) Barack Obama followed in the foot steps of FDR in elevating various issues – such as economic recovery and health care reform – over issues of human rights including TJ; and (3) successful terrorism calls into question whether even Western governments with liberal tendencies, like the Obama Administration, can use law to restrain the darker side of nationalism. When important political forces are aroused in the name of national security, human rights, especially the rights of enemy prisoners, are not likely to be trumps – or even fare well – in the policy making process.

This analysis leaves those interested in human rights facing an uphill battle to defend such rights in times of perceived national emergency. The struggle for human rights – including humanitarian law – will surely continue, but only the demise of militant Islam and similar threats to the international order are likely to secure the enlightenment project of applied universal human rights. When major powers believe they face an existential threat, or when elected leaders face domestic pressures demanding an end to national insecurity, many human rights are likely to suffer – especially those rights designed to protect enemy prisoners.

Transitional justice: a thumbnail sketch

Modern TJ was originally made possible by two developments: the collapse of brutal national security states in the southern cone of South America in the 1980s, and the collapse of European communism by 1991. These developments made possible on a broad scale criminal prosecutions, truth commissions, and other mechanisms, both national and international, that sought primarily (among other objectives) to prevent reoccurrence of the gross violations of human rights that had characterized past regimes.

Events in South America and somewhat later Central America were characterized by many developments at the national level, too many to recount here. In international relations, events were fueled by such decisions as the UN Security Council's creation of the International Criminal Tribunal for the Former Yugoslavia (ICTY, 1993) and the International Criminal Tribunal for Rwanda (ICTR, 1994). Other internationally approved criminal courts, the mixed or transnational courts, soon followed for Sierra Leone, Kosovo, East Timor, and Cambodia. These developments fed into the creation of the permanent International Criminal Court (ICC) in 1998, a tribunal that began to operate in 2002 and which commenced its first trial in 2008. Thus in particular the idea of internationally approved prosecution of individuals for war crimes, crimes against humanity, and genocide was resurrected after a fifty-year hiatus in the wake of the earlier criminal trials associated with Nuremberg and Tokyo at the close of the Second World War.

In an important development British courts reaffirmed the principle of universal jurisdiction in relation to torture, holding in 1999 that the former Chilean dictator Augusto Pinochet could indeed be extradited from Britain to Spain to face charges stemming from his brutal rule in Chile that included torture.[2]

There was, however, no sea change in political morality – appearances to the contrary not withstanding. The resurrection of international criminal justice started not with a human rights epiphany, similar to Saul on the road to Damascus, with world leaders suddenly discovering how to enforce human rights and humanitarian law. Rather, it started with a political maneuver that represented an attempted escape from responsibility. State members of the UN Security Council, above all the Clinton Administration speaking for the United States, were looking for some way to demonstrate concern about atrocities in the Balkans, being under considerable pressure to do so, but also looking for a way to avoid decisive intervention that might prove costly in terms of Western military personnel killed or wounded. Much of the American public and Congress had reacted critically to the deaths of

[2] For an overview of TJ, one of the best short treatments remains Martha Minow, *Between Vengeance and Forgetting* (Boston: Beacon, 1998). See also Naomi Roht-Arriaza and Javier Mariezcurrena, eds., *Transitional Justice in the Twenty-First Century: Beyond Truth versus Justice* (Cambridge: Cambridge University Press, 2006). I have two short essays on TJ being published in the *International Studies Review* during 2011.

With regard to individual criminal responsibility for waging aggressive war, rather prominent at the major Nuremberg trial even if most convictions were for war crimes, this crime has become something of a footnote in contemporary developments – ostensibly due to disagreements on how to define the offense. An underlying problem is that the major military powers and other war-prone states do not want to have to answer to an international court regarding their decision to resort to force. They therefore really do not want an agreed-upon definition that could lead to enforcement.

some eighteen American military personnel in an effort at coercive nation-building in Somalia in the Fall of 1992. Key UN member states, led by the United States, therefore settled on the option of creating an International Criminal Court for the Balkans, the ICTY.[3]

Human rights groups and "like-minded states" then seized the opportunity to press for more – not only to make the ICTY a serious venture but to expand and systematize the recourse to internationally approved criminal tribunals. There is some truth to the argument that states tend to articulate lofty statements to deal with a particular crisis, but then it is advocacy groups and others who follow up by insisting that important states indeed take seriously the promises they have made and the intentions they have announced.[4]

The UN Security Council, and particularly its permanent members, having said that international criminal justice was appropriate for the Balkans, then found it difficult to say, at least with a metaphorical straight face, why it was not appropriate for other situations. The point for the United States is this: if gross violations of human rights and humanitarian norms properly lead to criminal prosecution for the likes of Augusto Pinochet from Chile and Slobodan Milošević from Serbia, for Charles Taylor from Nigeria and Omar al-Bashir from Sudan, why not for President Bush and Secretary of Defense Rumsfeld, among other US officials? After all, Pinochet thought his tough measures were necessary to save Chile from Communist

[3] On the less-than-glorious reasons for the renaissance of international criminal justice, see David P. Forsythe, "Politics and the International Tribunal for the Former Yugoslavia," in Roger S. Clark and Madeleine Sann, eds., *The Prosecution of International Crimes* (New Brunswick: Transaction, 1996), pp. 185–206. For an overview of international criminal justice from that time forward, see Jordan L. Paust, *International Criminal Law: Cases and Materials* (Durham: Carolina Academic Press, 3rd edn., 2006).

[4] FDR and Churchill, having put out the Atlantic Charter to justify the Second World War in terms of liberal principles, then found it difficult – in the face of various pressures – to back away from those principles in subsequent years. See especially Roger Normand and Sarah Zaidi, *Human Rights at the UN: The Political History of Universal Justice* (Bloomington: Indiana University Press, 2008). Forsythe, "Politics," is also relevant. The United States pushed the idea of the ICTY in order to avoid military intervention in Bosnia in 1993, and then it and the world wound up with an operating ICC by 2002 because other actors developed further the idea that the Clinton Administration had earlier found politically convenient – namely that the international community should resurrect the idea of international criminal justice.

subversion. He, too, was motivated by his view of homeland security and the good society (notwithstanding his subsequent graft and corruption featuring, like many other dictators, money stashed in secret bank accounts).

This logic of prosecution was often quite reasonably articulated by international lawyers, even if anathema to many in the United States when applied at home. As demonstrated by the early Serb response to the ICTY, it is not broadly popular to prosecute one's own nationals for war crimes. Serb compliance, to the extent that it occurred, was primarily brought about by the pressures of a powerful transnational network.[5] Serbia's interest in bringing to justice Ratko Mladić, the immediate author of the Serb massacre at Srebrenica in 1995, in which perhaps 8,000 Bosnian Muslim males were executed, waxed and waned depending on shifting Western pressure.[6] It was unlikely that a similar network could be effective in the face of a US desire to avoid TJ measures after the post-9/11 torture and other cruelties.[7]

As part of TJ there had always been the option of national criminal proceedings, and after the Cold War these, too, came into play in places like Poland after communism – or even before the end of the Cold War in places like Argentina after military rule. These rarely worked well in newly emerging democracies either because of blatant retribution which made the judicial proceedings seem like political show trials (e.g. in Poland, particularly the trial of the former military leader Wojciech Jaruzelski; and in Iraq, particularly the trial of the dictator Saddam Hussein and some of his top officials); or because the new democratic authorities were weak and the old authoritarians had their continuing supporters (e.g. in Argentina after the junta, in Chile after Pinochet). These latter situations raised the question of whether national trials were worth the prospect of renewed national tensions and maybe the collapse of the new democratic regime. There could be sometimes the

5 Patrice C. McMahon and David P. Forsythe, "The ICTY and Serbia: Judicial Romanticism meets Network Politics," *Human Rights Quarterly*, 30, 2 (May 2008), pp. 412–435.

6 Dan Bilefsky and Doreen Carvajal, "Europe Tested as War Crimes Suspect Remains Free," *New York Times*, October 21, 2010, www.nytimes.com/2010/10/22/world/europe/mladic-timeline.html.

7 For a trenchant defense of human rights in times of national emergency utilizing the two notions of torture and lesser cruelties, see Alberto Mora, "Law, Foreign Policy, and the War on Terror," Carnegie Council on Ethics, November 2, 2006, www.carnegiecouncil.org/resources/publications/morgenthau/5284.html.

hell of good intentions. On the other hand, persistence sometimes paid off. The former military president of Argentina, Reynaldo Benito Bignone, aged eighty-two, was sentenced in 2010 to twenty-five years in prison for kidnapping and torture in that country's "dirty war" which had ended in 1983.[8]

Developments pertaining to TJ were also pushed along by the establishment of truth commissions, with the South African Truth and Reconciliation Commission (TRC, 1995–1998) as a leading example. Legal justice was not the only form of possible justice after atrocities, and in South Africa, El Salvador, Guatemala, and many other places a decision was taken to avoid prosecutions for violations of human rights and humanitarian norms. Criminal trials were necessarily backward-looking, could exacerbate continuing national and regional divisions, and with their complicated rules of evidence not always clearly superior to other measures in terms of establishing an accurate record of wrongful action. Truth commissions offered one way of giving attention to victims and establishing that what had been done was indeed wrong, but not in a penal process. Some places like Sierra Leone tried both internationally sanctioned criminal proceedings (via a mixed tribunal of international and national judges) and a truth commission.[9]

Then there were apologies, reparations, and lustration (denying public office to those involved in past gross violations of human rights) – all intended to help close the books on history, promote satisfaction and reconciliation, deter repetition of proscribed behavior in the future, and help institutionalize protection of human rights and humanitarian standards. Apologies and reparations were sometimes combined with truth commissions and sometimes not. For example, in the 1980s the

[8] Charles Newbery and Alexei Barrionuevo, "25 Years for Leader of Argentine Dictatorship," *New York Times*, April 20, 2010, www.nytimes.com/2010/04/21/world/americas/21argentina.html.

[9] On truth commissions in relation to criminal justice, three good starting points are Edel Hughes *et al.*, *Atrocities and International Accountability: Beyond Transnational Justice* (Tokyo: UNU Press, 2007); Steven Ratner and Jason Abrams, *Accountability for Human Rights Atrocities in International Law: Beyond the Nuremberg Legacy* (New York and Oxford: Oxford University Press, 3rd edn., 2009); and Rachel Kerr, *Peace and Justice: Seeking Accountability after War* (Cambridge: Polity, 2007). While the South African Truth and Reconciliation Commission (TRC) has become something of an icon and gold standard in the field, closer study reveals much debate about process and effect. See Audrey Chapman *et al.*, *Truth and Reconciliation in South Africa: Did the TRC Deliver?* (Philadelphia: University of Pennsylvania Press, 2008).

United States issued an official apology for, and paid reparations to family members of, those Japanese-Americans arbitrarily interned during the Second World War. Canada has apologized and paid reparations for the wrongful detention and torture of the terror suspect Maher Arar (whereas the United States has refused).

Also available was the option of doing nothing special, as chosen by Spain and Portugal after the end of brutal dictatorships. Both joined the Council of Europe (CoE), with its human rights norms and procedures, which served as the antechamber to the European Union with its own human rights norms and procedures. Thus these two countries conducted no special aspects of TJ but rather "moved on" and locked themselves into regional arrangements that presumably guaranteed no back sliding into the degradations of the past. This was not a perfect solution, as Spain in the twenty-first century engaged in a delayed debate about TJ, in particular whether specific measures should be taken to reconsider atrocities in the Spanish Civil War, 1936–1939, and the resulting Franco era of Fascist rule, 1939–1975.

In the varied measures of TJ that one saw from especially 1993 to current times, there was a certain double standard at work. The small states of the Balkans, Rwanda, Sierra Leone, Liberia (e.g. the trial of Charles Taylor in a special chamber of the Sierra Leone criminal court), East Timor, Cambodia, El Salvador, Guatemala, etc. were all expected by leading UN member states and human rights organizations to do something special. They were expected to do something particular to institutionalize protection of human rights and humanitarian law besides rewriting the national constitution and ratifying certain treaties. In fact, when the UN Security Council mandated criminal courts under Charter Chapter VII, which was binding in international law, they had no legal choice but to do something special.

But the story was otherwise for powerful states or those that had powerful protectors. There was no sustained pressure on China after the massacre at Tiananmen Square in 1989, as the repressive elite remained in power and covered up events. Short-term, symbolic reactions from abroad gave way to accommodating growing Chinese power. Moreover, states were aware that China could use its permanent seat on the UN Security Council to make life difficult for any state that openly challenged the various decisions of the Chinese elite. Nor did Russia take responsibility for or pay a heavy price for its scorched earth policy in Chechnya. Certainly the Europeans were not going to jeopardize their oil and gas supplies from Russia, and the United States needed Russian cooperation on issues relating to Iraq, Iran, Georgia, etc. UK officials faced little official opprobrium after their sometimes brutal efforts to suppress "the troubles" in Northern Ireland, although the United Kingdom did have to contend with the human rights organizations of the CoE. Israel was not greatly inconvenienced by allegations of war crimes in southern Lebanon (2006) and Gaza (2008), given that the United States could be counted on to veto any muscular resolutions of criticism emanating from the UN Security Council. So when powerful states, including those with clients, chose not to focus on some aspect of TJ, "the international community" could do little to compel these states to rethink their policies.

With regard to all of these examples of double standards regarding TJ, while some might agonize over the unfairness of it all, others might paraphrase the patron saint of realism, Thucydides, who remarked of earlier struggles, not entirely approvingly: the strong do what they will, and the weak do what they must.[10]

The discussion above sets the stage for addressing the question of the proper policy for the United States after the torture and inhuman treatment of the Bush Administration. Were major states to be let off the hook after gross violations of human rights? Were only small and weak states, those without powerful patrons, expected to engage in TJ?

Obama: ban major abuse, avoid transitional justice

President Barack Hussein Obama, upon taking office in January 2009, declared an intention to close Guantánamo, did close down the Black Sites where forced disappearances had been managed by the CIA, declared null and void the various legal memos about enemy prisoners that had been issued during the Bush II Administration, discarded the concept of "unlawful enemy combatant," and forbad the use of most "enhanced interrogation techniques" which had amounted to much inhumane treatment and sometimes torture. He created a new interrogation unit made up of various agencies to interrogate HVDs, a step forward in professionalism and legal process. Obama's policy was to

[10] *On Justice, Power, and Human Nature: The Essence of Thucydides' "History of the Peloponnesian War,"* trans. Paul Woodruff (Bloomington: Indiana University Press, 1993), p. 103.

embrace something close to the first view of political morality that we noted at the outset of this book in Chapter 1: the absolute and total prohibition of torture and CID treatment of those suspected of militant opposition to the United States.

Here we should note that while much political discussion and some law focuses on the distinction between torture and CID: (1) the distinction is not always clear in the real world of anguish; (2) some persons who undergo greater physical abuse may not suffer long-term disorders because of a strong character; (3) some who undergo supposedly lesser forms of abuse may have various forms of post-traumatic stress disorders; and (4) what seems to matter is a situation of total control and intensity of distress.[11] The political and legal point is that both torture and CID need to be barred, if the concern is the wellbeing of persons. Simply put, cutting with a knife or pulling out finger nails is not necessarily worse than combined forms of no touch torture or torture lite. The "intensity of pain" does not depend on simply whether the abuse was physical or mental, or whether the abusive measures were seen as limited by those who authorized them.

Obama's executive decisions were consistent with the revised Army and Marine field manual's sections on interrogation,[12] sections rewritten and then endorsed by Gen. David Petraeus and his advisors and superiors, even as they dealt with continuing practical needs for intelligence particularly in Iraq and Afghanistan. After all, the key to counterinsurgency operations, or undermining the civilian base of terrorists, is to drive a wedge between civilians and the insurgents/terrorists, not alienate civilians via such policies as indiscriminate detention and harsh interrogation. The point is to get civilians to turn in violent radicals, not look the other way because of disdain for those on the side of order. Petraeus and his advisors vetted the new draft manual with human rights organizations, dropping language in early versions that might have permitted some abuse in "the lesser evil" or "ticking time bomb" approach to interrogation.[13] While the revised manual was

[11] See the scientific evidence reported in Nicholas Bakalar, "The Line Between Torture and Cruelty," *New York Times*, March 6, 2007, p. D 6. And see the legal/policy point based on this research in Manfred Nowak, "What Practices Constitute Torture?," *Human Rights Quarterly*, 28, 4 (November 2006), pp. 809–841.

[12] US Department of Defense, FM 3–24/MCWP3033.5 (2006).

[13] Confidential interviews.

clearly a step forward in humanitarian terms, some analysts were not sure that all abusive measures had been proscribed.[14] As noted earlier, in Afghanistan Petraeus required notification of military capture to the ICRC within fourteen days, including special operations detention centers.[15] (There were, however, reports of continued secret detention in Afghanistan.[16]) So there were some important changes in favor of human rights and humanitarian law as Bush II gave way to Obama, even if some of these changes started before 2009, and even if Obama continued some controversial measures such as renditions[17] and Military Commissions. Obama's counter-terrorism policies displayed some continuity with Bush's, but they were far from being identical.

As for TJ, Obama indicated that he was not interested in criminal prosecutions of Bush officials, most CIA operatives, or high military personnel. He wanted to be "forward-looking." Despite the fact that the Torture Convention affirms that state parties are obligated to try or extradite for trial those alleged to be linked to torture or CID policies, and that under the 1949 Geneva Conventions states parties are obligated to pursue legal action against those who have committed "grave breaches," Obama was steadfast in his opposition to pursuing any criminal action against top Bush officials. Scrambling to deal with criticisms of his position from liberal supporters and human rights organizations, he said that he would defer to his Attorney General, Eric Holder, on the matter of criminal proceedings against Bush lawyers who enabled torture. As noted earlier, an ethics report by a unit of the DOJ recommended that the cases of John Yoo and Steven Bradbury be referred to the relevant bar associations for possible professional sanctions, but this conclusion was not accepted by the relevant official of the DOJ. Obama and Holder, not to mention most of Congress and the country, seemed quite content to let the matter fade away.

[14] Matthew Alexander, "Torture's Loopholes," *New York Times*, January 21, 2010, www.nytimes.com/2010/01/21/opinion/21alexander.html.

[15] Eric Schmitt, "U.S. Shifts, Giving Detainee Names to the Red Cross," *New York Times*, August 23, 2009, www.nytimes.com/2009/08/23/world/middleast/23detain.html.

[16] Alissa J. Rubin, "Afghans Detail a Secret Prison Still Operating on a US Base," *New York Times*, November 29, 2009, www.nytimes.com/2009/11/29/world/asia/29bagram.html.

[17] David Johnston, "U.S. Says Rendition to Continue, but With More Oversight," *New York Times*, August 25, 2009, www.nytimes.com/2009/08/25/us/politics/25rendition.html.

Holder then appointed a special prosecutor to inquire into possible criminal behavior by CIA operatives, including contractors, who might have exceeded what had been authorized. This was seen as going too far by the American political right and not going far enough by the American political left. The former saw the decision as motivated by partisan politics and unwise in the light of national security needs. The latter saw the decision as once again scapegoating the little fish while letting the policy makers and their lawyers off the hook.[18] In 2010 Jay Bybee, the DOJ lawyer who had signed off on several controversial legal memos about abuse, testified to Congress that several CIA interrogators had exceeded what he had authorized.[19] And so that particular issue, among others, refused to fade away.

It was obvious enough that Obama wanted to focus on economic recovery, health care reform, and other questions for which he desired Republican cooperation in Congress. Regardless of treaty obligations, Obama knew that criminal proceedings against those in the Executive Branch under Bush II would make his legislative agenda much more difficult to achieve, given the widespread tendency among congressional Republicans to avoid criminalizing detainee policy during the Bush Administration. After all, it was a Republican Congress that in 2006 had passed the Military Commissions Act (MCA) that decriminalized degrading and humiliating treatment as far as US law was concerned. While torture and cruel and inhuman treatment remained a criminal offense in US law, lesser forms of serious abuse did not – whatever treaty language might say.

In general the Republican Party, both the executive and congressional wings, saw at least CID if not torture as necessary in an age of terrorism. Treaty language prohibiting CID made little difference.[20] Some

18 See David Johnston, "Justice Dept. Report Advises Pursuing C.I.A. Abuse Cases," *New York Times*, August 24, 2009, www.nytimes.com/2009/08/24/us/politics/24detain.html. Jeffrey H. Smith, "CIA Accountability," *Washington Post*, August 24, 2009, www.washingtonpost.com/wp-dyn/content/article/2009/08/23/AR2009082302038. Also Howard Kurtz, "Torture, Back in Play," *Washington Post*, August 29, 2009, www.washingtonpost.com/wp-dyn/content/article/2009/08/26/AR2009082601017.

19 Charlie Savage and Scott Shane, "Bush Aide Says Some C.I.A. Methods Unauthorized," *New York Times*, July 15, 2010, www.nytimes.com/2010/07/16/us/politics/16interrogation.html.

20 At times in US politics it could be shown that those making a pure legal argument about international law (the law requires *X*) did not fare very well in policy debates. For example, in the debate on US payment of UN dues, State Department lawyers did go to Congress and say that the UN Charter requires no withholding.

Republican Members of Congress like Senators John McCain and Lindsey Graham, while they might be opposed to serious abuse of enemy prisoners, nevertheless did not favor criminal prosecutions under the "strained" legal interpretations of the past. Such were the workings of party loyalty and perceptions about what was best for the country.[21] McCain argued that prosecutions, in reopening the abuses of the past, would harm the image of the country in the world.[22] Others argued just the opposite, that the United States could restore its moral authority by holding trials. There was also the view, mostly articulated by Republicans, that criminal prosecutions of CIA officials, whether high or low, might make the Agency cautious and risk averse, or *more* cautious and risk averse. This would arguably be detrimental to national security.

While there was some support for criminal prosecutions of Bush officials in the House of Representatives that was under Democratic control after the November 2006 elections, no doubt the Obama White House was aware that in the public at large there was scant support for the option of criminal proceedings.[23] The public, too, was more interested in economic growth, restoring jobs, reducing health care costs,

But a majority in Congress did not care. So when it came to international law as soft law, not adjudicated in a US court but argued about in the political process, quoting the logic of the law in the face of self-interested concerns otherwise did not always carry the day. See further David P. Forsythe, *The Politics of International Law: U.S. Foreign Policy Reconsidered* (Boulder: Lynne Rienner, 1990). As noted earlier, State Department lawyers might have written that API, Art. 75 regarding humanitarian protections for a wide range of captured fighters had passed into customary law, but some in the ICRC knew that the Bush Administration simply did not accept that view and hence it was unwise to press that particular legal argument.

21 See further Bobby Ghosh, "Partisan Passions Dominate Interrogation Hearings," *Time*, May 13, 2009, www.time.com/time/printout/0,8816,1898125,00.html.

22 Scott Shane, "Obama Faces a New Push to Look Back," *New York Times*, July 13, 2009, www.nytimes.com/2009/07/13/us/politics/13intel.html.

23 PIPA (Program on International Public Attitudes), University of Maryland, electronic news release, June 25, 2009. This poll was consistent with one in 2006 that found that 57 percent of those sampled opposed prosecution of high Bush officials, and 65 percent opposed to prosecution of CIA and military officials. Chris Cillizza, Washington Post blog, May 7, 2006, http://voices.washingtonpost.com/thefix/white-house/polling-the-torture-debate.html. Those figures were consistent with a poll in April 2009 that found a clear majority of Americans opposed to prosecutions. Peter Wallsten and Greg Miller, "Obama gives Nuanced Defense of his Stance on Torture," *Los Angeles Times*, April 30, 2009, www.latimes.com/news/nationworld/nation/la-na-obama-assess30-2009apr30,0,1904.

and controlling federal spending, among other concerns, than in prosecuting for possible past errors of judgment in the "GWOT." Similar to the issue of the invasion of Iraq, a majority of the public might have come around to a critical view of the Bush record on detainee affairs, but there was virtually no grass roots movement for criminal prosecution in relation to either *jus ad bellum* (law for the start of war, under which an aggressive war is a crime) or *jus in bello* (law for the process of war, entailing attention to the Geneva Conventions, etc.). In the 2010 congressional election campaigns, foreign policy, terrorism, and human rights hardly surfaced at all. The clear emphasis was on economic recovery, deficit spending, and health care.

A central reason for forgetting about past prisoner abuse is not difficult to discern and was essentially the same for the French public concerning the Algerian War. The French experience provoked this *cri de coeur* by Jean Paul Sartre:

> But now when we raise our heads and look into the mirror we see an unfamiliar and hideous reflection: ourselves. Appalled, the French are discovering this terrible truth: that if nothing can protect a nation against itself, neither its traditions nor its loyalties nor its law ... then its behavior is not more than a matter of opportunity and occasion ... Happy are those who died without every having to ask themselves: "if they tear out my fingernails, will I talk?" But even happier are others ... who have not had to ask themselves that *other* question: "If my friends, fellow soldiers, and leaders tear out an enemy's fingernails in my presence, what will I do?"[24]

Any American who wanted to know could know that the Bush Administration established the *policy* of abusive treatment – and sometimes torture – of many enemy prisoners. But this abusive interrogation had been established to try to protect the country, not to achieve partisan advantage or give rein to personal deviancy.

In retrospect, especially when further catastrophes had not materialized (or in the French case when the Algerian War had been lost), a majority of the public might agree that wrong decisions had been taken. But much of the public thought the intentions had been understandable in context. No French official ever resigned because of torture in

[24] Introduction to Henri Alleg, *The Question* (Lincoln: University of Nebraska Press, 2006).

Algeria, and no French official was ever prosecuted for torture.[25] Of course that was the 1960s, before concern for internationally recognized human rights became a more potent force. But even some Obama officials were on record as indicating a reluctance to pass firm judgment on past decisions about interrogation. They noted that the absence of other activated sleeper cells and of other successful Al-Qaeda attacks on the homeland were now clearer than in the past. According to Dennis Blair, Director of National Intelligence for Obama, "I like to think I would not have approved those methods in the past, but I do not fault those who made the decisions at that time ..."[26] A sizable part of the public remained supportive of not just CID but even torture if that was required for national security.[27]

Thomas Friedman, prominent columnist for the *New York Times*, concisely summarized why he supported the President's "unsatisfying" policy position despite the military having tortured to death about thirty prisoners in Afghanistan and Iraq: Al-Qaeda was a brutal enemy which, had it been successful in other attacks, would have stimulated strong public pressure to "do whatever it takes" to stop further attacks; and, responsibility for abuse led to President Bush and other high officials, whose prosecution would "rip the country apart."[28] Just as President

25 Raphaelle Branche, "Torture of Terrorists?," *International Review of the Red Cross*, no. 867 (September 2007), pp. 543–560.

26 Eugene Robinson, "Where 'Those Methods' Lead," *Washington Post*, April 24, 2009, www.washingtonpost.com/wp-dyn/content/article/2009/04/23/AR2009042303717.

27 *Ibid*. In a BBC global survey, those believing in the necessity of some torture were: 43 percent Israel; 42 percent Iraq; 40 percent Indonesia; 40 percent Philippines; 39 percent Nigeria; 38 percent Kenya; 37 percent China; 37 percent Russia; 36 percent United States. At the other end of the scale were Italy, 14 percent; Spain, 16 percent; France, 19 percent, http://newsvote.bbc.co.uk/news.bbc.co.uk/1/hi/world/6063386.stm.

Research indicated that belief in the necessity of torture was strongly affected by (1) party identification and (2) gender. In the United States, Republican males were most likely to support torture. Donald P. Haider-Markel and Andrea Vieux, "Gender, Partisanship, and Conditional Support for Torture in the War on Terror," paper presented at the University of Nebraska, 2007. One version was published as "Gender and Conditional Support for Torture," *Politics and Gender*, 4, 1 (2008), pp. 5–33.

28 "A Torturous Compromise," *New York Times*, April 29, 2009, www.nytimes.com/2009/04/29/opinion/29friedman.html. Obama's opposition to prosecution of high officials, consistent as it was with majority public opinion, also received support from the widely read and respected columnist David Broder, as in "Stop

Gerald Ford had pardoned Richard Nixon after the crimes of Watergate so as to restore national stability and unity, so President Obama wanted to bypass the alleged crimes of Bush officials.

Obama was also opposed to an independent "truth commission" about treatment of enemy prisoners, the champion of which in the Senate was Patrick Leahy (D, VT). This idea had considerable support in various liberal circles.[29] The same calculation prevailed in the Obama White House on truth commissions as on trials, namely that it was best for the country to "move forward" rather than look to the past. Obama held to this policy position despite the fact that some in his Administration, such as CIA Director Leon Panetta, who strongly protected his Agency and jousted with Attorney General Holder, were initially in favor of a truth commission.[30] Conventional wisdom held that some congressional Democrats were not too keen on Leahy's push for such a commission because a few of them might be implicated in Bush decisions for abusive interrogation. Some Democratic MCs had sat on various oversight committees, and clearly the Joint Committee on Intelligence had been briefed by the CIA on detention and interrogation matters. While the CIA and various Republican MCs claimed that the briefings had been explicit about the details of harsh interrogation, House Speaker Nancy Pelosi (D, CA) and some others claimed otherwise. The subject of Democratic support for Republican policies after 9/11 remained sensitive, as per our discussion in Chapter 2.

Some also supported a truth commission because so much remained unknown about US detention and interrogation after 9/11, and because without some authoritative overview there would be a long stream of leaks and forced disclosures akin to the drip, drip, drip of the so-called Chinese water torture. So, it was argued, Obama could only get the subject behind him via a truth commission.[31]

Scapegoating," *Washington Post*, April 26, 2009, www.washingtonpost.com/wp-dyn/content/article/2004/04/24/AR2009042402902.

29 See, e.g., Nicholas D. Kristof, "Time to Come Clean," *New York Times*, April 26, 2009, www.nytimes.com/2009/04/26/opinion/26kristof.html.

30 Jane Mayer, "Leon Panetta's C.I.A. Challenge," *The New Yorker*, June 22, 2009, p. 53.

31 For a list of unanswered questions about US prisoner policies, see Jane Mayer, "Ten Unsolved Mysteries in the 'War on Terror,'" *The New Yorker*, December 16, 2009, www.newyorker.com/onlline/blogs/newsdesk/2009/12/unsolved-mysteries.

At the time of writing, the Senate Armed Services Committee under the Chairmanship of Carl Levin (D, MI) had produced a thorough and critical report on military detention and interrogation whose legitimacy or moral authority was enhanced by the support of Republicans on the committee – including John McCain and Lindsey Graham. Joe Lieberman, the conservative Democrat/Independent who had advised McCain in his presidential bid, also supported the study's conclusions. The Levin report restricted itself to analysis of policy decisions and did not address issues of TJ. The Senate Intelligence Committee under the leadership of Dianne Feinstein (D, CA) undertook a review of the record of the CIA on detainee and other matters. But that report, unlike the Levin report, was compiled in a secret and very lengthy process.

Any prospect for an independent commission on detainee affairs like the 9/11 Commission, or for a special prosecutor to inquire into possible criminal offenses by high officials, was of more interest to human rights and civil liberties organizations than to most elected officials – particularly since American public opinion was not engaged, and indeed mostly divided, on the issues. Certain commentators might criticize Obama for pursuing politics as usual rather than TJ,[32] but as noted American public opinion was otherwise. There were plenty of voices in the national media calling for criminal prosecutions, but Obama's "politics as usual" was in tune with the public, which had a braking effect especially on the Senate. Certain White House advisors thought that prosecutions were not politically viable early in the Obama's Administration.[33] In France in the past, it had taken quite some time for the country to be ready for a fully open debate about French torture and murder in the Algerian conflict.

In the meantime, Obama continued to wrestle with carryover issues from the Bush period: whether to release or block additional photos of US abuse of enemy prisoners, whether to continue with revised Military Commissions, whether to endorse lengthy administrative detention for some not tried or released, whether to transfer some Gitmo detainees to American soil, whether to use the state secrets doctrine to try to block

[32] Jorge Heine, "Closing Guantánamo," *The Hindu*, May 27, 2009, www.hindu.com/2009/05/27/stories/2009052754790800.htm. Heine was Chilean, active in Chilean politics after Pinochet, and Chilean Ambassador to South Africa at the time of the TRC.

[33] Mayer, "Leon Panetta's C.I.A. Challenge."

court proceedings, whether to continue any form of extraordinary renditions, and so on. We return to some of these subjects later in this chapter.

Cheney: defend going to the "dark side," no transitional justice

Making life difficult for Obama was the fact that former Vice President Cheney, upon leaving office, undertook an extraordinarily public campaign to defend Bush policies on detention and interrogation of enemy prisoners. Cheney's central argument was that Obama was playing fast and loose with US national security by his early decisions closing the CIA Black Sites and prohibiting the "enhanced interrogation techniques" that had been used by especially the CIA but also in reality by the military during 2002–2005. Cheney argued that these techniques had worked – providing valuable intelligence, and were legal – falling short of torture.[34] Obama's Director of National Intelligence also indicated the abusive measures had "provided a deeper understanding of the al Qa'ida organization . . ."[35] There is every indication that Cheney was a true believer in the necessity of very tough measures in a dangerous world.[36] It was increasingly clear that some kind of actionable intelligence had been gained through abusive interrogation, as noted in Chapter 5.

Clearly Cheney had been the driving force in establishing the Bush policy of abusive interrogation, even if it was his staff lawyer David Addington who managed the various details. It was also known that NSA Rice and others had come around to a different view after the Abu

[34] American Enterprise Institute, "Remarks by Richard B. Cheney," May 21, 2009, www.aei.org/print?pub=speech&pubId=100050&authors=RichardB.Cheney. Also PBS NewsHour, "Cheney Reflects on Legacy, Defends Interrogation Policy," January 14, 2008, www.pbs.org.newshour/bb/politics/jan-june09/cheney_01-14.html.

[35] Peter Baker, "Banned Techniques Yielded 'High Value Information,' Memo Says," *New York Times*, April 22, 2009, www.nytimes.com/2009/04/22/us/politics/22blair.html.

[36] Debate continued on whether it was abusive interrogation of Zubaydah that produced important intelligence, or whether that information was obtained through humane interrogation – a productive process that was aborted via the start of abuse. See Scott Shane, "Inside a 9/11 Mastermind's Interrogation," *New York Times*, June 22, 2008, www.nytimes.com/2008/06/22/washington/22ksm.html.

Ghraib scandal and moved President Bush in a more moderate direction on detainee affairs, as we noted in Chapters 3, 4, and 5. Cheney's public campaign was also, therefore, a defense of a major part of his own legacy. He was, in effect, attacking the more moderate elements in the Bush Administration as well as several of Obama's new decisions.[37]

Others in the Bush Administration may have agonized over their role in prisoner abuse, even if Cheney definitely did not. Apparently Bush and Tenet also did not. We noted in Chapter 5 that each endorsed abusive interrogation in his memoirs, although neither addressed the critique that the harsh methods did more harm than good to national security. We do not yet know about Rice, although as noted in Chapter 3 she did work to moderate Bush policies on detention and interrogation. Colin Powell had always been opposed to abusive interrogation by the military, and after leaving office he made clear his view that particularly Guantánamo should be closed. He did not, however, believe he should have resigned over the issue, any more than he thought he should have resigned over the invasion of Iraq.[38]

According to one biography of Donald Rumsfeld, the Secretary of Defense was "haunted" by what had transpired on the military side.[39] Apparently Rumsfeld took the position that he was not directly responsible for the abuse that occurred, especially at Abu Ghraib in Iraq. Rather, he thought the problem lay with field commanders and lower-ranking individuals. But if so, this does not accord with the facts.

Rumsfeld had both direct and indirect responsibility for the abuse itself by: (1) directly authorizing and supervising the tortuous interrogation of al-Qahtani at Gitmo; (2) allowing his harsh instructions for Gitmo to "migrate" to Afghanistan and Iraq; and (3) not tightly supervising Stephen Cambone and Douglas Feith in his office who had responsibility for intelligence and prisoner matters. It was Rumsfeld's office, if not Rumsfeld himself, who authorized Carolyn Wood and

[37] See especially Jack Goldsmith, "The Cheney Fallacy," *The New Republic*, May 28, 2009, www.tnr.com/story/print.html?id=le733cac-c273-48e5-9140-80443ed1f5e2.

[38] Karen De Young, *Soldier: The Life of Colin Powell* (New York: Vintage, for Random House, 2006, 2007), pp. 364–372, 430–431.

[39] Bradley Graham, *By His Own Rules: The Ambitions, Successes, and Ultimate Failure of Donald Rumsfeld* (New York: Public Affairs, 2009), p. 371 and *passim*.

Geoffrey Miller to go to Iraq in 2003 and give advice on how to abuse prisoners, as noted in Chapter 4.

Moreover, Rumsfeld was directly involved in the response to the Abu Ghraib controversy, ensuring that the various military investigations did not look upward at the civilian and military chain of command. Rumsfeld was central to the cover-up that transpired. That it was indeed a cover-up is now established by the Levin report on military detainees, as well as by accurate commentary by various human rights organizations and astute journalists. Colin Powell was disappointed that Bush did not insist on command responsibility for Abu Ghraib.[40] Of course Rumsfeld and Cheney had marginalized Powell in the first Bush II Administration.

The emerging picture seems to indicate that while Rumsfeld was a hands-on manager regarding combat and transformation of the US military, he was negligent regarding many post-combat and non-combat matters like occupation and interrogation.[41] He uncharacteristically turned over the non-security details of Iraqi occupation to Jerry Bremer, not defending his DOD turf as he usually did, and he was progressively uninterested in prisoner affairs after about the Spring of 2003 until the Abu Ghraib scandal. Cambone, Feith, and DOD Legal Counsel Jim Haynes were able to effectuate what Cheney and Addington wanted by way of abusive interrogation because from about Spring 2003 Rumsfeld was not paying proper attention. As late as August 2004, Rumsfeld was trying to deny US military abuse in interrogations.[42] As per the *Yamashita* v. *Styer* case after the Second World War, an established principle of law is that those in the upper reaches of the chain of command can be held responsible for war crimes if they knew, *or should have known*, about illegal action.[43]

If we return to Cheney's public defense of waterboarding and other measures of torture and CID, the danger for Obama was that the former Vice President's campaign charging the new President with playing fast and loose with US security could prove a rallying cry for critics in the event of another 9/11, or something similar to it. There was, after all,

[40] De Young, *Soldier*, p. 518. [41] See especially Graham, *By His Own Rules*.

[42] Eric Schmitt, "Rumsfeld Denies Details of Abuses at Interrogations," *New York Times*, August 28, 2004, p. A 1.

[43] Library of Congress, "The Case of General Yamashita: A Memorandum," Military Legal Resources, www.loc.gov/rr/frd/Military_Law/Yamashita_case.htm.

establishment support for the Cheney position. For example Michael Gerson of the Council on Foreign Relations argued that (1) decisions about human rights and national security were not always easy to reconcile; and (2) harsh interrogation that left no permanent damage was a reasonable policy.[44] Gerson had been an activist in Republican politics and had worked at the conservative Heritage Foundation. He was an example of a Christian evangelical who, similar to George W. Bush, was not squeamish about abusive interrogation. Another former Republican activist of very conservative bent, Marc Thiessen, argued that torture was permitted by Catholic theology.[45] As already noted in Chapter 6, various members of the Cheney camp tried to stigmatize as unpatriotic those helping to defend detainees at Gitmo and in the federal courts, even if some Republicans thought this went too far.[46] And some Republican members of Congress introduced legislation that would make it difficult for defense lawyers to work for due process and a fair trial.[47]

When a Nigerian, Umar Farouk Abdulmutallab, slipped through security procedures and tried to blow up a Delta airliner arriving in Detroit on Christmas Day 2009, the Obama team processed him through the criminal justice system. Despite the fact that the Bush Administration had also prosecuted numerous would-be terrorists under criminal law, and despite the fact that Abdulmutallab responded to humane detention and interrogation by confessing and cooperating, Obama's Republican critics used events to berate the President for being

44 "Lines on a Slippery Slope," *Washington Post*, April 27, 2009, www.washingtonpost.com/wp-dyn/content/article/2009/04/26/AR2009042601516. For a further defense see Heather MacDonald, "How to Interrogate Terrorists," in Karen Greenberg, ed., *The Torture Debate in America* (Cambridge: Cambridge University Press, 2006), pp. 84–97. The Gerson view assumes that the interrogation techniques used by the United States leave no psychological trauma. This may be untrue for certain detainees.

45 Marc Thiessen, *Courting Disaster: How the CIA Kept America Safe and How Barack Obama is Inviting the Next Attack* (Washington, DC: Regnery Press, 2010). The book has been strongly critiqued by most terror experts. Regnery Press has published a number of anti-Obama, anti-liberal, pro-conservative books. It is apparent it does not aspire to the objectivity of a university press.

46 John Schwartz, "Attacks on Detainee Lawyers Split Conservatives," *New York Times*, March 9, 2010, www.nytimes.com/2010/03/10/us/politics/10lawyers.html.

47 Charlie Savage, "Bill Puts Scrutiny on Detainee's Lawyers," *New York Times*, May 25, 2010, www.nytimes.com/2010/05/26/us/politics/26gitmo.html.

soft on terrorism. The domestic uproar was such that several commentators argued that the critics were doing the work of Al-Qaeda by helping to terrorize the country through partisan or panicked overreaction.[48] The Obama team eventually moved to try to change the law on "Miranda rights," pushing Congress to pass a new law that would allow the authorities to delay informing a detainee of his right to consult an attorney and to remain silent, *inter alia*.[49] ("Miranda rights" refer to the judgment in the1966 case of *Miranda* v. *Arizona*: public authorities are required to inform a detained suspect of his constitutional right to remain silent during interrogation and that any statement may be used in legal proceedings, among other rules.)

Journalists have yet to record Obama's frustration level when several congressional Democrats joined Republicans in blocking efforts to close Guantánamo. This, despite the fact that President Bush had indicated his desire to close the island prison as well, and that numerous military officials had testified that the prison was detrimental to US national security concerns. Still, enough MCs opposed moving the remaining detainees to a prison in Illinois so Obama gave up on making closure a signature event in his administration. Republican desires to block a high-profile Obama initiative and Democratic hysteria about terrorists on American soil, among other factors, sufficed to prevent much movement on that issue.[50] This congressional stand forced Obama into adopting the policy of open-ended administrative detention for some at Gitmo, and probably in Afghanistan, albeit with new procedures for prisoners to challenge their detention.

Some thought Obama should endorse the creation of a truth commission, with perhaps immunity from legal prosecution in return for full

[48] Fareed Zakaria, "Don't Panic: Fear is al-Qaeda's Real Goal," *Washington Post*, January 11, 2010, p. A 15. Scott Shane, "A Year of Terror Plots, Through a Second Prism," *New York Times*, January 13, 2010, www.nytimes.com/2010/01/13/us/13intel.html.

[49] Charlie Savage, "Proposal Would Delay Hearings in Terror Cases," *New York Times*, May 14, 2010, www.nytimes.com/2010/05/15/us/politics/15miranda.html.

[50] Charlie Savage, "Closing Guantánamo Fades as a Priority," *New York Times*, June 25, 2010, www.nytimes.com/2010/06/26/us/politics/26gitmo.html. Also Charlie Savage, "Vote Hurts Obama's Push to Empty Cuba Prison," *New York Times*, December 22, 2010, www.nytimes.com/2010/12/23/us/politics/23gitmo.html. The latter story refers to congressional legislation prohibiting the transfer of Gitmo prisoners to US soil, even for trials in federal courts.

cooperation, on the assumption that such a non-partisan or bipartisan body would endorse Obama's position of no torture or CID. The assumption could be based on an anticipated commitment to traditional American values and self-proclaimed role in the world – the city on a hill representing individual freedom, human rights, and genuine democracy. It could also be based on fidelity to rule of law, Geneva Conventions, other treaties duly ratified, etc. Such a commission conclusion could give Obama political cover in the event of a successful terrorist attack on the homeland. Otherwise, as noted in Chapter 1, critics like Cheney could continue to charge that the President had not done *everything* to forestall such an attack, and that trying to stay within the bounds of *humane* interrogation was naïve. In the event of another 9/11, one would no doubt hear again the refrain that it was not moral to subject innocent civilians to deadly attack.

It was precisely this kind of security consideration that led Obama to alter some of his campaign rhetoric and endorse the use of Military Commissions, as revised to afford more due process, and to accept the idea of extended administrative detention for dangerous detainees who could not be tried because of tainted evidence (from abuse) or other reasons. President Obama as compared to Candidate Obama was obviously sensitive to his responsibility to protect the nation from attack.[51]

Obama and others did sometimes pose a serious comeback to Cheney's position, based on self-interest.[52] This took three forms. First, a reputation for abusing detainees actually aided the enemy.[53] According to an interrogator with US Special Operations in Iraq, "I learned in Iraq that the No. 1 reason foreign fighters flocked there to

[51] For an accurate overview of Obama's liberal tendencies but his awareness of political pressures and tendency to compromise, see Peter Baker, "Obama's War Over Terror," *New York Times Magazine*, January 17, 2010, www.nytimes.com/2010/01/17/magazine/17Terror-t-html.

[52] Like William F. Schulz, former Executive Director of AI-USA, as per *In Our Own Best Interest: How Defending Human Rights Benefits Us All* (Boston: Beacon, 2001), some argue that one has to sell human rights and humanitarian norms primarily on the basis of self-interest. For a different view, arguing for a moral or ideological commitment to IHL, see W. Michael Reisman, "Holding the Center of the Law of Armed Conflict," *American Journal of International Law*, 100, 4 (October 2006), pp. 852–860 . His argument is that, absent moral commitment to core IHL values, when a state begins to consider its self-interest in this or that part, the entire edifice will collapse.

[53] See for example Wallsten and Miller, "Obama Gives Nuanced Defense."

fight were the abuses carried out at Abu Ghraib and Guantánamo. Our policy of torture was directly and swiftly recruiting fighters for al-Qaeda in Iraq . . ."[54] Dennis Blair of the Obama team testified in similar fashion in Congress, telling MCs that "the detention center at Guantánamo has become a damaging symbol to the world and that it must closed. It is a rallying cry for terrorist recruitment and harmful to our national security . . ."[55] Had those in Washington had a better grasp of history, they might have noted that France faced exactly this same problem in Algeria, as its torture inflamed the other side. This was noted by Albert Camus, among others.[56]

Second, abusing enemy prisoners endangered American military lives as reciprocity was undercut. In 2006, twenty-seven retired military officials of high rank testified in Congress in favor of continued attention to, and proper enforcement of, Geneva Convention Common Article 3: "If degradation, humiliation, physical and mental brutalization of prisoners is decriminalized or considered permissible under a restrictive interpretation of Common Article 3, we will forfeit all credible objections should such barbaric practices be inflicted upon American prisoners."[57] Reciprocity from militant Islamists was not likely, however, which was characteristic of the weaker side in asymmetrical warfare. If reciprocity had a role to play, it might be long-term and "diffuse" reciprocity among all states in building an effective international legal order.[58] Specific reciprocity between the United States and Al-Qaeda was not probable. The ICRC established some rapport with certain Taliban factions regarding prisoners, but not many. Due in part to the US emphasis on force protection, not many US military personnel were captured in Afghanistan, or in Iraq. This made specific reciprocity on prisoner matters difficult.

Third, abuse of enemy prisoners undercut US counter-insurgency operations, as already noted. A key to counter-insurgency was getting

[54] Quoted in Human Rights First, Law and Security Digest, no. 225, December 5, 2008.

[55] Hearing before Senate Committee on Intelligence, 109th Cong, January 22, 2009.

[56] Introduction, *Chroniques Álgériennes 1939–1958* (Paris: Gallimard, 1958).

[57] Quoted in Dan Fromkin, "A Defining Moment for Congress," *Washington Post*, September 14, 2006, www.washingtonpost.com/wp-dyn/content/blog/2006/09/14/BL2006041500784_pf.

[58] See further Mark Osiel, *The End of Reciprocity: Terror, Torture, and the Law of War* (New York and Cambridge: Cambridge University Press, 2009).

a civilian population to turn in terrorists, not give them sanctuary. Torturing enemy prisoners hence actually played into the hands of Al-Qaeda and other extremist groups.[59] This refrain was articulated by the mainstream media, as per an editorial in *USA Today*: the war on terrorism could not be won when the history of Guantánamo and Abu Ghraib was ruining the US image in the Muslim Middle East.[60] As former Secretary of State Colin Powell told Fareed Zakaria of *Newsweek* in 2006, in the latter's words: "After Guantánamo, Abu Ghraib, Haditha [site of alleged US military massacre in Iraq] and more, America desperately needs a symbol that showcases its basic decency. Quibbling with the Geneva Conventions is the wrong signal, by the wrong administration, at the wrong time."[61] David Cole and Jules Lobel argued at length that abusive interrogation, unfair treatment of immigrants, pre-emptive war, and other Bush measures all undercut the US effort to win the long fight against radical Islam.[62]

Splitting the difference: prosecution and reduced sentence

In Washington after Bush II, no prominent voice took up Alan Dershowitz's idea about torture warrants, or the related idea of a new security body to supervise detention and interrogation of terror suspects and similar prisoners. Prominent human rights advocates like Kenneth Roth of Human Rights Watch criticized both ideas, noting that the Foreign Intelligence Surveillance Court (FISA Court), designed to oversee security wiretaps, almost always gave the Executive what it wanted with regard to electronic surveillance. Until 2003, out of 10,000 requests, only four were denied.[63] Roth argued that a formal regulator of abusive interrogation would act in similar fashion – namely, would be captured by the logic of those supposedly regulated and give them mostly what they wanted.

Bush policies might be presented as this third, intermediate way between no torture and widespread torture. Certainly on the military

[59] See particularly James Fallows, "We Win: Declaring Victory," *The Atlantic*, September 2006, starting at p. 60.

[60] February 17, 2006.

[61] *Newsweek*, September 25, 2006.

[62] David Cole and Jules Lobel, *Less Safe, Less Free* (New York: The New Press, 2008).

[63] Kenneth Roth, "Getting Away with Torture," *Global Governance*, 11, 3 (2005), pp. 389–406.

side, especially at Gitmo, in Rumsfeld's mind his policy had been one of limited coercion, falling far short of torture and even CID. With regard to the CIA, Bush seemed to genuinely think that the coercion applied to the HVDs fell short of torture, even if it did cross over at times to CID. If one deciphers the comments of Attorney General Mukasey and others, it seems they believed that most terror suspects might have been roughed up a bit, and several HVDs like KSM had received a CID treatment that was merited, but none were supposed to be tortured. If torture happened, it was because the rules were not followed.

Of course this view would have to consider waterboarding as a technique short of torture, which had not been true in US law and practice. As noted, the United States considered waterboarding a crime when practiced by the Japanese in the Second World War. Even the "manly" Teddy Roosevelt objected to US use of waterboarding in US counter-insurgency efforts in the Philippines.[64] It was considered a war crime under US legislation until 2006, as we have noted. In fact, waterboarding had been widely considered torture since the Catholic inquisition.[65]

But if this was indeed the Bush vision, it suffered the fate of most attempted intermediate approaches. What was limited in theory did not turn out to be so limited in fact, as "force drift" kicked in. The supposedly limited techniques when used in combination, especially when used by interrogators who lost control and gave in to basic drives of hatred and domination, resulted in torture and the closely related upper end of inhuman treatment.[66] Thus KSM and Zubaydah were waterboarded

[64] Paul Kramer, "The Water Cure," *The New Yorker*, February 25, 2008, www.newyorker.com/reporting/2008/02/25/080225fa_fact_Kramer. One reads Kramer's account of US abuse of prisoners in the Philippines with awareness of similarities between post-1898 and post-9/11: torture was attributed to a few bad apples, the overall US cause was said to be just by leaders in Washington, and public interest waned which allowed the question of prosecution or other response to fade away.

[65] For one source among many, see James Reston, Jr., *Dogs of God: Columbus, the Inquisition, and the Defeat of the Moors* (New York: Anchor, 2006).

[66] On the general tendency of total control and domination to produce gratuitous abuse, see references to the famous "Stanford prison experiment," as reviewed in David Luban, "Liberalism, Torture, and the Ticking Bomb," in Greenberg, ed., *The Torture Debate*, p. 51 and *passim*. On the role of domination and anger leading to US abuse in Iraq, see Tony Lagouranis and Allen Mikaelian, *Fear Up Harsh: An Army Interrogator's Dark Journey Through Iraq* (New York: American Library, 2007).

far beyond any notion of limited and controlled procedures. Thus about thirty prisoners at Bagram and Abu Ghraib were fatally abused. Many Iraqis were beaten, burned with cigarettes, and otherwise mistreated after capture.[67]

The same fate seems to have befallen "intermediate" approaches in Israel, and the Israeli experience is highly relevant to the US record on abuse of prisoners. It is now very clear that in the wake of the 1987 Landau report legitimating "moderate physical pressure" on foreign enemy prisoners, widespread abuse, including torture, occurred in Israeli detention. A figure much tossed about for that era is that 80–90 percent of Palestinian detainees were abused in various ways.[68] But even after the 1999 Israeli Supreme Court judgment rejecting the "moderate physical pressure" standard and imposing a total prohibition on torture and CID, it appears to be the case that not so much changed.

There has been no formal request for a "necessity defense" exception to the total ban on torture and CID, and thus no formal application of the 1999 articulated standard through court cases. Moreover, reliable human rights organizations have reported that abuse of enemy prisoners remains widespread in Israeli detention, even if perhaps not as prevalent as before 1999. According to one source now widely quoted, from 1999 until mid-2002 there were some ninety "ticking time bomb" situations in which Israeli interrogators resorted to abusive treatment of highly suspicious detainees. In not one of these "cases" was there a formal application for an exception to the total ban on torture, and thus in not one of these "cases" did the Israeli courts rule on whether the abuse was justifiable as an exception to the total ban. The follow-up to the 1999 judgment has been deficient.[69]

Thus in both the US and Israeli cases, it appears to be true that theories of limited coercion of prisoners have not worked very well in practice. US authorization of coercion by the CIA was not very limited to start with and did not stay very limited in the case of several HVDs.

[67] Human Rights Watch, "New Accounts of Torture by US Troops," September 24, 2005, http://hrw.org/english/docs/2005/09/25/usint11776_txt.htm.

[68] Roth, "Getting Away with Torture," p. 403.

[69] Dinah Pokempner, "Command Responsibility for Torture," in Kenneth Roth *et al.*, eds., *Torture: Does It Make Us Safer?* (New York: The New Press, for HRW, 2005), pp. 158–172. Also Yuval Ginbar, *Why Not Torture Terrorists? Moral, Practical, and Legal Aspects of the "Ticking Bomb" Justification for Torture* (Oxford and New York: Oxford University Press, 2008), pp. 220–222.

On the military side, intended limitations gave way to high-level demands for actionable intelligence, and in some cases collapsed entirely because of confused guidelines and lack of proper supervision. In Israel, the Landau approach was clearly a failure, and the Supreme Court approach has apparently failed to significantly rein in the abusive measures practiced by the military and security services.

The Israeli 1999 model for controlling torture, limiting it to some exceptions required by genuine national security, and maintaining an absolute ban while providing for reduced sanction for justified violation, requires committed legal officials such as prosecutors and judges. John T. Parry thinks that even in liberal democracies the legal order relies heavily on violence and coercion, especially in times of perceived national emergency. Even if democracies have tended to formally proscribe torture, they have tended to accept CID and humiliating treatment, and in various ways even to limit the rules against torture such as by saying the prohibition does not apply to officials abroad. In noting such things as the US Senate's narrow definition of torture when consenting to ratification of the UN Convention against Torture and the tendency of British courts to balance abuse of prisoners against the needs of national security, he remains skeptical about the will of even consolidated liberal democracies to truly ban serious abuse. He finds violence integral to the construction of certain identities, arguing that much US abuse after 9/11 was central to establishing US superiority over violent Muslim opponents.[70] It follows that he would be skeptical about the ability of courts to restrain these strong political trends. Certainly the dominant trend for US courts is a reluctance to take on the role of opposing the President on issues said by him to be necessary for national security.[71]

A larger perspective: national and cosmopolitan views

Driving debates about both abuse and TJ after abuse was a fundamental dialectic. There is an inherent, which is to say inescapable, tension between on the one hand international human rights and humanitarian

[70] John T. Parry, *Understanding Torture: Law, Violence, and Political Identity* (Ann Arbor: University of Michigan Press, 2010), p. 13 and *passim*.

[71] For one source among many see Thomas Franck, *Foreign Relations and National Security Law* (St. Paul: West Publishing, 1987).

law, and on the other hand the nation-state system of world affairs featuring insecure governments fearful about their safety and existence. Human rights and humanitarian law mandate rights for all, some of which, like freedom from torture and CID, are absolute and inviolable. National concerns tend to be the real trumps in the policy making game, however, producing even in democratic governments the violation of even the core, non-derogable, *jus cogens* standards so hallowed in legal theory.

The point is well put by Paul W. Kahn, who notes the widely held view after 9/11: "The West must defend itself against enemies who oppose its political form, its moral beliefs, its power, and its religions – who oppose, in short, its liberalism. We are in a 'clash of civilians.' Our enemies, we are told, hate us 'for our freedom.' They are 'Islamo-fascists.' To these contemporary realists, none of the lessons about torture – legal, historical, or moral – amounts to a compelling reason not to be open to its use if it proves to be necessary for self defense."[72] After all, should one respect IHL if it means defeat?[73] Such thinking explains why in the Korean War US military forces attacked apparent refugees approaching US lines because of a fear of North Korean infiltrators.

This pessimistic line of thinking is why French Foreign Minister Bernard Kouchner, a Socialist Foreign Minister in the conservative Nicholas Sarkozy government, said that he regretted pushing for a cabinet-level human rights minister, because states really can't do proper human rights policy. He was quoted as saying, "there is a permanent contradiction between human rights and the foreign policy of a state, even in France ... One cannot decide the foreign policy of a country only as a function of human rights. To lead a country obviously distances one from a certain utopianism ..."[74] Meaning: national governments have to pursue the national interest, and the national interest is often defined in a way that contradicts human rights. As soon as President Jimmy Carter announced that human rights would be the

[72] Paul W. Kahn, *Sacred Violence: Torture, Terror, and Sovereignty* (Ann Arbor: University of Michigan Press, 2008), p. 5.

[73] See further *ibid.*, p. 7.

[74] Steven Erlanger, "French Foreign Minister Voices Doubts on Human Rights Push," *International Herald Tribune*, December 10, 2008, *New York Times*, December 11, 2008, www.nytimes.com/2008/12/11/world/europe/11france.html?_r=1&ref=bernardkouchner.

cornerstone, centerpiece, and soul of his foreign policy, keen observers knew that this would be highly problematical.[75] Carter, like Reagan, had an optimistic view of humanity's capacity to change for the better, whereas analysts like Paul Kahn read history not as the progressive march of human rights but as the evolution of WMD in the context of total war thinking. For them, as for Kouchner, avoidance of torture is utopian.

This tension between national security, read broadly to mean a national prerogative to determine vital needs, and universal human rights is at times especially pronounced in the United States in part because the ultra-nationalists, of which there are many, see the country as always a force for good in the world. They are prone to overlook various Faustian bargains leading to considerable evidence to the contrary.[76] Notable was the US alignment with many despots during the Cold War, especially in much of Latin America where governments aligned with Washington killed tens of thousands of their own citizens (plus others) in places like Guatemala, Chile, Argentina, El Salvador, and elsewhere. The list of American despotic allies is long, and in a search for egregious cases one could also mention US support for Mobutu in Zaire, despite his brutalities and kleptocracy, or Ceausescu in Romania despite his repressive megalomania. Ultra-nationalists everywhere tend to believe in lots of things that are just not so.[77] Washington's ultra-nationalists consistently overstate Washington's beneficial impact on the rest of the world. But their enthusiasm for unrestrained American power takes time to change, often only under the impact of some disaster.[78]

This ultra-nationalist orientation was especially strong in the era of Bush II. One saw this clearly in the DOD National Security Strategy

[75] Sandy Vogelgesang, *American Dream, Global Nightmare: The Dilemma of US Human Rights Policy* (New York: Norton, 1980).

[76] See Joan Hoff, *A Faustian Foreign Policy from Woodrow Wilson to George W. Bush: Dreams of Perfectibility* (Cambridge: Cambridge University Press, 2008).

[77] See further especially J. Hobsbawm, *Nations and Nationalism since 1780* (Cambridge: Cambridge University Press, 1990), p. 12.

[78] I subscribe to the view that major learning in public affairs all too often takes the form of reacting to some débâcle – like the Abu Ghraib scandal or the fiasco of occupation in Iraq. For an accurate overview in general, see John Stoessinger, *Nations in Darkness, Nations at Dawn* (New York: McGraw-Hill, 6th edn., 1994).

statement of 2002 in which international law *per se* was attacked as part of lawfare against the United States. And one saw it clearly in the ease with which Bush, Cheney, Rumsfeld, and others all played fast and loose with the 1949 Geneva Conventions and the 1984 Torture Convention. It may be true that all Great Powers are not terribly excited about the restraints of international law and international organization when they are Great Powers,[79] but the Goldwater–Reagan–Bush wing of the Republican Party has been exceptional in its doctrinaire unilateralism and exemptionalism – as discussed in Chapters 2 and 3. The United States to them was so obviously a force for good in the world that it should not be restrained by the rules which applied to others.

During the tenure of Bush II and immediately thereafter, there were no lack of statements by UN human rights officials about the need to alter detainee policy and indeed to punish those who had engaged in policies that violated international law. The UN High Commissioner for Human Rights and the UN Special Rapporteur on the Promotion and Protection of Human Rights while Countering Terrorism, among others, all commented critically on various aspects of US policy pertaining to enemy detainees. None of this got much play in the American news media, even when it fitted with the commentary of leading human rights organizations, and none of it had discernible impact on Bush policy in the first Administration. In fact, the commentary on Guantánamo by Mary Robinson and Louise Arbour, as UN High Commissioner for Human Rights, put them in the Bush doghouse. The Bush team went through the normal exercises of reporting to, and taking questions from, the UN committees that supervised the Torture Convention and the ICCPR, but again one is hard pressed to find evidence that such processes had any impact on policy making. The ICRC was certainly offering its view of international humanitarian law and policy. The Organization certainly believes that it had some impact on US views over time, and points out that Bush officials engaged with it on many levels. The ICRC, the EU, and NATO may have had some impact over time.

Certain officials in the Pentagon and State Department were progressively sensitive to various forms of international criticism of Bush detainee policies. Indeed, after the Abu Ghraib photos surfaced in

[79] Josef Joffe, *Überpower: The Imperial Temptation of America* (New York: Norton, 2006).

2004, some officials from both Departments sought to effectuate more attention to the Geneva Conventions and other international standards, particularly after an Office of Detainee Affairs was created in the DOD. The short-term result of these efforts was that Cheney and Addington, Rumsfeld and Haynes were able to block most meaningful changes. The revolt of the likes of Philip Zelikow, Matthew Waxman, and Gordon England was aborted, as noted in Chapter 3.

In the longer run, however, those in the Pentagon with more sensitivity to military honor than Rumsfeld and Myers, or Haynes, Cambone, and Feith, were able to crack down on military abuse. The downside of civilian control over the military, so evident during Rumsfeld's tenure, was eventually altered. Rice became more sensitive to international pressures in Bush's second term after she moved to the State Department, as were others close to her like Zelikow and Bellinger.[80] The growing drumbeat of criticism, both multilateral and bilateral, both international and domestic, did finally make a difference. What really counted in the last analysis, however, was action by Congress and the courts especially in 2005 and 2006, not directly the international blowback. Admittedly it was in the context of international blowback that Congress reacted, but arguably notions of US self-interest, American identity, and military honor were most important. Purely legal arguments played a minor role in Congress, but not of course in the US Supreme Court.

In legal theory all states possess the right to exercise universal jurisdiction in relation to war crimes, crimes against humanity, and genocide – among other violations of international law like piracy. But in diplomatic practice most states shy away from activating this principle against nationals of Great Powers. David Cole had it exactly right: what state wanted to take on the powerful United States, especially after Obama was elected President, by activating universal jurisdiction in order to go after Bush, Cheney, Tenet, Rumsfeld, or anyone else in relation to US detainee policy?[81] Would such a move help in the coordinated response to terrorism, or the coordinated approach to Iran or North Korea? Just as most governments did not like to sue each other in international courts, so

[80] See the excellent commentary on US self-interest in humane interrogation by Philip Zelikow, "A Dubious C.I.A. Shortcut," *New York Times*, April 24, 2009, www.nytimes.com/2009/04/24/opinion/24zelikow.html.

[81] David Cole, "What to Do About the Torturers," *New York Review of Books*, 56, 1 (January 15, 2009), www.nybooks.com/articles/22232.

most governments did not like to rock the boat and open Pandora's box by encouraging their legal officials to go after US officials alleged to have been involved in criminal behavior.

Of course one could ask foreign courts to exercise universal jurisdiction in order to try to publicize and harass, even if there was little expectation of serious legal action, and some of that activity related to civil proceedings transpired.[82]

True, Judge Baltasar Garzón in Spain initiated an investigation into possible criminal behavior by several Bush officials.[83] This step was applauded in some human rights circles and was the type of action that had been forecast by Philippe Sands in his book on the subject.[84] It is important to keep several points in mind, however. (1) There are not so many national legal officials like Garzón, who is regarded as either highly principled or a loose cannon, depending on one's view. He was criticized by other Spanish officials including those in his own justice department for opening the investigation about US officials.[85] High Spanish authorities did not even support his efforts against Pinochet in the United Kingdom, much less his initiatives regarding Bush officials. And the Spanish parliament debated revising Spain's law on universal jurisdiction to limit cases to those involving some Spanish connection. This debate was similar to restricting the law on universal jurisdiction in Belgium.[86] (2) Even if Garzón's steps proceeded further, he would face the problem of obtaining physical control over the defendants if indicted, not to mention the problem of obtaining documents necessary for obtaining convictions. So while Sands and others might hold out the threat of foreign or international

[82] Mark Landler, "12 Detainees Sue Rumsfeld in Germany, Citing Abuse," *New York Times*, November 15, 2006, p. A 17.

[83] Marlise Simons, "Spanish Court Weights Inquiry on Torture for 6 Bush-Era Officials," *New York Times*, March 29, 2009, www.nytimes.com/2009/03/29/world/europe/29spain.html.

[84] Philippe Sands, *Torture Team: Rumsfeld's Memo and the Betrayal of American Values* (London: Palgrave Macmillan, 2008). See also Michael Ratner, *The Trial of Donald Rumsfeld: A Prosecution by Book* (New York: The New Press, 2007).

[85] Marlise Simons, "Spanish Prosecutors Formalize Objections to Torture Indictments," *New York Times*, April 18, 2009, www.nytimes.com/2009/04/18/world/europe/18spain.html.

[86] When Belgian law led to a series of claims filed in Belgian courts regarding alleged crimes linked to US and Israeli officials, *inter alia*, Belgium revised its law to limit petitions to cases manifesting some Belgian connection. The United States had leaned hard on the Belgian government, threatening to move NATO headquarters out of Brussels if the law on universal jurisdiction was not changed.

prosecution of Bush officials in relation to torture and/or war crimes, in reality this threat was not very likely to be widely activated – especially if the targeted individuals stayed within the United States.

There was also the possibility of more civil litigation. At the time of writing a civil process had been initiated by José Padilla, a former security detainee, against John Yoo for, essentially, complicity in torture. The Federal District Judge had ruled in favor of the petitioner in the sense of allowing the case to proceed to the substantive phase. Other civil cases were likely to follow against various former officials.[87] It was difficult to believe, however, that an increasingly conservative US Supreme Court was going to allow this process to result in substantial penalty for former US officials, should such cases get to that level of the judiciary. Among various defenses there was the defense of sovereign immunity – that as state officials they were personally immune to civil legal action for decisions taken as public officials.

There were other actions possible, such as petitions to legal regulatory bodies questioning the role of officials like Yoo and others involved in establishing abusive interrogation. Various organizations were trying to make it difficult for Yoo and others to continue with their practice of law, or teaching law. The CIA consultants who had devised and implemented abuse in secret prisons were also the targets of petitions trying to block their practice of psychology in states like Texas.[88] None of these steps, of course, amounted to a formal US position on TJ after torture and CID, whether pertaining to high Bush officials, DOD personnel, or CIA personnel. So elites in Washington continued to avoid what international law required, namely holding to account those responsible for gross violations of human rights including humanitarian norms.

Final thoughts

In terms of norms, one can appreciate the intent of the Israeli Supreme Court to reinstate an absolute ban on torture and CID, especially in the

[87] Binyam Mohamed, a British resident released from Gitmo and other prisons, had filed civil lawsuits in several courts. Bob Egelko, "U.S. Battling CIA Rendition Case in 3 Courts," *San Francisco Chronicle*, August 20, 2009, www.sfgate.com/cgi=bin/article.dgi?f=/c/a/2009/08/10/BAHZ195SJR.DTL.

[88] Morgan Smith, "Psychologist in Terror War is Subject of Complaint," *New York Times*, November 13, 2010, www.nytimes.com/2010/11/14/us/14ttlawsuit.html.

wake of the failure of the Landau approach based on some supposedly intermediate way allowing limited abuse of enemy prisoners. The Bush era confirms that attempts at limited abuse do not stay limited – or not very limited. Thus a strong case can be made for reaffirming the total prohibition on torture and CID. It is consistent with treaties duly ratified. It confronts the problem of "force drift." It also seems to be acceptable to a majority of the American public that across time showed about 60 percent opposition to torture (with variation depending on the question asked and the particular technique discussed).[89] Importantly, an absolute ban is clear and workable in large bureaucracies like the DOD that depend on clear rules and following orders, and is consistent with military honor, military law, and military cohesion and effectiveness. It is also consistent with much opinion in professional intelligence circles that emphasizes humane rapport between interrogator and suspect as the route to reliable intelligence.

To the extent that multiple damaging attacks on a country, or the proven existence of multiple sleeper cells, practically push a government into considering exceptions to a total and absolute ban on major mistreatment of suspects, then one should profit from the failure of Israeli developments and emphasize the core need to address truly necessary exceptions. The resulting abuse of detainees, when and if it occurs, should therefore remain illegal, but could lead to the possibility of mitigating considerations in judicial punishment. This is already the situation in military law, where military personnel have a duty to object to an illegal order, but where there is recognition that in certain situations the soldier has no choice but to carry out an illegal act. If the commanding officer is prepared to enforce his order with force, then there is no real option but to obey. But in that situation, while an illegal act has been committed, it is recognized there should not be a harsh punishment – at least for the person directly committing the act. Similar logic is at the heart of the "necessity" defense.

We might remember that Michael Walzer, when noting that national officials have a tendency to override personal legal rights for the sake of

[89] See further Paul Gronke *et al.*, "US Public Opinion on Torture, 2001–2009," *PS*, 43, 3 (July 2010), pp. 437–444. Some polls showed that a majority of Americans wanted an absolute and total ban on torture, even if a sizable segment of the country also saw such a total ban as too stringent for the needs of national security. In short, they wanted an absolute ban even if it had to be violated on occasion. This maybe paradoxical but is not unreasonable.

national security, also argued that "they can only prove their honor by accepting responsibility for those decisions and by living out the agony."[90] To some this would mean facing the legal music, or at least some other formal review like a truth commission. The issue might not be Walzer's "honor," but rather deterrence. By holding officials legally responsible, even if given a light sanction, one might somewhat deter future force drift and a tendency, evident in the past, to exaggerate when cruelty was "necessary." Why did realists like Henry Kissinger try to explain their support for Pinochet's brutal regime? They thought it was "necessary" during the Cold War.[91]

This scenario requires a country as a whole, and particularly judicial authorities, to exercise real discretion and judgment as to what is truly a necessary exception to the absolute ban, and what is not. Unfortunately Israel has not been successful at this second stage, which does indeed require a significant adjustment in typical nationalistic thinking, which normally concludes that almost any argument for national defense always trumps the human rights of enemy prisoners. It is difficult for national judges to second guess national security officials, but that is required in combining a total ban with a proper "necessity" defense in order to mitigate punishment. This process has in fact transpired in the related domain of administrative detention. US judges have ordered the release of numerous Gitmo detainees said by the Executive to be dangerous to the country as "unlawful enemy combatants." The judges have exercised their integrity and overruled Executive decisions based on shoddy evidence.[92] True, they have not addressed the legal culpability of Executive officials, but they have often overruled them with regard to Gitmo detention.

[90] Michael Walzer, *Just and Unjust Wars* (New York: Harper, 1977), p. 326.

[91] For the tip of the iceberg see PBS NewsHour, "Kissinger on Chile, Pinochet," February 6, 2001, www.pbs.org/newshour/bb/latin_American/chile/documents/kissinger_02-06-01.html. Kissinger argued that his decisions had to be seen in the life-and-death context of struggle with the Soviet Union; it was not a graduate seminar.

[92] For a good overview see Chisun Lee, "Their Own Private Guantánamo," *New York Times*, July 23, 2009, www.nytimes.com/2009/06/23/opinion/23lee.html. Also Del Quentin Wilber, "Judge Orders Guantánamo Detainee's Release," *Washington Post*, June 23, 2009, www.washingtonpost.com/wp-dyn/content/articles/2009/06/22/AR2009042201302. Also William Glaberson, "Evidence Faulted in Detainee Case," *New York Times*, July 1, 2008, www.nytimes.com/2008/07/01gitmo.html.

The United States has declared the prohibition on torture to be an imperative and pre-emptory rule of law against which no contradictory law or policy is permitted.[93] The argument here is that one must protect the absolute nature of the ban on torture *and* CID, while allowing room for political reality in the matter of adjusted punishment for well-considered exceptions. But if there is no real grappling with what is truly necessary and what is not, then the legal regime based on the necessity defense will not work – as appears to be the case in Israel. If most security threats are said to be existential threats, then efforts to rein in torture are not likely to succeed.

There is a tendency among certain state officials, of whatever nationality, to elevate many security threats to the level of existential threats – threats to the very survival of the state. Pinochet (and Nixon and Kissinger) saw Allende in Chile and his model of democratic socialism as an existential threat to the American model of capitalism. Violent regime change and torture followed. There is no way to legislate against paranoid security policies, but one must struggle against such distorted views nevertheless. Some type of court system is about the only line of potentially effective defense. It is clear that Congress cannot be expected to do the right thing, witness deference to the President at the start of the Korean War, the Gulf of Tonkin resolution giving the President open-ended authorization in the Vietnam War, and the 2001 AUMF that repeated the mistakes of the Gulf of Tonkin resolution. Moreover, it has completely failed to impose a statutory framework on detention policies after 9/11.

It seems clear enough that Cheney, Rumsfeld, and ultimately President Bush seized upon 9/11 to overstate the threat from particularly Saddam. Al-Qaeda was never in a position to conquer or cause the demise of the United States, only to harass it with mostly civilian attacks. Absent nuclear weapons, Al-Qaeda was not really an existential threat, only a major nuisance: "to put the terrorist threat in perspective, of the roughly 14,000 Americans who were murdered in the United States in 2009, just 14 (or 0.001 percent) died as a result of terrorism . . ."[94] One can debate the fundamental source of this hysteria,

[93] Restatement of the Foreign Relations Law of the United States, section 702 (d).

[94] Michael C. Desch, "The More Things Change, the More They Stay the Same: The Liberal Tradition and Obama's Counterterrorism Policy," *PS*, 43, 3 (July 2010), p. 427.

but repeatedly US governments have engaged in threat exaggeration concerning national security.

Without some kind of official pronouncement on all of this, similar threat exaggeration is likely to happen again – and thus to repeat the various paranoid episodes of the past. We saw American hysteria against German Americans during the First World War, similar hysteria against suspected communists during McCarthyism in the 1950s, false claims about Soviet superiority in missiles in the 1960s, and misrepresentation in the Cuban missile crisis in the form of the assertion that Soviet missiles were inherently aggressive (even though they were approximate in nature to US missiles in Turkey aimed at the USSR). There needs to be some reliable process of saying what is necessary for national security and what is not when torture and CID are involved.

We have noted some skepticism that civilian judges may not be able to play this role. Often they do not feel comfortable – and not trained for – contesting the Executive Branch concerning security issues. Even a normally liberal Appellate Court in the *Jeppesen Dataplan* case caved in to Executive requests for secrecy and dismissal on national security grounds. There are exceptions, of course, as in the 2006 *Hamdan* ruling by the Supreme Court asserting that resort to war was not a blank check for the Executive, and the 2010 *Ghailani* ruling in which a District Court asserted that the Constitutional protections for prisoners were not to be discarded just because national security concerns were involved.

If the civilian courts are not up to the task, the one remaining option in contesting unfettered Executive judgment would actually be some officials in the Military Commissions. The JAG Corps has a long record of independence in speaking legal truth to political power,[95] even if the occasional JAG like Diane Beaver at Gitmo buckled to political pressure and gave the Bush Administration the desired legal memo. But the JAGs are more typically represented by the likes of Admiral Alberto Mora who forced a change in Rumsfeld's decisions by his principled opposition to abusive treatment of prisoners at Gitmo.[96] And several officials

[95] Osiel, *The End of Reciprocity*, and Peter Jan Honigsberg, *Our Nation Unhinged: The Human Consequences of the War on Terror* (Berkeley: University of California Press, 2009).

[96] Recall his strong defense of human rights and humanitarian law in the face of a US policy of "cruelty" toward enemy prisoners, Carnegie Council on Ethics.

in the Military Commission system have either thrown out charges, or reduced sentences, because defendants were mistreated. Because of their traditions and because they have some military standing, JAG officials may actually be in a better position than civilian prosecutors and judges to address the central issue of humanitarian values in the context of the necessities of national security. They are part of the Executive, but they do have military standing and a tradition of independence. They do not, however, have jurisdiction over the CIA.

There is no avoiding the difficulty of the cosmopolitan project to make torture and CID truly exceptional. We live in a world of nation-states, and often nationalism is strong to the point of becoming jingoistic or chauvinistic. Fearful nationalism is a potent and dangerous force. There are those who believe we have not advanced very far from the time of the Dreyfus case in 1895, when French nationalistic maneuvers resulted in false charges being brought against a Jewish officer in the French army. One reading of that case serves as a "reminder of how fragile the standards of civilized conduct prove in moments of national panic" and how "that national panic makes bad policy and false prisoners."[97] Even democracies have a sizable history of torture, as Darius Rejali has shown, and as we noted in Chapter 1. The Administration of Bush II, through its fear and threat exaggeration, has gravely wounded the cosmopolitan project to protect the human rights of all, especially the rights of personal integrity, whether seen as part of human rights or humanitarian law. UN officials have noted the spread of secret detention in the wake of US policies, as already remarked. Off the record, ICRC officials regard Bush policies after 9/11 as a disaster for humanitarian affairs.

Conor Gearty has argued that regarding the United States and the United Kingdom: "in the field of counter-terrorism and human rights, these two secure, stable democracies make the weather, creating the climate in which human rights activists of the world must work. In the way that these states conduct themselves vis-à-vis human rights, they matter out of all proportion to their sovereign space."[98] Keeping in mind that the British were complicit in the Bush policy of authorized and

[97] Adam Gopnik, "Trial of the Century," *The New Yorker*, September 28, 2009, p. 72.

[98] Conor Gearty, *Can Human Rights Survive?* (Cambridge: Cambridge University Press, 2006), p. 107.

monitored abuse, just as they were complicit in the invasion of Iraq, these two important states have done tremendous damage to human rights and humanitarian law. In that the British have promised an inquiry into their role in supporting US detention, interrogation, and rendition policies, London may be able to make a contribution to undoing some of the damage done.

Kenneth Roth of Human Rights Watch drove the point home: "When most governments breach international human rights [and humanitarian] law, they commit a violation – the breach is condemned or prosecuted, but the rule remains firm. Yet when a government as dominant and influential as the United States openly defies that law and seeks to justify its defiance, it also undermines the law itself, and invites others to do the same. That shakes the very foundations of the international system for the protection of human rights that has been carefully constructed over the past sixty years."[99]

It will take considerable courage by the US Executive, the Congress, the court system, and the Military Commissions to repair the damage. There has already been, at least sometimes, a significant push back against the Bush record in these circles. If these forces coordinate with UN human rights officials and other cosmopolitan forces, it is possible some of the damage can be repaired. But none of the contemplated responses is free from controversy. There are no perfect solutions. Terror and torture feed off each other, and at the present stage of world history it is not clear that law can control torture.[100] But if we do not try, we will end up worse off.

Ramesh Thakur is quite right: "The robustness and resilience of the civilized world's commitment to human rights norms and values will be judged in the final analysis not by the breaches in the aftermath of 9/11, but by the reversal and attenuation of the breaches through the judicial and political process as well as the pressure of domestic and international civil society."[101]

[99] Roth, "Getting Away with Torture," p. 391.
[100] See further Kahn, *Sacred Violence.*
[101] *The Hindu*, July 20, 2007, www.thehindu.com/2007/07/20/stories/2007072055110000.htm.

ANNEX A
Cast of principal characters

David Addington, Office of the Vice President, Legal Counsel (2001–2005); Chief of Staff (2005–2009)

John D. Ashcroft, US Attorney General (2001–2004)

Diane E. Beaver, Lt. Col., US Army, Staff Judge Advocate, Joint Task Force-170, Guantánamo Naval Base (2002–2004); Deputy General Counsel for International Affairs, Department of Defense (2004–2009)

John B. Bellinger, III, Senior Associate Counsel to the President and Legal Advisor, National Security Council (February 2001–January 2005); Legal Advisor, US Department of State (April 2005–January 2009)

Cofer Black, Director, CIA's Counter-terrorism Center (CTC) (1999–2001); Ambassador-at-large for Counter-terrorism, State Department (2002–2004); Vice Chairman, Blackwater (Xe), USA (2005–2008); Chairman, Total Intelligence Solutions (2008–)

Steven G. Bradbury, Principal Deputy Assistant Attorney General (Department of Justice) Office of Legal Counsel (April 2004–June 2005); Acting Assistant Attorney General, Office of Legal Counsel (June 2005–January 2009)

L. Paul (Jerry) Bremer, III, Head, Coalition Provisional Authority, Iraq (May 2003–June 2004)

George W. Bush, 43rd President of the United States (2001–2009)

Jay S. Bybee, Assistant Attorney General, Office of Legal Counsel, Department of Justice (November 2001–March 2003)

Stephen Cambone, Special Assistant to the Secretary of Defense and Deputy Secretary of Defense (January 2001–July 2001); Principal Deputy Undersecretary of Defense for Policy (July 2001–July 2002); Director, Program Analysis and Evaluation, Office of the Secretary of Defense (July 2002–March 2003); Undersecretary of Defense for Intelligence (March 2003–December 2006)

Richard B. Cheney, Vice President of the United States (2001–2009)

Robert Delahunty, Special Counsel, Office of Legal Counsel, Department of Justice (1992–2002); Deputy General Counsel, White House Office of Homeland Security (2002–2003)

Daniel Dell'Orto, Principal Deputy General Counsel, Defense Department (2000–2009)

Michael E. Dunlavey, Maj. Gen., US Army, Commander, Joint Task Force-170, Guantánamo Naval Base (Spring 2002–November 2002)

Gordon England, Secretary of the Navy (May 2001–January 2003, October 2003–December 2005); Deputy Secretary of Homeland Security (January 2003–October 2003); Deputy Secretary of Defense (May 2005–January 2009)

George R. Fay, Maj. Gen., US Army, co-author of report on Military Intelligence at Abu Ghraib Prison, Iraq.

Douglas J. Feith, Undersecretary of Defense for Policy (July 2001–August 2005)

Timothy E. Flanigan, Deputy Counsel to the President (2001–December 2002)

Tommy Franks, Gen., US Army, Commander, US Military Central Command (July 2000–July 2003); Commander, US Military Forces, Iraq (2003)

Robert Gates, US Secretary of Defense (December 2006–)

Jack Goldsmith, Assistant Attorney General, Office of Legal Counsel, Department of Justice (October 2003–July 2004)

Alberto R. Gonzales, Counsel to the President (2001–2005); US Attorney General (February 2005–September 2007)

Lindsey Graham, Senator (R, SC) (2002–)

Michael Hayden, Director, National Security Agency (1999–2005); Principal Deputy Director, CIA (April 2005–May 2006); Director, CIA (May 2006–February 2009)

William J. Haynes, II, Legal Counsel, Defense Department (May 2001–February 2008)

John L. Helgerson, Inspector General, CIA (2002–2009)

James T. Hill, Gen., US Army, Commander, US Military Southern Command (2002–2004)

Eric Holder, US Attorney General (January 2009–)

Bruce Jessen, Co-founder, Mitchell Jessen Associates, a private contractor with the CIA (2002–2009); formerly associated with the US military's SERE program

Anthony R. Jones, Lt. Gen., US Army, co-author of report on Military Intelligence at Abu Ghraib prison, Iraq
Janis Karpinski, Brig. Gen. (demoted to Col., May 2005), US Army Reserves (2003–2005); Head, Military Police, Iraq, 2003
Patrick Leahy, Senator (D, VT) (1980–)
John McCain, Senator (R, AZ) (1982–)
Geoffrey D. Miller, Maj. Gen., US Army, Commander, Guantánamo Naval Base (November 2002–September 2003); transferred to be advisor, Abu Ghraib prison, Iraq (September 2003)
James Mitchell, Co-founder, Mitchell Jessen Associates, a private contractor with the CIA (2002–2009)
Alberto J. Mora, Adm., US Navy (ret.), Legal Counsel, US Navy (2001–2006)
Michael B. Mukasey, US Attorney General (November 2007–January 2009)
Richard B. Myers, Gen., US Army, Chair, Joint Chiefs of Staff, Defense Department (October 2001–September 2005)
Barack Obama, 44th President of the United States (January 2009–)
Leon E. Panetta, Director, CIA (February 2009–)
Thomas M. Pappas, Col., US Army, Head of Military Intelligence, Abu Ghraib prison, Iraq (2003), later demoted and fined
James L. Pavitt, CIA Deputy Director for Operations (under George Tenet) (1999–2004)
Colin L. Powell, US Secretary of State (2001–2005)
Condoleezza Rice, National Security Advisor (2001–2005); Secretary of State (2005–2009)
John Rizzo, Acting General Counsel, CIA (2006–2009), formerly career staff lawyer for the Agency
Donald R. Rumsfeld, Secretary of Defense (2001–2006)
Ricardo S. Sanchez, Lt. Gen., US Army, V corps, Commander of Coalition Forces, Iraq (June 2003–June 2004) (ret. November 2006)
Randall M. Schmidt, Lt. Gen., US Air Force (ret. September 2006), author of report on Geoffrey Miller and abusive interrogation at Guantánamo
William Howard Taft, IV, Legal Advisor, State Department (2001–2005)
Antonio M. Taguba, Maj. Gen., US Army (ret. January 2007), author of report on Military Police at Abu Ghraib prison, Iraq
George J. Tenet, Director, CIA (July 1997–June 2004)

Mary Walker, US Air Force General Counsel (2001–), head of legal study team on military abusive interrogation, 2003; formerly head of study team that issued controversial report minimizing alleged command misbehavior at US Air Force Academy

John Warner, Senator (R, VA) (January 1979–January 2009)

Matthew Waxman, Deputy Assistant Secretary of Defense, Detainee Affairs (2004–2005)

Paul D. Wolfowitz, Deputy Secretary of Defense (2001–2005); President, World Bank (June 2005–June 2007)

John C. Yoo, Deputy Assistant Attorney General, Office of Legal Counsel, Department of Justice (2001–2003)

Philip D. Zelikow, Senior White House Staffer, National Security Council (1989–1991); Director, 9/11 Commission (November 2002–August 2004); Counselor, State Department (February 2005–January 2007)

ANNEX B

Reports on US policy toward enemy prisoners

1 US reports on prisoner abuse after 9/11

(The US reports cited in section 1 are in ascending date order so that the unfolding picture from 2003 to 2010 may be followed; the NGO and other reports cited in sections 2 and 3 are in descending date order from 2010. A given report may be found at more than one site on the internet.)

a Miller report: "Assessment of DOD Counter-Terrorism Interrogation and Detention Operations in Iraq," September 2003

The report was prepared by Maj. Gen. Geoffrey Miller in September 2003 as part of his assessment of the Abu Ghraib detention facility. The report recommends the adoption of harsh practices employed at Guantánamo Bay, where Miller was then the commander, as a model for personnel in Iraq. The key to his approach was the integration of MP with MI, so that MP could soften up prisoners for interrogation. Detainees at Guantánamo had been designated "illegal enemy combatants" to whom the 1949 Geneva Conventions supposedly did not apply. The Bush Administration acknowledged that the 1949 Geneva Conventions applied to the invasion and occupation of Iraq. Yet Miller recommended Gitmo's harsh approach in Iraq.

www.publicintegrity.org/docs/AbuGhraib/Abu3.pdf

b Ryder report: "Report on Detention and Corrections Operations in Iraq," November 2003

Maj. Gen. Donald Ryder investigated conditions in US-run prisons in Iraq prior to the publication of the Abu Ghraib photographs. He found problems throughout the system, such as inadequate training of prison guards in the 800th Military Police Brigade at Abu Ghraib.

www1.umn.edu/humanrts/OathBetrayed/Ryderpercent20Report.pdf

c "Taguba" report: "Article 15–6 Investigation of the 800th Military Police Brigade," March 2004

The report presents findings from an investigation of detainee abuse involving military police personnel and the policies, procedures and command climate of the 800th Military Police Brigade at Abu Ghraib by Maj. Gen. Antonio M. Taguba. The report concluded that numerous incidents of "sadistic, blatant, and wanton criminal abuses" were inflicted intentionally on detainees, many of which had already been referred for criminal investigation. The report finds abuse to be a systemic problem. Taguba was later to say that the United States was responsible for war crimes at Abu Ghraib.

www1.umn.edu/humanrts/OathBetrayed/Taguba-Report.pdf

d Helgerson report: "Counter-terrorism Detention and Interrogation Activities," May 2004

Findings from the report by the Agency's Inspector General John L. Helgerson suggest that some CIA-approved interrogation procedures appeared to constitute cruel, inhuman, or degrading treatment (CID), if not torture. The report suggests that certain CIA interrogations exceeded their instructions. The report also raises questions about the effectiveness of certain Agency techniques.

http://luxmedia.vo.llnwd.net/o10/clients/aclu/IG_Report.pdf

e Jacoby report: "Combined Forces Command–Afghanistan Area Operations (CFC–A AO) Detainee Operations Report of Inspection," June 2004

The Jacoby report focused on prisons in Afghanistan. The report findings suggest that detention operations are functional, but lack cohesive direction, and are constrained by friction at critical junctures. This report was largely discounted and played a small role in developments.

www1.umn.edu/humanrts/OathBetrayed/Jacobypercent20Report.pdf

f Mikolashek report: "Department of the Army Inspector General Inspection Report on Detainee Operations," July 2004

The report prepared by the Army Inspector General finds that abuse of detainees mainly in Iraq resulted from the failure of individuals to follow known standards of discipline and, in some cases, the failure of a few leaders to enforce those standards of discipline. The report was unable to identify systemic failures that resulted in detainee abuses. Parts of this report are contradicted by the "Taguba," Schlesinger, and Fay–Jones reports.

www.washingtonpost.com/wp-srv/world/iraq/abughraib/detaineereport.pdf

g Fay–Jones report: "Investigation of intelligence activities at Abu Ghraib," August 2004

Lt. Gen. Anthony R. Jones and Maj. Gen. George R. Fay investigated intelligence activities of the 205th Military Intelligence Brigade at Abu Ghraib and reported that dozens of military personnel and contractors were responsible for abuses. This report on MI complements the "Taguba" report on MP, and fits with the Schlesinger report on Abu Ghraib as a whole. All these reports are carefully constructed by officials in Washington to avoid addressing the role of the Secretary of Defense and other civilian policy makers.

www1.umn.edu/humanrts/OathBetrayed/Fay-Jonespercent20Report.pdf

h Schlesinger report: "Final Report of the Independent Panel to Review DoD Detention Operations," August 2004

The panel led by former Defense Secretary James Schlesinger described the migration of harsh techniques from Afghanistan through Guantánamo to Iraq. The report concluded that commanding officers and their staffs at various levels failed in their duties that contributed directly or indirectly to detainee abuse. While finding personal and institutional responsibility for the abuses at Abu Ghraib in Iraq, the panel did not focus on the Office of the Secretary of Defense or other high political and military leaders. The report stressed that much abuse at Abu Ghraib had little relation to serious intelligence gathering and was the result of lower-ranking individuals running amok, but within a permissive context.

www.defense.gov/news/Aug2004/d20040824finalreport.pdf

i Church report: "Review of Department of Defense Detention Operations and Detainee Interrogation Techniques," February 2005

Vice Adm. Albert T. Church, the Navy's Inspector General, investigated detainee conditions in Afghanistan, Guantánamo, and Iraq at the request of Secretary of Defense Rumsfeld. According to the Executive Summary, this inquiry found seventy-one cases of abuse resulting in six deaths which had been perpetrated by a variety of active duty, reserve, and national guard personnel from three services on multiple occasions in all three locations investigated. The report also found that "there was a failure to react to early warning signs of abuse" but did not identify systemic problems. The report, long classified, is widely regarded as ducking the issue of command responsibility and played little role in subsequent developments.

www1.umn.edu/humanrts/OathBetrayed/Churchpercent20Report.pdf

j Army Surgeon General report: "Assessment of Detainee Medical Operations for OEF (Operation Enduring Freedom), GTMO (Guantánamo Bay Detention Facility), and OIF (Operation Iraqi Freedom)," April 2005

This report presents findings from an extensive assessment of detainee medical operations in Iraq, Guantánamo, and Afghanistan. It raises questions mostly about using psychiatrists on Behavioral Science Consultation Teams (BSCTs) in interrogations. The report finds ninety-four incidents of confirmed or possible detainee abuse in US prison facilities throughout Iraq and Afghanistan.

It found only two cases where interviewees were aware of claims of abuse but did not report them. These cases were reported to the Criminal Investigation Division. The report did not sharply differentiate conditions and policies early on after 9/11 compared to 2004–2005, but it did suggest that training and sensitivity to prisoner needs improved over time. The report is not entirely consistent with various accounts of harsh forced feeding at Guantánamo, or with an ICRC report questioning the role of US military medical personnel in abusive interrogation.

www1.umn.edu/humanrts/OathBetrayed/Armypercent20Surgeon percent20Generalpercent20Report.pdf

k Schmidt report: "Army Regulation 15–6: Investigation into FBI Allegations of Detainee Abuse at Guantánamo Bay, Cuba Detention Facility," July 2005

This military report prepared by Lt. Gen. Randall M. Schmidt and Brig. Gen. John T. Furlow looked into FBI allegations of abuse at

Guantánamo and found that while policies were violated, the resulting treatment was not "inhumane." The report covers over 24,000 interrogations over a period of three years and found that only three interrogations violated interrogation policies and in one case of a suspected high-value detainee (HVD) the interrogation resulted in degrading and abusive treatment but it did not reach the level of being "inhumane." The report criticized Comm. Geoffrey Miller for allowing combined abusive techniques of interrogation to be used on a prisoner, thus being negligent about limits. The report recommended sanctions for Miller. No such sanctions transpired. The report documents much abuse at Gitmo, while avoiding independent judgment about the abuse, repeatedly saying the abuse was authorized.

www.defense.gov/news/Jul2005/d20050714report.pdf

l Formica report: "Article 15–6": Investigation of CJSOTF–AP (Combined Joint Special Operations Task Force – Arabian Peninsula) and 5th SF (Special Forces) Group Detention Operation," June 2006

The report is based on an investigation led by Brig. Gen. Richard Formica into three specific allegations against the Combined Joint Special Operations Task Force – Arabian Peninsula, which operates throughout Iraq. Formica's report concludes that detainees who report being sodomized or beaten are seeking sympathy and better treatment, and thus are not credible. The investigation found no evidence of any detainees being abused by Army personnel in Iraq as of that date.

www1.umn.edu/humanrts/OathBetrayed/Formicapercent20Report.pdf

m McCaffrey report: "Academic Report Trip to JTF (Joint Task Force) Guantánamo," June 2006

The report by Gen. Barry R. McCaffrey, Adjunct Professor of International Affairs at the United States Military Academy based on visits to the Southern Command (SouthCom) of JTF Guantánamo between June 18 and 19, 2006 finds no physical or mental abuse of prisoners in this facility by either guard personnel or military intelligence interrogator as of that date.

www1.umn.edu/humanrts/OathBetrayed/McCaffreyReport.pdf

n Department of Defense, Office of Inspector General report: "Office of Inspector General Review of DoD-Directed Investigations of Detainee Abuse," August 2006

The report reviews detainee investigations and concludes that allegations of detainee abuse were not consistently reported, investigated, or managed in an effective, systematic, and timely manner by US authorities in Iraq. The report further suggests that no single entity within any level of command was aware of the scope and breadth of detainee abuse and that interrogation support in Iraq lacked unity of command and unity of effort.

www1.umn.edu/humanrts/OathBetrayed/OIGpercent202006percent20 Report.pdf

o Department of Justice, Inspector General report: "A Review of FBI's Involvement in and Observations of Detainee Interrogations in Guantánamo Bay, Afghanistan and Iraq," May 2008

The report found that complaints by FBI agents about interrogation techniques at Guantánamo were brought to the attention of White House officials, but ignored. The report suggests that the FBI was somewhat slow in responding to events and did not fashion a clear policy on detainee abuse and communicate it to staff for considerable time. Nevertheless, the Bureau did, for the most part, distance itself from abusive interrogation, with only a few agents acting otherwise.

www.justice.gov/oig/special/s0805/final.pdf

p Levin report: "Senate Armed Services Committee Inquiry into the Treatment of Detainees in US Custody," December 2008

The report investigated the origins of detainee abuse by the US military after 9/11 and found that the actions of former Defense Secretary Donald H. Rumsfeld were a direct cause of abuse through unclear and confusing guidelines plus lack of follow-up and supervision. The report was backed by both Democratic and Republican members of the committee.

http://levin.senate.gov/newsroom/supporting/2008/Detainees.121108.pdf

q Department of Justice, Office of Professional Responsibility report: "Investigation into the Office of Legal Counsel's Memoranda Concerning Issues Relating to the Central Intelligence Agency's use of 'Enhanced Interrogation Techniques' on suspected Terrorists," July 2009

The report by the Justice Department's Office of Professional Responsibility (OPR) looked into the conduct of the lawyers in the Office of Legal Counsel (OLC), regarding their role in approving the use of abusive interrogation techniques. The report concludes that the primary author of the memos, John Yoo, an OLC lawyer and the senior official who signed the August 1, 2002 memos, Assistant Attorney General Jay S. Bybee were guilty of "professional misconduct." The report, however, was not accepted by higher DOJ authorities on grounds that the standards for misconduct were not clear in the report.

http://judiciary.house.gov/hearings/pdf/OPRFinalReport090729.pdf

r Margolis' memo to Attorney General Eric Holder: "Memorandum for the Attorney General: Memorandum of Decisions Regarding the Objections to Findings of Professional Misconduct in the Office of Professional Responsibility Report of Investigation into the Office of Legal Counsel's Memoranda Concerning Issues Relating to the Central Intelligence Agency's use of 'Enhanced Interrogation Techniques' on suspected Terrorists," January 5, 2010

In a sixty-nine-page memo to Attorney General Eric Holder, Associate Deputy Attorney General David Margolis asserted that Yoo and Bybee had only shown "poor judgment" but not negligence or misconduct in facilitating abusive interrogation by CIA and military officials.

http://judiciary.house.gov/hearings/pdf/DAGMargolisMemo100105.pdf

2 NGO reports

a Amnesty International, selected reports, 2001–2002

USA – Missing from the United States' "human rights agenda": Accountability and remedy for "war on terror" abuses (AMR 51/005/2010, January 2010)

One year into the Obama Administration, almost 200 individuals remain detained without fair trial at the Guantánamo prison camp, and accountability and remedy for the human rights violations committed against these and other detainees in what the United States previously called the "war on terror" remain more myth than reality. This report calls for concrete action, including accountability, remedy, and ending the Guantánamo detentions in line with its international human rights obligations.

www.amnesty.org/en/library/asset/AMR51/005/2010/en/0b982b8b-a730-49b5-8d0a-1ad4f6bd25eb/amr510052010en.pdf

USA – Trials in error: Third go at misconceived military commission experiment (AMR 51/083/2009, July 2009)

This report outlines that even if some of the shortcomings of the Military Commissions are addressed through reforms, there would remain a number of reasons why they would remain incompatible with international standards.

www.amnesty.org/en/library/asset/AMR51/083/2009/en/7cd7b5c8-d9f4-4415-b9fa-2ca47fe59a9f/amr510832009eng.pdf

USA – President Obama defends Guantánamo closure, but endorses "war" paradigm and indefinite preventive detention (AMR 51/072/2009, May 2009)

In a recent major speech on national security, President Barack Obama restated his commitment to closing the Guantánamo detention facility and to ending the use of "enhanced interrogation techniques." However, President Obama restated his support for Military Commissions and confirmed his opposition to an independent commission of inquiry. Amnesty International remains concerned that this Administration continues to invoke the laws and means of war without recognizing its international legal obligations to ensure and respect the human rights of every individual.

www.amnesty.org/en/library/asset/AMR51/072/2009/en/9d5f4bfb-e356-488d-9cfc-ccb971668d54/amr510722009en.pdf

USA – Facts and figures: Illegal US detentions (AMR 51/147/2008, December 2008)

This document presents facts and figures about illegal US detentions. On January 11, 2009 it will be seven years since the first detainees were transferred to Guantánamo and approximately 250 were still held in December 2008. Elsewhere dozens have been held in secret and hundreds of people remain detained without charge at the US air base in Bagram, Afghanistan.

www.amnesty.org/en/library/asset/AMR51/147/2008/en/99c5c1c4-cde2-11dd-b0c5-1f8db3691f48/amr511472008en.pdf

USA – Way of life, way of death: Capital charges referred against five former secret detainees (AMR 51/041/2008, May 2008)

On May 13, 2008, the United States opened another chapter in its relationship with the death penalty when it referred capital charges against five Guantánamo detainees for joint trial by Military Commission. The five are accused of involvement in the September 11, 2001 attacks in the United States. The Administration should turn to the existing federal courts for any trials of the detainees and release those who are not to be charged.

www.amnesty.org/en/library/asset/AMR51/041/2008/en/159f2575–2660-11dd-b995-f7269e5ea55f/amr510412008eng.pdf

USA – Law and executive disorder: President gives green light to secret detention program (AMR 51/135/2007, August 2007)

On July 20, 2007, President George W. Bush issued an executive order determining that Article 3 common to the four Geneva Conventions of 1949 "shall apply to a program of detention and interrogation operated by the Central Intelligence Agency" (CIA). This report provides some background to the development of the secret CIA program and to the issuing of this executive order more than five years later. It concludes that both the executive order and the CIA program itself fail to comply with the USA's international obligations.

www.amnesty.org/en/library/asset/AMR51/135/2007/en/16c3d1a9-d371-11dd-a329-2f46302a8cc6/amr511352007en.pdf

USA – Off the record: US responsibility for enforced disappearances in the "war on terror" (AMR 51/093/2007, June 2007)

This briefing paper presents information about at least thirty-nine detainees, all of whom are still missing, who are believed to have been held in secret sites run by the US government overseas. The paper provides basic information about these individuals, including facts concerning the circumstances of their apprehension, evidence concerning US involvement, and any information available concerning their current whereabouts. This document is based on research by six major human rights groups: Amnesty International; Cageprisoners; the Center for Constitutional Rights; the Center for Human Rights and Global Justice at NYU School of Law; Human Rights Watch; and Reprieve.

www.amnesty.org/en/library/asset/AMR51/093/2007/en/466435a8-d38b-11dd-a329-2f46302a8cc6/amr510932007en.pdf

USA – Justice delayed and justice denied? Trials under the Military Commissions Act (AMR 51/044/2007, March 2007)

A few people held in the US Naval Base at Guantánamo Bay in Cuba are now facing trial by Military Commission, which system mirrors the Combatant Status Review Tribunals (CSRTs). Amnesty International is calling on the US government to abandon the Military Commissions and to bring any Guantánamo or other "war on terror" detainees it charges to trial in the ordinary federal courts, without recourse to the death penalty. The Guantánamo detention facility should be closed down.

www.amnesty.org/en/library/asset/AMR51/044/2007/en/48cca375-d3a8-11dd-a329-2f46302a8cc6/amr510442007en.pdf

USA – Five years on "the dark side": A look back at "war on terror" detentions (AMR 51/195/2006, December 2006)

In this document Amnesty International continues to press for the closure of Guantánamo and the ending of secret detentions and renditions. Human rights organizations support the tireless efforts of the US legal community to restore the rule of law. Amnesty International will continue to call on Congress to establish a full commission of inquiry into the United States' "war on terror" detention policies and practices, to repeal or substantially amend the Military Commissions Act and to amend the Detainee Treatment Act, as well as to withdraw treaty reservations and seal loopholes for torture and other ill-treatment.

www.amnesty.org/en/library/asset/AMR51/195/2006/en/725a2ddc-d3ca-11dd-8743-d305bea2b2c7/amr511952006en.pdf

USA – Close Guantánamo. Guantánamo's Military Commissions: a travesty of justice (AMR 51/184/2006, December 2006)

On October 17, 2006 President Bush signed the Military Commissions Act, which codifies in US law a substandard and discriminatory system of justice for those held in Guantánamo Bay, Afghanistan and elsewhere. This document shows how the Military Commissions Act disregards the standards of justice set out in the US Constitution, federal law and military justice system, as well as in international treaties that the United States has ratified.

www.amnesty.org/en/library/asset/AMR51/184/2006/en/8945443e-d3cc-11dd-8743-d305bea2b2c7/amr511842006en.pdf

USA – "War on terror" detentions at a crossroads: New AI report on detentions and trials following the US Supreme Court's *Hamdan* v. *Rumsfeld* ruling (AMR 51/148/2006, September 2006)

This document accompanies the issue of an Amnesty International report (AI index AMR 51/146/2006) that comes at a time when the US Congress is considering legislation with major implications for the treatment of persons held in the context of "the war on terror." In June 2006 the Supreme Court concluded that the commissions as constituted under a Military Order in November 2001 were unlawful. Amnesty International welcomed the ruling. The organization called on the government to use the ruling for real change in the United States' "war on terror" detention practices that had systematically violated international law and standards.

www.amnesty.org/en/library/asset/AMR51/148/2006/en/2dbe375c-d3f2-11dd-8743-d305bea2b2c7/amr511482006en.pdf

USA – No impunity for war crimes: US administration seeking to amend the War Crimes Act (AMR 51/136/2006, August 2006)

Amnesty International is concerned that the US Administration is seeking to persuade Congress to narrow the scope of the US War Crimes Act to prevent prosecutions of US personnel for humiliating and degrading treatment of detainees in the "war on terror." The organization believes that any such measure would undermine the rule of law and send a dangerous message about impunity. Torture and ill-treatment thrive on impunity.

www.amnesty.org/en/library/asset/AMR51/136/2006/en/ac8a2dcc-d403-11dd-8743-d305bea2b2c7/amr511362006en.pdf

USA – Updated briefing to the Human Rights Committee on the implementation of the International Covenant on Civil and Political Rights (AMR 51/111/2006, July 2006)

This briefing builds on Amnesty International's previous submission to the supervising Committee from September 2005, which summarized the organization's principal concerns regarding the counter-terrorism measures taken by the United States following the attacks of September 11, 2001 as they related to the state party's obligations under the Covenant. It expands on a number of the issues raised in the earlier submission and provides additional information relevant to other areas of the implementation of the Covenant by the state party, which is not directly related to the United States' counter-terrorism measures.

www.amnesty.org/en/library/asset/AMR51/111/2006/en/5629ea1d-d412-11dd-8743-d305bea2b2c7/amr511112006en.pdf

Amnesty International submits memorandum to the US government on torture and Guantánamo (AMR 51/096/2006, June 2006)

This document accompanies a major report (AMR 51/093/2006) and calls for the closure of Guantánamo detention camp. On 22 June 2006, the Optional Protocol to the Convention against Torture came into force after the twentieth country ratified it. The UN Committee Against Torture issued its recommendations on 19 May. It found serious violations of the United States' obligations under the Convention against Torture and Other Cruel, Inhuman, or Degrading Treatment or Punishment. Amnesty International is concerned by the Administration's initial negative reaction to the Committee's findings and the organization's memorandum seeks to persuade the government to adopt a more positive stance.

www.amnesty.org/en/library/asset/AMR51/096/2006/en/3822e859-d41b-11dd-8743-d305bea2b2c7/amr510962006en.pdf

USA – Memorandum to the US Government on the report of the UN Committee Against Torture and the question of closing Guantánamo (AMR 51/093/2006, June 2006)

The UN Committee Against Torture has recently made recommendations on the United States' compliance with its obligations under the Convention against Torture and the future of the Guantánamo detention camp. Amnesty International here details its recommendations, a framework, for an alternative to continued detentions at Guantánamo. In brief, those held in the base should be released unless they are to be charged and tried in accordance with international standards of fair trial. No detainees who are released should be forcibly sent to their country of origin or other countries where they may face serious human rights abuses.

www.amnesty.org/en/library/asset/AMR51/093/2006/en/267dd10c-d41e-11dd-8743-d305bea2b2c7/amr510932006en.pdf

USA – Below the radar: Secret flights to torture and "disappearance" (AMR 51/051/2006, April 2006)

In this report Amnesty International brings together critical evidence about the US-led rendition programme. Its recommendations include: the United States should end its practice of renditions; all governments should ensure that rendition victims are protected from torture, and that "war on terror" detainees are charged and given a fair trial, or released; all governments should prohibit the transfer of people to places where they are at risk of ill-treatment; all governments should ensure that their airports and airspace are not being used in renditions;

and all private aircraft operators should refrain from leasing planes where they might be used in renditions.

www.amnesty.org/en/library/asset/AMR51/051/2006/en/b543c574-fa09-11dd-b1b0-c961f7df9c35/amr510512006en.pdf

Iraq – Abu Ghraib torture victims still seeking redress (**MDE 14/019/2006, April 2006**)

The release of photographs showing detainees being tortured and ill-treated by US military personnel at Abu Ghraib prison in Iraq shocked and horrified the world. Despite repeated calls, the US authorities have failed to conduct proper investigations to ensure that all those responsible, including at the highest levels, are held to account. The survivors are still seeking redress.

www.amnesty.org/en/library/asset/MDE14/019/2006/en/d5abe737-d439-11dd-8743-percent20d305bea2b2c7/mde140192006en.pdf

USA – Guantánamo. Lives torn apart: The impact of indefinite detention on detainees and their families (**AMR 51/007/2006, February 2006**)

In this document, Amnesty International relates the continuing plight of detainees, and summarizes developments related to the ongoing hunger strike and suicide attempts. The organization assesses the situation of nine men who remain detained despite no longer being considered "enemy combatants" by US authorities. It also examines the impact on some of the family members of the detainees, many of whom have suffered as a result of the detentions. Finally, Amnesty International describes the consequences for some detainees who were released from Guantánamo yet continue to suffer the direct results of their experiences in US detention in Guantánamo and elsewhere.

www.amnesty.org/en/library/asset/AMR51/007/2006/en/3acfbf3c-d46d-11dd-8743-d305bea2b2c7/amr510072006en.pdf

Iraq – Beyond Abu Ghraib: Detention and torture in Iraq (**MDE 14/001/2006, March 2006**)

In this report, Amnesty International focuses on human rights violations for which the US-led Multinational Force is directly responsible and those that are being committed by Iraqi security. Since the invasion in March 2003 tens of thousands of people have been detained by foreign forces without being charged. Many cases of torture and ill-treatment of detainees held in facilities controlled by the Iraqi authorities have been reported. Amnesty International is calling on the Iraqi,

US and UK authorities to take urgent, concrete steps to ensure that the fundamental human rights of all detainees in Iraq are respected.

www.amnesty.org/en/library/asset/MDE14/001/2006/en/a2b9a7ed-d46e-11dd-8743-d305bea2b2c7/mde140012006en.pdf

USA – Guantánamo and beyond: The continuing pursuit of unchecked executive power (**AMR 51/063/2005, May 2005**)

This report forms part of Amnesty International's campaigning on detentions in Guantánamo and other US facilities in the "war on terror." Along with other issues, the document considers the detentions in the context of the international legal framework; the Combatant Status Review Board; Military Commissions; deaths in custody; torture and ill-treatment; secrecy; transfers from Guantánamo. There are also appendixes on deaths in custody; witness testimonies; alleged detention and interrogation practices; recommendations based on Amnesty's 12-point Programme for the Prevention of Torture and Ill-treatment; and, selected AI documents on "war on terror" detentions.

www.amnesty.org/en/library/asset/AMR51/063/2005/en/0e3f8b95-d4fe-11dd-8a23-d58a49c0d652/amr510632005en.pdf

USA – Human dignity denied: Torture and accountability in the "war on terror" (**Summary report AMR 51/146/2004, October 2004**)

This is a summary of a report based on Amnesty International's 12-point Programme for the Prevention of Torture by Agents of the State. In the main 200-page report, Amnesty International seeks to provide a framework by which there can be a full accounting for any torture or cruel, inhuman, or degrading treatment by US agents, and to prevent future violations of international law and standards. Part One of the report gives an overview of the situation. Part Two is entitled "Agenda for Action," and begins with a reiteration of Amnesty International's call for a full commission of inquiry into all US "war on terror" detention and interrogation practices and policies. The remainder of Part Two is structured around Amnesty International's 12-point Programme for the Prevention of Torture by Agents of the State.

www.amnesty.org/en/library/asset/AMR51/146/2004/en/d22d6f0e-d56c-11dd-bb24-1fb85fe8fa05/amr511462004en.pdf

USA – The threat of a bad example (**AMR 51/118/2003, August 2003**)

The United States has displayed a troubling tendency to seek unchallengeable executive power for itself in the context of its "war on terror." It has created a parallel justice system in which the executive has the power to detain, interrogate, charge, or try suspects under the "laws of war."

www.amnesty.org/en/library/asset/AMR51/118/2003/en/0498ea30-face-11dd-b531-99d31a1e99e4/amr511182003en.pdf

b Human Rights Watch: Selected Reports, July 16, 2010

Locked Up Alone: Detention Conditions and Mental Health at Guantánamo, June 2008

The report documents the conditions in the various "camps" at the detention center, in which approximately 185 of the 270 detainees are housed in facilities akin to "supermax" prisons even though they have not yet been convicted of a crime.

www.hrw.org/sites/default/files/reports/us0608webwcover.pdf

Double Jeopardy: CIA Renditions to Jordan, April 2008

The report documents how Jordan's General Intelligence Department (GID) served as a proxy jailer and interrogator for the CIA from 2001 until at least 2004. While a handful of countries received persons rendered by the United States during this period, no other country is believed to have held as many as Jordan.

www.hrw.org/sites/default/files/reports/jordan0408webwcover.pdf

Off the Record: US Responsibility for Enforced Disappearances in the "War on Terror," June 2007

The briefing paper, published by six leading human rights organizations, includes the names and details of thirty-nine people who are believed to have been held in secret US custody abroad and whose current whereabouts remain unknown.

www.hrw.org/legacy/backgrounder/usa/ct0607/ct0607web.pdf

The Omar Khadr Case: A Teenager Imprisoned at Guantánamo, June 2007

This report documents the case of Omar Khadr who was just fifteen when he was arrested. The report finds that the United States has completely ignored his juvenile status throughout his detention and incarcerated him with adults, reportedly subjected him to abusive interrogations, failed to provide him any educational opportunities, and denied him any direct contact with his family.

www.hrw.org/legacy/backgrounder/usa/us0607/us0607web.pdf

The "Stamp of Guantánamo": The Story of Seven Men Betrayed by Russia's Diplomatic Assurances to the United States, March 2007

The report reconstructs the experiences of the detainees after being returned to Russia in March 2004, based on interviews with three of the detainees, their family members, lawyers, and others.

www.hrw.org/sites/default/files/reports/russia0307webwcover.pdf

Cases Involving Diplomatic Assurances against Torture, January 2007

This document sets out developments in the use of diplomatic assurances in select individual cases since the publication of a previous report "Still at Risk: Diplomatic Assurances No Safeguard Against Torture in 2005" (United States: *Maher Arar* and *Bekhzod Yusupov* cases).

www.hrw.org/sites/default/files/reports/eu0107.pdf

"No Blood, No Foul": Soldiers' Accounts of Detainee Abuse in Iraq, July 2006

Based on accounts from soldiers, the report findings suggest that torture and other abuses against detainees in US custody in Iraq were authorized and routine, even after the 2004 Abu Ghraib scandal.

www.hrw.org/sites/default/files/reports/us0706web.pdf

By the Numbers: Findings of the Detainee Abuse and Accountability Project, April 2006

The report presents findings of the Detainee Abuse and Accountability Project, a joint project of New York University's Center for Human Rights and Global Justice, Human Rights Watch, and Human Rights First. The project is the first comprehensive accounting of credible allegations of torture and abuse in US custody in Iraq, Afghanistan, and Guantánamo.

www.hrw.org/sites/default/files/reports/ct0406webwcover.pdf

List of "Ghost Prisoners" Possibly in CIA Custody: List of Detainees Published by Human Rights Watch, November 2005

The Human Rights Watch list of persons believed to be in US custody as "ghost detainees" – detainees who are not given any legal rights or access to counsel, and who are likely not reported to or seen by the International Committee of the Red Cross. The list is compiled from media reports, public statements by government officials, and from other information obtained by Human Rights Watch.

www.hrw.org/legacy/english/docs/2005/11/30/usdom12109_txt.htm

Leadership Failure: Firsthand Accounts of Torture of Iraqi Detainees by the US Army's 82nd Airborne Division, September 2005

This report provides soldiers' accounts of abuses against detainees committed by troops of the 82nd Airborne stationed at Forward Operating Base Mercury (FOB Mercury), near Fallujah

www.hrw.org/sites/default/files/reports/us0905.pdf

US/Canada – Transfer of Maher Arar to Torture: Human Rights Watch Report to the Commission of Inquiry on Maher Arar, June 2005

Using the case of Maher Arar, a Canadian citizen, the report suggests that the US government has come under increasing scrutiny for its policy of accepting assurances of proper treatment from countries that routinely use torture.

www.hrw.org/legacy/backgrounder/eca/canada/arar/arar_testimony.pdf

Getting Away with Torture? Command Responsibility for the US Abuse of Detainees, April 2005

The report presents substantial evidence warranting criminal investigations of Rumsfeld and Tenet, as well as Lt. Gen. Ricardo Sanchez, formerly the top US commander in Iraq, and Gen. Geoffrey Miller, the former commander of the prison camp at Guantánamo Bay, Cuba.

www.hrw.org/sites/default/files/reports/us0405.pdf

Still at Risk: Diplomatic Assurances No Safeguard Against Torture, April 4, 2005

The report documents the growing practice among Western governments – including the United States, Canada, the United Kingdom, and the Netherlands – of seeking assurances of humane treatment in order to transfer terrorism suspects to states with well-established records of torture.

www.hrw.org/sites/default/files/reports/eca0405.pdf

Guantánamo: Detainee Accounts, October 2004

A compilation of accounts by thirty-three former detainees at Guantánamo of their experiences there.

www.hrw.org/legacy/backgrounder/usa/gitmo1004/gitmo1004.pdf

Interrogation Techniques for Guantánamo Detainees, August 19, 2004

The report questions the secrecy of the interrogation techniques used by US personnel on detainees at the naval base at Guantánamo Bay, Cuba.

www.hrw.org/legacy/english/docs/2004/08/19/usdom9248_txt.htm

Table of Interrogation Techniques Approved by US Officials

www.hrw.org/legacy/backgrounder/usa/0819interrogation.htm

Making Sense of the Guantánamo Bay Tribunals, August 2004

Brief outlines of the Military Commissions, the combatant status review panels, and the administrative review procedures adopted by the US Department of Defense (DOD) for use at Guantánamo Bay, Cuba.

www.hrw.org/legacy/english/docs/2004/08/16/usdom9235_txt.htm

Military Investigations into Treatment of Detainees in US Custody, July 2004

The report presents an overview of internal investigations into the abuse of detainees at Abu Ghraib.

www.hrw.org/sites/default/files/reports/071604investigations.pdf

The Road to Abu Ghraib, June 2004

The report examines how the Bush Administration adopted a deliberate policy of permitting illegal interrogation techniques on Iraqi prisoners at Abu Ghraib prison and then spent two years covering up or ignoring reports of torture and other abuse by US troops.

www.hrw.org/sites/default/files/reports/usa0604.pdf

Presumption of Guilt: Human Rights Abuses of Post-September 11 Detainees, August 15, 2002

After the 9/11 attacks, the report establishes that the United States has witnessed a persistent, deliberate, and unwarranted erosion of basic rights against abusive governmental power that are guaranteed by the US Constitution and international human rights law. Most of those directly affected have been non-US citizens who have been subjected to arbitrary detention, violation of due process in legal proceedings against them, and a system that ran roughshod over the presumption of innocence.

www.hrw.org/legacy/reports/2002/us911/USA0802.pdf

c *Human Rights First, July 16, 2010*

In Pursuit of Justice: Prosecuting Terrorism Cases in the Federal Courts, 2008

The report analyzes more than 100 cases brought in federal court that involve terrorism that is associated organizationally, financially, or ideologically with self-described jihadist or Islamist extremist terrorist groups like Al-Qaeda. The findings suggest that the justice system has capably handled these cases, and continues to evolve to meet the challenge terrorism cases pose.

www.humanrightsfirst.info/pdf/080521-USLS-pursuit-justice.pdf

Tortured Justice: Using Coerced Evidence to Prosecute Terrorist Suspects, 2008

The report finds that the Bush Administration has undercut its own intended use of the Military Commission system at Guantánamo Bay by allowing the admission of coerced evidence. It focuses on six Guantánamo prisoners who have alleged abuse while in custody, some of which has been documented by military investigations and detainee interrogation logs, and some of which has been publicly acknowledged by administration officials.

www.humanrightsfirst.info/pdf/08307-etn-tortured-justice-web.pdf

Command's Responsibility: Detainee Deaths in US Custody in Iraq and Afghanistan, 2006

The report provides an account of the US government's handling of the nearly 100 cases of detainees who have died in US custody since 2002.

www.humanrightsfirst.info/pdf/06221-etn-hrf-dic-rep-web.pdf

Ending Secret Detentions, 2004

The report outlines the scope of the global network of US detention facilities holding suspects in the "war on terrorism."

www.humanrightsfirst.org/us_law/PDF/EndingSecretDetentions_web.pdf

Assessing the New Normal: Liberty and Security for the Post-September 11 United States, 2003

This report documents the continuing erosion of basic human rights protections under US law and policy since September 11. The expansion of executive power and abandonment of established civil and criminal procedures have become part of a "new normal" in American life.

www.humanrightsfirst.org/pubs/descriptions/Assessing/AssessingtheNewNormal.pdf

Year of Loss: Reexamining Civil Liberties Since September 11, 2002

In the twelve months after the September 11 attacks, the US government took a series of actions that eroded basic human rights protections in the United States, fundamental guarantees that have been central to the US constitutional system for more than 200 years. The report covers the period from September 2001 to September 2002.

www.humanrightsfirst.org/pubs/descriptions/loss_report.pdf

d Center for Constitutional Rights July 16, 2010

Closing Guantánamo and Restoring the Rule of Law, January 2009

The report includes comprehensive numbers of detainees at Guantánamo, by status, and by nationality. It recommends three steps to closing Guantánamo: (1) send those home who can go home, (2) secure safe haven for those who cannot, and (3) charge those who can be charged and try them in ordinary federal criminal court.

http://ccrjustice.org/files/12.01.09_CCRpercent20Report_Closing percent20Guantánamo.pdf

Guantánamo Six Years Later, January 2008

The report reviews the six years since January 11, 2002 and shows that the total number of detainees rose to more than 750, making Guantánamo a symbol of the US government's deeply flawed "war on terror," a place where the rule of law does not apply.

http://ccrjustice.org/files/GuantánamoSixYearsLater.pdf

Rendition to Torture, 2008

The report presents the story of Maher Arar, a Canadian citizen of Syrian descent who was sent by US officials to be detained and interrogated under torture in Syria under a program known as "extraordinary rendition."

http://ccrjustice.org/files/FINALpercent20updatedpercent20rend-itionpercent20topercent20torturepercent20reportpercent20decper cent2008.pdf

Abandoned at Guantánamo, November 2008

The report describes the issue of transfer of detainees by the United States from Guantánamo to high-risk countries despite credible individualized fears of persecution or torture upon their repatriation. It also covers some of the men at Guantánamo who continue to be wrongfully detained simply because no country has offered them refuge.

http://ccrjustice.org/files/Guantánamo'spercent20Refugeespercent203d percent20edpercent20_FINAL_.pdf

Guantánamo and its Aftermath: US Detention and Interrogation Practices and Their Impact on Former Detainees, November 2008

The report reveals the cumulative effect of Bush Administration policies on the lives of sixty-two released detainees. Many of the prisoners were sold into captivity and subjected to brutal treatment in US prison camps. Once in Guantánamo, prisoners were denied access to civilian courts to challenge the legality of their detention. Almost two-thirds of the former detainees interviewed reported having psychological problems since leaving Guantánamo.

http://ccrjustice.org/files/Report_GTMO_And_Its_Aftermath_0.pdf

US Government Allows Security Forces from Brutal Human Rights Abusing Regimes to Threaten Prisoners at Guantánamo, 2008

The report highlights numerous instances of threats and abuse of prisoners at Guantánamo by interrogators from brutal human rights-abusing regimes who are given full access by the United States and the deteriorating mental health of the overwhelming majority of Guantánamo prisoners relegated to solitary confinement at the prison.

http://ccrjustice.org/files/Foreignpercent20Interrogatorspercent20inpercent20Guantánamopercent20Bay_1.pdf

The Faces of Guantánamo: Guantánamo's Many Wrongly Imprisoned, April 2007

The report discredits the Bush Administration's attempts to reshape the image of Guantánamo and the men detained there as the "worst of the worst." Instead, findings show that hundreds of men do not fit into the "enemy combatant" definition under the Geneva Conventions.

http://ccrjustice.org/files/report_FacesOfGuantánamo.pdf

Torture and Cruel, Inhuman, and Degrading Treatment of Prisoners at Guantánamo Bay, July 2006

This report recounts the experiences of prisoners inside Guantánamo Bay prison from the accounts of torture and cruel, inhuman, and degrading treatment drawn directly from habeas counsels' unclassified notes.

http://ccrjustice.org/files/Report_ReportOnTorture.pdf

The Guantánamo Prisoner Hunger Strikes and Protests, February 2002–August 2005, 2005

The report chronicles the history of prisoner protests at the detention center at Guantánamo Bay Naval Station from February 2002 to August 2005.

http://ccrjustice.org/files/Finalpercent20Hungerpercent20Strikepercent20Reportpercent20Septpercent202005.pdf

"Tipton Three" Detention in Afghanistan and Guantánamo Bay

The report presents a composite of the experiences of three men from Tipton in the West Midlands, United Kingdom, and sets out details of their treatment at the hands of UK and US military personnel and civilian authorities during the time of their detention in Kandahar in

Afghanistan in late December 2001 and throughout their time in American custody in Guantánamo Bay Cuba.

http://ccrjustice.org/files/report_tiptonThree.pdf

e International Commission of Jurists July 16, 2010

Report: Assessing Damage, Urging Action: Report of the Eminent Jurists Panel on Terrorism, Counter-terrorism and Human Rights, International Commission of Jurists

The report presents results of a worldwide investigation into the impact of counter-terrorism laws and practices on human rights that draw on sixteen hearings covering forty countries in all regions of the world. The report concludes that many governments have confronted the threat of terrorism with ill-conceived measures that have undermined cherished values and resulted in serious violations of human rights. It illustrates the devastating effects that notorious counter-terrorism measures such as extraordinary rendition, torture, arbitrary detention, and unfair trials have had on human rights worldwide. It warns of the increasing secrecy preventing accountability, and the danger of "temporary" measures becoming permanent features of law and practice in many states, including in democratic societies. The report calls for the rejection of the war paradigm in the United States as a basis for its counter-terrorism policy.

http://ejp.icj.org/IMG/EJP-Report.pdf

f American Civil Liberties Union, July 16, 2010

The Torture Report, 2009

The Torture Report, an initiative of the ACLU's National Security Project, gives an account of the Bush administration's enemy prisoner program, from its origins to "the systematized, lawyer-rationalized maltreatment of hundreds of prisoners in US custody around the world."

www.thetorturereport.org/

Chapter 1: Origins

www.thetorturereport.org/report/chapter-1-origins

Chapter 2: Experimenting With Torture

www.thetorturereport.org/report/chapter-2-experimenting-torture

Chapter 3: Black Sites, Lies, and Videotapes

www.thetorturereport.org/report/chapter-3-black-sites-lies-and-videotapes

3 Other reports: ICRC and UN reports, July 16, 2010

International Committee of the Red Cross

ICRC Report on the Treatment of Fourteen "High Value Detainees" in CIA Custody, February 2007

The report includes findings and recommendations of the ICRC to the CIA on the fourteen "High-Value Detainees" (HVDs) who were held for several years under the CIA secret detention program before finally being transferred to Guantánamo in September 2006. The report was intended to be non-public but was leaked to the press, probably by persons within the US government. The report is based on ICRC confidential interviews with each transferred prisoner. The ICRC concluded that the treatment meted out to the prisoners constituted torture and cruel, inhuman, or degrading (CID) abuse, without specifying in the report which prisoner was tortured and which the victim of CID.

www.nybooks.com/icrc-report.pdf

Report of the International Committee of the Red Cross (ICRC) on the Treatment by the Coalition Forces of Prisoners of War and Other Protected Persons by the Geneva Conventions in Iraq during Arrest, Internment and Interrogation, February 2004

The report documents a number of serious violations of international humanitarian law that warrant attention and corrective action by the Coalition Forces on treatment of prisoners of war, civilian internees, and other persons protected by the Geneva Conventions in Iraq between March and November 2003. The report was intended to be non-public but was leaked to the press, probably by persons within the US government. Despite its content, the summary report appears to have had little effect on US policies. Only with the circulation of unauthorized photos of US abuse of prisoners at Abu Ghraib in the Spring of 2004 did civilian and military authorities in Washington begin to curtail mistreatment of prisoners held by the United States in Iraq – and then in Afghanistan.

www.globalsecurity.org/military/library/report/2004/icrc_report_iraq_feb2004.pdf

United Nations Independent Experts

UN Report: Situation of Detainees at Guantánamo Bay, February 2006, E/CN.4/2006/120

Report by the Chairperson of the Working Group on Arbitrary Detention, the Special Rapporteur on the independence of judges and lawyers, the Special Rapporteur on torture and other cruel, inhuman, or degrading (CID) treatment or punishment, the Special Rapporteur on freedom of religion or belief, and the Special Rapporteur on the right of everyone to the enjoyment of the highest attainable standard of physical and mental health.

The joint report presents findings of the five holders of mandates of special procedures of the Commission on Human Rights (now the UN Human Rights Council) who had been jointly following the situation of detainees held at the United States of America Naval Base at Guantánamo Bay from January 2002 to January 2006. The report provides a legal analysis common to all mandates, outlines the legal framework specific to each mandate, as well as the particular allegations of human rights violations that concern them. The report not only asserts the preferred legal framework for prisoners held at Gitmo, but also makes recommendations for changes in US policy.

http://daccess-dds-ny.un.org/doc/UNDOC/GEN/G06/112/76/PDF/G0611276.pdf?OpenElement

Joint Study on Global Practices in Relation to Secret Detention in the Context of Countering Terrorism of the Special Rapporteur on the Promotion and Protection of Human Rights and Fundamental Freedoms While Countering Terrorism, the Special Rapporteur on Torture and Other Cruel, Inhuman or Degrading Treatment or Punishment, the Working Group on Arbitrary Detention, and the Working Group on Enforced or Involuntary Disappearances, A/HRC/13/42. Advance Unedited Version, January 2010

The report's findings suggest that secret detention continues to be used in the name of countering terrorism around the world. The evidence shows that many states, referring to concerns relating to national security – often perceived or presented as unprecedented emergencies or threats – resort to secret detention characterized by complete arbitrariness and uncertainty about the duration of the secret detention. The report also addresses the use of secret detention in the context of the "global war on terror" following the events of September 11, 2001.

The report describes the progressive and determined elaboration of a comprehensive and coordinated system of secret detention of persons suspected of terrorism, involving not only US authorities, but also other states in almost all regions of the world and criticizes the policy of extraordinary rendition. The report concludes that international law clearly prohibits secret detention, which violates a number of human rights and humanitarian law norms that may not be derogated from under any circumstances.

www.ediec.org/uploads/media/A-HRC-13-42.doc

ANNEX C

Some relevant legal norms: selected provisions

1 Common Article 3, 1949 Geneva Conventions, 12 August (War Victims)

Note by author

The four interlocking Geneva Conventions of 1949 dealt mostly with international armed conflict, being largely a reaction to the Second World War. An identical article no. 3 in each, hence Common Article 3, dealt with non-international armed conflict, being largely a reaction to the Spanish civil war of 1936–1939. In several subsequent armed conflicts, the war in Southeast Asia during the 1960s and 1970s being a leading example, different governments saw the conflict through different legal prisms. Some saw the fighting as international, while others saw it as an essentially internal conflict, but with outside participation. There was thus controversy over which set of rules applied, the law of international armed conflict or only Common Article 3. There were other examples of what some commentators referred to as "internationalized civil wars." The US Supreme Court in 2006 ruled in the *Hamdan* case that Common Article 3 applied in all armed conflicts, as the minimum humanitarian standard. It is widely believed that Common Article 3 is declarative of customary international law. It has been supplemented by Additional Protocol II (APII), added to the Geneva Conventions in 1977, also for internal war, but with a different field of application from Common Article 3.

In the case of armed conflict not of an international character occurring in the territory of one of the High Contracting Parties, each Party to the conflict shall be bound to apply, as a minimum, the following provisions:

(1) Persons taking no active part in the hostilities, including members of armed forces who have laid down their arms and those placed *hors de combat* by sickness, wounds, detention, or any other cause, shall in all circumstances be treated humanely, without any adverse distinction founded on race, colour, religion or faith, sex, birth or wealth, or any other similar criteria.

To this end the following acts are and shall remain prohibited at any time and in any place whatsoever with respect to the above-mentioned persons:

(a) violence to life and person, in particular murder of all kinds, mutilation, cruel treatment and torture;

(b) taking of hostages;

(c) outrages upon personal dignity, in particular humiliating and degrading treatment;

(d) the passing of sentences and the carrying out of executions without previous judgment pronounced by a regularly constituted court, affording all the judicial guarantees which are recognized as indispensable by civilized peoples.

(2) The wounded and sick shall be collected and cared for.

An impartial humanitarian body, such as the International Committee of the Red Cross, may offer its services to the Parties to the conflict . . .

2 1949 Geneva Convention III (POW Convention)

Note by author

Among the four treaties making up the 1949 Geneva Conventions, Geneva Convention III is commonly called the POW Convention. It seeks to provide humanitarian protection and assistance to regular military forces made captive by capture, surrender, or illness. It is based largely on the experiences during the Second World War. During that war the then-existing 1929 Geneva Convention was widely seen as having had an ameliorative effect on Allied and Fascist prisoners of war, in comparison to the harsh and often fatal conditions of detention that obtained between German and Russian POWs (not regulated by the 1929 Convention). States added Additional Protocol I (API) in 1977, parts of which dealt with detained fighters of various types, not just regular military personnel in uniform but also various militias and irregular forces loosely associated with one of the fighting parties. So the view of fighters or combatants found in 1949 Geneva Convention III was updated and expanded in 1977 via API. The United States has never ratified API, whereas it consented to all four 1949 Geneva Conventions in the mid-1950s.

Article 4

A. Prisoners of war, in the sense of the present Convention, are persons belonging to one of the following categories, who have fallen into the power of the enemy:

(1) Members of the armed forces of a Party to the conflict, as well as members of militias or volunteer corps forming part of such armed forces.
(2) Members of other militias and members of other volunteer corps, including those of organized resistance movements, belonging to a Party to the conflict and operating in or outside their own territory, even if this territory is occupied, provided that such militias or volunteer corps, including such organized resistance movements, fulfill the following conditions:
   (a) that of being commanded by a person responsible for his subordinates;
   (b) that of having a fixed distinctive sign recognizable at a distance;
   (c) that of carrying arms openly;
   (d) that of conducting their operations in accordance with the laws and customs of war.
(3) Members of regular armed forces who profess allegiance to a government or an authority not recognized by the Detaining Power.

Article 5

The present Convention shall apply to the persons referred to in Article 4 from the time they fall into the power of the enemy and until their final release and repatriation.

Should any doubt arise as to whether persons, having committed a belligerent act and having fallen into the hands of the enemy, belong to any of the categories enumerated in Article 4, such persons shall enjoy the protection of the present Convention until such time as their status has been determined by a competent tribunal.

Article 13

Prisoners of war must at all times be humanely treated. Any unlawful act or omission by the Detaining Power causing death or seriously endangering the health of a prisoner of war in its custody is prohibited, and will be regarded as a serious breach of the present Convention. In particular, no prisoner of war may be subjected to physical mutilation or to medical or scientific experiments of any kind which are not justified by the medical, dental or hospital treatment of the prisoner concerned and carried out in his interest.

Likewise, prisoners of war must at all times be protected, particularly against acts of violence or intimidation and against insults and public curiosity.

Measures of reprisal against prisoners of war are prohibited.

Article 17

Every prisoner of war, when questioned on the subject, is bound to give only his surname, first names and rank, date of birth, and army, regimental, personal or serial number, or failing this, equivalent information.

If he willfully infringes this rule, he may render himself liable to a restriction of the privileges accorded to his rank or status.

Each Party to a conflict is required to furnish the persons under its jurisdiction who are liable to become prisoners of war, with an identity card showing the owner's surname, first names, rank, army, regimental, personal or serial number or equivalent information, and date of birth. The identity card may, furthermore, bear the signature or the fingerprints, or both, of the owner, and may bear, as well, any other information the Party to the conflict may wish to add concerning persons belonging to its armed forces. As far as possible the card shall measure 6.5 × 10 cm and shall be issued in duplicate. The identity card shall be shown by the prisoner of war upon demand, but may in no case be taken away from him.

No physical or mental torture, nor any other form of coercion, may be inflicted on prisoners of war to secure from them information of any kind whatever. Prisoners of war who refuse to answer may not be threatened, insulted, or exposed to unpleasant or disadvantageous treatment of any kind.

Article 99

No prisoner of war may be tried or sentenced for an act which is not forbidden by the law of the Detaining Power or by international law, in force at the time the said act was committed.

No moral or physical coercion may be exerted on a prisoner of war in order to induce him to admit himself guilty of the act of which he is accused.

No prisoner of war may be convicted without having had an opportunity to present his defense and the assistance of a qualified advocate or counsel.

3 1949 Geneva Convention IV (Civilian Convention)

Note by author

Among the four Geneva Conventions of 1949, Geneva Convention III pertained to combatants and Geneva Convention IV pertained to civilians, both to apply in international armed conflict or occupied territory as a result of belligerence. There is now universal legal acceptance of the 1949 Geneva Conventions, including by the United States (1955). If one consults Geneva Convention III (1949) and API (1977), one finds international law regulating various types of combatants in international armed conflict such as regular fighters in uniform but also irregular militias and other fighting groups associated with a party to the conflict. Geneva Convention IV always dealt only with civilians. None of the legal instruments under consideration mention "terrorists," that term being subject to varying definitions. The legal status of those appearing to be civilians but taking up arms from time to time has not been entirely agreed upon across different states and during different eras. The US official position during the Vietnam War was first of all that not only North Vietnamese regular fighters, but also irregular or guerrilla fighters aligned with them, such as various cadres of the VC, were to be treated as prisoners of war or at least covered by Common Article 3. Those persons appearing to be civilians, and thus not displaying weapons openly during attack or just prior to attack, but taking some violent action against South Vietnamese or American personnel or property, were to be regarded as civilians. So even apparent civilians who took violent action were seen as protected by Geneva Convention IV.

Article 27. Protected [civilian] persons are entitled, in all circumstances, to respect for their persons, their honour, their family rights, their religious convictions and practices, and their manners and customs. They shall at all times be humanely treated, and shall be protected especially against all acts of violence or threats thereof and against insults and public curiosity.

Article 31. No physical or moral coercion shall be exercised against protected persons, in particular to obtain information from them or from third parties.

Article 143. Representatives or delegates of the Protecting Powers shall have permission to go to all places where protected persons are, particularly to places of internment, detention and work.

They shall have access to all premises occupied by protected persons and shall be able to interview the latter without witnesses, personally or through an interpreter.

Such visits may not be prohibited except for reasons of imperative military necessity, and then only as an exceptional and temporary measure. Their duration and frequency shall not be restricted.

Such representatives and delegates shall have full liberty to select the places they wish to visit. The Detaining or Occupying Power, the Protecting Power and when occasion arises the Power of origin of the persons to be visited, may agree that compatriots of the internees shall be permitted to participate in the visits.

The delegates of the International Committee of the Red Cross shall also enjoy the above prerogatives. The appointment of such delegates shall be submitted to the approval of the power governing the territories where they will carry out their duties.

Note by author

Protecting Powers are rarely appointed any longer. In the past they were neutral states appointed by the belligerents to assist in implementing the law of armed conflict.

4 Protocol Additional to the Geneva Conventions of 12 August 1949, and Relating to the Protection of Victims of International Armed Conflicts (Protocol I), 8 June 1977

Note by author

Additional rules for international armed conflict were added to the 1949 Geneva Conventions by a diplomatic conference concluding its four sessions in Geneva in 1977. By February 2010, 160 states had given their consent to this Additional Protocol I. The material field of application for the Protocol was controversial. In general, the Protocol sought to bring irregular or asymmetrical or guerrilla warfare within the regulation of international humanitarian law (IHL). The Protocol was largely a reaction to the French–Algerian War and the United States–Vietnamese War, both wars featuring fighters not in uniform and not always displaying arms openly, among other characteristics. While many states were interested in conferring greater status and protection on such fighters engaged against colonial and racist regimes, some states like Israel and the United States were concerned about encouraging terrorism. The United States has not given its consent to be so bound. However, several US officials have indicated in writing that in their view several provisions of API had passed into customary international law and were thus binding on the United States. In this view, IHL now covers guerrilla fighters as protected combatants when falling under the control of opponents. Also in this view, civilians who take up arms are not protected fighters but protected civilians when detained. In the view of the ICRC, only spies are not covered by IHL in international war. Among the key provisions of API was Art. 75. Some justices of the US Supreme Court in rendering the *Hamdan* judgment of 2006 discussed Art. 75 and customary international law, without the Court as a whole taking a definitive position on the matter. The ICRC, the guardian of IHL, also known as the law of armed conflict, is among those who believe API, Art. 75, among other provisions, is now part of customary international law.

Article 75. Fundamental guarantees

1. In so far as they are affected by a situation referred to in Article 1 of this Protocol, persons who are in the power of a Party to the conflict and who do not benefit from more favourable treatment under the Conventions or under this Protocol shall be treated humanely in all circumstances and shall enjoy, as a minimum, the protection provided by this Article without any adverse distinction based upon race, colour, sex, language, religion or belief, political or other opinion, national or social origin, wealth, birth or other status, or on any other similar criteria. Each Party shall respect the person, honour, convictions and religious practices of all such persons.

2. The following acts are and shall remain prohibited at any time and in any place whatsoever, whether committed by civilian or by military agents:
   (a) violence to the life, health, or physical or mental well-being of persons, in particular:
      (i) murder;
      (ii) torture of all kinds, whether physical or mental;
      (iii) corporal punishment; and
      (iv) mutilation;
   (b) outrages upon personal dignity, in particular humiliating and degrading treatment, enforced prostitution and any form of indecent assault;
   (c) the taking of hostages;
   (d) collective punishments; and
   (e) threats to commit any of the foregoing acts.
3. Any person arrested, detained or interned for actions related to the armed conflict shall be informed promptly, in a language he understands, of the reasons why these measures have been taken. Except in cases of arrest or detention for penal offences, such persons shall be released with the minimum delay possible and in any event as soon as the circumstances justifying the arrest, detention or internment have ceased to exist.
4. No sentence may be passed and no penalty may be executed on a person found guilty of a penal offence related to the armed conflict except pursuant to a conviction pronounced by an impartial and regularly constituted court respecting the generally recognized principles of regular judicial procedure, which include the following:
   (a) the procedure shall provide for an accused to be informed without delay of the particulars of the offence alleged against him and shall afford the accused before and during his trial all necessary rights and means of defence;
   (b) no one shall be convicted of an offence except on the basis of individual penal responsibility;
   (c) no one shall be accused or convicted of a criminal offence on account of any act or omission which did not constitute a criminal offence under the national or international law to which he was subject at the time when it was committed; nor shall a heavier penalty be imposed than that which was applicable at the time when the criminal offence was committed; if,

after the commission of the offence, provision is made by law for the imposition of a lighter penalty, the offender shall benefit thereby;

(d) anyone charged with an offence is presumed innocent until proved guilty according to law;

(e) anyone charged with an offence shall have the right to be tried in his presence;

(f) no one shall be compelled to testify against himself or to confess guilt;

(g) anyone charged with an offence shall have the right to examine, or have examined, the witnesses against him and to obtain the attendance and examination of witnesses on his behalf under the same conditions as witnesses against him;

(h) no one shall be prosecuted or punished by the same Party for an offence in respect of which a final judgement acquitting or convicting that person has been previously pronounced under the same law and judicial procedure;

(i) anyone prosecuted for an offence shall have the right to have the judgement pronounced publicly; and

(j) a convicted person shall be advised on conviction of his judicial and other remedies and of the time-limits within which they may be exercised.

5 Protocol Additional to the Geneva Conventions of 12 August 1949, and Relating to the Protection of Victims of Non-International Armed Conflicts (Protocol II), 8 June 1977

Note by author

The 1949 Geneva Conventions recognized two types of armed conflicts regulated by international law: international and non-international (internal). Thus not only situations like the Second World War but also situations like the Spanish Civil War were to be regulated by international law. Additional Protocol II (APII) was initially drafted with the intent to develop international law beyond 1949 Common Article 3 (the same Article 3 common to the four Geneva Conventions of 1949), which was the only part of the 1949 Geneva Conventions that pertained to internal war. APII was approved by a diplomatic conference meeting in Geneva and concluding its four sessions in 1977. By February 2010, 165 states had consented to be bound by APII. Its material field of application differed in some respects from, and was more restricted than, Common Article 3. Thus, among internal armed conflicts, one could have Common Article 3 situations and APII situations. Common Article 3 pertains to all internal armed conflicts, whereas for APII to apply, various conditions have to be met by the non-state fighting party, such as controlling a certain amount of territory. The United States has never consented to APII. Several legal authorities have indicated in writing that they believe several articles found in APII have become part of customary international law. The US Supreme Court, in its *Hamdan* judgment of 2006, ruled that Common Article 3 is now applicable in all armed conflicts as the baseline standard for minimal humanitarian protections. Since 1977, no state has ever declared that it was involved in an APII situation. Several have stated that they faced a Common Article 3 situation. The dividing line between internal wars, regulated by Common Article 3 and perhaps also APII, and forms of national instability such as internal troubles and tensions, riots or rebellions, is often not a matter of complete agreement.

Part II Humane Treatment

Article 4. Fundamental guarantees

1. All persons who do not take a direct part or who have ceased to take part in hostilities, whether or not their liberty has been restricted, are entitled to respect for their person, honour and convictions and religious practices. They shall in all circumstances be treated humanely, without any adverse distinction. It is prohibited to order that there shall be no survivors.
2. Without prejudice to the generality of the foregoing, the following acts against the persons referred to in paragraph 1 are and shall remain prohibited at any time and in any place whatsoever:
   (a) violence to the life, health and physical or mental well-being of persons, in particular murder as well as cruel treatment such as torture, mutilation or any form of corporal punishment;
   (b) collective punishments;
   (c) taking of hostages;
   (d) acts of terrorism;

   (e) outrages upon personal dignity, in particular humiliating and degrading treatment, rape, enforced prostitution and any form or indecent assault;
   (f) slavery and the slave trade in all their forms;
   (g) pillage;
   (h) threats to commit any of the foregoing acts.
3. Children shall be provided with the care and aid they require, and in particular:
   (a) they shall receive an education, including religious and moral education, in keeping with the wishes of their parents, or in the absence of parents, of those responsible for their care;
   (b) all appropriate steps shall be taken to facilitate the reunion of families temporarily separated;
   (c) children who have not attained the age of fifteen years shall neither be recruited in the armed forces or groups nor allowed to take part in hostilities;
   (d) the special protection provided by this Article to children who have not attained the age of fifteen years shall remain applicable to them if they take a direct part in hostilities despite the provisions of subparagraph (c) and are captured;
   (e) measures shall be taken, if necessary, and whenever possible with the consent of their parents or persons who by law or custom are primarily responsible for their care, to remove children temporarily from the area in which hostilities are taking place to a safer area within the country and ensure that they are accompanied by persons responsible for their safety and well-being.

Article 5. Persons whose liberty has been restricted

1. In addition to the provisions of Article 4 the following provisions shall be respected as a minimum with regard to persons deprived of their liberty for reasons related to the armed conflict, whether they are interned or detained;
   (a) the wounded and the sick shall be treated in accordance with Article 7;
   (b) the persons referred to in this paragraph shall, to the same extent as the local civilian population, be provided with food and drinking water and be afforded safeguards as regards health

and hygiene and protection against the rigours of the climate and the dangers of the armed conflict;

(c) they shall be allowed to receive individual or collective relief;

(d) they shall be allowed to practise their religion and, if requested and appropriate, to receive spiritual assistance from persons, such as chaplains, performing religious functions;

(e) they shall, if made to work, have the benefit of working conditions and safeguards similar to those enjoyed by the local civilian population.

2. Those who are responsible for the internment or detention of the persons referred to in paragraph 1 shall also, within the limits of their capabilities, respect the following provisions relating to such persons:

   (a) except when men and women of a family are accommodated together, women shall be held in quarters separated from those of men and shall be under the immediate supervision of women;

   (b) they shall be allowed to send and receive letters and cards, the number of which may be limited by competent authority if it deems necessary;

   (c) places of internment and detention shall not be located close to the combat zone. The persons referred to in paragraph 1 shall be evacuated when the places where they are interned or detained become particularly exposed to danger arising out of the armed conflict, if their evacuation can be carried out under adequate conditions of safety;

   (d) they shall have the benefit of medical examinations;

   (e) their physical or mental health and integrity shall not be endangered by any unjustified act or omission. Accordingly, it is prohibited to subject the persons described in this Article to any medical procedure which is not indicated by the state of health of the person concerned, and which is not consistent with the generally accepted medical standards applied to free persons under similar medical circumstances.

3. Persons who are not covered by paragraph 1 but whose liberty has been restricted in any way whatsoever for reasons related to the armed conflict shall be treated humanely in accordance with Article 4 and with paragraphs 1 (a), (c) and (d), and 2 (b) of this Article.

4. If it is decided to release persons deprived of their liberty, necessary measures to ensure their safety shall be taken by those so deciding.

Article 6. Penal prosecutions

1. This Article applies to the prosecution and punishment of criminal offences related to the armed conflict.
2. No sentence shall be passed and no penalty shall be executed on a person found guilty of an offence except pursuant to a conviction pronounced by a court offering the essential guarantees of independence and impartiality. In particular:
   (a) the procedure shall provide for an accused to be informed without delay of the particulars of the offence alleged against him and shall afford the accused before and during his trial all necessary rights and means of defence;
   (b) no one shall be convicted of an offence except on the basis of individual penal responsibility;
   (c) no one shall be held guilty of any criminal offence on account of any act or omission which did not constitute a criminal offence, under the law, at the time when it was committed; nor shall a heavier penalty be imposed than that which was applicable at the time when the criminal offence was committed; if, after the commission of the offence, provision is made by law for the imposition of a lighter penalty, the offender shall benefit thereby;
   (d) anyone charged with an offence is presumed innocent until proved guilty according to law;
   (e) anyone charged with an offence shall have the right to be tried in his presence;
   (f) no one shall be compelled to testify against himself or to confess guilt.
3. A convicted person shall be advised on conviction of his judicial and other remedies and of the time-limits within which they may be exercised.
4. The death penalty shall not be pronounced on persons who were under the age of eighteen years at the time of the offence and shall not be carried out on pregnant women or mothers of young children.
5. At the end of hostilities, the authorities in power shall endeavour to grant the broadest possible amnesty to persons who have participated in the armed conflict, or those deprived of their liberty for reasons related to the armed conflict, whether they are interned or detained.

6 1984 Convention against Torture and Other Cruel, Inhuman, or Degrading Treatment or Punishment

Note by author

This multilateral treaty was approved by the UN General Assembly in 1984. It came into legal force for consenting states in 1987, the required number of ratifications having been obtained. The United States became a full party in 1990, but with reservations, understandings, and declarations (RUDs) attached by the Senate when giving its advice and consent. In 1996 the Congress passed and the President signed into law the War Crimes Act, presumably incorporating the treaty into US federal law. However, the terms of that act differed from the wording of the treaty in important respects. Because of US Declaration no. 3, the words of the treaty were not legally controlling within US jurisdiction. A non-self-executing treaty does not immediately take legal effect within US jurisdiction but must be incorporated into US law by statute, in which case the language of the statute is controlling. In this matter international law and national law comprise dual systems of law. International law is supposed to inform national law. But if any discrepancy occurs, national law is controlling within that state's jurisdiction. Hence in ratifying the UN Convention against Torture, the United States insisted on certain interpretations not always shared by other states, and not always shared by the main authors of the treaty. In general, Senate action sought to restrict the impact of the treaty on the United States. The Senate agreed to be associated with the treaty but refined and indeed restricted the terms of the treaty.

Article 1

1. For the purposes of this Convention, torture means any act by which severe pain or suffering, whether physical or mental, is intentionally inflicted on a person for such purposes as obtaining from him or a third person information or a confession, punishing him for an act he or a third person has committed or is suspected of having committed, or intimidating or coercing him or a third person, or for any reason based on discrimination of any kind, when such pain or suffering is inflicted by or at the instigation of or with the consent or acquiescence of a public official or other person acting in an official capacity.

It does not include pain or suffering arising only from, inherent in or incidental to lawful sanctions.

2. This article is without prejudice to any international instrument or national legislation which does or may contain provisions of wider application.

Article 2

1. Each State Party shall take effective legislative, administrative, judicial or other measures to prevent acts of torture in any territory under its jurisdiction.
2. No exceptional circumstances whatsoever, whether a state of war or a threat or war, internal political instability or any other public emergency, may be invoked as a justification of torture.
3. An order from a superior officer or a public authority may not be invoked as a justification of torture.

Article 3

1. No State Party shall expel, return ("refouler") or extradite a person to another State where there are substantial grounds for believing that he would be in danger of being subjected to torture.
2. For the purpose of determining whether there are such grounds, the competent authorities shall take into account all relevant considerations including, where applicable, the existence in the State concerned of a consistent pattern of gross, flagrant or mass violations of human rights.

Article 4

1. Each State Party shall ensure that all acts of torture are offences under its criminal law. The same shall apply to an attempt to commit torture and to an act by any person which constitutes complicity or participation in torture.
2. Each State Party shall make these offences punishable by appropriate penalties which take into account their grave nature.

Article 7

1. The State Party in territory under whose jurisdiction a person alleged to have committed any offence referred to in article 4 is found, shall in

the cases contemplated in article 5, if it does not extradite him, submit the case to its competent authorities for the purpose of prosecution.

Article 8

1. The offences referred to in article 4 shall be deemed to be included as extraditable offences in any extradition treaty existing between States Parties. States Parties undertake to include such offenses as extraditable offences in every extradition treaty to be concluded between them.
2. If a State Party which makes extradition conditional on the existence of a treaty receives a request for extradition from another State Party with which it has no extradition treaty, it may consider this Convention as the legal basis for extradition in respect of such offenses.

US reservations to Torture Convention

I. The Senate's advice and consent is subject to the following reservations:
 (1) That the United States considers itself bound by the obligation under Article 16 to prevent "cruel, inhuman, or degrading treatment or punishment," only insofar as the term "cruel, inhuman, or degrading treatment or punishment" means the cruel, unusual, and inhumane treatment or punishment prohibited by the Fifth, Eighth, and/or Fourteenth Amendments to the Constitution of the United States.

II. The Senate's advice and consent is subject to the following understandings, which shall apply to the obligations of the United States under this Convention:
 (1)(a) That with reference to Article 1, the United States understands that, in order to constitute torture, an act must be specifically intended to inflict severe physical or mental pain or suffering and that mental pain or suffering refers to prolonged mental harm caused by or resulting from:
  1 the intentional infliction or threatened infliction of severe physical pain or suffering;
  2 the administration or application, or threatened administration or application, of mind altering substances or other procedures calculated to disrupt profoundly the senses or the personality;

3 the threat of imminent death; or
4 the threat that another person will imminently be subjected to death, severe physical pain or suffering, or the administration or application of mind altering substances or other procedures calculated to disrupt profoundly the senses or the personality.

III. The Senate's advice and consent is subject to the following declarations:
1 That the United States declares that the provisions of Articles 1 through 16 of the Convention are not self-executing.

7 1966 International Covenant on Civil and Political Rights, GA res. 2200A (XXI), 21 UN GAOR Supp. (No. 16) at 52, UN Doc. A/6316 (1966), 999 UNTS 171, *entered into force* March 23, 1976

Note by author

This multilateral treaty was approved by the UN General Assembly in 1966 and came into legal force for consenting states in 1976, the requisite number of ratifications being obtained. As of February 2010, there were 159 states that were full parties to this instrument. The United States accepted this treaty in 1990, but the Senate, in giving its advice and consent as required by the US Constitution, attached a number of reservations, understandings, and declarations (RUDs). The United States has never produced a statute incorporating this treaty into US federal law. That being the case, given Declaration no. 1, individuals within US jurisdiction cannot litigate the treaty in US judicial proceedings. A number of other states have objected to US acceptance with RUDs, arguing that the United States is trying to give the appearance of accepting the treaty but reserving to itself the right not to make the required changes in its national law and public policy. In international law, it is not allowed to submit reservations that defeat the "object and purpose" of the treaty. Understandings and declarations are also considered the equivalent of reservations.

Article 2

1. Each State Party to the present Covenant undertakes to respect and to ensure to all individuals within its territory and subject to its jurisdiction the rights recognized in the present Covenant, without

distinction of any kind, such as race, colour, sex, language, religion, political or other opinion, national or social origin, property, birth or other status.

2. Where not already provided for by existing legislative or other measures, each State Party to the present Covenant undertakes to take the necessary steps, in accordance with its constitutional processes and with the provisions of the present Covenant, to adopt such legislative or other measures as may be necessary to give effect to the rights recognized in the present Covenant.
3. Each State Party to the present Covenant undertakes:
   (a) To ensure that any person whose rights or freedoms as herein recognized are violated shall have an effective remedy, notwithstanding that the violation has been committed by persons acting in an official capacity;
   (b) To ensure that any person claiming such a remedy shall have his right thereto determined by competent judicial, administrative or legislative authorities, or by any other competent authority provided for by the legal system of the State, and to develop the possibilities of judicial remedy;
   (c) To ensure that the competent authorities shall enforce such remedies when granted.

Article 4

1. In time of public emergency which threatens the life of the nation and the existence of which is officially proclaimed, the States Parties to the present Covenant may take measures derogating from their obligations under the present Covenant to the extent strictly required by the exigencies of the situation, provided that such measures are not inconsistent with their other obligations under international law and do not involve discrimination solely on the ground of race, colour, sex, language, religion or social origin.
2. No derogation from articles 6, 7, 8 (paragraphs 1 and 2), 11, 15, 16, and 18 may be made under this provision.
3. Any State Party to the present Covenant availing itself of the right of derogation shall immediately inform the other States Parties to the present Covenant, through the intermediary of the Secretary-General of the United Nations, of the provisions from which it has derogated and of the reasons by which it was actuated. A further

communication shall be made, through the same intermediary, on the date on which it terminates such derogation.

Article 7

No one shall be subjected to torture or to cruel, inhuman, or degrading treatment or punishment. In particular, no one shall be subjected without his free consent to medical or scientific experimentation.

Article 16

Everyone shall have the right to recognition everywhere as a person before the law.

US reservations to ICCPR

(3) That the United States considers itself bound by article 7 to the extent that "cruel, inhuman, or degrading treatment or punishment" means the cruel and unusual treatment or punishment prohibited by the Fifth, Eighth, and/or Fourteenth Amendments to the Constitution of the United States.

DECLARATIONS:

(1) That the United States declares that the provisions of articles 1 through 27 of the Covenant are not self-executing.

8 2006 International Convention for the Protection of All Persons from Enforced Disappearance

Note by author

This multilateral treaty was adopted by the UN General Assembly in late 2006. It is not yet in force for states giving their consent, with 20 ratifications needed to activate it. As of February 2010, there were 81 signatures and 18 ratifications. The United States has not signed or otherwise accepted this instrument, although some of its major allies, such as France, Germany, Japan, Spain, etc. have. A number of Latin American states like Argentina, Chile, Uruguay, etc. have ratified, having their own experience with disappearances and not wanting to repeat that history. Given the US policy of forced disappearance after 9/11 especially via the CIA but also the military, both of which "ghosted" prisoners and at times did not allow the ICRC to visit them, it seemed unlikely that given the continuing terroristic attacks the United States would accept this treaty anytime soon. A UN report in 2010 by human rights experts indicated that secret detention was on the increase around the world in the context of counter-terrorism policies.

Article 1

1. No one shall be subjected to enforced disappearance.
2. No exceptional circumstances whatsoever, whether a state of war or a threat of war, internal political instability or any other public emergency, may be invoked as a justification for enforced disappearance.

Article 2

For the purposes of this Convention, "enforced disappearance" is considered to be the arrest, detention, abduction or any other form of deprivation of liberty by agents of the State or by persons or groups of persons acting with the authorization, support or acquiescence of the State, followed by a refusal to acknowledge the deprivation of liberty or by concealment of the fate or whereabouts of the disappeared person, which place such a person outside the protection of the law.

Article 3

Each State Party shall take appropriate measures to investigate acts defined in article 2 committed by persons or groups of persons acting without the authorization, support or acquiescence of the State and to bring those responsible to justice.

Article 4

Each State Party shall take the necessary measures to ensure that enforced disappearance constitutes an offence under its criminal law.

Article 5

The widespread or systematic practice of enforced disappearance constitutes a crime against humanity as defined in applicable international law and shall attract the consequences provided for under such applicable international law.

Article 11

1. The State Party in the territory under whose jurisdiction a person alleged to have committed an offence of enforced disappearance is found shall, if it does not extradite that person or surrender him or her to another State in accordance with its international obligations or surrender him or her to an international criminal tribunal whose jurisdiction it has recognized, submit the case to its competent authorities for the purpose of prosecution.

Article 16

1. No State Party shall expel, return ("refouler"), surrender or extradite a person to another State where there are substantial grounds for believing that he or she would be in danger of being subjected to enforced disappearance.
2. For the purpose of determining whether there are such grounds, the competent authorities shall take into account all relevant considerations, including, where applicable, the existence in the State concerned of a consistent pattern of gross, flagrant or mass violations of human rights or of serious violations of international humanitarian law.

9 ICRC Statement, Fundamental Guarantees of International Humanitarian Law Found in Customary International Law

Note by author

International law comprises primarily treaty law and customary law. International customary law results from widespread practice that over time acquires the additional characteristic of being perceived as legally obligatory. It is often not clear to all how much practice constitutes widespread practice, or what constitutes evidence of *opinio juris* meaning a sense that the practice must be continued as a matter of legal obligation. Nevertheless courts and other authorities do in fact utilize customary international law. In an effort to clarify customary international law with regard to international humanitarian law or the international law of armed conflict, the International Committee of the Red Cross (ICRC), the guardian of international humanitarian law (IHL), undertook a comprehensive study of the subject. It submitted its conclusions to states for their comments and reactions, hoping to bring greater clarity to the subject. The United States, like certain other states, responded to the ICRC initiative by agreeing with or contesting various ICRC statements. What follows is the ICRC version of the fundamental guarantees found in customary IHL. The parenthetical references refer to International Armed Conflict (IAC) and Non-International (Internal) Armed Conflict (NIAC).

Chapter 32. Fundamental Guarantees

Rule 87. Civilians and persons *hors de combat* must be treated humanely. [IAC/NIAC]
Rule 88. Adverse distinction in the application of international humanitarian law based on race, colour, sex, language, religion or belief, political or other opinion, national or social origin, wealth, birth or other status, or on any other similar criteria is prohibited. [IAC/NIAC]
Rule 89. Murder is prohibited. [IAC/NIAC]
Rule 90. Torture, cruel or inhuman treatment and outrages upon personal dignity, in particular humiliating and degrading treatment, are prohibited. [IAC/NIAC]
Rule 91. Corporal punishment is prohibited. [IAC/NIAC]
Rule 92. Mutilation, medical or scientific experiments or any other medical procedure not indicated by the state of health of the person concerned and not consistent with generally accepted medical standards are prohibited. [IAC/NIAC]
Rule 93. Rape and other forms of sexual violence are prohibited. [IAC/NIAC]
Rule 94. Slavery and the slave trade in all their forms are prohibited. [IAC/NIAC]
Rule 95. Uncompensated or abusive forced labour is prohibited. [IAC/NIAC]
Rule 96. The taking of hostages is prohibited. [IAC/NIAC]
Rule 97. The use of human shields is prohibited. [IAC/NIAC]
Rule 98. Enforced disappearance is prohibited. [IAC/NIAC]
Rule 99. Arbitrary deprivation of liberty is prohibited. [IAC/NIAC]
Rule 100. No one may be convicted or sentenced, except pursuant to a fair trial affording all essential judicial guarantees. [IAC/NIAC]
Rule 101. No one may be accused or convicted of a criminal offence on account of any act or omission which did not constitute a criminal offence under national or international law at the time it was

committed; nor may a heavier penalty be imposed than that which was applicable at the time the criminal offence was committed. [IAC/NIAC]

Rule 102. No one may be convicted of an offence except on the basis of individual criminal responsibility. [IAC/NIAC]

Rule 103. Collective punishments are prohibited. [IAC/NIAC]

Rule 104. The convictions and religious practices of civilians and persons *hors de combat* must be respected. [IAC/NIAC]

Rule 105. Family life must be respected as far as possible. [IAC/NIAC]

Chapter 34. The Wounded, Sick and Shipwrecked

Rule 109. Whenever circumstances permit, and particularly after an engagement, each party to the conflict must, without delay, take all possible measures to search for, collect and evacuate the wounded, sick and shipwrecked without adverse distinction. [IAC/NIAC]

Rule 110. The wounded, sick and shipwrecked must receive, to the fullest extent practicable and with the least possible delay, the medical care and attention required by their condition. No distinction may be made among them founded on any grounds other than medical ones. [IAC/NIAC]

Rule 111. Each party to the conflict must take all possible measures to protect the wounded, sick and shipwrecked against ill-treatment and against pillage of their personal property. [IAC/NIAC]

Chapter 35. The Dead

Rule 112. Whenever circumstances permit, and particularly after an engagement, each party to the conflict must, without delay, take all possible measures to search for, collect and evacuate the dead without adverse distinction. [IAC/NIAC]

Rule 113. Each party to the conflict must take all possible measures to prevent the dead from being despoiled. Mutilation of dead bodies is prohibited. [IAC/NIAC]

Rule 114. Parties to the conflict must endeavour to facilitate the return of the remains of the deceased upon request of the party to which they belong or upon the request of their next of kin. They must return their personal effects to them. [IAC]

Rule 115. The dead must be disposed of in a respectful manner and their graves respected and properly maintained. [IAC/NIAC]
Rule 116. With a view to the identification of the dead, each party to the conflict must record all available information prior to disposal and mark the location of the graves. [IAC/NIAC]

Chapter 36. Missing Persons

Rule 117. Each party to the conflict must take all feasible measures to account for persons reported missing as a result of armed conflict and must provide their family members with any information it has on their fate. [IAC/NIAC]

Chapter 37. Persons Deprived of their Liberty

Rule 118. Persons deprived of their liberty must be provided with adequate food, water, clothing, shelter and medical attention. [IAC/NIAC]
Rule 119. Women who are deprived of their liberty must be held in quarters separate from those of men, except where families are accommodated as family units, and must be under the immediate supervision of women. [IAC/NIAC]
Rule 120. Children who are deprived of their liberty must be held in quarters separate from those of adults, except where families are accommodated as family units. [IAC/NIAC]
Rule 121. Persons deprived of their liberty must be held in premises which are removed from the combat zone and which safeguard their health and hygiene. [IAC/NIAC]
Rule 122. Pillage of the personal belongings of persons deprived of their liberty is prohibited. [IAC/NIAC]
Rule 123. The personal details of persons deprived of their liberty must be recorded. [IAC/NIAC]
Rule 124.

A. In international armed conflicts, the ICRC must be granted regular access to all persons deprived of their liberty in order to verify the conditions of their detention and to restore contacts between those persons and their families.
B. In non-international armed conflicts, the ICRC may offer its services to the parties to the conflict with a view to visiting all persons

deprived of their liberty for reasons related to the conflict in order to verify the conditions of their detention and to restore contacts between those persons and their families. [IAC (A)/NIAC (B)]

Rule 125. Persons deprived of their liberty must be allowed to correspond with their families, subject to reasonable conditions relating to frequency and the need for censorship by the authorities. [IAC/NIAC]
Rule 126. Civilian internees and persons deprived of their liberty in connection with a non-international armed conflict must be allowed to receive visitors, especially near relatives, to the degree practicable. [IAC/NIAC]
Rule 127. The personal convictions and religious practices of persons deprived of their liberty must be respected. [IAC/NIAC]
Rule 128.

A. Prisoners of war must be released and repatriated without delay after the cessation of active hostilities.
B. Civilian internees must be released as soon as the reasons which necessitated internment no longer exist, but at the latest as soon as possible after the close of active hostilities.
C. Persons deprived of their liberty in relation to a non-international armed conflict must be released as soon as the reasons for the deprivation of their liberty cease to exist.

The persons referred to may continue to be deprived of their liberty if penal proceedings are pending against them or if they are serving a sentence lawfully imposed. [IAC (A), (B)/NIAC (C)]

Chapter 38. Displacement and Displaced Persons

Rule 129.

A. Parties to an international armed conflict may not deport or forcibly transfer the civilian population of an occupied territory, in whole or in part, unless the security of the civilians involved or imperative military reasons so demand.
B. Parties to a non-international armed conflict may not order the displacement of the civilian population, in whole or in part, for reasons related to the conflict, unless the security of the civilians involved or imperative military reasons so demand. [IAC (A)/NIAC (B)]

Rule 130. States may not deport or transfer parts of their own civilian population into a territory they occupy. [IAC]
Rule 131. In case of displacement, all possible measures must be taken in order that the civilians concerned are received under satisfactory conditions of shelter, hygiene, health, safety and nutrition and that members of the same family are not separated. [IAC/NIAC]
Rule 132. Displaced persons have a right to voluntary return in safety to their homes or places of habitual residence as soon as the reasons for their displacement cease to exist. [IAC/NIAC]
Rule 133. The property rights of displaced persons must be respected. [IAC/NIAC]

Chapter 39. Other Persons Afforded Specific Protection

Rule 134. The specific protection, health and assistance needs of women affected by armed conflict must be respected. [IAC/NIAC]
Rule 135. Children affected by armed conflict are entitled to special respect and protection. [IAC/NIAC]
Rule 136. Children must not be recruited into armed forces or armed groups. [IAC/NIAC]
Rule 137. Children must not be allowed to take part in hostilities. [IAC/NIAC]
Rule 138. The elderly, disabled and infirm affected by armed conflict are entitled to special respect and protection. [IAC/NIAC]

10 1996 US War Crimes Act, as amended by the relevant parts of the Military Commissions Act (2006) 18 USC 2441, and 18 USC 2340: Selected articles

Note by author

The United States, having become a party to the 1949 Geneva Conventions (in 1955) and the 1984 UN Convention against Torture (in 1990), as well as other international instruments, adopted several legislative acts that were presented as incorporating certain provisions of these instruments into US law. In reality, as of 2010 the US War Crimes Act (WCA) as amended differed significantly from the wording of international law on several important matters. The political point of the wording adopted by a Republican Congress in the Fall of 2006 was to make it difficult to prosecute US nationals for much of the abusive interrogation and harsh detention measures adopted by the George

W. Bush Administration after 9/11. However, in that some of the wording in the 1996 WCA and the 2006 Military Commissions Act (MCA) reflects previous legislation, the latest acts can be seen as a continuation of congressional wrestling with legal semantics over two decades.

The fact remains that whereas international law forbids torture for any reason, the US WCA as amended forbids torture resulting from the intention to inflict severe pain. Severe pain that is the result of the intention to gain intelligence for security purposes is not made clearly illegal. Also, US wording emphasizes physical pain and mind altering drugs, but is largely silent about severe mental pain that arises from mainly psychological pressures – e.g. prolonged solitary confinement. Also US law mandates that inflicting severe mental pain that is criminal must result in permanent psychological impairment. Moreover, US wording decriminalizes humiliating treatment, while leaving the prohibitions on torture and cruel treatments. But the latter appear to have narrow definitions or high thresholds for illegality.

2441. War crimes

(a) **Offense.** – Whoever, whether inside or outside the United States, commits a war crime, in any of the circumstances described in subsection (b), shall be fined under this title or imprisoned for life or any term of years, or both, and if death results to the victim, shall also be subject to the penalty of death.

(b) **Circumstances.** – The circumstances referred to in subsection (a) are that the person committing such war crime or the victim of such war crime is a member of the Armed Forces of the United States or a national of the United States (as defined in section 101 of the Immigration and Nationality Act).

(c) **Definition.** – As used in this section the term "war crime" means any conduct –

  (1) defined as a grave breach in any of the international conventions signed at Geneva 12 August 1949, or any protocol to such convention to which the United States is a party;

  (2) prohibited by Article 23, 25, 27, or 28 of the Annex to the Hague Convention IV, Respecting the Laws and Customs of War on Land, signed 18 October 1907;

(3) which constitutes a grave breach of common Article 3 (as defined in subsection (d)) when committed in the context of and in association with an armed conflict not of an international character; or

(4) of a person who, in relation to an armed conflict and contrary to the provisions of the Protocol on Prohibitions or Restrictions on the Use of Mines, Booby-Traps and Other Devices as amended at Geneva on 3 May 1996 (Protocol II as amended on 3 May 1996), when the United States is a party to such Protocol, willfully kills or causes serious injury to civilians.

(d) **Common Article 3 Violations. –**

(1) **Prohibited conduct.** – In subsection (c)(3), the term "grave breach of common Article 3" means any conduct (such conduct constituting a grave breach of common Article 3 of the international conventions done at Geneva August 12, 1949), as follows:

(A) **Torture. – [see p. 275 for changed language]**

(B) **Cruel or inhuman treatment.** – The act of a person who commits, or conspires or attempts to commit, an act intended to inflict severe or serious physical or mental pain or suffering (other than pain or suffering incidental to lawful sanctions), including serious physical abuse, upon another within his custody or control.

(C) **Performing biological experiments.** – The act of a person who subjects, or conspires or attempts to subject, one or more persons within his custody or physical control to biological experiments without a legitimate medical or dental purpose and in so doing endangers the body or health of such person or persons.

(D) **Murder.** – The act of a person who intentionally kills, or conspires or attempts to kill, or kills whether intentionally or unintentionally in the course of committing any other offense under this subsection, one or more persons taking no active part in the hostilities, including those placed out of combat by sickness, wounds, detention, or any other cause.

(E) **Mutilation or maiming.** – The act of a person who intentionally injures, or conspires or attempts to injure, or injures whether intentionally or unintentionally in the course of committing any other offense under this subsection, one or more persons taking no active part in the hostilities, including those placed out of combat by sickness, wounds, detention, or any other cause, by disfiguring the person or persons by any mutilation thereof or by permanently disabling any member, limb, or organ of his body, without any legitimate medical or dental purpose.

(F) **Intentionally causing serious bodily injury.** – The act of a person who intentionally causes, or conspires or attempts to cause, serious bodily injury to one or more persons, including lawful combatants, in violation of the law of war.

(G) **Rape.** – The act of a person who forcibly or with coercion or threat of force wrongfully invades, or conspires or attempts to invade, the body of a person by penetrating, however slightly, the anal or genital opening of the victim with any part of the body of the accused, or with any foreign object.

(H) **Sexual assault or abuse.** – The act of a person who forcibly or with coercion or threat of force engages, or conspires or attempts to engage, in sexual contact with one or more persons, or causes, or conspires or attempts to cause, one or more persons to engage in sexual contact.

(I) **Taking hostages.** – The act of a person who, having knowingly seized or detained one or more persons, threatens to kill, injure, or continue to detain such person or persons with the intent of compelling any nation, person other than the hostage, or group of persons to act or refrain from acting as an explicit or implicit condition for the safety or release of such person or persons.

(2) **Definitions.** – In the case of an offense under subsection (a) by reason of subsection (c)(3) –

(A) the term “severe mental pain or suffering” shall be applied for purposes of paragraphs (1)(A) and (1)(B) in accordance with the meaning given that term in section 2340 (2) of this title;

(B) the term “serious bodily injury” shall be applied for purposes of paragraph (1)(F) in accordance with the meaning given that term in section 113 (b)(2) of this title;

(C) the term “sexual contact” shall be applied for purposes of paragraph (1)(G) in accordance with the meaning given that term in section 2246 (3) of this title;

(D) the term “serious physical pain or suffering” shall be applied for purposes of paragraph (1)(B) as meaning bodily injury that involves –

(i) a substantial risk of death;

(ii) extreme physical pain;

(iii) a burn or physical disfigurement of a serious nature (other than cuts, abrasions, or bruises); or

(iv) significant loss or impairment of the function of a bodily member, organ, or mental faculty; and

(E) the term “serious mental pain or suffering” shall be applied for purposes of paragraph (1)(B) in accordance with the meaning given the term “severe mental pain or suffering” (as defined in section 2340 (2) of this title), except that –

(i) the term “serious” shall replace the term “severe” where it appears; and

(ii) as to conduct occurring after the date of the enactment of the Military Commissions Act of 2006, the term “serious and non-transitory mental harm (which need not be prolonged)” shall replace the term “prolonged mental harm” where it appears.

2340. Definitions

As used in this chapter –

(1) “torture” means an act committed by a person acting under the color of law specifically intended to inflict severe physical or mental pain or suffering (other than pain or suffering incidental to lawful sanctions) upon another person within his custody or physical control;

(2) “severe mental pain or suffering” means the prolonged mental harm caused by or resulting from –

(A) the intentional infliction or threatened infliction of severe physical pain or suffering;

(B) the administration or application, or threatened administration or application, of mind altering substances or other procedures calculated to disrupt profoundly the senses or the personality;

(C) the threat of imminent death; or

(D) the threat that another person will imminently be subjected to death, severe physical pain or suffering, or the administration or application of mind altering substances or other procedures calculated to disrupt profoundly the senses or personality; and

(3) "United States" means the several States of the United States, the District of Columbia, and the commonwealths, territories, and possessions of the United States.

ANNEX D

Timeline, selected events, prisoner abuse after 9/11, Bush Administration

2001

9/11 Al-Qaeda attacks on New York and Washington. Almost 3,000 persons killed, mostly civilians.

9/14 President Bush declares state of national emergency; Congress passes Authorization to Use Military Force (AUMF) in response to attacks; general, vague authorization for Executive to take broad but unspecified actions.

9/16 Vice President Cheney gives interview about "going to the dark side," United States having to use all means to respond to terrorism.

9/17 President Bush authorizes CIA to act against Al-Qaeda and its supporters, including secret detention.

9/25 Attorney John Yoo of DOJ sends memo to attorney Tim Flanigan in the White House saying President has unlimited authority to act for national security. President said not to be restrained by treaties or statutes.

10/7 United States launches armed attacks in Afghanistan.

11/6 DOJ attorneys provide memo saying 1949 Geneva Conventions do not apply to Taliban and Al-Qaeda prisoners in Afghanistan; Bush Administration reverses early decisions by military commanders in favor of laws of war and prisoners of war; broad pattern of abuse of prisoners follows in Kandahar, Bagram, and elsewhere, both by military and CIA. DOJ view eventually rejected by Supreme Court.

11/9 William Haynes, top civilian lawyer in the Pentagon, moves to establish system of Military Commissions to provide justice to enemy prisoners; minimizes concerns by military lawyers (JAGs).

11/13 Bush announces use of Military Commissions in bypassing federal civilian courts for terror defendants, although civilian courts will sometimes be used; no systematic policy evolves on this bifurcation.

11/19 Haynes ask private consultants to help design interrogation program for Pentagon, drawn up for SERE training, which abuses US military personnel in limited ways to prepare them for harsh captivity by enemies. Consultants have no experience in interrogation or Arab world.

11/24 The American John Walker Lindh is captured while fighting for Taliban in Afghanistan; he is subsequently abused during interrogation on instructions from the Pentagon; held in an irregular process and denied proper medical treatment for a time, he eventually strikes a plea bargain in federal court and gets twenty years in a US prison as he drops his claims of mistreatment.

12/18 With US help, Sweden "renders" two terror suspects to Egypt, where they subsequently claim torture; at about same time, United States captures terror suspect Ibn al-Shaik al-Libi and renders him to Egypt, where he claims torture and later recants his story that Saddam Hussein had substantive ties with Al-Qaeda. Nevertheless, US officials later use story in the run-up to invasion of Iraq.

12/27 Secretary of Defense Rumsfeld announces the naval base at Guantánamo as the "least worst place" to hold "the worst of the worst" among US enemy prisoners; designed to be a legal black hole where no legal judgments can be made by US courts. No reference made to CIA detention that is supposed to hold high-value detainees (HVDs).

12/28 DOJ attorneys Yoo and Patrick Philbin advise the White House that federal courts have no jurisdiction at Guantánamo. Supreme Court later rejects this argument.

2002

1/9 Yoo and Robert Delahunty provide memo again saying 1949 Geneva Conventions do not protect Taliban and Al-Qaeda detainees.

1/16 Guantánamo opens.

1/19 Rumsfeld tells Pentagon that "Geneva" covers no one at Gitmo but detention should be appropriately humane. At Gitmo, officials not sure what is permitted and what is out of bounds. ICRC invited to do visits at Gitmo by middle-level military officials, not by Pentagon.

1/24 State Department tries to get greater attention to "Geneva" with regard to detainees held by the military, but Secretary of State Colin Powell and Legal Advisor William Taft, IV are unsuccessful.

2/7 Bush declares that he has the right to suspend "Geneva" as between the United States and Afghanistan, but declines to do so for the moment. Statement thus asserts that President is not bound by international law. Says US policy is humane detention but limited by "military necessity," thus indicating publicly that some prisoners will not be treated humanely.

3/30 Abu Zubaydah, terror suspect, captured, taken to CIA Black Site in Thailand; interrogated humanely by FBI and CIA; later CIA ordered to use coercion. FBI withdraws. Controversy follows about his importance and whether coercion was necessary to get important information.

4/16 Former SERE personnel advise CIA on Zubaydah interrogation; abusive techniques discussed and approved by top officials in Bush Administration, including Powell who opposed abusive interrogation by the military. Harsh interrogations videotaped; discussion follows as to whether to keep tapes.

8/1 Yoo and Jay Bybee produce extensive memo detailing CIA harsh interrogation techniques and arguing all are legal; techniques already in use; DOJ attorneys have been giving advice to CIA already. State Department and JAG lawyers not involved in August 1 "torture memo."

9/16 Abusive techniques based on SERE are taught to military as well as CIA interrogators.

9/25 Group of Administration high officials make secret trip to Gitmo in order to get military personnel to request harsher techniques for the military; Gitmo JAG Diane Beaver complies, sends memo up chain of command; later a high-level legal review of Beaver memo is blocked by Haynes at request of David Addington, the latter from Cheney's office.

11/23 Rumsfeld oversees abusive interrogation of Mohammed al-Qahtani at Gitmo, having made several changes of local command to institute harsh detention and interrogation;

Comm. Geoffrey Miller does as Rumsfeld wishes, is later subjected to a review which recommends sanctions for use of combined techniques without limits; sanctions never imposed. (Bush later gives Miller medal for exemplary service.)

12/2 Rumsfeld approves long list of abusive techniques allowed to military interrogators; when Navy legal counsel objects, some techniques recalled. Thus begins confusion on military side about what is allowed and what is not. Original long list of abusive measures "migrates" to Afghanistan.

2003

1 CIA Inspector General John Helgerson begins investigation into CIA interrogation, in response to deaths while in CIA custody, reports in May that interrogators have exceeded instructions, continuing debates about videotapes and their destruction.

1/17 Haynes names pliable Mary Walker to lead military study about interrogation techniques; Yoo advice influential; JAG concerns bypassed; eventually Walker group produces a list of approved abusive techniques for the military. By this time abuse is widespread at Bagram military base in Afghanistan, under the supervision of Carolyn Wood. More confusion about military guidelines.

3/1 Khalid Sheikh Mohammed (KSM), claimed brains behind 9/11 attack, captured. Increases in number of HVDs held by the CIA who are waterboarded and otherwise seriously abused. Total number of CIA HVDs disputed.

3/20 US invades Iraq. Slightly later Abu Ghraib, Saddam's notorious prison, selected as main prison by invading coalition; as chaotic occupation unfolds and insurgency erupts, the word circulates that United States must get actionable intelligence to combat insurgency. Abu Ghraib overcrowded, dangerous, badly organized and managed. Bush Administration statement that "Geneva" applies to invasion and occupation does not lead to careful and lawful detention and interrogation.

8/31 Rumsfeld's office transfers Miller from Gitmo to Abu Ghraib to advise on how to make the latter conform to the former, despite the fact that "Geneva" was not supposed to apply at Gitmo but was supposed to regulate Abu Ghraib. Carolyn Wood also transferred to Abu Ghraib, despite, or because of, systematic abuse at Bagram. Abuse spins out of control at Abu Ghraib, also prevalent in many other parts of Iraq.

10/9 ICRC makes public statement about concern for mental health of detainees at Guantánamo, absent a clear legal framework for their detention that would cover rights to challenge detention and prospects for trial or release.

11/5 The Ryder report, a military report reviewing US detention in Iraq, finds numerous problems and recommends separation of Military Intelligence (MI) from Military Police (MP), which is precisely the combination that Miller had instituted at Guantánamo with approval of Rumsfeld's office. Report thus challenges using MP to soften up prisoners for MI.

11/24 The ICRC, having temporarily suspended its prison visits to Abu Ghraib to indicate its concern about detainees there, and having resumed visits at various places in Iraq, compiles a summary report about detention during occupation. This critical report had slight impact on the United States.

2004

1/13 Joseph Darby of the US Army gives photos of abuse at Abu Ghraib to the Army's Criminal Investigation Department. Pentagon officials increase attention to prisoner affairs. At approximately the same time, the CIA Inspector General's report (the Helgerson report) begins to circulate inside the executive branch, questioning the CIA's abusive interrogations.

3/9 The "Taguba" report, commissioned by the military in response to growing concern about detention in Iraq, candidly confirms abuse by US MI in Iraq in detail, especially at Abu Ghraib. Notes permissive culture about abuse, thus implicating higher authorities.

4/28 CBS breaks Abu Ghraib story with photos.

5/7 Congress holds hearings on Abu Ghraib and detention policies.

6/2 Tenet resigns as head of CIA.

6/28 US Supreme Court issues *Hamdi* judgment asserting court jurisdiction at Guantánamo based on US *de facto* sovereignty; says detainees entitled to contest their detention before a neutral decision maker.

7/7 Bush team announces CSRT military review system at Gitmo, controlled by the Pentagon. System finds that detainees are properly held in overwhelming number of proceedings. Questions arise about fairness of system.

8/23 The Fay–Jones report, a military investigation, finds misconduct by MI in Iraq.

8/25 The Schlesinger report, headed by a former Secretary of Defense and other establishment figures, finds both individuals out of control and institutional responsibility for abuses at Abu Ghraib. Emphasis is on lower-level personnel, and Congress under Republican control does not follow up on command responsibility.

2005

5/10 After CIA Inspector General report questions abusive interrogation, Steven Bradbury for DOJ issues secret memo, followed by other memos, continuing to authorize severe abuse by CIA, even as Bush begins to move in a more moderate direction regarding detainees, as pushed by Rice and others; Cheney's influence waning on some prisoner matters, although he remains Administration leader for CIA abusive interrogation on the Hill.

11/1 *Washington Post* breaks story of CIA Black Sites.

11/9 CIA confirms that videotapes of waterboarding and other major abuses have been destroyed, despite court order to preserve all documents relating to certain court cases. Slow investigation follows.

12/8 Secretary of State Condoleezza Rice says that all US representatives everywhere are bound to adhere to the prohibition not only on torture but also on cruel, inhuman, or degrading (CID) treatment. Her statement does not end the dispute over definitions of those terms, but does put pressure on Cheney camp which is in favor of continued tough approach.

12/30 Detainee Treatment Act passed by Congress becomes law as Bush signs but with "signing statement" raising question about implementation in all situations. Act prohibits serious abuse of detainees held by the military and by CIA in military facilities. So Congress joins Supreme Court in trying to change some Bush policies regarding detainees. CIA not clearly affected.

2006

6/29 US Supreme Court strikes down Military Commission system on narrow grounds that President cannot act alone; requires congressional role. Also in *Hamdan* judgment, holds that Geneva Conventions Common Article 3 applies to Guantánamo. In holding that Military Commissions must meet unspecified due process requirements, court also infers that no torture or other cruel or degrading treatment should be allowed there.

9/6 Bush moves fourteen HVDs from CIA Black Sites to Guantánamo, as recommended by Rice and others, thus confirming earlier assertions about US secret detention. ICRC interviews detainees and concludes that much CIA treatment was either torture or CID. ICRC notes that Bush authorized the program, which was directed by high officials.

10/17 Military Commissions Act signed into law, as Congress under Republican control largely gives Bush what he wants. Reforms are slight, habeas rights denied, and humiliating treatment removed from US war crimes definition. (Bush *de facto* argument is that US abusive interrogation was neither torture nor inhumane but merely humiliating, which is no longer a crime in US law.)

2007

3/26 The Australian David Hicks, who had fought for Taliban, strikes a plea deal in the Military Commission system, accepting a prison term to be served in his home country in exchange for dropping his charges about being abused in detention.

2008

6/12 US Supreme Court holds in *Boumediene* case that prisoners at Guantánamo have right of habeas corpus and can thus use US federal courts to challenge their detention. Habeas decisions follow that do not accept Executive claims about reasons for detention, and courts often order release of detainee.

8/6 Military Commission convicts Hamdan, Osama bin Laden's driver, but gives him a few months' sentence after which he is deported to Yemen. During Bush Administration Military Commissions only convict three persons, one of whom was Hicks who pleaded his way to prison in Australia. The other is a Yemeni who got a life sentence after failing to cooperate with the system.

2009

1/14 Susan Crawford, US official in the Military Commission system, drops charges against al-Qahtani, saying he was tortured at Gitmo. Rumsfeld and Miller had been directly involved in that interrogation, as well as other lower-level persons.

Index